Dark Voices

Dark Voices

W. E. B. Du Bois and American Thought, 1888–1903

Shamoon Zamir

The University of Chicago Press

Chicago & London

Shamoon Zamir teaches American literature and American studies at King's College, University of London.

Epigraph on page vii: "W. E. B. Du Bois at Harvard," first published in *The Homecoming Singer* (Corinth Books, 1971). © Jay Wright. Used by permission.

The University of Chicago Press, Chicago 60637
The University of Chicago Press, Ltd., London
© 1995 by The University of Chicago
All rights reserved. Published 1995
Printed in the United States of America
04 03 02 01 00 99 98 97 96 95   1 2 3 4 5

ISBN: 0-226-97852-4 (cloth)
0-226-97853-2 (paper)

Library of Congress Cataloging-in-Publication Data

Zamir, Shamoon.
    Dark voices : W. E. B. Du Bois and American thought, 1888–1903 / Shamoon Zamir.
        p. cm.
    Includes bibliographical references and index.
    1. Du Bois, W. E. B. (Williams Edward Burghardt), 1868–1963.
2. Afro-Americans. 3. United States—Race relations. I. Title.
E185.97.D73Z36   1995
305.896′073′0092—dc20   94-45847
                                                                    CIP

⊗ The paper used in this publication meets the minimum requirements of the American National Standard for Information Sciences—Permanence of Paper for Printed Library Materials, ANSI Z39.48-1984.

in memory of my father,
for my mother,
& for Marzia

In Harvard Square,
the designing locks
swing to your pace.
The bells push you
toward the teasing dons.
Bright boys begin to trill
their lamentable lessons.
It is too early for you.
All night, again, all night,
you've been at your
fledgling history,
passing through the old songs,
through the old laments.
But here, in Harvard Square,
the prosody of those dark voices
is your connection.
In any square,
the evening bell
may be your release.

Jay Wright,
"W. E. B. Du Bois at Harvard"

Teach us Forever Dead, there is no Dream
but Deed, no Deed but Memory.

W. E. B. Du Bois,
Autobiography

Contents

Acknowledgments

A grant from the Fulbright Commission made possible a period of research in the United States out of which the present project developed. I am grateful to the African and African American Studies Program at Yale University for their hospitality during the 1988–89 academic year and for allowing me access to the libraries at Yale. In particular I would like to thank Professor Vera Kutzinski. Without her early support and her continued friendship and encouragement this work might never have been started. Professor Werner Sollors offered support in the later stages of this project. A portion of chapter 5 has appeared in *The Black Columbiad,* a volume of essays edited by Werner Sollors and Maria Diedrich and published by Harvard University Press.

The Department of Literature at Sarah Lawrence College and the English departments at the University of Chicago, at the University of York, and at King's College London have provided encouraging work environments over the last five years.

My special thanks to Professor David Du Bois for permission to quote from previously unpublished material from the W. E. B. Du Bois archives, to Linda Sideman, librarian in charge at the Du Bois Archives at the University of Massachusetts at Amherst, and to the librarians at the Beinecke and Sterling Memorial Libraries at Yale for all their help. It has been a pleasure to have Alan Thomas as my editor at the University of Chicago Press. His advice and guidance have been well judged and unstinting.

Early versions of chapter 4 were presented at Yale, Nottingham University, Keele University, and the University of Chicago. I thank all respondents. Elizabeth O'Connor Chandler of the Continuing Education Program at the University of Chicago has been very generous in allowing me to present these and related materials at several conferences. The criticisms of those who have read various versions of these chapters have provided invaluable input into this work. I would like to thank Dick Davis, Stephen Fink, Robert Lee, and David Murray. Richard Godden and Gerd Hurm have been exemplary in the depth of their engagement and dialogue.

A handful of friends and colleagues on both sides of the Atlantic have in different ways helped sustain a dialogue in which the excitement and value of the life of the mind has been continuously nourished. The friendship, conversation, good humor, and seriousness of Hanne Bramness, Allen Fisher, Harriet Guest, Stephen Minta, Paige Mitchell, and Steven Want have been invaluable over the last few years. Arnold Krupat has been not only an extraordinary friend but also a model of critical engagement and commitment. My greatest debts are owed to four persons in particular. Clive Bush and Marzia Balzani continue to be the most uncompromising representatives of the value and purpose of knowledge and friendship. For many years now Marzia Balzani has pointed the way to a range of involvements. Clive Bush's book *Halfway to Revolution* has helped clarify several areas of the argument in the following chapters and it is, I fear, inadequately acknowledged in the notes. Katie Trumpener has been a careful reader and a rigorous critic. Without her scrutiny of early versions of the manuscript there would be many more weaknesses in the following pages than there are now. She remains unmatched in her kindness and openness and in her intellectual curiosity. Eric Mottram not only supervised the present study in its doctoral form but has been the single most important source of inspiration and encouragement since 1980. To engage in an ongoing reading and rereading of the work of Eric Mottram (and, equally, to accept the invitation to involvement offered by his teaching and conversation) is to engage, in the words of Allen Fisher, in "necessary business."

Abbreviations of Frequently Cited Works of W. E. B. Du Bois

Other abbreviations and full details of all manuscript materials are given in the text.

A   *The Autobiography: A Soliloquy on Viewing My Life from the Last Decade of Its First Century* (n.p.: International Publishers, 1968).

AR   *Against Racism: Unpublished Essays, Papers, Addresses, 1887–1961,* ed. Herbert Aptheker (Amherst: University of Massachusetts Press, 1985).

DD   *Dusk of Dawn: An Essay toward an Autobiography of a Race Concept* (1940), in Du Bois, *Writings,* pp. 549–801.

P4   Philosophy 4 notebook, manuscript.

PN   *The Philadelphia Negro: A Social Study,* with an introduction by E. Digby Baltzell (1899; New York: Schocken Books, 1967).

RE   "The Renaissance of Ethics," manuscript.

SAST   *The Suppression of the African Slave-Trade to the United States of America, 1638–1870* (1896), in Du Bois, *Writings,* pp. 1–356.

SBF   *The Souls of Black Folk* (1903), in Du Bois, *Writings,* pp. 357–548.

TT   "The Talented Tenth" (1903), in Du Bois, *Writings,* pp. 842–61.

Human enterprise has two aspects: it is both success and failure. The dialectical scheme is inadequate for reflecting upon it. We must make our vocabulary and the frames of our reason more supple. Some day I am going to try to describe that strange reality, History, which is neither objective, nor ever quite subjective, in which the dialectic is contested, penetrated, and corroded by a kind of antidialectic, but which is still a dialectic. But that is the philosopher's affair. One does not ordinarily consider the two faces of Janus; the man of action sees one and the poet sees the other. When the instruments are broken and unusable, when plans are blasted, and effort is useless, the world appears with a childlike and terrible freshness, without supports, without paths. It has the maximum reality because it is crushing for man, and as action, in any case, generalizes, defeat restores to things their individual reality. But, by an expected reversal, the defeat, considered as a final end, is both a contesting and an appropriation of this universe.

Jean-Paul Sartre,
What Is Literature? *(1948)*[1]

One

Race and Multiplicity

An Introduction

This book is an account of the ways in which certain traditions of American philosophical and social thought failed W. E. B. Du Bois in the violently racist last two decades of the nineteenth century, and of his imaginative response to this failure. The response is traced in his writings, from his undergraduate work in philosophy at Harvard University in the 1880s to the publication of *The Souls of Black Folk* in 1903. Born just three years after the end of the Civil War, Du Bois grew up a witness to the failure of Reconstruction, the retrenchment of legislative racism, and the brutal triumph of Jim Crow segregation and lynch law. At the same time he received a privileged education available to only a handful of African-Americans at that time. After a general undergraduate degree from Fisk University in Tennessee, Du Bois pursued further undergraduate and then graduate work at Harvard and the University of Berlin. Trained in philosophy by William James and George Santayana, and also in history and sociology, he was fully aware of the epistemological crises that dominated philosophy, science, and the social sciences in the late nineteenth and early twentieth centuries. Du Bois's early career is an attempt to investigate the relationship between the political crisis of race and understanding's failure of confidence. The present study is a description of

1

this attempt. To offer an account of this achievement is to undertake a
fresh reading of Du Bois's early career from a specific perspective, and to
offer a new reading of *Souls*—among the most widely quoted works of
African-American literature, but also one of the most neglected.[2] It is also
to suggest ways in which the history of race in America may provide
critical perspectives for American intellectual history.

The conceptual frameworks of Du Bois's work in philosophy, history, and sociology at this time are derived mainly from European and
Euro-American intellectual traditions. But as Du Bois himself notes in
Dusk of Dawn, his autobiography from 1940, throughout the late nineteenth century his "education" was confronted again and again by "the
truth in the world," and the most immediate face of this "truth" was "the
problems of racial and cultural contacts" (*DD* 572).

> Had it not been for the race problem early thrust upon me and enveloping
> me, I should have probably been an unquestioning worshipper at the shrine
> of the social order and economic development into which I was born. But
> just that part of that order which seemed to most of my fellows nearest
> perfection, seemed to me most inequitable and wrong; and starting from
> that critique, I gradually, as the years went by, found other things to ques-
> tion in my environment. At first, however, my criticism was confined to
> the relation of my people to the world movement. I was not questioning
> the world movement in itself. What the white world was doing, its goals
> and ideals, I had not doubted were quite right. What was wrong was that
> I and people like me and thousands of others who might have my ability
> and aspirations, were refused permission to be a part of this world. It was
> as though moving on a rushing express, my main thought was as to the
> relations I had to other passengers on the express, and not to its rate of
> speed and its destination. (*DD* 573–74)

The "truth of the world" opens a breach in the idealist optimisms
and cohesions of Du Bois's "education," and it is the relation of the two,
of a system of beliefs and ideologies and the concrete particulars of a
life lived and understood historically, that constitutes—to borrow Louis
Althusser's term—the *problematic* of Du Bois's work and also the focus
of the present study.[3] In the prefatory remarks to *Dusk of Dawn* Du Bois
insisted that "my life had its significance and its only deep significance
because it was part of a Problem; but that problem was, as I continue to
think, the central problem of the greatest of the world's democracies and
so the Problem of the future world" (*DD* 551). The opening chapter of the

autobiography sketches in broad outline the historical form and content of this problem: "In the folds of this European civilization I was born and shall die, imprisoned, conditioned, depressed, exalted and inspired. Integrally a part of it and yet, much more significant, one of its rejected parts; one who expressed in life and action and made vocal to many, a single whirlpool of social entanglement and inner psychological paradox, which always seem to me more significant for the meaning of the world today than other similar and related problems" (*DD* 555). The self is carefully located both inside and out, but this duality is to be understood as a "single" process. The dramatic accumulation of adjectives in the first sentence registers the experienced effects of power but also the possibilities of freedom within the interstices of the existing order. Instead of narratives of transcendence that attempt to cut through the Gordian knot of history, Du Bois presents the facts of relation and mediation as the conditions of necessity and action, not defeat. The self is, therefore, made an exemplar of the contradictions and multiplicities of the age, not a representative of its official culture and ideology.

This is Du Bois writing at the end of the Depression and on the eve of the Second World War in Europe, his nineteenth-century faiths severely tested by the first half of the twentieth century. He has also by this time adopted a loosely Marxist position, and his turn-of-the-century vitalist programs for an elite African-American leadership have been modified by the critical understanding made available by political economy. He resists essentializing both epistemology and self-consciousness and struggles instead to describe the shape of a life's imaginative investigations of its own contexts. Only such description can be simultaneously open to the unique and the universal, which together constitute the imaginative life. At the end of the 1930s Du Bois thinks that he is facing "a world whose foundations seem to be tottering" (*DD* 572). From this perspective of a seventy-year-old man, it seems that the young Du Bois's belief in the "onsweep of civilization" and in "progress" in the nineteenth century was "unquestioned and unquestionable" (*DD* 572). While the periodized distinctions are true in some crude way, this vision of an earlier self and an earlier age offers an exaggerated sense of cohesion and uniformity from within the experiences of later crisis. Peter Conn is right to suggest that Henry Adams's self-styling as a "conservative Christian anarchist" can be taken as "an epigraph to the cultural history" of America at the turn of the century.[4] One would have to substitute some other term for "anarchist" in describing Du Bois and modify "Christian" for the unreligious New

Englander who remained deeply Puritan in his attitudes. But Adams's bold confrontation of the failures of law and systems of knowledge and his description of the subsequent fragmentations of the self in his *Education of Henry Adams* are instructive points of comparison for thinking about Du Bois at the turn of the century.

In the first chapter of the *Education* Adams writes that "the problem of running order through chaos, direction through space, discipline through freedom, unity through multiplicity, has always been, and always must be, the task of education, as it is the moral of religion, philosophy, science, art, politics, and economy."[5] But by the end of his autobiography Adams concludes that "the new American" must "think in contradictions," and that the ever-accelerating transformation of society requires "a new social mind" (*EHA* 497–98). In moving from unity to multiplicity and fragmentation the narrative of the *Education* reverses the transition from modernism to progressivism that has been given as one possible way of describing a generational shift in American social thought at the end of the nineteenth century. Taking the 1890s as the key decade for this transition, Donald Bellomy writes:

> In certain aspects, the crisis appeared urgent, particularly on the social front. Depression, strikes and riots, the poverty of the slums, the unrest among farmers, the concentration of wealth, and the consolidation of big business all seemed to have brought America to a crossroads. Yet the Progressive generation responded with surprising confidence. The juncture occurred as a culmination of forces that had been building for over a quarter of a century; by 1900 the process of industrialization and urbanization began to stabilize. They realized this, or at least decided that the time had arrived when people could act rather than react. They could replace conflict with control and mindless expansion with efficient management of human and natural resources.[6]

But "the older group" of modernists, by contrast, "proceeded after 1890 to plunge ever deeper into the meaning of science, relativism, and historical change."[7]

In Du Bois's work from this period there is not a transition from one to the other of the poles described by Bellomy or Adams but a perpetual flux between the two. In the writings up to and including *Souls* there is a constant movement between a typically nineteenth-century affirmation of heroic vitalism and natural law as twin guarantors of a progressive historical process and a complex description of the fracture of this confi-

dence and of consciousness's struggle to survive the collapse. Vitalist teleologies promise the African-American people salvation from the disas-
trous setbacks of post-Reconstruction history, but it is this very history
that repeatedly undermines the philosophical schematizations of historical experience and challenges Du Bois's program for an elite African-
American leadership.

A set of reference points for Du Bois's attraction to different versions
of vitalism can be given quickly: his undergraduate admiration for Bismarck as a nation builder; his efforts to understand William James's notions of will and action in his (previously unexamined) lecture notes; his
attempt in a thesis written for James to formulate a science of ethics that
edges into an idealist philosophy of history; the simultaneous outline of
a program of political and cultural leadership and a philosophy of history
in the seminal essay "The Conservation of Races" (1897); the quest as
sociologist for a science of society that will reveal universal laws of social
causality; and finally the well-known essay "The Talented Tenth" (1903),
a plan for an African-American vanguard pulling the black masses into
modernity.

The points of doubt and questioning in the early career can be equally
easily mapped. In "A Vacation Unique," an undergraduate story discussed and published here for the first time, Du Bois parodies not only
James's volitionist ethics but also his own quest for a metaphysics of
history. "Jefferson Davis as Representative of Civilization," Du Bois's
Harvard commencement speech, appears at first to be a reaffirmation
of the "Great Man" theory of history. But embedded in it is a parodic
ambivalence that draws on "A Vacation Unique" and suggests Du Bois's
nervousness about the hero as the engine of historical transformation.
"Strivings of the Negro People" was published the same year as "The
Conservation of Races" but presents a very different prospect. In "Strivings" the talented elite are caught in "double-consciousness" and the
"contradiction of double aims" (*SBF* 364–65). A year later, in 1898, Du
Bois published his groundbreaking sociological study *The Philadelphia
Negro*. Here a positivist defense of scientific objectivity cautions against
the kind of idealist philosophizing of the laws of history that is present in
"Conservation."

But if *The Philadelphia Negro* qualifies the metaphysical urge of "The
Conservation of Races" it also posits a positivist argument against the
radical sense of subjectivity and introspection that dominates "Strivings."
The publication of "The Conservation of Races" and "Strivings of the

Negro People" in the same year, and of *The Philadelphia Negro* the following year, provides a nodal point at which the contradictory pulls in Du
Bois's work can be clearly seen. These contradictions can be described
through the three very different ways in which Du Bois engages with the
world around him at the turn of the century. He can be an empirical
scientist building a scientific basis for reform and higher understanding
of the problems of race. He can be an idealist philosopher of history. And
he can also be a literary artist who resists generalization. The first part of
this study looks at the continuous three-way pull in the early career. The
second part examines *Souls,* Du Bois's finest literary achievement, in the
context of American thought. "Strivings" later became "Of Our Spiritual
Strivings," the famous first chapter of *Souls.* It is in *Souls* that the crisis
of confidence and the struggle to gather up the self out of chaos are most
imaginatively and complexly dramatized. Here Du Bois is able to describe
a history in which, to use Sartre's terms, "the instruments are broken and
unusable" and "plans are blasted." In this defeat Du Bois the theorist of
action and Du Bois the idealist philosopher of history begin to give way
to Du Bois the poet who tries to contest and appropriate the new universe.
Certainly *Souls* is concerned with the simultaneously objective and subjective nature of "that strange reality, History," but as literature, not as
philosophy. It is one of the achievements of *Souls* that its descriptive
strategies remain "supple" and do not become reductively schematic.

Souls can be described by locating it between the subtitle of *Dusk of
Dawn* and Adams's initial subtitle for his *Education:* "An Autobiography
of a Race Concept" and "A Study of Twentieth Century Multiplicity"
(*EHA* xxvii). In *Dusk of Dawn,* in a chapter called "The Concept of Race,"
Du Bois describes his lifelong struggle to define the idea of race. The
discussion is framed by an account of Du Bois's own complicated family
genealogy, going back to French Huguenot, Dutch, African, and even
Native American sources. The cultural and geographical range of this
ancestry provides the context in which a recollection of an African song
heard in family circles during childhood is described. The pieces of the
past are brought back by Du Bois as a prelude to a description of his visit
as an official representative of the American government to Liberia in the
1920s. The account of the visit combines a romantic sense of affiliation
to Africa with a sense of the historical formation of racial politics and
identity within a capitalist and imperialist world system. Pan-Africanism
is brought into dialogue with a broader "Third World" perspective, and
the boundaries of race and labor become blurred. At the heart of the

chapter is a meditation on the relationship of the black and the white worlds and of the black leader to the black masses. The meditation is dramatized through a reworking of the allegory of the cave from Plato's *Republic,* where the relationship of the guardians of the republic to those imprisoned in the cave is considered. As the discussion of this chapter from *Dusk of Dawn* in chapter 5 demonstrates, this reworking is itself a revision of the final chapter of *Souls,* where Du Bois uses the same Platonic allegory as part of his dramatization of his own relationship to those who sing the spirituals. At the conclusion of "The Concept of Race" Du Bois writes that "perhaps it is wrong to speak of it at all as 'a concept' rather than as a group of contradictory forces, facts and tendencies" (*DD* 651). It is the sense of this retrospective meditation on the relation of unity and multiplicity that is built upon in the reading of the early writings in the following chapters.

An account of the multiplicity of knowledge and experience requires more than addition; it requires the invention of daring literary structure. Like the *Education, Souls* is a kind of *Bildungsbiographie* that combines autobiography with collective history and a broad range of cultural commentary. The analogical procedures of the *Education* allow Adams to move freely between international and national politics, contemporary economic theory and history, the philosophy of science and the history of technology, meditations on the nature of religious faith, considerations of sexuality in nineteenth-century America, and deeply felt accounts of love, friendship, and loss. Du Bois likewise locates accounts of the development of self-consciousness and of personal tragedy within a series of reflections on race in America that draw upon a range of materials from philosophy, psychology, economics, sociology, political history, educational theory, religion, and cultural anthropology. However, *Souls* is not, as has usually been assumed, merely a loose collection of fourteen essays. Just as Adams undertakes a set of speculative discussions inside the ironic structure of a third-person autobiography, Du Bois frames his diverse cultural commentaries within a subdued autobiographical narrative that moves from his childhood in chapter 1 to his adulthood in the final chapter. The function of this narrative is not to give coherence to the process of fragmentation. The interplay of the autobiographical narrative and structures of juxtaposition and displacement suggests instead that fragmentation can be understood and described without reduction to unity. It is in this sense that *Souls,* like the *Education,* can be taken as an "index of the twentieth century."[8] It is true that *Souls* confronts the issues of multiplicity and fragmentation more allusively than the *Education,* which is very explicit in its self-reflexivity and its theoretical and philosophical meditations. The *Education* was first printed privately by Adams and circulated among his friends. By contrast, nine out of the fourteen chapters of *Souls* appeared in popular middle-class journals like the *Atlantic Monthly* and the *Dial* prior to their publication in book form.[9] Given the forcefulness of Du Bois's primary intention, the exposure to a predominantly white audience of the conditions of black life in America, it is easy to ignore the complexity and subtlety of his writing. Comparison with Adams's work is therefore intended as an aid to description.

The usefulness of such a comparison may seem questionable given the social differences between Adams and Du Bois. Though both men were New Englanders, Du Bois was a black American, the son of a domestic and a barber, born at a time when the promise of Emancipation had been effectively reversed; he was not the descendent of presidents nor a member of America's patrician elite, as Adams was. Du Bois was also too committed to collective political action to adopt Adams's stance of watcher rather than player (*EHA* 405). Like Adams, Du Bois eventually gave up university teaching, but only to become more active in the political and cultural struggle for African-American rights. Du Bois's sense of the contradictions between political activism and the life of the mind is always more acute and direct than Adams's, and is dramatized without the sense of ironic distance that is so characteristic of the posture of "conservative Christian anarchist" in the *Education.* The comparisons between Adams and Du Bois are not proposed in order to wipe out these differences. If Du Bois's sense of cultural crisis has any genuine parallels with Adams's, it is reached through the particulars of a very different history. *Souls* deserves a place in the history of American literary modernism just as Du Bois's early career should be included in accounts of American modernity, but not because the work transcends the particulars of race. It deserves this kind of reassessment precisely because Du Bois can use the history of race in America as an entrance into issues of modernity. Du Bois's claim at the start of *Souls* that "the problem of the Twentieth Century is the problem of the color-line" (*SBF* 359) is still valuable despite the exaggeration. The focus on race is not in Du Bois a sign of provincialism, but the particular through which the general is also engaged.

Though the social differences between Adams and Du Bois are wide, it is also worth noting that their respective political stances shared a conservative common ground. Du Bois was always aristocratic in his bearing and attitudes, never more so than in his early life, when his politics upheld a clear distinction between the patrician and the plebeian classes. August Meier's history of African-American thought at the turn of the century places Du Bois's conservatism in the context of the aftermath of Reconstruction's failure. Meier argues that after the compromise of 1877 there was a general shift in African-American thought away from politics and toward an emphasis on economics, self-help, and racial solidarity. Meier takes Alexander Crummell, the Episcopal divine who founded the American Negro Academy and who was such a major influence on Du Bois in his early thought, as exemplary of this reorientation. Meier demonstrates the ways in which this shift led to both accommodationist and radical positions, and his detailed account of the diversity of political positions adopted in the period makes it clear that the popular opposition of Booker T. Washington and Du Bois cannot be accepted as a characterization of the age.[10] At a time when radicals like T. Thomas Fortune believed that "the revolution is upon us" and that African-Americans "should take sides with the labor forces in their fight for a juster distribution of the results of labor," most other "radical Negroes were chiefly 'radical' on the race question, and most of them remained 'conservative' in their broader economic and social outlook."[11] Washington and Du Bois shared a more conservative stance.

> Both tended to blame Negroes largely for their condition, and both placed more emphasis on self-help and duties than on rights. Both placed economic advancement before universal manhood suffrage, and both were willing to accept franchise restrictions based not on race but on education and/or property qualifications equitably applied. Both stressed racial solidarity and economic co-operation. Du Bois was, however, more outspoken about injustices, and he differed sharply with Washington in his espousal of the cause of higher education.[12]

By the 1890s Fortune was to abandon his radicalism and to go over to Washington's camp. Du Bois, on the other hand, became more radicalized in the early years of the twentieth century and moved toward a form of socialism in the first decade of the new century. Something of this shift may be visible in *Souls,* but it was only in the middle decades of the twentieth century that Du Bois adopted what could safely be called a Marxist position. But if at the turn of the century Du Bois's radicalism did not take the form of anticapitalist political and economic programs, it needs also to be defined in terms that extend beyond his engagement with the race question as Meier and others have described it. As far as political programs are concerned, Du Bois tended to accept as unproblematic the unities of collectivity and his own cultural and political position as a horizon of normative value. As Sartre says, "action" tends to "generalize." But at the same time that Du Bois as political activist has to work from generalization, he is also forced by the particularities of the history of race to acknowledge the collapse of *communitas* and his own confident subjectivity as terms of generalization. Most accounts of Du Bois's life that have focused on his political and academic career have marginalized *Souls* at the cost of simplifying the range of doubt and self-interrogation in his early life.[13]

At its best, Du Bois's early work, like Adams's *Education,* is characterized by an acute and highly trained intelligence that describes from within a conservative outlook a set of cultural and psychological points of crisis. If one side of Du Bois can be described in terms of a radicalism on the race question tied to a fairly uncritical acceptance of the economic and social status quo, description of another side of Du Bois requires a different set of terms. On this side critical self-examination regarding his own position on the race question and his relationship to the black masses leads Du Bois to a questioning of the broader status quo. Without the support of his later understanding of political economy he cannot adequately theorize the link between the race question and the American economic system, nor propose radical transformation. But he does dramatize his growing unease about the ways in which his own conceptual frameworks may help sustain this system and its supporting ideologies.

Du Bois's continued attraction to heroic vitalism and progressivist ideologies and his sense of their instability, as well his dramatization of the crisis of his own consciousness in relation to the "black folk," are the borders within which his repeated investigations of a set of philosophical and political issues can be mapped. Through successive transitions from philosophy to history to sociology to literature, Du Bois is preoccupied with the problems of freedom and historical necessity, activity and passivity, submission and power, the potentialities of will and the promise of a national culture. He explores the meaning and nature of black self-consciousness and the role of the black intellectual and scholar inside the cultural and political crises of late-nineteenth-century America. Du Bois's exploration of these problems and his use of these different modes of knowledge are used in this study as a forum in which to discuss his relationship to developments in American thought. The primary focus is on a dialogue between Du Bois's work and the theorization of action, will, and consciousness in the ethical pragmatism of William James, though Du Bois's relation to the reactionary implications of the growth of positivism in the social sciences, the uses of Hegelian idealism in defense of manifest destiny, and the revivals of exceptionalist accounts of the nation in several arenas of thought are also considered at length. The choices are not arbitrary. They are determined by the course of Du Bois's career. There are certain specific points of contact between these diverse traditions that will be discussed in detail in the chapters that follow. But the philosophical and social common ground between them can be given here as a theoretical generalization to be refined later. These traditions offer accommodation, not resistance, to the social process, and their accounts of historical process and of consciousness and its relation to the past—and so also to the present and future—are impoverished. At various stages of his early career Du Bois was pulled toward each of these traditions, and they all, in different ways, confirmed in him the desire for hero and system. But those texts in which the doubtings are plotted, from "A Vacation Unique" to *Souls*, provide critiques of these contemporary intellectual positions.

In *The American Evasion of Philosophy* (1989), Cornel West, following the contemporary revival of the pragmatic attitude in America, has traced "a genealogy of pragmatism" from Emerson to Richard Rorty and given Du Bois a branch on the family tree, characterizing him as a Jamesian intellectual and *Souls* as a work "in the Emersonian grain."[14] Looking back at his undergraduate years, the older Du Bois himself acknowledged that James had an immediate impact on him and that he "became a devoted follower of James at the time he was developing his pragmatic philosophy" (*A* 133). James guided him "out of the sterilities of scholastic philosophy to realist pragmatism" (*A* 133). This study argues that scholars have accepted these autobiographical statements too uncritically.[15] David Levering Lewis's recent biography of Du Bois has made clear the significance of the gaps between the facts of the life and the accounts given of them in Du Bois's autobiographies.[16] This study tests the autobiographical recollections against the early writings themselves and proposes that neither Du Bois's student writings nor *Souls* reveal an emotional tenor or intellectual orientation that can be termed unproblematically Jamesian. Robert Gooding-Williams is one scholar who *has* offered a cogent critique of West's genealogy and of his distorted reading of Du Bois. But Gooding-Williams opposes an idealist Du Bois, aligned with the Hegelianism of Josiah Royce, to the anti-idealist James.[17] These oppositions are themselves problematic. It is argued here that Du Bois does not turn from James to idealism, but that there is in his work a crisis of idealism parallel to the fracture of a pragmatic ethics.

The following chapters argue that both James and Emerson conceive of consciousness as passive perception and of action as unreflective activity, and so fail to give an adequate account of the location of the subject in the world. Views of consciousness that describe it primarily as a faculty of seeing (Emerson) or of registering objects (James) imply an absolutely conditioned actor who can only submit unquestioningly to the given social and political order. James is celebrated for his account of a pluralistic universe, but his propositions are not radical in the way that Adams's account of multiplicity is. In *The Principles of Psychology* (1890), James puts "the Multiplicity with the Reality" outside of consciousness and so hopes to "leave the mind simple."[18] For James the mind chooses single options from the pluralist flux and chooses inside the groove of habit, not creative imagination, whereas for Adams consciousness and the problem of choice are not simple structures, and the final proposition is not for a retreat into the security of habit but for "a new social mind." Equally, to imagine action (as both James and Emerson do) as a willed transcendence or perpetual becoming, divorced from memory and oriented toward the future, is to produce a wholly unconditioned agent who can neither locate the self in relation to history nor critically examine the relation of self to dominant law and the forms of representation that govern the present. As Ross Posnock says of James, "He does not seem to consider either the possibility that his basic premise of monadic subjectivity may be too simple and constricted a model or that the self is a social construct dependent on and conditioned by others." One consequence of this failure to locate the self is a reductively utilitarian dismissal of contemplative intellection because James's "unshakable dualism of doing versus being blinds him to the possibility of the former taking a variety of forms beyond the 'manly concrete deed.'"[19] The refusal of reflective thought or of creative consciousness in such an attitude goes hand in hand, therefore, with an inability to describe or understand the nature of the experience of power and mediation, and also with the failure to imagine genuinely transformative activity.

Souls, by contrast, offers a series of dramatizations of a self-consciousness struggling for self-realization and freedom within the confining violence of a history of racism, and also in dialogue with a romantically conceived folk who embody their own survival in the great spirituals. The self is mediated by power and terror, but also by positive social location among others. At the heart of the book is an exploration of the dilemma of the black intellectual and artist caught between *communitas* and solitude, between the necessities of political activism and the requirements of the contemplative life. This is not a polarization between passivity and activity, as James would assume, but a dialectics of two different kinds of activity. In its refusal to simplify the issue and its repeated dramatizations of the failure of progressivism, *Souls* cuts not only against the grain of James's, and indeed Du Bois's, own voluntaristic faiths, but also against James's and Emerson's psychologies. Where James urges an either/or choice, Du Bois, like Adams, faces both the anxiety and the challenge of a multiple self.

"Of Our Spiritual Strivings," the first chapter of *Souls,* illustrates the contrasts. A brief look at it can be used to sketch an outline of propositions and conclusions about the work of James and Du Bois and about nineteenth-century American philosophy and social science that will be delineated in greater detail later. In "Strivings" Du Bois draws heavily on the middle chapters of Hegel's *Phenomenology of Mind,* particularly the account of the "unhappy consciousness," as a resource not only for his famous description of African-American "double-consciousness" but for his entire narrative.[20] The turn to Hegel is a curious move for a supposed follower of James. In his early essays James rejected the subjectivism of Romantic philosophy. He singled out Hegel for his fiercest attacks because Hegel was the source of both pessimistic introspection and the system-building of metaphysical idealism.[21] In focusing on the "unhappy consciousness" rather than on the metaphysical schema of history in the *Phenomenology,* Du Bois is also rejecting idealist teleologies. His use of Hegel can be read against the widespread adoption of Hegel in support of American nationalism and manifest destiny in America in the nineteenth century, from the voluminous productions of the St. Louis Hegelians to the essays of the young John Dewey. But by concentrating attention on the unhappy consciousness in his account of both autobiographical and African-American historical experience, Du Bois also goes counter to James's rejection of introspective accounts of self-consciousness. And by dramatizing African-American psychology inside a particular history of terror and violence, Du Bois locates the self with greater complexity than James. The implications of such a location extend, in fact, beyond an alternative to James to considerations of American exceptionalist theorizations of the atomistic individual and the nation beyond history.

Du Bois's turn to Hegel also has critical implications for Du Bois's own work. The turn occurs at a time when he is working on his sociological study of Philadelphia and on "The Conservation of Races." The reworking of Hegel in "Of Our Spiritual Strivings" is closer to Marx's, Sartre's, and Alexandre Kojève's existentialist and materialist commentaries on Hegel than to any other accounts of Hegel.[22] It therefore challenges the idealist philosophy of history that is proposed in the "Conservation" essay, a philosophy that could be seen as a very different kind of Hegelianism. "Of Our Spiritual Strivings" can also be read in opposition to Du Bois's adoption of sociological positivism in *The Philadelphia Negro*. Hegel had intended those sections of his *Phenomenology* that Du Bois uses (sections that narrate the transformation of consciousness into self-consciousness) to be a critique of positivism or commonsense philosophy. In *The Philadelphia Negro* Du Bois tries strenuously to exclude from his objectivist stance any tinge of introspection or philosophical speculation. The sociological divorce of method and theoretical speculation in fact reproduces the anti-intellectualism of James and leads, like James's pragmatism, to the triumph of an instrumentalist logic that accepts the social order as natural rather than as a historical construction to be contested. There are direct links between James's pragmatism and the attitudes of the American social sciences at the turn of the century. Posnock points out that "at the time of his death [James] was hailed as a patron saint of the efficiency movement" and concludes: "James's critique of intellectualism can lead just as easily to social control as to his cherished anarchy of a 'tramp and vagrant world adrift.'"[23] The pragmatist anarchist is ironically aligned with a social science that, as Dorothy Ross puts it, "found fixed laws of history and nature that would perpetuate established national institutions."[24] Ross connects this abdication to the social process to the fact that "American social science owes its distinctive character to its involvement with the national ideology of American exceptionalism, the idea that America occupies an exceptional place in history, based on her republican government and economic opportunity."[25] Ross's commentary on the political import of exceptionalism is worth noting at greater length because it provides terms with which James's exceptionalism can also be analyzed later and because it helps clarify the significance of Du Bois's foregrounding of history and mediated subjectivity against the grain of American ahistoricisms of various kinds. It also suggests at least some of the possible limits of Du Bois's own sociological conceptualizations: "The models of the social world that have dominated American social science in the twentieth century invite us to look through history to a presumably natural process beneath. Here the social world is composed of individual behaviors responding to natural stimuli, and the capitalist market and modern urban society are understood, in effect, as part of nature. We are led toward quantitative and technocratic manipulation of nature and an idealized liberal vision of American society."[26] Along with Ross's history of American social science, chapters 2 and 3 use critiques of pragmatist instrumentalism (Max Horkheimer) and theoretical analyses of sociological positivism (Gillian Rose, H. T. Wilson) to suggest the possible connections between James's pragmatism and the social sciences, and so also to describe a possible continuity between Du Bois's philosophical and sociological works. This continuity is seen not only as the turn, via James, from the vagueness of metaphysical idealism to pragmatic engagement with the world, but also in terms of a persistence of potentially reactionary theoretical frameworks.

In his pragmatist genealogy West writes that "the evasion of epistemology-centered philosophy—from Emerson to Rorty—results in a conception of philosophy as a form of cultural criticism in which the meaning of America is put forward by intellectuals in response to distinct social and cultural crises. In this sense, American pragmatism is less a philosophical conversation initiated by Plato and more a continuous cultural commentary or set of interpretations that attempt to explain America to itself at a particular historical moment."[27] This liberal pragmatist version of Marx's call for a return of philosophy to the real world reproduces the classic dichotomizations of Europe and America that underlie American self-fashioning, from Emerson's rejection of "the sepulchers of the [European] fathers" for the renewed vision of the "transparent eyeball" in the opening pages of *Nature* (1836),[28] to James's exceptionalist playing-off of American "healthy-minded" objective action against the subjective thought of Europe's "sick soul."[29] Such a dichotomization supports a refusal of the creative and social import of speculative thought and leads to a false separation of action from consciousness, something that George Santayana, who also taught Du Bois, pointed out long ago. A later commentator on America, Louis Hartz, concluded in *The Liberal Tradition in America* (1955) that "the psychic heritage of a nation 'born equal' is . . . a colossal liberal absolutism, the death by atrophy of the philosophic impulse." In the face of this wasting away Hartz is uncertain that a people imagining itself so born can "ever understand peoples . . . who have to become so" or "ever understand itself."[30] What Hartz lamented in the aftermath of the Second World War has, at least since the 1970s, been celebrated with renewed vigor as the triumph of liberal American pragmatism over European, post-Cartesian philosophy, most notably in the work of Rorty.[31] It is in this context that West can celebrate rather than lament "the American *evasion* of philosophy." Clive Bush has ably analyzed Rorty's and West's brand of pragmatist anti-intellectualism. His conclusions, which should be read alongside Ross's commentary on American social science, are worth quoting at some length, since they outline an attitude to the life of the mind (rather than any one particular theoretical or ideological critical stance) to which this work is sympathetic:

> There seems to be a real American-European divide here. In the Western nation which has most seriously failed in relation to communal and public responsibility . . . there seems to be a sentiment according to which philosophy legitimates itself by a populist manner of address, not by whether it has sometimes difficult and complex things to say about nature, experience and culture. . . . In an anti-capitalist framework, thinking is not legitimated by material ends, simply because the greatest truth about the human condition lies elsewhere. And if the only alternative to that conceived of by capitalist philosophers is characterized as "European," superstitious airy-fairyness, in which the "real world" is ignored, then the paucity of those philosophers' imaginations aids and abets a betrayal not only of intellectual life, in which liberal behavior is substituted for radical thought, but of a whole range of values which distinguish freedom from necessity.[32]

The work of Du Bois as much as that of Adams seeks to sustain the relationship of creative imagination and speculative thought, not to evade it. In the commentary on the African-American spirituals in the final chapter of *Souls* Du Bois reflects on an art that imagines freedom in the midst of necessity. In that chapter Du Bois explores not only his own relationship to the folk but also the relationship of his writing (that is, the book called *Souls*) to the different art of the songs. Du Bois is pushed toward transformation through a contemplation of the songs that brings the songs into dialogue with Plato. A consideration of the songs leads to a dislocation of Plato, but also to the writing of a book in which Plato and the songs are both taken as intellective resources aiding survival through creative response to a history of necessity. In "Of the Sorrow Songs" Du Bois asserts that the spirituals are "the sole American music" and "the most beautiful expression of human experience born this side of the seas"

(*SBF* 356–57). But he also insists on his right to use whatever he finds useful from Western literary, philosophical, and political traditions:

> I sit with Shakespeare and he winces not. Across the color line I move arm in arm with Balzac and Dumas, where smiling men and welcoming women glide in gilded halls. From out the caves of evening that swing between the strong-limbed earth and the tracery of the stars, I summon Aristotle and Aurelius and what soul I will, and they come all graciously with no scorn nor condescension. So, wed with Truth, I dwell above the veil. Is this the life you grudge us, O knightly America? Is this the life you long to change into the dull red hideousness of Georgia? Are you afraid lest peering from this high Pisgah, between Philistine and Amalekite, we sight the Promised Land? (*SBF* 438)

As elsewhere in Du Bois, the purpleness of the prose here tends to date the writing. The transcendental vision of art edges toward idealism but should not be mistaken for an abdication of politics. Du Bois's political understanding of art is demonstrated by his commentary on the spirituals. Here the stance resists dogmatism and recognizes that creative life at its best is not reducible to ideological compartmentalization. In the above passage there is an American epic vision of past cultures, asserting against American anti-intellectualism a permission to read the achievements of pre-American experience. It differs from Emerson and Whitman in that it sees these earlier achievements as contemporaneous, not as part of a progressive teleological journey to American triumphalism. It also states a now unfashionable belief that in each era notions of truth and beauty may deserve renewed consideration as part of a politics of self-realization and cultural transformation.

Nowadays a study such as the present one that tries to examine the relationship of a minority cultural tradition to a dominant one is likely to be ill received by those who believe that to undertake such an examination is perforce to deny the minority the authenticity or uniqueness of its achievements. Such a charge, it is hoped, is adequately addressed by Du Bois himself in his reflections on his relationship to European and American culture with which this introduction began, and by his reflections on art quoted above. Du Bois makes it quite clear that to deny a black writer a catholicity of procedures and resources is, in effect, a kind of racism.

As Kenneth Warren has noted, an African-American criticism that asserts the *difference* of African-American literature within the history of

American literature aligns itself with the most "mainstream" form of American cultural self-fashioning: American exceptionalism.[33] Where it seeks to discover difference, this critical practice in fact produces ideological *identity*. Warren also observes accurately that, within the logic of the reproduction of American exceptionalism, this criticism's attempt to displace "that quite problematic American 'we'" only installs a no less problematic "racial 'we'" in which the "pluralism" of a "nonpolitical notion of black unity" attempts to bypass "politics and ideology."[34]

To draw false demarcations between black and white cultures does not help unveil the achievements of African-American art; rather, it obscures the full extent of that achievement. The drawing of such boundaries signals a failure of critical nerve. In his *Concluding Unscientific Postscript* Kierkegaard writes that "as soon as it is proposed to make [anything] serve as limit, in such a way that the limit is not itself again dialectical, we have superstition and narrowness of spirit. There always lurks some such concern in a man, at the same time indolent and anxious, a wish to lay hold of something so really fixed that it can exclude all dialectics; but this desire is an expression of cowardice."[35] In his invocation of Western art in *Souls* Du Bois seems to agree. Anyone who would draw a "color line" blocking dialogue between the spirituals and the traditions of Shakespeare, Aristotle, and the others is "afraid" of the possibilities of freedom and would return the black artist to "the dull red hideousness of Georgia."

In concentrating on the relation of Du Bois's thought to various Euro-American traditions this study does not propose that Du Bois's relation to the development of African-American thought be accorded secondary place. This is not a totalizing account of Du Bois's early career; it is an examination of a much-neglected aspect of that career. The connections between Du Bois's work and that of various African-American thinkers have already received considerable attention in several studies of his work, though much more needs to be done even in this area. At the same time it is worth stressing again that the concern of the present study is with the theoretical and conceptual underpinnings of Du Bois's early thought, and these *are* taken mainly from Euro-American traditions. The attraction to vitalism provides one instance. Crummell's proposals for an elite leadership and his theorizations of racial destiny are certainly a major source for Du Bois's adoption of similar ideas, and other African-American precedents could be invoked.[36] But on the conceptual level this kind of vitalism is a commonplace of the nineteenth century, most frequently associated with Carlyle and Emerson, and also of the Progressive Era in America.

Sources and influences understood in any deterministic sense are not the concern of the following chapters. As Raymond Williams has cautioned, "The history of ideas is a dead study if it proceeds solely in terms of the abstraction of influences. What is important in a thinker . . . is the quality of his direct response."[37] The discussion here tries above all to respect the quality of Du Bois's response and to read the inventiveness of his response politically and culturally, not as an Oedipal anxiety of influence. As the American poet George Oppen recognizes in his long poem *Of Being Numerous* (1967), it is both difficult and also crucial to speak

> about those who have recognized the range of choice or those who have lived within the life they were born to—. It is not precisely a question of profundity but a different order of experience. One would have to tell what happens in a life, what choices present themselves, what the world is for us, what happens in time, what thought is in the course of a life and therefore what art is, and the isolation of the actual.[38]

The *essential* facts of such a life and such a process can be grasped only through a description of the multiplicity through which they arise. Within such a description art is conceived of as neither a wholly conditioned nor a wholly unconditioned process (that is, neither as a mirror of the apparatus of ideology and the relations of production, nor as utopian transcendence), but as a process in which it is possible to imagine self-realization and freedom inside the realm of necessity.

Part I

From the South

to the

Seventh Ward

Two

"Great Men," "Great Laws," and the "Fourth Dimension"

The Crisis of Hero, System, and Nation

In June 1890 Du Bois graduated cum laude with a bachelor's degree in philosophy from Harvard University. He had transferred to Harvard in 1888 having already completed a general undergraduate degree at Fisk University, an African-American institution in Nashville, Tennessee.[1] During his time at Fisk Du Bois had gone into rural Tennessee to teach among the black poor and had been shocked by the appalling condition of black life, which he encountered more directly and concretely in the South than he had done in the Massachusetts of his childhood. At Harvard Du Bois appears to have made a separate peace. While he held "lively social intercourse" with the black community of "Boston and surrounding places," of Harvard Du Bois "asked nothing . . . but the tutelage of teachers and the freedom of the library," choosing "quite voluntarily and willingly [to be] outside its social life" (*DD* 579). Du Bois felt that Boston, though by no means free of racism, was the most comfortable Northern city for blacks to live in.[2] But Harvard itself was witnessing a period of greater social division while Charles Eliot Norton, its president, offered some support for students from public schools and for African-Americans and Jews.[3] At the same time that he recognized the effective segregation on campus, Du Bois seems also to have held the racial crises of the times at bay in order to pursue "the basis of knowledge and explore foundations and beginnings" (*A* 133). It was to prove difficult to sustain this artificial separation of the political and the pedagogical worlds.

This chapter examines work written by Du Bois during his first two years at Harvard in relation to the ethical and social thought of William James. James offered his students a spirited defense of a voluntaristic ethics in a pluralist world, and an equally lively critique of metaphysical and deterministic systems that made claims to be a science of ethics. It is clear from Du Bois's own account of these years that James had a liberating impact on him and helped him to move away from the conservatism of his religious background and his training at Fisk toward a more socially grounded, locally focused secular mode of social thought. But if Du Bois was at this time in the process of becoming something of a follower of James, then it is strange to find in these early writings both a retreat into metaphysical historicism and a radical science-fictional satirization of the Jamesian ethics of self-realization through a will to action.

The satire, available in the form of an incomplete draft of a previously unpublished short story, tests the political limits of voluntarism inside the nightmare arena of black life in America. The outlines of a deterministic philosophy of history that is also an ethics are given in a long thesis written for James, also unpublished. The flight from history into historicism is precisely a bid for security in the face of the unmastered present revealed in the story. The doubts and anxieties dramatized in these works are further developed in Du Bois's Harvard commencement speech on the topic of "Jefferson Davis as Representative of Civilization."

The Harvard commencement speech attempts to modify and critique some of the assumptions of the Great Man theory of history that were the bases of an earlier commencement speech by Du Bois, delivered at Fisk, on Bismarck as exemplary nation builder. However, the dawning critical awareness of all these early works does not lead Du Bois to any immediate sense of viable alternatives. Instead, he perpetually circles back to comforting guarantees of historical purpose and mastery promised by the Great Man theory. The contradictions between a developing sense of the nature of the historical experience of power and oppression and a commitment to voluntarism and historicism remain exemplary for the whole of the early career of Du Bois examined in this study. Nor do the doubts and contradictions coalesce into a systematically theorized and publicly articulated critique of James's philosophy. Rather, Du Bois's work from his first two years at Harvard begins to explore issues of power, politics, and alienation that are central to an understanding of African-American experience but that James inadequately addresses. The young Du Bois begins to ask questions that James's ethics cannot answer. What is only half articulate in the early writings considered here will be made devastatingly clear in *Souls*.

At the center of the discussion in this chapter is a consideration of the social and political limitations of James's philosophical thought as it is presented in his teaching and his essays in the 1880s and 1890s. James's conceptualization of individual freedom blocks the possibility of formulating radical opposition to the drift of social process. In the end, the will to believe and the will to action only confer a blessing on the status quo. An understanding of this failure will highlight the philosophical and political issues that are central to Du Bois's struggle to describe the nature of African-American self-consciousness using the tools made available to him by his education.

Du Bois came to Harvard wanting to be a philosopher. This desire signaled not a failure of engagement with the historical situation of the African-American people but a response to it. The undergraduate philosophical speculations can be seen as an attempt to address a set of issues arising out of the reality encountered in the South. It is with a brief account of Du Bois's experiences in Tennessee that the chapter begins.

Bismarck in Tennessee: Traveling in Time

Du Bois came to Tennessee from the small New England town of Great Barrington, Massachusetts. Although in his autobiographies Du Bois tends to paint a picture of his childhood that is a little too rosy, it is nevertheless true that his New England boyhood was relatively sheltered from both racism and the kind of black life and culture he was to encounter in the South and then in the slums of Philadelphia's Seventh Ward. David Levering Lewis, Du Bois's latest biographer, calculates that the population of Great Barrington at the end of the Civil War, just three years before Du Bois was born, was about four thousand, and that there were less than thirty African-American families in the region. There was as yet only a small influx of freed slaves from the South into the region. Most African-Americans in the area were farmers, and a few were substantial property owners. Those that left farming did not go into millwork like the new Catholic immigrants, who were looked down upon by both the African-Americans and their white Protestant neighbors, but into personal service.[4] Reviewing his life in his seventieth year, Du Bois wrote that he had "learned new things about the world" during his three years in Tennessee:

> My knowledge of the race problem became more definite. I saw discrimination in ways which I had never dreamed; the separation of passengers on the railways of the South was just beginning; the race separation in living quarters throughout the cities and towns was manifest; the public disdain and even insult in race contact on the street continually took my breath; I came in contact for the first time with a sort of violence that I had never realized in New England. (*DD* 575–76)

Violence against blacks was common, and at Fisk Du Bois met "men and women who had faced mobs and seen lynchings; who knew every phase of insult and repression" (*A* 108).

Feeling that the campus in Nashville provided a "protected vantage point" (*A* 114), Du Bois spent the summers of 1896 and 1897 teaching school among the poor rural blacks of east Tennessee. If in Nashville Du Bois had been witness to the emergence of the New South, in the "little valley near Alexandria" (*DD* 576) he found himself back in the Old South:

> I travelled not only in space but in time. I touched the very shadow of slavery. I lived and taught school in log cabins built before the Civil War. My first school was the second held in the district since Emancipation. I touched intimately the lives of the commonest of mankind—people who ranged from bare-footed dwellers on dirt floors, with patched rags for clothes, to rough, hard-working farmers, with plain, clean plenty. (*A* 114)

In *Souls,* which is plotted over a series of journeys across the American South, a timeless and dreamy South is evoked again and again only to be collapsed into the nightmare of its real past and present. "Once upon a time," Du Bois writes at the start of the fourth chapter, "I taught school in the hills of Tennessee, where the broad dark vale of the Mississippi begins to roll and crumple to greet the Alleghenies" (*SBF* 96). The young Du Bois "wandered beyond railways, beyond stage lines" to where "sprinkled over hill and dale lay cabins and farmhouses, shut out from the world by the forests and the rolling hills toward the east" (*SBF* 97). This is, of course, a particularly American version of the pastoral, a version of that tradition of romance writing that is best known through Washington Irving's mythologization of the Catskill Mountains and Sleepy Hollow. And Du Bois's awakening is as rude as Rip Van Winkle's. Having found a rural school to teach in, he is invited to dinner by the school commissioner only to be told to wait till the whites have eaten (*SBF* 98–99). The stay in Tennessee, which is the concern of the chapter on the "meaning of progress," ends with Du Bois riding back to Nashville in the Jim Crow car (*SBF* 108). Increasingly we see a landscape "forlorn and forsaken" (*SBF* 145), littered with the ruins of former plantations and populated by the poor and unemployed blacks.

> On we wind, through sand and pines and glimpses of old plantations, till there creeps into sight a cluster of buildings,—wood and brick, mills and houses, and scattered cabins. It seemed quite a village. As it came nearer and nearer, however, the aspect changed: the buildings were rotten, the bricks were falling out, the mills were silent, and the store was closed. Only in the cabin appeared now and then a bit of lazy life. I could imagine the place under some weird spell, and was half-minded to search out the princess. An old ragged black man, honest, simple, and improvident, told us the tale. The Wizard of the North—the Capitalist—had rushed down in the seventies to woo this coy dark soil. He bought a square mile or more, and for a time the field-hands sang, the gins groaned, and the mills buzzed. Then came a change. The agent's son embezzled the funds and ran off with them. Then the agent himself disappeared. Finally the new agent stole even the books, and the company in wrath closed its business and its houses, refused to sell, and let houses and furniture and machinery rust and rot. So the Waters-Loring plantation was stilled by the spell of dishonesty, and stands like some gaunt rebuke to a scarred land. (*SBF* 149–50)

Here, as in a similar passage on the economic basis and wealthy opulence of the antebellum South that follows a few pages later (*SBF* 152–53), Du Bois links the rupture of the pastoral with the history of the political economy of a new kind of slavery that followed the war, as if Emancipation had never taken place. For all the rudimentary broadness and melodrama of its analytic strokes, this point of rupture, like so many of the insights in *Souls,* is given a penetrating force, rather than weakened, by the moving sentimentalism of this condensed exemplary narrative.

A sensuous opening of the body to the natural landscape, and the disgust of the head and the heart against the history for which the geography has been a stage, also characterize Adams's vivid memories of his antebellum childhood visit to Maryland, Virginia, and Washington, D.C. It is one of the earliest and most powerful barriers encountered by progressive self-confidence in the *Education:* "What struck [Adams] most, to remain fresh in his mind all his lifetime, was the sudden change that came over the world on entering a slave State" (*EHA* 43).

> Slavery struck him in the face; it was a nightmare; a horror; a crime; the sum of all wickedness! Contact made it only more repulsive. He wanted to escape, like the negroes, to free soil. Slave States were dirty, unkempt, poverty-stricken, ignorant, vicious! He had not a thought but repulsion for it; and yet the picture had another side. The May sunshine and shadow had something to do with it; the thickness of foliage and the heavy smells had more; the sense of atmosphere, almost new, had perhaps as much again; and the brooding indolence of a warm climate and a negro population hung in the atmosphere heavier than the catalpas. (*EHA* 44)

These scenes are only a short train ride away from Capitol Hill, and they throw the young Adams into confusion about his own faith in Enlightenment politics.

> To the New England mind, roads, schools, clothes, and a clean face were connected as part of the law of order or divine system. Bad roads meant bad morals. The moral of this Virginia road was clear, and the boy fully learned it. Slavery was wicked, and slavery was the cause of this road's badness which amounted to social crime—and yet, at the end of the road and product of the crime stood Mount Vernon and George Washington. (*EHA* 47)

Adams does not know "how to deal with the moral problem that deduced George Washington from the sum of all wickedness" (*EHA* 48). The dream of reason and progress is built upon America's own version of feudal horror. As far as the struggle to conceptualize the direction of time and history in the *Education* goes, the effect of the South on Adams is the same as that of past-bound Rome: "Rome could not be fitted into an orderly, middle-class, Bostonian, systematic scheme of evolution. No law of progress applied to it" (*EHA* 91). For Adams, "in 1860 the lights and shadows were still medieval, and medieval Rome was alive": "the shadows breathed and glowed, full of soft forms felt by lost senses. No sand blast of science had yet skinned off the epidermis of history, thought, and feeling" (*EHA* 90). In the case of the South, the retreat in time is a return not to past glory, but to the brutal violence by which the nation was born into history. In the first chapter of the *Education,* Adams asks of himself, "What could become of such a child of the seventeenth and eighteenth centuries, when he should wake up to find himself required to play the game of the twentieth?" (*EHA* 4). The threat to the Enlightenment faith in the triumph of rationality in social and historical process comes not only from the future horizons of a fragmenting modernity, but also from the persistence of the past itself.[5]

Unlike Adams, Du Bois, for the most part, sees the new era as a political continuation of rational progress. He struggles to embody this progressive force himself, and to develop a program for leadership that will lift into modernity African-Americans trapped in the pre-Emancipation era. For Du Bois, it is not just the effects of slavery and Jim Crow that account for this time trap. In "Of the Faith of the Fathers," the tenth chapter of *Souls,* Du Bois characterizes "the double life of every American negro" as being "swept on by the current of the nineteenth while yet struggling in the eddies of the fifteenth century" (*SBF* 502). Du Bois is describing the nature of African-American religious beliefs. The fifteenth century is meant to evoke the "heathen rites" of *pre*-slavery Africa (*SBF* 498). The collision of the nineteenth and fifteenth centuries suggests the retention within African-American Christianity of certain traits of what is "roughly designated" by Du Bois "as Voodooism" (*SBF* 498). According to Du Bois, the slave

> called up all the resources of heathenism to aid,—exorcism and witchcraft, the mysterious Obi worship with its barbarous rites, spells, and blood-sacrifice even, now and then, of human victims. Weird midnight orgies and mystic conjurations were invoked, the witch-woman and the voodoo-priest became the centre of Negro group life, and that vein of vague superstition which characterizes the unlettered Negro *even to-day* was deepened and strengthened. (*SBF* 499, emphasis added)

Although Du Bois is one of the first to grasp the continuities between the African religions of the slaves and some of the practices and beliefs of the black church, and also one of the first to analyze the political role of the church in black American life, in the passage above he aligns his mode of commentary with the moralistic regard of the exoticist white spectator. Where the burden of the Southern and Roman past undermines the rationalist foundations of Adams's education, the primitivization of "black folk" secures Du Bois's progressive confidence.

It is true that within the overall narrative structuring of *Souls,* the reversals and doubts do come and are honestly met. When Du Bois dramatizes his own responses to the "sorrow songs" in the final chapter of the book, the meanings of progress and knowledge are shifted. The songs, and the collective voice that sings them, pull Du Bois back in time, not toward ignorance and squalor, but toward a tragic understanding and a poetry of survival. Du Bois does not present his own crises of understanding with the nervous sharpness of Adams's ironies, but *Souls*'s dramatizations are as true as the *Education* in their sense of the process by which knowledge emerges from a living problematic of experience. But the first reaction of the young Du Bois witnessing the horrors of the South is not to undertake complex literary description but to propose ill-considered solutions of dramatic simplicity and force.

When Du Bois graduated from Fisk in June 1888 he chose as the topic of his commencement speech Bismarck as a model for African-American leadership. Bismarck was his "hero" because he "had made a nation out of a mass of bickering peoples. He had dominated the whole development with his strength until he crowned an emperor at Versailles." This "foreshadowed" in Du Bois's mind "the kind of thing that the American Negroes must do, marching forth with strength and determination under trained leadership" (*A* 126). The hero offers vitality and salvation within a parasitic structure. He is the force that moves history forward and the pattern inside which others can live by imitation. So history is reduced to the biographies of great men.[6] For Du Bois heroic vitalism offered an ideal of free will and agency in the face of the mounting racism, both legislative and public, that wiped out the gains of the Civil War and Reconstruction between the 1870s and 1890s and returned a disenfranchised black population to conditions of poverty, powerlessness, and terror that recalled the days of slavery.[7] The will to power holds obvious attractions in conditions of powerlessness and a vacuum of political alternatives. So it is hardly surprising that "the romantic vision of state, with its stress on the authentic *Geist,* spirit, or soul of the nation, appealed for a long time to Du Bois, as it tends to appeal to someone who is obsessed by his people's historic deprivation and disunity and who yearns for a greater national or racial future."[8]

Writing at the end of the 1930s, when he was increasingly attracted to socialist and Marxist thought, Du Bois understood that his choice of Bismarck as hero revealed "the abyss between [his] education and the truth in the world." In those earlier years he understood nothing "of current European intrigue, of the expansion of European power into Africa, of the Industrial Revolution built on slave trade and now turning into Colonial Imperialism." The young Du Bois was, in fact, "blithely European and imperialist in outlook; democratic as democracy was conceived in America" (DD 577). The older Du Bois is aware of the irony of his earlier espousal of Bismarck as political model at a time when the United States emerged, after the Spanish American War, as an imperial power in the Pacific and as the dominant influence in the Caribbean. It was a time when, in the words of Henry Steele Commager, "the piercing protests of the anti-imperialists were drowned out by the thunder of manifest destiny."[9]

From the vantage point of the late twentieth century the politics of the young Du Bois appear to be miscalculated and reactionary in the context of nineteenth-century America, but such obvious judgments are of little value. It is more important to try to understand what alternatives were available to Du Bois, why he made the choices he made, and what these decisions tell us about the culture in which he was working—in short, to watch as sympathetically as possible the committed investigations of a young man deeply engaged with the crises of his culture.

Other writings from the Fisk period suggest that the immediate inspiration for the "Bismarck" speech may have been Carlyle.[10] But the speech must also be located within a wider field of nineteenth-century obsessions with hero worship and heroic vitalism in America, from Emerson's "representative men" and William James's psychological and philosophical celebrations of will, to social Darwinism and other deterministic theories of force, and the revivals of nationalist ideologies and movements from the Civil War to the 1890s. The range of these permutations indicates that vitalism can appear in the shape of either *hero* or *system,* or as what Henry Adams called "lines of will" and "lines of force" (*EHA* 426). Adams saw the two as being in opposition, with force replacing will in the modern era. But though these two forms can be mutually opposed, in both cases the desire is for trajectories of vitalist power as the structures of historicism against mechanistic notions of power. As Harold Kaplan has noted, this dualism is "installed at the very center of naturalist thought":

One half of this dualism is deeply passive, submitting thought and choice to the dominant movement of history. The other, in contrast, assumes a kind of automatic conformity with the will of history and so becomes completely willful itself, in the manner of the leader who believes that he can and must control men's minds in order to empower them with the beliefs that change history. The result is a kind of convenient dialogue between passive followers and the activist cadres who speak for history. The conflict between naturalist politics and the older democratic tradition makes itself most evident here.[11]

At Harvard Du Bois found philosophical confirmations and alibis for his vitalist tendencies in James's ethics and theorizations of will. But he then tried to transform the hero as force of history into an impersonal metaphysics of history in which the teleological unfolding of history is governed by universal laws, though without Adams's always sardonic mistrust of that process.

Pluralism as Mind-Cure:
The Accommodation of William James

Du Bois had come to Harvard with the intention of pursuing philosophy as a "life career, with teaching for support" (*A* 133), and he stuck to this goal with a distinguished seriousness, picking demanding courses and organizing his days around a rigorous work schedule.[12] These were Harvard's golden years, and Du Bois noted accurately in his *Autobiography* that "seldom, if ever, has any American university had such a galaxy of great men and fine teachers as Harvard in the decade between 1885 and 1895" (*A* 132). All the faculties in which Du Bois took courses contained distinguished scholars, but this was particularly true of the philosophy department. Besides James and Santayana, there were Josiah Royce and George Herbert Palmer.[13] Although Du Bois met and talked with Royce (with whom he also did forensics) and Palmer, he took courses in philosophy only with James and Santayana—with James in his first year, and with both James and Santayana in his second.

In his first year of philosophy Du Bois had signed up for Palmer's course on ethics. But Palmer was on sabbatical and was replaced by the younger James, who represented greater philosophical and psychological radicalism compared with Palmers's Christian moralism. Philosophy 4 was a course on "recent English contributions to theistic ethics," and James used as required texts the second volume of James Martineau's *Types of Ethical Theory* (1885) and his *Study of Religion* (1888).[14] James's lectures, however, followed neither the announced focus of the course nor the work of Martineau in any narrow sense. Each lecture used an assigned portion of Martineau's work as a point of departure for broad philosophical speculation largely determined by James's own current concerns. Although James had not published any of his major books by the first year that Du Bois studied with him (1888–89), he *had* formulated most of his key ideas: this much is evident from Du Bois's surviving notebook for the course (the only surviving notebook from the Harvard period and previously unexamined),[15] from James's own lecture notes,[16] and from the works James had already published (particularly several of the essays that were later included in *The Will to Believe* [1897]) and those that appeared soon after.[17]

In keeping with his already published work and much of his later work, James's lectures offered a defense of contingent ethics, free will, and the relativity of all systems of knowledge set against an ongoing critique of absolutist programs, particularly Spencerian evolutionary determinism and Hegelian idealist monism, and their undermining of human volition.[18] James insisted that "we must *experiment* in morals. We live under the sword of the future.["](19) The last words of the notes read: *"Man must act"* (P4). James rejected Kant's relegation of freedom to the noumenal world and told his students that the neo-Kantian Charles Bernard Renouvier was the great man who had upheld a theory of free will in the phenomenal world (P4).[20] James referred to idealism as "transcendental optimism" or "Indifferentism" because the system of Martineau, or that of a Royce or a Hegel, made the individual indifferent to strife in the world—and James had insisted throughout the course on the need to strive as a cornerstone of ethics.

Within what James later in his career called the "pluralistic universe" there could not be any scientifically grounded *"system* of ethics."[21] The only attempt to unite science and ethics (apart from "mysticism" or "Gnosticism") has been, James concludes, Hegelianism, but this he dismisses as, in the final count, "sophistical" (P4). It is clear from Du Bois's notes for Philosophy 4 and from James's own notes for various lecture courses given during the late 1870s and throughout the 1880s that, for James, the idealist metaphysical tradition he labeled Hegelianism included not only the work of contemporary philosophers like his colleague Royce, but also Spencer's attempt to construct a science of ethics based on an evolutionary theory whose progressive teleology falsely reconciled rationalism and empiricism by recourse to the prime cause, which Spencer called "the Unknowable." Spencer explained in *The Data of Ethics* (1879) that the "ultimate aim" behind the epic project of his "System of Philosophy," begun with *First Principles* in 1862, was "that of finding for the principles of right and wrong in conduct at large, a scientific basis."[22] But for James, evolutionary science could not be the basis for ethics because the analogy between the human and natural spheres falsely attempted to deduce the higher categories from the lower ones (P4). For James there were no deterministic "laws of history," and Spencer's system was a "metaphysical creed" masquerading as science.[23]

Building on his critique of determinism and his defense of will and action, James wound up the course with an argument for the relativity of all systems of knowledge. He tried to assess the rival claims of philosophy, science, religion, skepticism, and poetry. A few lectures later James went on to consider the different conceptions of God possible in the realms of religion, science, ethics, and poetry, something like Kierkegaard's different modes of existence. He argued that, although these various conceptualizations may appear to be compatible on some generalized level, an investigation of the concrete particulars of each realm reveals them to be fundamentally irreconcilable. In insisting that the world was a *"plurality,"* not a *"unity"* (P4), James was offering his students philosophy as an ethical and epistemological negative capability.

James's defense of plurality, his sense of energy and openness of process, shows him at his most radical and creative, but this is also a radicalism from which James retreats. The critique of Spencerian determinism is sound, even if sometimes overly caricaturish. But James's own arguments in support of free will and relativism are far from rigorous in their theorizations of the nature of agency and value.

In his own notes for the Philosophy 4 course for the year that Du Bois studied with him, James writes:

So far as I feel anything good, I make it so. It *is* so, for me. . . . *Prima facie,* goods form a multifarious jungle. Must we so leave them, or can they be unified? . . . The abstract best would be that *all* goods should be realized. That is physically impossible, for many of them exclude each other. The whole difficulty of the moral life consists in deciding, when this is the case, which good to sacrifice and which to save. . . . The solution is [to] consider *every* good as a real good, and *keep as many as we can.* That act is the best act which *makes for the best whole,* the best whole being that which prevails at least cost, in which the vanquished goods are least completely annulled. . . . Follow the common traditions. Sacrifice all wills which are not organizable, and which avowedly go against the whole. No one pretends in the main to revise the decalogue, or to take up offenses against life, property, veracity, or decency into the permanent whole. If those are a man's goods, the man is not a member of the whole we mean to keep, and we sacrifice both him and his goods without a tear. When the rivalry is between real organizable goods, the rule is that the one victorious should so far as possible keep the vanquished somehow represented. Find some innocent way out.[24]

These notes reveal the instrumentalist logic of James's thought. Value is defined as the exercise of self-interest within the conservative parameters of "common traditions." The notion that the collective will may be malign and may need to be opposed is never considered. Evil is simply not taken up "into the permanent whole." The belief in the regulatory functioning of collective choice against individual "offenses" is a version of the social Darwinist explanation of social process. It can lead in James not only to a simplistic faith in the containment of evil but also to an undermining of the individual creativity of which he is seen as a champion. In "Great Men and Their Environment" (1880), for example, he writes that "the relation of the visible environment to the great man is in the main exactly what it is to the 'variation' in the Darwinian philosophy. It chiefly adopts or rejects, preserves or destroys, in short *selects* him" (GM 226). Individual "initiatives," the equivalents of Darwinian spontaneous variation, are subsumed within environmental selection. Since the environment can "reject" or "destroy" individual "variation," the individual creativity is always under threat from potential social conservatism.[25] The same accommodation to a social Darwinist process is evident in all the talk of sacrifice and conquest in the Philosophy 4 notes. The only chance of self-fulfillment that the "vanquished" can have in James's world is dependent upon the good will of the victors. James's final appeal to innocence is a disgraceful evasion.

James is so comfortable theorizing the creation of value as a matter of the relationship of "authority" and "submission" because he cannot imagine the experience of power and terror.[26] Against those who argue that Sicily and Sardinia "stagnated because they never gained political autonomy, being always owned by some Continental power," James argues that they did not gain autonomy "simply because no individuals were born there with patriotism and ability enough to inflame their countrymen with national pride, ambition, and thirst for independent life" (GM 241–42).

James's conceptualization of the relationship of history and action leaves no way to describe a self-consciousness struggling for critical understanding and self-realization in the midst of alienation and the mediations of power. All that James dismisses as pessimistic subjectivism. The exemplary text is "The Dilemma of Determinism" (1884). Here James remarks on "how inevitably the question of determinism and indeterminism slides us into the question of optimism and pessimism, or, as our fathers called it, 'the question of evil.' "[27] Pessimism is a passive acceptance of the status quo that does not move beyond epistemology, and therefore does not confront being and doing. According to James, for a pessimist,

> the world must not be regarded as a machine whose final purpose is the making real of any outward good, but rather as a contrivance for deepening the theoretic consciousness of what goodness and evil in their intrinsic natures are. Not the doing either of good or of evil is what nature cares for, but the knowing of them. Life is one long eating of the fruit of the tree of *knowledge*. (DoD 165)

This attitude James labels "*gnosticism*" or "*subjectivism*" (DoD 165). As examples of this subjectivism James trots out caricatures of the *Sturm und Drang* of consciousness in Romanticism (DoD 169) or "the last runnings of the romantic school, as we see them in that strange contemporary Parisian literature, with which we of the less clever countries are so often driven to rinse out our minds after they have become clogged with the dulness and heaviness of our native pursuits" (DoD 172). The threat to American native simplicities comes specifically from the antitheological aestheticism and stoic speculativeness of Joseph Ernest Renan and from the naturalism of Emile Zola (DoD 172). The opposition between pessimism and optimism, determinism and indeterminism, is, then, a polarization (to use James's own terms from *The Varieties of Religious Experience* [1904]) of the "sick soul" of Europe and the "healthy mindedness" of America, or between European introspection and American action. James, of course, draws no distinction between decadent self-regard and creative reflection on the relationship of self and history; for James, apparently, thought is something that does not clog American "minds."

Not surprisingly James includes "Hegelian gnosticism" and the "disciples of Hegel" (DoD 171; 145) in the pessimist camp. But James's experiential and actional critique of Hegel should not be equated with either Marx's shifting of Hegelian epistemology toward materialist understanding or Sartre's ontological revisions of Hegel.[28] James's answer to the impasse of passivity and activity in idealist philosophy is a celebration of the Carlylean will to power. Despite reservations about many aspects of Carlyle's writings, James shares his sense that "the heart of romantic utterance" is a "whimpering of wail and woe" from which "the only escape is by the practical way" (DoD 173). The most important thing Carlyle says to James is: " 'Hang your sensibilities! Stop your snivelling complaints, and your equally snivelling raptures! Leave off your general emotional tomfoolery, and get to WORK like men!' But this means a complete rupture with the subjectivist philosophy of things. It says conduct, and not sensibility, is the ultimate fact for our recognition" (DoD 174). The polarization of "conduct" and "sensibility" is a false dualism that denies reflection because it cannot distinguish between emotional excess and active consciousness. Within this confusion, there can be no thinking, only doing—and doing *right* at that. James is happy to argue that "no matter how we feel; if we are only faithful in the outward act and refuse to do wrong, the world will in so far be safe, and we be quit of our debt toward it." Thus, "at a stroke we have passed from the subjective into the objective philosophy of things, *much as one awakens from some feverish dream, full of bad lights and noises, to find one's self bathed in the sacred coolness and quiet of the air of night*" (DoD 174, emphasis added). The earlier dichotomization of decadent Europe and healthy America here appears as an escape from terror and its manifestations in the unconscious workings of the mind into the reassuring securities of a sacred stillness. James's "heroic" ethical action unfolds and is tested not in the world of Emily Dickinson or of Poe or Melville, but somewhere between the early Emerson's hunger for transcendence and the reassuring moral sentimentalism of Louisa May Alcott's *Little Women*.

For all of James's insistence on the world as an indeterminate plurality that cannot be described through the singular and teleological schematizations of a Spencer or Hegel, his own reduction of action to "conduct" is itself an escape from the challenge of plurality. For James, "our responsibility ends with performance of that duty [which is conduct], and the burden of the rest we may lay on higher powers" (DoD 175) because "the essence of this philosophy of objective conduct" is "the recognition of limits, foreign and opaque to our understanding" (DoD 174). What appears as a just and modern recognition of the relativity of human knowledge in James, amounts in fact to a suppression of the plurality of the world, and of the fragmentation of subject and epistemology alike. In the face of a world defined as a plurality the answer is not to *think* but to *act* with singular determination and to let thought and plurality take care of themselves. Reflective thought is evaded because it is seen as a hindrance to action.

James's espousal of action and right conduct and his attack on what he calls subjectivism need to be seen in the context of American culture in the last two decades of the nineteenth century. John Higham, in an account of the polarities of this culture, argues that although versions of pessimism and decadence did make inroads into the work of writers like Ambrose Bierce, Mark Twain, and Brooks and Henry Adams, pessimism never became "general or profound" in America.[29] Men like James and Frederick Jackson Turner, who "conceived of themselves as revitalizing values rooted in American life," are taken as more representative of the age. "Feeling that great reserves of energy lay all around them," these men "did not look so far afield as those Europeans who turned to primitive myth or to the international proletariat. Nor did they look so far beneath the surface as those Europeans who plunged into the depths of the private self." Higham concludes that "nothing seems more striking in comparative terms than the relative absence in the United States of the radical subjectivity that was entering European thought."[30]

Higham's is a useful sketch of the period but tends for the most part to celebrate the programs for the active and strenuous life as a resistance to materialist and scientific rationality and to give inadequate attention to the accommodationist potential of such attitudes. The extent to which James's strategies for self-recovery into the health of "sacred coolness" are a program of accommodation to the social process can be seen by comparing his strategies and rhetoric with those of the therapeutic mind-cure movement that came to great prominence in the second half of the nineteenth century in America as a response to widespread fears of ever-prevalent abulia (or neurasthenia). James's playings-off of action and passive thought, of health and debilitating pessimism, are commonplaces of the mind-cure movement. As Jackson Lears has shown, this movement did not so much resist the new managerial and corporate capitalist culture, which was perceived as a major cause of what George Miller Beard in 1880 called "American nervousness," as train people to live in harmony with it.[31]

James's own fear of a paralysis of will and nervous prostration in the late 1860s and early 1870s and his subsequent recovery after reading Renouvier are well-known episodes of his life.[32] As Lears points out, such a bout of neurasthenia was far from exceptional at the time among the urban bourgeoisie. The "respectable American" came to be perceived as "a creature who is . . . oversophisticated and effete—a being in whom the springs of action are, in greater or less degree, paralyzed or perverted by the undue predominance of the intellect."[33] These, like the attacks on the European Decadent movement and its supposed undermining of American moral fiber, were the terms James also adopted in his anti-intellectualism. And as in James's advice to the subjectivists, the stress on returning to health through vigorous activity played a crucial role in many of the mind-cure therapies. This was particularly true in the last two decades of the century of the therapies of "psychic abundance," which followed those therapies that had stressed "psychic scarcity"— the hoarding of valuable psychic energy in repose: "Many advised the overstrained to put themselves in touch with 'the great everlasting currents' of psychic energy in order to win back and perhaps even increase lost mental and emotional vigor." The order of the day was "continual psychic growth over adherence to prescribed norms."[34]

Again, the parallels between the therapies of abundance and James's notions of self-realization are not hard to see. But it is Lears's alignment of mind-cure therapies and the capitalist linking of a culture of consumption with personal growth and self-expression that suggests one way in which the political and social meanings of James's defense of free choice and healthy-mindedness inside a plural universe can be read.

> Mind-curists were brothers under the skin to a new breed of corporate liberal ideologues—social engineers who spoke of economic rather than psychic abundance but who shared the interest of mind-curists in liberating repressed impulses. The economist Simon Nelson Patten, for example, argued at the turn of the century that the era of economic scarcity was over and that the "new basis of civilization" would be self-expression rather than self-denial. "Men must enjoy" would be the watchword of the emerging economy of abundance. "The new morality does not consist in saving but in expanding consumption," he asserted. Patten's deification of "self-expression" and "experience" as ends in themselves, his rejection of ultimate values in favor of perpetual growth and process—these qualities allied him with abundance therapists and with other social theorists like John Dewey and Walter Lippmann.[35]

Although Lears does not mention him, James would provide an even more appropriate alignment here. James's vision of an unhampered exercise of free choice within a pluralistic universe where all values are contingent begins as a challenge to orthodoxy and dogma but ends up as a mirror of the operations of consumer choice within a free market. The overriding logic of James's ethics is utilitarian. Therefore all values become equal and truth is defined as the satisfaction of self-interest. Precisely the relativity of truth and personal profitability, use value and abundant wealth, as well as the alignment of the technological benefits of capitalist society and therapy, provide the framework in which James himself defends the mind-cure movement in *The Varieties of Religious Experience* (1904).

> The obvious outcome of our experience is that the world can be handled according to many systems of ideas, and is so handled by different men, and will each time give some characteristic kind of profit, for which he cares, to the handler, while at the same time some other kind of profit has to be omitted or postponed. Science gives to all of us telegraphy, electric lighting, and diagnosis, and succeeds in preventing and curing a certain amount of disease. Religion in the shape of mind-cure gives to some of us serenity, moral poise, and happiness, and prevents certain forms of disease as well as science does, or even better in a certain class of persons. Evidently, then, the science and the religion are both of them genuine keys for unlocking the world's treasure-house to him who can use either of them practically.[36]

As Max Horkheimer notes with characteristic insight in his commentary on this passage, "In face of the idea that truth might afford the opposite of satisfaction and turn out to be completely shocking to humanity at a given historical moment and thus be repudiated by anybody, the fathers of pragmatism made the satisfaction of the subject the criterion of truth. For such a doctrine there is no possibility of rejecting or even criticizing any species of belief that is enjoyed by its adherents."[37] Horkheimer understands that while the "bourgeois idea of tolerance" can mean "freedom from the rule of dogmatic authority," it can also further "an attitude of neutrality toward all spiritual content, which is thus surrendered to relativism. Each cultural domain preserves its 'sovereignty' with regard to universal truth."[38] Secure within its liberal sense of tolerance and its optimism, pragmatism is "quite unable to deal with the cultural debacle of our day."[39]

Horkheimer is writing in the immediate aftermath of the Second World War. His assessment of the possible alignments between liberal pragmatism and the forces of reaction is animated by a sense of informed urgency.[40] Almost an identical critique of pragmatism's political failure, with an even greater sense of urgency and disillusionment, was offered from within America by a one-time admirer of pragmatism in the shadow of the First World War. It was John Dewey's support for the war that led Randolph Bourne to reassess the limitations of pragmatist optimism and to articulate a sharp critique in his essay "Twilight of Idols."

> Dewey's philosophy is inspiring enough for a society at peace, prosperous and with a fund of progressive good will. It is a philosophy of hope, of clear-sighted comprehension of materials and means. Where institutions are at all malleable, it is the only clue for improvement. It is scientific method applied to "uplift." But this careful adaptation of means to desired ends, this experimental working out of control over brute forces and dead matter in the interests of communal life, depends on a store of rationality, and is effective only where there is strong desire for progress.[41]

For Bourne the war had shattered the bases for Dewey's liberal optimism. Pragmatism sought "adjustment" to the individual's given "situation, in radiant cooperation with reality," but the war had revealed a reality that demanded a radical alternative, not adjustment or accommodation.[42]

It is true that in the 1890s, in a series of public lectures and essays, James spoke out against imperialism, particularly against the American intervention in the Philippines, and with increasing sympathy for cultural and social diversity.[43] These statements have been taken as a demonstration that James's ethics of individualism in a pluralistic world is a basis for a viable social thought and politics—a basis, in fact, for cultural and ethnic pluralism.[44] The two key essays from the 1890s are "On a Certain Blindness in Human Beings" and "What Makes a Life Significant?"—both published in *Talks to Teachers on Psychology* in 1899. In the introduction to this volume of his essays, James himself tried to argue that the social philosophy of these essays was based directly on his philosophy of individualism and that the two taken together amounted to a defense of the democratic faith. Discussing the "Certain Blindness" essay, he wrote that it was more than a "mere piece of sentimentalism. . . . It connects itself with a definite view of the world and of our moral relations to the same. . . . I mean the pluralistic or individualistic philosophy. . . . The practical consequence of such a philosophy is the well-known democratic respect for the sacredness of individuality."[45] But these essays are worth looking at again because what they reveal is not a rigorous social philosophy moving toward the transformation of a culture in which extreme economic and racial inequalities were the norm. They in fact enact little more than a genteel extension of sympathy to the dispossessed and disempowered, nostalgically imagined as *fellahin* whose energies could revive the lost vigor of an enfeebled bourgeoisie. And what James offers the powerless and the poor is an acceptance of their material lot in return for the joy and freedom promised by the possession of higher spiritual ideals.

"On a Certain Blindness" and "What Makes a Life Significant?" constitute a single argument. James proposes that a life is significant wherever the content and living of a life brings happiness to whoever lives it. Because individuals are blind to those different from themselves they tend not to grasp this fact. So what James advocates is toleration of those different from ourselves and a nonjudgmental attitude toward those whose lives differ from ours.

What James is urging is sympathetic understanding. In the famous chapter "The Consciousness of Self" in the first volume of *The Principles of Psychology* (1890), James places the stoic and the sympathetic selves in opposition. Where stoicism is, for James, a "mode of protecting the Self by exclusion and denial,"[46] sympathy is altogether more social and proceeds "by the entirely opposite way of expansion and inclusion." James acknowledges that in sympathetic expansion the "outline" of the self "often gets uncertain enough, but for this the spread of contentment more than atones" (*PP* 1:313).[47] It is through the exercise of sympathy that James, in "What Makes a Life Significant?" can confidently open himself up to the "great fields of heroism lying about me . . . in the daily lives of the laboring classes."[48]

James's overwhelming sense of "a wave of sympathy with the common life of common men" was transformed, as Alan Trachtenberg has described, into a deeply felt critique of the middle class's cultural ideals as these were enshrined in summer retreats like the famous Chautauqua, sanitized enclosures cut off from the outside world, where the middle class could go for self-education and cultural refinement.[49] The pervasive belief in "the healing properties identified with high culture" as an ameliorative economic and political force reflected anxieties about "changes in social structure, the polarization of rich and poor, and the growth of a salaried middle class anxious about its own status":[50] "Stock notions of the 'other half' were implanted in the evolving middle-class consensus, notions that served the negative purpose of claiming what the true America was not, what it must exclude or eradicate in order to preserve itself. Thus, incorporation spawned a normative ideal of culture which served as protection against other realities."[51]

But if by advocating sympathetic understanding James was trying to trouble the moral conscience of a self-enclosed middle class, what did sympathy have to offer the lower classes? In the passage on sympathy in the first volume of *Principles of Psychology* the idea of sympathy ends up as an apology for social hegemony and the economic status quo. The "expansive nature" of sympathetic people, writes the politically idealist and genteel James, "can feel a sort of delicate rapture in thinking that, however sick, ill-favored, mean-conditioned, and generally forsaken they may be, they yet are integral parts of the whole of this brave world, have a fellow's share in the strength of the dray-horses, the happiness of the young people, the wisdom of the wise ones, and are not altogether without part or lot in the good fortunes of the Vanderbilts and the Hohenzollerns themselves" (*PP* 1:313). And there is a similar dressing up of cold comfort as spiritual well-being inside a defense of ultra-gradualist reform in the social essays of the 1890s.

> Society has . . . to pass toward some newer and better equilibrium, and the distribution of wealth has doubtless slowly got to change; such changes have always happened, and will happen to the end of time. But if, after all that I have said, any of you expect that they will make any *genuine vital difference* on a large scale, to the lives of our descendants, you will have missed the significance of my entire lecture. The solid meaning of life is always the same eternal thing,—the marriage namely of some unhabitual ideal, however special, with some fidelity, courage and endurance; with some man's or woman's pains.—And, whatever or whenever life may be, there will always be the chance for that marriage to take place.[52]

For James "the nightingale" sang "its eternal meaning in all sorts of different men's hearts" quite unaffected by any material or social changes in the lives of these men: "If the poor and the rich could look at each other in this way, *sub specie aeternitatis,* how gentle would grow their disputes! What tolerance and good humor, what willingness to live and let live, would come into the world!"[53]

Such was James's solution to social inequality and class conflict at a time when 12 percent of the population owned more than 90 percent of the nation's wealth; when the Pacific, Missouri, and Homestead strikes had brought the labor question to the fore of political debate; and when (between 1881 and 1900) Massachusetts alone experienced over eighteen hundred strikes and lockouts.[54] In offering the "sick, ill-favored, mean-conditioned, and generally forsaken" only a spiritual share in "the happiness of the young people" or "the good fortunes of the Vanderbilts and the Hohenzollerns," James was in fact offering them a therapy of abundance; his panacea for the poor and the oppressed was to sell them a mind-cure.

It is true that James himself registers the potential flimsiness of sympathy in the face of violence when, in the second volume of *Principles of Psychology,* he notes that "sympathy is peculiarly liable to inhibition from other instincts" such as love, hate, and belligerency: "This accounts for the cruelty of collections of men hounding each other on to bait or torment a victim. The blood mounts to the eyes, and sympathy's chance is gone" (*PP* 2:411). But this remains characteristically evasive since instinct subsumes a historically specific politics into biology. James could here be describing a lynching, but it is clear that his ethical and social thought can offer little opposition to a culture that was, in the 1890s, to witness unprecedented violence against African-Americans and the rapid institution of severe Jim Crow segregation. Bourne was right that pragmatism "is inspiring enough for a society at peace," but America was not a society at peace at the turn of the century. As most African-Americans knew then and know today, the history of racial contact in America is more likely than not to be a history of continuing violence and disgrace.

Sympathy, of course, can be invoked in support of projects radically different in their political and social orientations. In late-nineteenth-century America, sympathy formed an important element in social theorization in both the radical cultural relativism of Franz Boas and the conservative sociologies acquiescing in the status quo formulated by men like Frank Giddings. Du Bois's own recourse to sympathetic understanding, examined in chapter 3, is closer to Boasian attempts at cross-cultural understanding than it is to James's attitudes. Despite appearances, James is much closer to Giddings than he is to Boas.

In his early major work, *The Principles of Sociology* (1896), Giddings, one of the founding figures of the new sociology in the 1880s and 1890s,[55] adapted Adam Smith's theorizations of sympathetic feeling toward a defense of the normative values of a liberal and competitive capitalist society. Smith, also a major source for James, had examined the operations of sympathetic "fellow feeling" experienced by the "impartial spectator" (a white, male, bourgeois consciousness) in *The Theory of Moral Sentiments*

(1759; 1790),[56] an ethical companion to the economic program of *The Wealth of Nations* (1776).[57] Giddings, building on Smith, proposed that "the original and elementary fact in society is *the consciousness of kind*." That is to say, "a state of consciousness in which any being, whether low or high in the scale of life, recognizes another conscious being as of like kind with itself."[58] It was Giddings's argument that association through consciousness of kind led to adaptation to "social life" and the pursuit of self-interest through imitation.[59] Giddings used the idea of sympathy to theorize not only what draws human beings together but also what splits them apart through class and race prejudice. He combined Smith's classical conception of liberal society with an evolutionary sociology. As Dorothy Ross has argued, in doing so Giddings offered a progressive alibi for industrial society by arguing that social conflicts would eventually disappear, but at the same time he fixed these conflicts into "natural law."[60]

Giddings stresses likeness and a resistance to displacement of the self where James appears to stress difference and a relativization of the self. But, as the preceding discussion has tried to demonstrate, such displacement is momentary at best in James and is always undertaken from within the security of a self anchored in self-confidence submitting to the logic of the social process. In James, no less than in Giddings, sympathy oils the smooth operations of social process imagined as natural law.

The account of James's thought given here is not meant to suggest an assessment of the American philosopher shared by Du Bois. As has already been pointed out, the social and political thought of the young Du Bois is, in many ways, fairly conservative. He cherishes many of the genteel values of New England culture, and elitist social programmatics readily appeal to him. For Du Bois, it is an exceptional vanguard made up largely of Northern African-Americans who will uplift the black masses. James believes that history is made by "the Grants and Bismarcks" (GM 218), and Du Bois, despite some equivocation, tends to agree.[61] James is willing to go as far as to demonstrate his "greatest respect" for those who explain the cultural and political "failure" of a Sicily or a Sardinia by arguing that "a subordinate race cannot possibly engender a large number of high-class geniuses" (GM 242). Du Bois is even willing to follow James here. He asserts in "The Talented Tenth" that "slavery" is "the legalized survival of the unfit and the nullification of the work of natural internal leadership." "Negro Leadership" needs, therefore, "to rid the race of this awful incubus that it might make way for natural selection and the survival of the fittest" (TT 842–43). So there is much in James's thought that will attract him.

But what these alignments and the account of James given here are meant to suggest is that the neopragmatist readings of James, of Du Bois, and of their relationship present, at best, a highly distorted picture. Cornel West's and others' attempts to confirm Du Bois's place within a viable pragmatist tradition proceed by first affirming the positive values of the pluralistic doctrine and then signaling toward Du Bois's studentship under James, thereby sealing Du Bois inside a "genealogy of pragmatism" as a confirmation of a progressive and liberal tradition of American cultural thought. But if the critique of James's pluralism offered here has any validity, then this confirmation of the continuing health of the liberal tradition needs to be held in some suspicion. Not only are many of the alignments between James and Du Bois confirmations of conservative leanings in both, but also the pluralistic doctrine that represents the more radical side of James can easily feed into a reactionary politics—a problem that present-day liberal defenses of pluralism and relativism must also negotiate.

It is not that James offers Du Bois nothing that can today be recuperated as positive value. James's emphasis on contingency and striving in the real world does play a significant part in turning Du Bois toward politically committed social science work (discussed in the next chapter), though here again the alignment between James's ethics and a conservative functionalist sociology also needs to be noted. But what is most radical in Du Bois's early work is his ability to confront, through complex descriptions of the outer contours and inner torments of black life in America, what Horkheimer in a different context called the "debacle of our days." In this endeavor James is of little help to him. The discussion now turns to an early attempt by Du Bois to undertake such a description.

"Fourth Dimension" and "Great Laws": Satire and Historicism

Sometime in 1889, probably in the late spring or early summer when Du Bois was coming to the end of his Philosophy 4 course with James and working on a long thesis on ethics as a final project for the course, Du Bois drafted a long sketch for a work of fiction (possibly a short story, possibly a novel) titled "A Vacation Unique." A bitter satire on American racism and Teutonic nationalist self-fashioning, the fiction engages directly and critically with the argument of James's lectures on ethics and begins to question Du Bois's own undergraduate theorizations of a philosophy of history. Previously unpublished and unstudied, this work offers an invaluable insight into Du Bois's relationship to James and his work in philosophy at Harvard. Since the content and narrative of the fiction also prefigure in important ways both the first chapter of *Souls* (with its dramatization of the life across the color line and of "double-consciousness") and many of the major preoccupations and literary strategies of twentieth-century African-American fiction, it is also a significant document for African-American literary history.

"A Vacation Unique" survives as a series of manuscript fragments in Du Bois's hand in the Du Bois archives at the University of Massachusetts at Amherst and in a transcription, part summary and part direct quotation, made by Francis Broderick in the 1950s and now among Broderick's research notes for his book on Du Bois housed at the Schomburg Institute in New York. The relation of Du Bois's own handwritten text and Broderick's transcription is a complicated one and is discussed in detail, along with issues of dating and editing, in the Appendix, where the full text of the fiction is also given. It is clear that Broderick has had access to parts of the work that are now lost. For the sake of convenience the following discussion treats Du Bois's manuscript fragments and Broderick's transcription as a single work. A "D" or a "B" after quotations indicates whether the Du Bois or the Broderick version is being used.

Du Bois's fiction tells of a black protagonist who suggests to a white classmate that he undergo an operation that will make him temporarily black. The two will then spend the summer touring "the Land of the Free and Home of the Brave as two readers giving 40 or 50 entertainments" (D) in order to defray academic expenses. By September, when the white student will be restored to his former self, they will return to Harvard. In this way, the white companion will get a chance to enter an unknown region, a "Fourth Dimension" (D) (what Du Bois later called the life behind the veil), from which he can observe the "world's intestines from a new point of view" (B).

As the two students begin their touring they encounter racist hostility. The narrator gives an account of his attempt to approach the rector of a certain white church for an opportunity to give readings. He describes the stares he receives and satirizes the "god-given right of American ladies to eye a social inferior from head to foot and still retain their self-respect" (B). The story then narrates the main protagonists' condescending reception at the hands of the hostess at the rectory, her praises for all the charitable work the Anglo-Saxon race has done for the blacks, and her shock at finding out that there are now "Niggers in *Harvard!*" (D). The request for readings is, of course, politely refused.

Although it is not possible to say how much of this is based on Du Bois's direct experience, it is clear that there is a large autobiographical content in the story, and the intense resentment against racism at Harvard and in Boston's white well-to-do community that Du Bois voices in his autobiographical writing is here channeled into fiction.[62] The clearest evidence of autobiographical experience having provided the grounds for the bitterness of the satire is to be found in one of the key scenes of the story, set in the dining hall of a large American hotel where black waiters are serving. The protagonist now sits at dinner with his transformed companion: "Don't yell at the waiter in that manner, or I'll knock you down. I'm a former waiter myself, and if there is one foul and festering sore on civilization which more characteristically shows the rottenness beneath it [it] is your American Hotel. Teuton loves his belly better than his Christ" (B).

The scene is based largely on Du Bois's own experiences in the Midwest. In the summer months between leaving Fisk and coming to Harvard, Du Bois had joined a few other Fisk students who had formed a glee club. The group went to work in a resort hotel on Lake Minnetonka near Minneapolis as singing waiters. Du Bois wanted to supplement his scholarship for Harvard and agreed reluctantly to act as the business manager of the group. The group chose to go to Minnesota because one of its members had made the summer trip a few times previously. But the choice may also have been influenced by the fact that a good number of Du Bois's teachers at Fisk were "from the New Englandized Middle West" (*A* 108).

The Midwest experience proved both disagreeable and humiliating for Du Bois, though the unpleasantness appears to have been exaggerated in his autobiographies.[63] He found the Midwestern clientele of the hotel rude, coarse, and loose in morals. The Fisk students spent most of their time working as waiters—or rather, being inexperienced waiters, as busboys. Du Bois later recalled one incident in particular:

> I stood staring and thinking, while the other boys hustled about. Then I noticed one fat hog, feeding at a heavily gilded trough, who could not find his waiter. He beckoned me. It was not his voice, for his mouth was too

full. It was his way, his air, his assumption. Thus Caesar ordered his legionaries or Cleopatra her slaves. Dogs recognize the gesture. I did not. He may be beckoning yet for all I know, for something froze within me. I did not look his way again. Then and there I disowned menial service for me and my people.[64]

In the story Du Bois directly reworks this particular incident when a white guest at the hotel calls a waiter "darky" and "John" when the waiter's real name is "Edward" (B), Du Bois's own second Christian name.

Du Bois uses the incidents at the hotel to initiate an extensive satire and critique of Teutonism (*Anglo-Saxon* and *Teuton* are interchangeable terms for Du Bois), and this at a time when theories about the Teutonic origins of the United States still had widespread currency.[65] "Anglo-Saxon civilization," proclaims the black protagonist, is "built upon the Eternal I," and the "high Episcopal Nicene creed" of the Anglo-Saxon is "to put heel on neck of man down." The last lines of the sketch read: "I don't deny A[nglo]-Sax[on] civ[ilization] has done much; I just deny that it has done all. Only the self-forgetful Quakers still remember God. Among rest, 'not that I is above Thee but that I despises Thee'—there is the death warrant of Teutonic civilization" (B). These lines are a rewording of an earlier section in the sketch in which the Teutonic satire is located within a broader mockery of Germanic metaphysical historicism. In the earlier part Du Bois wrote that for the Teuton it is not that the "I is above you but that the I despises You . . . : that is the little worm that gnawing at the vitals of the *World Soul* shall . . . [one word not clear] drown him in the Deep Sea" (emphasis added).

Where Du Bois's later autobiographical writings offer evidence in hindsight that it was not always easy for Du Bois to maintain his separate peace between politics and pedagogy, the story is a more contemporary and visceral indication that there were, from the very start, cracks in Du Bois's stoic divorce from white society. What is important for the present argument is that these cracks should begin to open up with such force at the very time that Du Bois was taking his first course with James and immersing himself in the philosophical speculation discussed in the previous section.

The phrase "Fourth Dimension," which recurs in "A Vacation Unique," is a direct reference to C. H. Hinton's "What Is the Fourth Dimension?" (1884), the first of Hinton's *Scientific Romances* and a text that, according to Du Bois's notebook, James referred to and adapted in his lectures on ethics. Using a rather protracted demonstration based on mathematical logic, Hinton argued for at least conceiving the possibility of a fourth dimension. While he acknowledged that this argument remained abstract, he also stressed the practical utility of such an abstraction. Hinton's aim was "to show that, by supposing away certain limitations of the fundamental conditions of existence as we know it, a state of being can be conceived with powers far transcending our own." From this perspective one could "investigate what relations would subsist between our mode of existence and that which will be seen to be a possible one."[66] The idea of a fourth dimension helped express in intelligible terms that for which we have no image. In other words, it provided a kind of "scaffolding" on which "many philosophical ideas and doctrines could be well illustrated"—"Much of Spinoza's Ethics, for example, could be symbolized" this way.[67]

James picked up the relativist and ethical implications of Hinton's argument, suggesting that "we live in a 4th moral dimension separating us from animals" (P4). This fourth moral dimension is the realm in which the will to believe negotiates its defense of a conditional, "common sense" God against the "absolute" God of "speculative" theories such as Martineau's (P4). Since we cannot ever have access to the whole universe, we cannot ever have full knowledge of God. As such, the absolutist's attempt to explain away all evil in the world within alibis of divine purpose is unacceptable to James—suffering, for James, cannot be explained away by being made theologically purposeful. The speculative argument for an absolute God is, James suggests, part of an over-intellectualization characteristic of contemporary culture: "We are too suckled o'er with the pale cast of thought," he laments, "to be given over to the abdominal joyousness of the Middle Ages" (P4).

"A Vacation Unique" appears to conclude on a reaffirmation of James's ethical teachings. After repeated satirizations of academic philosophizing through parodies of disputations in mathematical logic that nod toward Hinton's work (several professors apparently debate the different factors by which a multiplication table with the result 6930 can be arrived at), the narrator concludes: "I seriously doubt if there is any truth after all your blatant world-search. Truth is not the object of knowledge nor even consistency. It is the best knowable hypothesis" (B). But if Du Bois wants, through this relativist argument, to reassert an allegiance to a Jamesian ethical heroism in which "the moral equation" is the only thing that makes philosophical meaning relevant to the conduct of living, this is not the overall effect achieved by his story.

The story in fact takes the body of Hinton's and James's four-dimensional world and turns it inside out. James's adaptation of Hinton suggests that the fourth dimension is a kind of Kantian a priori, a negative horizon in dialogue with which the objects of pragmatic and practical ethical reason are constructed. The fictive dramatizations of "A Vacation Unique" suggest that this pragmatic realism may in itself be too ahistorical and abstract. Du Bois's story confronts James's longing for medieval "*abdominal* joyousness" with the racial suffering of black people that lies in the "*intestines*" of white America. Such a confrontation immediately highlights the fact that James's refusal to explain away evil is, in its own way, only a *theoretical* acknowledgment of its existence and an *acceptance* of suffering, since the acknowledgment is divorced from any sense of the concrete particulars of historical and political experience. Where, for James, the fourth dimension of the moral life separates human from animal, for Du Bois it separates white from black. Where Hinton argues from the higher plane of the fourth dimension down to the human sphere, Du Bois's story in effect dramatizes the resurfacing of the repressed political content of white America's collective psyche. Where for Hinton the human appears abstract when seen from the perspective of the fourth dimension, for Du Bois the self-legitimations of white American culture appear as hollow forms masking a more concrete and disgraceful history.

The model for Du Bois's inversion of James's and Hinton's four-dimensional worlds, and for his playing-off of mathematical and philosophical sophistry against the experience of racism, is a contemporary science-fictional satire of American social inequalities. When Du Bois's protagonist invites his white companion to enter the "Fourth Dimension" of color, he tells him that his "view of mankind in general will have a striking resemblance to the view which Mr. Field of Flatland had of . . . Lineland intestines" (D). The reference here is to Edwin A. Abbott's popular late-nineteenth-century science fiction novella *Flatland,* which had appeared in a second edition in 1884.

Flatland is narrated by a geometrical personification, a square, who describes not only life in the two-dimensional world of Flatland, but also his travels through the one-dimensional world of Lineland and the three-dimensional world of Spaceland. Abbott's aim is to satirize strategies of enforced conformity, fears of difference, and anxieties about social revolution. The narrator, having returned from Spaceland, has tried to tell his fellow Flatlanders about the possibilities of a life in the third dimension, only to be imprisoned for sedition and heresy.

Much of the novella is given to the description of the authoritarian regime that governs Flatland. The priestly order of Circles tolerates no irregularity of shape in Flatland, since irregularities are seen as signs of moral degeneracy. Each gender, social class, and profession is assigned a specific shape, and the citizenry is trained in the recognition through sight and touch of these two-dimensional shapes. Precise training in the skills of seeing and feeling is essential in Flatland since all that is visible in a two-dimensional world are lines and the only way to tell shapes apart is by being able to judge the length of lines exactly and feel shapes with equal exactitude. The most serious challenge to this social order has come in the distant past during a time known as the "Color Period." This period began when an enlightened Pentagon started to paint "first his house, then his slaves, then his Father, his Sons, and Grandsons, lastly himself."[68] The trend soon catches on, but the aesthetic gains rapidly translate themselves into social revolution because the rise of color leads to the decay of the arts of recognition by sight and by touch, thus making it possible to confuse certain different shapes that are identically colored.

> Year by year the Soldiers and Artisans [and Abbott soon adds Women] began more vehemently to assert—and with increasing truth—that there was no great difference between them and the very highest class of Polygons, now that they were raised to an equality with the latter, and enabled to grapple with all the difficulties and solve all the problems of life, whether Statical or Kinetical, by the simple Process of Color Recognition. Not content with the natural neglect into which Sight Recognition was falling, they began boldly to demand the legal prohibition of all "monopolizing and aristocratic Arts" and the consequent abolition of all endowments for the studies of Sight Recognition, Mathematics, and Feeling. Soon, they began to insist that inasmuch as Color, which was a second Nature, had destroyed the need of aristocratic distinctions, the Law should follow in the same path, and that henceforth all individuals and all classes should be recognized as absolutely equal and entitled to equal rights. (*F* 34–35)

The ironies of Abbott's treatment of color as a means of social leveling—a means by which the identities of the slaveowner, his family, and his slaves become indistinguishable—in the segregated America of the late nineteenth century should be obvious. The last decades of the nineteenth century and the first of the twentieth were to see a spate of cultural commentaries defending the color line in America and providing alibis for the rising legal and physical violence against African-Americans.[69] For Abbott's narrator the Period of Color evokes not fears of racial blending and the descent of civilization into barbarism, but a time when "the commonest utterances of the commonest citizens . . . seem to have been suffused with a richer tinge of word and thought; and to that era we are even now indebted for our finest poetry and for whatever rhythm still remains in the more scientific utterances of these modern days" (*F* 34). But the course of history is as grim in Flatland as it is in the America of "A Vacation Unique." When the orphaned daughter of a Polygon commits suicide after she has been deceived by the confusions of color into marrying a lowly Tradesman, the priests whip up fears about the relationship of color and sexuality that would have been familiar to an American audience and secure the support "of a large number of reactionary Women" for their cause (*F* 39). A vast and treacherous massacre ensues, guaranteeing the "triumph of Order" (*F* 41) in which the square narrator finds himself imprisoned at the end of the book. As Abbott's narrator moralizes in his Preface, "how strong a family likeness runs through blind and persecuting humanity in all Dimensions! . . . We are all liable to the same errors, all alike the Slaves of our respective Dimensional prejudices" (*F* Pref., n.p.).

The narrator of *Flatland* makes it quite clear from the start that his book is addressed to the human beings of Spaceland. He is concerned that life in the second dimension represents just one of many realities ignored by Spaceland historians "in whose pages (until very recent times) the destinies of Women and of the masses of mankind have seldom been deemed worthy of mention and never of careful consideration" (*F* Pref., n.p.). The sense of exclusion from the narratives of history is also central to "A Vacation Unique." And it is this sense that most clearly animates the fiction's meditations on those philosophical issues that preoccupy Du Bois in his early career: the nature of freedom, consciousness, and self-realization, and their relationship to the historical process.

Du Bois drives home the message of his dramatization of racism by divesting the epitome of historical agency, a white, Anglo-Saxon male of "distinguished ancestry" (D), of all freedom. After the operation that transforms the white friend into black, the narrator tells him that his "Anglo-Saxon lips, of the Sir Walter Scott pretty red pouting variety have gained thickness with color" and that his "countenance," once "winning," "has suddenly become to the last degree repulsive" (D). This rude and surreal initiation across the limen of what Du Bois would later call the color line is also a divestiture of all agency. "Hold your tongue," the black narrator now commands his "fool," "*your* feelings have played but small part in history" (D). Following on from the slave narratives and prefiguring so much of twentieth-century minority and postcolonial writing, voicelessness becomes a primary sign of the enforced denial of fundamental freedoms.

Du Bois's narrator's first response to this imposed passivity is to fantasize an escape from history. In a passage of meditative introspection that is characteristic of many parts of Du Bois's story, he notes that "other things being equal I prefer a man with no ancestry at all not even a father—I should have been pleased to make the acquaintance of Adam" (D). This regressive fantasy resurfaces in the final sections of the story as the narrator and his transformed companion drive through the Berkshire hills. It is a curious (and confused) episode in which a primal, cyclical pastoralism seems to be intended to obliquely mock the Christian promise of historical novelty and therefore also the promise of redemption. The narration of the scene is indebted to the traditions of romance, appropriately so since romance is a mode in which American literature has investigated the nature of historical experience and the desire for transcendence.

> To the Berkshire Hills! we are sitting and the world is flying past. O I love this grimly unconscious old world this conservative old [crossed-out word] Widower whose son persists in setting yesternight just as it did 6000 years ago & who has never added an extra tint to the rainbow. It is a beautiful day: the rain does not come down in a raging flood as if angry with its task it sought to choke the Earth—but it comes lovingly in a drizzle and the parched forests drink slowly and thankfully and only Man is discontented—see now in the West it is breaking away—grey, pink, red, blue—back! now comes your sun to dazzle and glare—see my Fool this is life in a nut-shell. (D)

The section that follows this one is the scene at the rectory where the narrator encounters the polite racist hypocrisy of the hostess, a scene that provides a rude awakening for the narrator as the spell of pastoral romance is broken.

If the persistent shock of real historical experience leads Du Bois to a satirical description of both ethical voluntarism and transcendent flight, it also nudges him into a parody of metaphysical system building. At one point in "A Vacation Unique" the black narrator explains to his white friend that he can, once he experiences being black, solve the intricate problems of introspection and the fourth dimension: "Outside of mind you may study mind, and outside of matter by reason of the fourth dimension of color you may have a striking view of the intestines of the fourth great civilization" (B). It is immediately following this passage that the narrator tells his transformed companion that his "feelings no longer count, they are no part of history" (B).

As with many other passages in Du Bois's rough and fragmentary draft, the meaning here is obscure. But as is so often the case with "A Vacation Unique," a sense of the relevant context and referentiality of this passage can greatly clarify matters. The idea of "introspection," the study of "mind," the relation of mind and matter, as well as the overall concern with "history" throughout the story, all refer to the concluding Spencerian-Hegelian section of "The Renaissance of Ethics," the thesis Du Bois wrote for James at the end of the Philosophy 4 course.[70]

> We must study, not *my* mind, but the great universal mind, in its millions of manifestations past and present, using introspection, not as a hindrance to science, but as an additional help; this largely invalidates the objection of the scientist, for in the wonderful panorama of history, in the throbbing world of today are multitudinous facts as to the working of the most wonderful of forces, mind; they only need to be scientifically treated to yield fruit in *great laws*. (RE; emphasis added)

In reusing the language of this passage in his fictional satire Du Bois opens up his own thesis to the same kind of parodic reading that he aims at his other targets. In the thesis Du Bois conceives of history as "the great universal mind" unfolding along lines of development governed by what he calls "great laws." But if in the thesis history is a kind of history of universal consciousness that offers security through the guarantee of progressive teleologies, in "A Vacation Unique" the experiences of black consciousness are seen to be categorically excluded from history as conceived by the "fourth civilization."

Some years later, in writing the first chapter of *Souls* in the midst of his work on *The Philadelphia Negro*, Du Bois would again confront the relationship of "thought and feeling" (*SBF* 487) to science. The confrontations of African-American consciousness and either metaphysical historicism or sociological positivism present similar though by no means identical polarities. In neither case do they represent a simple opposition. In both cases the different attempts to describe the world are undertaken simultaneously. And if the different approaches represent conflicting understandings, then it is the very contradictions and struggles, not the straightforward triumph of one option over another, that must be accepted as the truth of Du Bois's thought. "A Vacation Unique" does not represent a clear-cut rejection of the historicism of Du Bois's thesis. It is written at the same time as the thesis and at best registers a certain nervousness about the easy neatness of the thesis's conclusions. Du Bois's flirting with a metaphysical historicism shows the more conservative side of his struggle with the philosophy of history and is just as much a retreat from the extreme voluntarism of James as is "A Vacation Unique."

The quest for "great laws" in fact reproduces Spencer's claims, in the conclusion of *First Principles,* for a "synthetic philosophy" based on a "science" that "from the beginning, has been grouping isolated facts under laws, uniting special laws under more general laws, and so reaching on to laws of higher and higher generality; until the conception of universal laws has become familiar to it."[71] In his comments on the above passage on teleology and Christianity in Du Bois's thesis, James underlined "Christian teleology" and asked: "How expressed? As by scholasticism—or by Christ, or by whom?" It is surprising that by the end of the thesis James had not recognized the Spencerian source or the Hegelian overtones. He himself had, in the first lecture of the second half of his course, referred his students not only to Hegel but also to the fourth chapter of *First Principles,* "The Relativity of All Knowledge." Du Bois in fact owned copies of both *First Principles* and *The Data of Ethics.* But his thesis reproduces the argument not of the fourth chapter of *First Principles,* but of its fifth, "The Reconciliation," in which science and religion are rescued from eternal incompatibility by "the Unknowable." In staging this reconciliation on the site of a universal consciousness or "mind," Du Bois pushes the Spencerian narrative more firmly toward German metaphysical idealism than Spencer himself would have liked.

The Spencer scholar J. D. Y. Peel has noted the appeal of such historicism in his claim that Spencerian theory was a kind of nineteenth-century "theodicy": "At a time of unprecedented, seemingly uncontrolled and terrifying change, Spencer reassured the bewildered by interpreting the transition that men had experienced and setting it within a longer arc of change covering all nature."[72] Henry Adams had also thought that "unbroken evolution under uniform conditions . . . was the very best substitute for religion; a safe, conservative, practical, thoroughly Common Law deity" (*EHA* 225). But Adams also grasped that such a uniform system promised a false sanctuary from political disaster and responsibility. Adams's commentary on Darwinian thought occurs in the chapter of the *Education* devoted to the years 1867–68. It is part of a series of meditations that follow the chapters on the Civil War years. In the chapter dealing with 1861, Adams writes that "the law, altogether, as path of education, vanished in April, 1861, leaving a million young men planted in the mud of a lawless world, to begin a new life without education at all" (*EHA* 110). In the chapter on Darwinism, Adams notes with sharp irony that evolutionary theory promised "some great generalization which would finish one's clamor to be educated" (*EHA* 224). Neo-Darwinian notions of uniform evolution seemed to offer "a working system for the universe suited to a young man who had just helped to waste five or ten thousand million dollars and a million lives, more or less, to enforce unity and uniformity on people who objected to it; the idea was only too seductive in its perfection; it had the charm of art" (*EHA* 225–26).

"The Renaissance of Ethics" seems to begin with a Jamesian resistance to such seduction but ends up arguing for the unification of science and ethics inside a secure historicism. The thesis *appears* to postulate the need for a science of ethics free from metaphysical abstractions and rooted firmly in the phenomenal world, and guaranteed by scientific objectivity. But Du Bois still wants through "fact" to discover the "ultimate cause." It is only through such a science, argues Du Bois, that the divorce between reason and teleology can be repaired: "The only way to find *why* the world [is] is to find *what* it is—the only path to teleology is science." It is by wedding the *what* securely to the *why* that Du Bois proposes to discover the absolute basis of the *ought,* or ethical ends.

While the concern with human ends throughout Du Bois's thesis very much reflects the preoccupations of James's course, the following excerpt demonstrates more clearly than the passage on "the great universal mind" just how Du Bois can slide from a Jamesian uncertain plurality and relativism into metaphysical securities:

What are the Ends? Shall I be St. Paul, Jeremy Bentham, or Walt Whitman? Thus the world answers—further than which I cannot go: "So act that the Ends of the best Universe of which you can conceive the world a part, may best be realized." In thus acting . . . you may be a fool, but in the Hereafter, be it Elysian fields, or deepest oblivion, you will be a moral hero, who, if the World is the Kingdom of God, shall see the King in his beauty, and if it is a mere farce, shall have risen infinitely above it. One momentous fact . . . future science must not forget: Christian teleology is the only one yet presented which seems worthy of a man. This is the true status of ethics and this status it will only attain when, ceasing to be a department of metaphysics, it becomes the aim of teleologic search, and metaphysics ceases to usurp the place of science. Above and beyond is this beacon light: that gradually, year by year, science will narrow the field, more and more will our thoughts converge upon eternal Truth. (RE)

The leap of faith assuring that "the fool" will inevitably be a "moral hero" is characteristically Jamesian. It is the same leap of faith that underlies James's defense of the will to believe and of religious experience, or the will to action and right conduct discussed earlier. In his marginal comments James notes that Du Bois does not explain how to get from the "what" to the "why." The relationship of means and ends is certainly inadequately theorized by Du Bois, but it is, of course, equally poorly thought through in James's own instrumentalist logic. "Ascertain what the facts are! that is truly the beginning of the method," James comments in the margin, but he adds that Du Bois does not "make clear its later course." When Du Bois writes of the work of James and Royce as "another attempt to base ethics upon fact—to make it a science," James offers a denial: "I doubt whether we do seek to make it a *science*—to me that seems impossible."

As Daniel Wilson has demonstrated, the increasing dominance of science in American universities in the second half of the nineteenth century led to a crisis in academic philosophy. The crisis was manifested especially as a decline in interest in moral philosophy, which had been central to the philosophy curriculum in the ante-bellum period.[73] In "Renaissance of Ethics" Du Bois is trying to recuperate the project of moral philosophy, placing it on a supposedly scientific footing. James argued against the viability of such a synthesis, but the undergraduate Du Bois clearly has not fully grasped the Jamesian argument. In any case, what sustains and propels Du Bois's thesis is not so much logical demonstration as a passionate religiosity manifest as a typically late-nineteenth-century faith in "the intelligible design and purpose of history,"[74] a secularization of the Christian plot. Teleologic narrative and the universal absolute of "eternal Truth" are structures within which moral heroism is *permitted,* not achieved, a mockery James had outlined in great detail (notwithstanding the problems with his own theorizations of will); they are the alibis for a redemptive, vitalist historicism.

The conservatism of Du Bois's retreat from Jamesian relativism needs, however, to be qualified in one important respect: the uneasy attempt to wed voluntarism and historicism, James and Spencer, was itself a liberalizing departure from Du Bois's previous orthodox philosophical training at Fisk. At Fisk Du Bois had studied John Bascom's *Science of Mind* (1881), James McCosh's *Laws of Discursive Thought* (1870), James Fairchild's *Moral Philosophy* (1869), and George Frederick Wright's *Logic of Christian Evidences* (1880).[75] As Arnold Rampersad has pointed out, "Du Bois' experience in philosophy at Fisk reflected the attempt of philosophers of conservative persuasion to deal with enduring questions concerning the nature of man and the theories and discoveries of the Darwinian age."[76] Du Bois recalled that "at Fisk a very definite attempt was made to see that we did not lose or question our Christian orthodoxy," and for some time Du Bois was untroubled by this (*DD* 577). But he was deeply "affronted" by Wright's book, which he saw as "a cheap piece of special pleading," and he could not accept the then current anti-evolutionary heresy trials (*DD* 577–78).[77] Wright's book attempted "to revitalize the appeal of Christianity, especially for the liberally educated, younger generation, by a new and more 'scientific' examination of traditional evidences of Christian belief."[78] McCosh's work was more openly "hostile to the sensationalism, empiricism, and religious skepticism of the positivists" and "saw the methods of John Stuart Mill, Comte, and Spencer as 'infected throughout' by the principles expounded in Kant's *Critique of Pure Reason,* which he repudiated in favor of a basically Aristotelian rationalism."[79] The same religious conservatism marked Fairchild's book, which was indebted to "Jonathan Edwards' *The Nature of True Virtue* and to Edwards' friend and disciple Samuel Hopkins, founder of Du Bois' church in Great Barrington." Only Bascom "tried to bring conventional theology into closer relationship with nineteenth-century science, especially evolution, [and] allowed for some empiricism and for those *a priori* principles of thought which McCosh had denied."[80]

Du Bois's historicism in "The Renaissance of Ethics" is in fact an attempt to resolve the dualism in nineteenth-century psychology of will and science, of an unconditioned free volition and a physiologically overdetermined self, by changing the definition of science from physiology (the study of "*my* mind") to metaphysics (the study of "universal mind") while keeping the name of science as an "objective" guard against Jamesian charges of idealism. As Lorraine Daston argues in her survey of the struggle between the "theory of will" and the "science of mind" in nineteenth-century psychology, James tried to mediate between the two.

He was attracted to the physiological approach but also suspicious of the totalizing and reductive arguments of people like Huxley. "Eventually, James declared the problem of will to lie outside the purview of psychology and the personal choice between 'this whole goodly universe' implied by voluntarism and 'the world without a purpose of mechanical philosophy' to lie beyond the reach of empirical evidence. James himself opted for voluntarism, but he did so on avowedly ethical rather than scientific grounds."[81] Du Bois's attempts to adopt a Jamesian position of voluntarism also indicate a desire on his part to freely choose will on ethical grounds. But the drift from ethical relativism into historicism, and the simultaneous satirization of both, clearly indicate that, for one who understood the politics of repeated mediation and constraint, agency was not simply a matter of exercising free choice.

Jefferson Davis at Harvard: Representing Civilization

It is hardly surprising to find that the philosophic contradictions of "The Renaissance of Ethics" and the doubts of "A Vacation Unique" translate themselves for Du Bois into questions about the nature of individual action within the historical process and reflections on the purpose and direction of his own life. In the thesis on ethics he had asked, "What are the Ends? Shall I be St. Paul, Jeremy Bentham, or Walt Whitman?" The positing of the apostolic evangelicalism of St. Paul as a possible model suggests the attraction to shifting vitalism from the political to the religio-ethical. In the "Bismarck" speech delivered at Fisk Du Bois concludes that the life of the Prussian leader "carries with it a warning lest we sacrifice a lasting good to temporary advantage; lest we raise a nation and forget the people, become a Bismarck and not a Moses."[82] The move from Bismarck to Moses is an instance of that incorporation of the vitalist tradition into the messianisms of the Christian church or the Nation of Islam that has been characteristic of black American political leadership, from Alexander Crummell to Martin Luther King, Jr., Malcolm X, Louis Farrakhan, and Jesse Jackson. A Benthamite utilitarian ethics offers the option of secularizing this ethics toward (in the phrase popularized by Bentham) "the happiness of the greatest number." This suggests something like James's argument for harnessing the largest number of goods toward what he called "the best whole" in the Philosophy 4 course. But if the attraction to St. Paul and to Bentham is easy enough to explain in the context of Du Bois's early intellectual development, the presence of Whitman here seems surprising and anomalous.[83] How are the ends toward "the best Universe" conceived by a *poet* comparable to the ends conceived by evangelical-messianic or utilitarian programs? (As is well known, Whitman himself had differentiated the poet and the democratic "gangs of kosmos" from the priestly order in his 1855 Preface to *Leaves of Grass*). The most likely appeal of Whitman is his bardic address singing the tale of the tribe and the nation. That this is so will be suggested by the ways in which *Souls* revises the models of Whitmanian and Emersonian prophecy.

In *Souls* Du Bois will be able to conceive of complex and multiple models of agency by contrasting the requirements of political leadership with the life of the mind. While an undergraduate at Harvard, Du Bois never gets much beyond conceiving of leadership in terms provided by the Great Man theory of history. However, in his commencement speech titled "Jefferson Davis as Representative of Civilization," a meditation on the meaning and significance of the Confederate president's career that must have been unexpected and surprising, coming as it did from a black speaker before a northern and white audience, Du Bois does manage to offer an ethical critique of the theory. The speech is another document from Du Bois's early writings that reveals much about his early thought and that has received almost no critical attention. The criticisms of the speech are fairly conservative, but the performance of it was both daring and witty. Seemingly a balanced and impartial assessment of the meaning of Davis's career, the speech in fact subtly turns its criticisms of Davis into a veiled attack on the northern audience. The extent and nature of this designed reversal can be easily grasped if the satire of Teutonism in "A Vacation Unique" is kept in mind while reading the speech. Written about a year after the fiction, the speech repeatedly cannibalizes parts of the earlier satire for its own parodic purposes.

In order to understand the full range of meanings and hidden intentions of Du Bois's speech, it is necessary to keep the performance context in mind. In coming to Harvard, Du Bois had returned from the South to New England and to the major urban and institutional center of its intellectual and cultural life. At the commencement he is addressing not a gathering at a black Southern university but an audience made up of members of a white, largely New England elite—culturally, politically, and economically the most powerful social group in America at that time—including Mrs. Grover Cleveland, wife of the former president (*AR* 13).[84] He is doing so after two years of intense work in philosophical studies and as the very first black commencement speaker at the nation's most prestigious institution of higher learning (a fact duly noted by the national press in its annual coverage of the event), and that at a time of rising nationalism, imperialist expansion, and racist reaction.

Du Bois began the speech with two propositions that accept the Great Man theory of history: "Jefferson Davis was a typical Teutonic Hero; the history of civilization during the last millennium has been the development of the idea of the Strong Man of which he was the embodiment" (*AR* 14). The audience's curiosity and surprise can hardly have decreased as Du Bois followed up this bold opening with a laudatory portrait of Davis: "A soldier and a lover, a statesman and a ruler; passionate, ambitious and indomitable; bold reckless guardian of a people's All." Davis, Du Bois argued, could "have graced a medieval romance" (*AR* 14). But this literary compliment turns out to be closer to Mark Twain's numerous deflations of the South's self-fashioning in the image of Walter Scott's historical romances.

While Du Bois acknowledged that "judged by the whole standard of Teutonic civilization, there is something noble in the figure of Jefferson Davis," he also added that "judged by every canon of human justice, there is something fundamentally incomplete about the standard" (*AR* 14). Coming at the end of an inflated encomium, the very moderateness of the qualifying tone in which standards of cultural and ethical judgment are relativized, and "civilization" and "justice," "Teutonic" and "human" calculatedly opposed, guarantees an arresting deflation. But if this promises the kind of anti-South critique the audience could have expected from Du Bois, he once again defeats these expectations by making his argument more complex.

Du Bois broadens the focus of his speech by stating that he wishes "to consider not the man, but the type of civilization which his life represented" (*AR* 14). The combination of "individualism" and "might" supplies the deadly logic of such a civilization, transforming "a naturally brave and generous man" into a leader "advancing a civilization by murdering Indians, now a hero of a national disgrace called by courtesy, the Mexican War; and finally, as the crowning absurdity, the peculiar champion of a people fighting to be free in order that another people should not be free" (*AR* 14).

Whenever this idea has for a moment, escaped from the individual realm, it has found an even more secure foothold in the policy and philosophy of the State. The Strong Man and his mighty Right Arm has become the Strong Nation with its armies. Under whatever guise, however, a Jefferson Davis may appear as man, as race, or as nation, his life can only logically mean this: the advance of a part of the world at the expense of the whole; the overweening sense of the I, and the consequent forgetting of the Thou. (*AR* 14)

By making Davis an embodiment of the very "policy and philosophy of the State" (*AR* 14), Du Bois presents him as something more than the aberrant product of southern culture. Davis appears, in fact, as the logical outcome of a nationalist ideology that supports imperialist expansion and racial violence.

Du Bois in fact quietly implicates the culture of his victorious northern audience in his political critique. The deployment of a vocabulary of "representativeness" and typicality in the speech and its title is a displacement of the Emersonian mythology of democratic nationalism. The characterization of Davis as "representative" refers the audience, in a stroke of superb irony, to Emerson's *Representative Men* (1851), itself an American version of Carlyle's *On Heroes, Hero Worship, and the Heroic in History* (1840). The traditional labeling of Carlyle as aristocratic and of Emerson as democratic simplifies both writers' attempts to occupy more complex and sometimes mutually contradictory positions.[85] Nevertheless, Emerson did intend his book to be an American and democratic "reply" to Carlyle. Representativeness for Emerson meant the symbolic representation of things and ideas. This was the basis for the unconvincing attempt to transform the hero into a *democratic* representative by arguing that the true representative man embodies the universal and abolishes individualism. As Robert Hume notes, in American national mythology American heroes, unlike the heroes of Carlyle and of previous cultures, "stood out, paradoxically, by their typicality, by their emphatic embodiment of the very traits most characteristic of the society that had temporarily elevated them."[86]

By making Davis the apotheosis of this nationalist idealism Du Bois punctures its self-legitimations. In choosing Davis he chooses the leader of the defeated and racist South, a figure heavy with symbolic resonance and the memory of national division, as the logical telos of an unselfconscious New England idealism, and that at a time of rising nationalism.

And Du Bois adds insult to injury by making a military figure the embodiment of American representativeness, thus aligning Emerson more closely with the martial emphasis of Carlyle where Emerson had tried to distance himself from such an alignment.

The satiric thrust of the speech is, of course, also a self-critique to some extent, a distancing from an earlier self that had adopted Bismarck as a personal ideal. Both Bismarck and Davis embody the same vitalist conception of history, but where the former had tried to unite "a mass of bickering people," the latter had sown disunity; where the former had created a nation through the power of his individual will, the latter had been the agent of forces moving toward the dissolution of the nation. The individual will-to-power cannot guarantee black Americans an equitable place in the historical unfolding of a national cultural identity, and Du Bois now attempts to use an ethical qualification of the Great Man theory of history to propose an alternative model to "might makes right."

In the advance of one part of the world at the expense of others, argued Du Bois, the "overweening sense of the I" has led to the "consequent forgetting of the Thou" (*AR* 14). The "incomplete" ideal represented by Davis needs to be "checked by its complementary ideas" (*AR* 15). As this complement Du Bois proposed "the doctrine of the Submissive Man" as personified by "the Negro" (an "idea of submission apart from cowardice, laziness or stupidity," he quickly added) (*AR* 15).

Despite first appearances, Du Bois is not offering an alibi for slavery. He still accepts that the "world has needed and will need its Jefferson Davises" (*AR* 15). He even goes so far as to accept that, under certain circumstances perhaps, slavery is "not wholly despicable" (*AR* 15). But the meaning of submission in the speech is far from obvious. Du Bois is in fact proposing "the submission of *the strength of the Strong* to the advance of all," a rechanneling of the energies of the assertive "I" into a "submission to the Thou" as "the highest individualism" (*AR* 15, emphasis added). Submission means, then, a kind of Christian-Hegelian recognition of duty and collective debt as the basis of the state—not subservience. It is in this sense that blacks, African or American, are mythologized as an ideal against which Teutonic aggression and its alibis can be judged and exposed. The "highest individualism" is the Mosaic ideal democratized, Du Bois's own representative maneuver.

Du Bois, clearly anxious about the racist implications of heroic vitalism, attempts to rehabilitate the ideal through an ethical critique. Moralism and nervous satire are the only available modes of resistance at this stage. The desperate moral pleading of the speech gives an indication of Du Bois's continued commitment to the dominant culture's ideology within an increasing alienation from this ideology. Predictably, the audience heard only the plea for moral rehabilitation, not the sharper ironies. Both the national press and the audience wholeheartedly applauded Du Bois. An editorial in the *Nation* covering the 1890 Commencement Day noted that Du Bois "handled his difficult and hazardous subject with absolute good taste, great moderation, and almost contemptuous fairness" (*AR* 13).[87]

Du Bois's positing of the problem of progressive history and national destiny as a problem of the relationship of the "I" and the "Thou" frames the ethical issues in terms recalling Carlyle's *Sartor Resartus* (1831).[88] Within this frame, as in the conceptualization of the relation of self and other as one of a complementarity of submission and domination in which the issues of power and politics are suppressed, a blend of Christian moralism and Kantian ethics appears to have been filtered through Carlyle. Du Bois had studied Kant with William James and George Santayana, had taken a course on the ethics of social reform (with special reference to Native Americans) with Francis Greenwood Peabody, and, at about the same time that he gave his "Jefferson Davis" speech, had written a speech on Carlyle. The Carlyle of this speech is not only the admirer of Bismarck and the author of *Hero Worship,* but also the critic of industrialization and advocate of ethical culture. In his Carlyle speech Du Bois addresses the architects of a new nation. He champions Carlyle's resistance to the dangers of industrialization and his opposition to the values of a commercial culture. Along with Carlyle, Du Bois advocates the gospel of true and hard work.[89] Having suggested the shift from Bismarck to Moses two years earlier, Du Bois is clearly already moving toward his later formulation of the ideal of an elite and benign leadership for black Americans that he will, in 1903, name the "Talented Tenth."[90]

The continued admiration for Carlyle and the very nomenclature of the "Talented Tenth," as much as Du Bois's own sense of the continuity of New England influence on his education,[91] is a caution against overinterpreting the satirical thrust of the "Jefferson Davis" speech into a systematic rejection of New England traditions. If the play on "representative" was intended as a deflationary strategy in 1890, by 1903 Du Bois had, in part, circled back to Emersonian vitalism. The "talented" in the "Talented Tenth" is as much a reference to Emerson as "representative" in the commencement speech. Where Carlyle had distinguished

between "Great" and "Noted" men, Emerson had referred to "Representative" and "Talented" men.[92] The shifts between the categories represent,
at best, a certain leveling out of the elitist hierarchies.

However, Du Bois's ability to criticize Davis and the political realities
he typified, and at the same time to uphold the ideals of Bismarck, Moses,
"the Higher Individualism," and the "Talented Tenth," is a sign not so
much of hypocritical inconsistency as of the inadequacy of available radical
theoretical political discourses. The fact that Du Bois, like many other
nineteenth-century naturalists, continues to conceive the historical shape
of vitalist force in terms of individualism or as the collectivities of race or
nation ("a Jefferson Davis may appear as man, as race, or as nation" [*AR*
14]) also indicates the extent to which he is caught in the "conflict between
naturalistic politics and the older democratic traditions" noted in the introduction to this study. Furthermore, Bismarck in a poor black university
in Tennessee and Davis at Harvard *could* have very different meanings for
Du Bois. If Du Bois is as yet unable to deconstruct the politics of ideological *form*, that is only an indication of the problematic already outlined:
that Du Bois is inside cultural formations he is trying to get out of, but
with the ambiguous potentialities of these very formations as the only
available tools of analysis and rupture.

The contradictory impulses of Du Bois's philosophic thought during
the Harvard years and his reaction to the teachings of James have been
mapped in this chapter as the conflict between two divergent strategies:
on the one hand the building of a system or philosophy of history that
will be a vehicle for the hero's historical and racial mission, and on the
other a nervous laughter that leaves the available philosophical frameworks in tatters. Describing his experience of being "a thing apart" from
"the white world" in *Dusk of Dawn*, Du Bois writes:

> It was impossible for any time and to any distance to withdraw myself and
> look down upon these absurd assumptions with philosophical calm and
> humorous self-control. If, as happened to a friend of mine, a lady in a
> pullman car ordered me to bring her a glass of water, mistaking me for a
> porter, the incident in its essence was a joke to be chuckled over; but in its
> hard, cruel significance and its unending inescapable sign of slavery, it was
> something to drive a man mad. (*DD* 653–54)

The power of Du Bois's early satire lies in its refusal of "philosophical
calm" and resigned chuckling alike, and in its harnessing the rage of
madness into radical exposure. It is not Du Bois's science of universal

mind, nor his Jamesian admiration for great men, but the honesty of his ridicule that continues to speak the truths of African-American experience. In the next stage of Du Bois's career the tension between philosophical frameworks and a description of the particulars of black lives was to be more successfully resolved. But even in his turning away from metaphysics to the locally grounded knowledges of historiography and sociology, Du Bois was to reexperience the struggle, this time between the abstractions of positivist methodologism and the necessity of describing the nature of African-American consciousness in a more complex and tragic sense than is available in "A Vacation Unique."

Three

Local Knowledge in the

Shadow of Liberty

Science, Society, and Legitimacy

There is a fundamental shift in Du Bois's thought between his under-graduate work in philosophy and the publication of his books *The Suppression of the African Slave Trade to the United States of America, 1638–1870* (1896) and *The Philadelphia Negro* (1899). This shift is signaled by the transformation of the truth of "science" and scientific legitimation from the metaphysical quest for "great laws" to the empirical positivism of the "scientific method." After Du Bois's return from his two years of study in Germany in 1894, there emerged in his work a clear formulation of a positivist methodology that rejected the vagueness of the waning theodicy of Spencer's sociology for a more radically empirical and localized focus. Recalling the years after his return in *Dusk of Dawn,* Du Bois wrote that the main result of his schooling had been "to emphasize science and the scientific attitude" (*DD* 590). While the new discoveries of the natural and physical sciences thrilled him, Du Bois also recognized that "the difficulties of applying scientific law and discovering cause and effect in the social world were still great."

> Social thinkers were engaged in vague statements and were seeking to lay down the methods by which, in some not too distant future, social law

analogous to physical law would be discovered. Herbert Spencer finished his ten volumes of Synthetic Philosophy in 1896 [the year Du Bois began work on *The Philadelphia Negro*]. The biological analogy, the vast generalizations were striking, but actual scientific accomplishment lagged. For me an opportunity seemed to present itself. I would not lull my mind to hypnosis by regarding a phrase like "consciousness of kind" as a scientific law. But turning my gaze from fruitless word-twisting and facing the facts of my own social situation and racial world, I determined to put science into sociology through a study of the conditions and problems of my own group. (*DD* 590)[1])

Du Bois is here attacking not only Spencer but Frank Giddings, one of the leading figures in the new sociology of the 1880s and 1890s, who coined the phrase "consciousness of kind." The political orientation of Giddings's sociology of the laws of social association and the alignment of his ideas with the social commentaries of James have already been considered in the previous chapter. The issue raised by Du Bois in *Dusk of Dawn* concerns methodology. As Dorothy Ross has illustrated, Giddings was a chief spokesman for a largely ahistorical sociology that continued to subscribe to grand evolutionary schemas and rather vague formulations of so-called laws of social process. The claims to scientific status put forward by this sociology were opposed by an alternative sociology committed to historical and analytical method. Giddings's main opponent was Albion Small, who dismissed Giddings's method as a "pre-Platonic metaphysical fabrication" and argued that sociology must be based on an inductive method that built generalizations on a careful process of classification. The debate between Small and Giddings was raging at important conferences and in important journals in 1896.[2] Not only did Spencer complete his Synthetic Philosophy and Du Bois start his study of Philadelphia's black population in this year but Giddings also published his *Principles of Sociology*. It is clear from Du Bois's unpublished writings from around the turn of the century that he not only knew of Giddings's work but was critical of its methodology.[3]

Du Bois himself participated in the development of the inductive and historical empiricism advocated by Small and others. What was needed in sociology, he argued, was "the minute study of limited fields of human action, where observation and accurate measurement are possible and where real illuminating knowledge can be had."[4] Du Bois entered this project "primarily with the utilitarian object of reform and uplift," but still wanted to do the work with "scientific accuracy" (*DD* 591). He "was going to study the facts" of black life and history, "and by measurement and comparison and research, work up to any valid generalization" (*DD* 591).

> Amid a multitude of interesting facts and conditions we are groping after a science—after reliable methods of observation and measurement, and after some enlightening way of systematizing and arranging the mass of accumulated material. Moreover the very immensity of the task gives us pause. What after all are we trying to do but to make a science of human action? And yet such a task seems so preposterous that there is scarce a sociologist the world over that would acknowledge such a plan.[5]

Du Bois himself was, of course, a sociologist who *did* acknowledge such a plan. He is here describing his own plans to establish at Atlanta University, where he began teaching in 1897, a series of sociological studies of black American life. The intention was to reexamine each subject after ten years, with the whole project running for a hundred years, and to systematize the data gathered toward the formulation of laws of society (*DD* 600–601).

There is a continuity between Du Bois's work in philosophy and his social-scientific work. The attempt to synthesize voluntarism and determinism within a systematic science of history and human action, evident in "The Renaissance of Ethics" and to some extent in Du Bois's ambivalence about the Great Man theory of history, is not abandoned in Du Bois's turn to the scientific method; rather, it is reframed. The model for the systematization of laws now becomes not teleological metaphysics but a historicized version of the methodology of the physical and natural sciences where the concern with teleology and system is made secondary to and dependent on a concrete local knowledge. It is through a meticulously researched legislative documentary history and a statistical and historical sociology based on intense fieldwork that Du Bois now sets out to further the understanding and amelioration of the conditions of African-American life. The adoption of the "scientific method" is characteristic of the dominant trend in American social science in the 1880s and 1890s. Du Bois's transition from metaphysical historicism to localized understanding is also typical of the reorientation of historical thought in the nineteenth century. Instead of philosophy commanding explanations of history's unfolding, historical experience itself now becomes the site on which philosophical meanings are discovered. Philosophy therefore moves "toward an understanding of history not as a means to knowledge but as an *end* of knowledge, as a complete knowledge in itself beyond which the human mind cannot and need not go."[6]

This chapter examines Du Bois's theorization and practice of the scientific method from three different perspectives. The first section demonstrates the extent to which Du Bois's struggle to synthesize a conceptualization of the scientific method out of the many disciplinary traditions made available to him by his education is a continuation of the philosophical problems he struggled with as an undergraduate, particularly the problem of the relationship of voluntarism and determinism thrown up by James's course. The second section describes the way in which Du Bois's practice of the scientific method, much like its use by other "outsider" social scientists such as Franz Boas and Thorstein Veblen, proves to be an effective tool for the critique and delegitimation of society. A comparison of Du Bois with Boas and Veblen and a contextualization of Du Bois's work within an account of the cultural and political orientation of social-scientific discourse in late-nineteenth-century America also exposes the scandal of the continuing neglect of Du Bois in histories of American social science.[7] More important for the argument of the present study, an examination of Du Bois's historiography and sociology helps describe a growing historical awareness and social critique in his work that feed directly into *Souls*. The last section of the chapter analyzes the way in which Du Bois's practice of positivist methodology returns him to the philosophical problem of consciousness and introspection and of the process of referral between the will to action and historical and social process first encountered in the teachings and writings of James. This circling back can be seen as partly the result of the neo-Kantian paradigms that underlie both James's ethical thought and the positivist methodology of the new social science. In examining the disjuncture between Du Bois's scientific method and what he, in *Souls,* calls a world of "thought and feeling" (*SBF* 487), this last section also opens the discussion onto the detailed investigation of *Souls* in the second part of this study.

Toward Science: Will and Law Revisited

In "Sociology Hesitant," an unpublished essay written just after the turn of the century, Du Bois argued that in order to explain human action "we must assume Law and Chance working in conjunction—Chance being the scientific side of inexplicable will. Sociology, then, is the Science that seeks [to measure] the limits of Chance in human conduct."[8] As Dan Green and Edwin Driver note in their commentary on this passage, "Du Bois's sociology stands between that school of thought that considered all human behaviors subject to laws and the proponents of free will who refused to conceive of man's behavior as governed by laws."[9] Du Bois's acknowledgment of the equal claims of both "Law" and "Chance" in any definition of "human action" is an attempt to synthesize the rival claims of voluntarism and determinism, of idealism and positivism, a synthesis that he also attempted in his earlier philosophical work.

Thomas Haskell, following Talcott Parsons, has argued that it was precisely this synthetic convergence, along with the emphasis on empiricism and objective distance, that characterized the new academic scientific sociology that displaced, in the last two decades of the nineteenth century, the older, more reform-oriented, and less professionalized social science represented by the American Social Science Association.[10] Haskell argues that the theory undergirding the new science tried to accommodate idealism by acknowledging "the authenticity of human freedom," and in doing so "rejected the radical positivist tendency to reduce the conscious, willing mind to little more than an epiphenomenal reflex of heredity and environment." At the same time the new social theory stressed "a wide range of external constraints upon human freedom." It "gave close attention to law-like regularities in human experience and reached for the power to predict and control, even as it admitted the authenticity of choice."[11]

The paradoxical harmonization here of "the authenticity of choice" and "law-like regularities in human experience" serving the ends of social prediction and control needs a more critical statement than Haskell gives it because (as will be argued later) the new sociology tended, in practice if not in theory, more toward social control and acquiescence to the status quo than toward a defense of individual freedom. A similarly strained harmonization marks not only Du Bois's own sociological writings but also "The Renaissance of Ethics." From the perspective of Haskell's account of the theoretical development of social science in the late nineteenth century, the thesis can clearly be seen as Du Bois's first attempt to transform philosophy, particularly James's ethical teachings, into the science of sociology. There too Du Bois had attempted to engineer nothing less than a synthesis of determinism and indeterminism in the name of a Spencerian "science" of human action. The drift to Huxlean determinism had been checked by an appeal to Jamesian voluntarism, but that itself had been subsumed within a faith in the possibility of a "science" of the "great laws" governing human development. Green and Driver's conclusion that Du Bois's sociology tends ultimately more toward "the positivistic argument and reductionism" than toward voluntarism is equally true of "The Renaissance of Ethics," though in the sociological and historiographic work Du Bois's emphasis is on the discovery of laws through a study *of* history, not the imposition of metaphysical laws *on* history.[12] What is equally important, however, is that within this difference there is a fundamental continuity of concern with related philosophical issues between Du Bois's undergraduate philosophical explorations of determinism, indeterminism, and heroic vitalism and his later theorization and practice of social science.

The process by which Du Bois arrives at his positivistic methodology is a complex one involving the convergence of many different and often seemingly contradictory influences and traditions. The particularities of this convergence can only inadequately be suggested by the philosophic schematization of the development of late-nineteenth-century social theory as a struggle between determinism and indeterminism. A more detailed examination of the synthesizing process will make possible a richer understanding not only of Du Bois's theorization and practice of the scientific method but also of the relationship of this method with James's philosophy and with *Souls*.

In his *Autobiography* Du Bois himself narrates the origins of his own conversion to the scientific stance as a struggle in which a radical ethics and methodology, represented by James and the historian Albert Bushnell Hart, triumph over a more conservative politics and less rigorous method, represented by the social science of Francis Peabody and the economics of Frank Taussig. But there are problems in this account. While there is some truth in the distinctions Du Bois draws, he tends to overemphasize the differences between his teachers where it is equally necessary to see fundamental continuities in both politics and methodology among the four Harvard professors. The retrospective coherence of Du Bois's account should not be taken as the final or only possible version of Du Bois's move from philosophy to sociology. James certainly played a crucial part in pushing Du Bois toward social science. But it would be too simplistic to see Du Bois's intellectual development in terms of a single trajectory of an organic narrative in which James plants the germ of pragmatism in the young Du Bois that later flowers into a radical-liberal social analysis and activism.[13] Du Bois's account of his education also implies a reading of his own social scientific work that aligns it with the supposed radicalism of James and Hart. But if it can be demonstrated that this account needs to be revised, then it is also necessary to look more carefully at Du Bois's own practice of the scientific method.

Du Bois had taken a wide range of courses in the natural and physical sciences at Fisk and at Harvard, but he felt that he had come "to the study of sociology, by way of philosophy and history rather than by physics and biology" (*A* 149).[14] As a student at Harvard Du Bois had "conceived the idea of applying philosophy to an historical interpretation of race relations," and this he understood as his "first steps towards sociology as a science of human action" (*A* 148). Near the end of his life Du Bois wrote that it was "James with his pragmatism," as well as "Albert Bushnell Hart with his research method," who turned him "back from the lovely but sterile land of philosophic speculation, to the social sciences as the field for gathering and interpreting that body of fact which would apply to my program for the Negro" (*A* 148). Earlier in the *Autobiography* this same account of the move from philosophy to social science is made by distinguishing the influences of James and Hart from those of Peabody and Taussig: "William James guided me out of the sterilities of scholastic philosophy to realist pragmatism; from Peabody's social reform with a religious tinge, I turned to Albert Bushnell Hart to study history with documentary research; and from Taussig with his reactionary British economics of the Ricardo school, I approached what was later to become sociology" (*A* 133).

The characterizations of Peabody and Taussig are certainly accurate enough. But what is problematic in Du Bois's account of his teachers at Harvard is not his characterization of Peabody and Taussig as reactionaries but his distancing of James from this conservatism and his drawing of a clear distinction between the methodologism of Hart and that of Peabody.

Under Taussig, Marxist and socialist economics were dismissed and Ricardo was "revered" at a time when Ricardean economics was "dying" (*A* 141).[15] Taussig, even though he tried to position himself somewhere between supporters of laissez-faire and the advocates of state intervention, was basically in favor of a laissez-faire and conservative economics and opposed to socialist trends (a position that rigidified after the Haymarket riot of 1886 and in the face of the continued labor unrest of the 1880s and 1890s).[16] Peabody represented a similar resistance to radicalism. His course considered "questions of Charity, Divorce, the Indians, Labor, Prisons, Temperance, etc., as problems of practical Ethics."[17] Peabody had wanted to redirect the study of ethics from abstraction to, in his own words, "the practical application of moral ideals" by approaching "the theory of ethics inductively through the analyses of great moral movements."[18] The limits of Peabody's reformism are clearly suggested by his conviction that the "reward of the plain, unnoticed man as he trudges home in the dark" is the possession of the knowledge that "he has done his duty well." This was the "Christian thought of duty, which grows out of the Christian thought of sonship."[19]

James's attempt to solve the problems of the dispossessed and powerless by offering them a sympathetic spiritual share in the well-being and privilege of the powerful, described in the previous chapter, is very much of a piece with Peabody's Christian evasions and Taussig's defense of the socioeconomic status quo. Sydney Kaplan has demonstrated that James's pragmatic ethics, Peabody's Christian moralism, and Taussig's economics in fact shared a common reactionary and ultragradualist politics.[20] As Kaplan points out, James admired Peabody, and James's own social essays of the 1890s (considered in the previous chapter) do little more than reproduce Peabody's (or Carlyle's) gospel of work and duty.

If the distinctions that Du Bois is pointing to are meant to distinguish positivist realism from a looser and more biased methodology, this opposition also needs some qualification. As Kaplan has also demonstrated, not only did Peabody, James, and Taussig share a conservative political and moral stance, they also shared a methodological predilection "to treat their discipline as tied up organically in the life complex with other disciplines; to stress historic and evolutionary development, flow and change; to emphasize scientific method on the hypothesis-verification level; to be concerned with the concrete and factual."[21] Hart, who is not considered by Kaplan, also strongly shared this methodological orientation. His stress on documentary research and the inductive method was in keeping with the enormous influence of Leopold von Ranke in American historiography in the last quarter of the nineteenth century, and he combined a defense of this positivism with the argument that scientific method in historiography should be modeled on the post-Darwinian natural sciences, an importation that historiography was to share with sociology in the late nineteenth century:

What we need is a genuinely scientific school of history which shall remorselessly examine the sources and separate the wheat from the chaff; which shall critically balance evidence; which shall dispassionately and moderately set forth results. For such a process we have the fortunate analogy of the physical sciences; did not Darwin spend twenty years in accumulating data, and in seeing typical phenomena before he so much as ventured a generalization? History, too, has its inductive method, its relentless concentration of the grain in its narrow spout, till by its own weight it seeks the only outlet. In history, too, scattered and apparently unrelated data fall together in harmonious wholes.[22]

This is from Hart's presidential address to the American Historical Association in 1910, but it is clear from Du Bois's descriptions of Hart's teachings that the principles outlined here were already formulated in the 1890s when Du Bois studied with him. Nowadays commentators are less sanguine about the "fortunate analogy of the physical sciences." Du Bois's own later theorization of a positivist method working toward general laws was to follow Hart's formulations closely. But before Du Bois arrived at his own formulations, he was to test what he had learned at Harvard in the more rigorously methodological and scientific arena of social science studies in Germany.[23] It was in Berlin that Du Bois was to clearly synthesize an antiradical, centrist politics with a positivist methodology.

Between completing his undergraduate studies in 1890 and leaving for Europe in 1892, Du Bois had already begun his graduate studies. He had received his M.A. in history in 1891 and had started research on the suppression of the slave trade in America (Hart suggested the topic). The cultivation of the new field of history led Du Bois, in keeping with the current academic fashion and Hart's Germanic emphasis on institutional history, to study in Germany.[24] He studied at the university of Berlin and toured through much of Europe between August 1892 and June 1894. In Berlin Du Bois "came in contact with several of the great leaders of the developing social sciences: in economic sociology and in social history," and his "horizon in the social sciences was broadened not only by teachers but by students from France, Belgium, Russia, Italy and Poland" (*A* 162). He studied politics under the great Hegelian nationalist historian Heinrich von Treitschke, Prussian state reform under Rudolph von Gneist, and Prussian constitutional history under Gustav von Schmoller. His other courses included "theoretical political economy and 'industrialism in society' under Adolph Wagner and, most important of all, a research seminar on method with Schmoller. These latter courses proved to be the crucial ones."[25]

As at Harvard, the teachers are important and are discussed in Du Bois's autobiographies. Du Bois even wrote an essay on Schmoller. The impact of Schmoller and Wagner is understandable, given that Du Bois felt that "Harvard had in the social sciences no such leadership of thought and breadth of learning as in philosophy, literature and physical sciences" (*A* 141). Du Bois's studies in Berlin fostered his search for liberal and ethical solutions to political problems. In Berlin Du Bois attended meetings of the local German Social Democratic party, and in his travels through Europe he encountered not only the high art of Western culture but also peasants and workers of many nations.[26] He was attracted to socialism but, given his academic training up to that time, he was unable to grasp Marxist ideas or those of "revisionists like Lassalle, Bernstein or Bakunin" (*A* 168). At Harvard, "Marx was mentioned but only incidently and as one whose doubtful theories had long since been refuted. Socialism as dream of philanthropy or as will-o-wisp of hotheads was dismissed as unimportant" (*A* 133). The graduate work in Berlin, particularly the work with Schmoller, led Du Bois away from both Ricardo and Marx toward a more liberal and positivist social science that tied its advocacy of state intervention to a belief in the evolutionary modification of the capitalist system, not a revolutionary transformation of it.[27] Henry Adams too found in the positivist tradition a sort of halfway house to Marx. Adams writes in the *Education* that "he should have been . . . a Marxist, but some narrow trait of New England nature seemed to blight socialism." Adams "did the next best thing; he became a Cometist, within the limits of evolution" (*EHA* 225).

Francis Broderick has assessed the significance of Du Bois's studies in Berlin for his intellectual development:

> Schmoller and Wagner were prominent figures in the emerging German school of historical economics. In revolt against the deductive method of Manchester economists, this "younger school" sought through historical studies to provide an empirical base for economic theory. Though not scornful of theoretical treatises, these economists put them in a secondary position. Schmoller, more totally committed to this school than Wagner, believed that innumerable small accurate studies of all phases of man's social life would accumulate a body of information on which social policy could be based. For him political economy was primarily a normative science, and the information once accumulated was to be used to establish "justice in the economic system" through state action. And yet research and social policy were to be sharply differentiated. Du Bois's notes on Schmoller's seminar quote the German as saying: "My school tries as far as possible to

leave the *sollen* for a later stage and study the *geschehen* as other sciences have done."[28]

Schmoller's major disagreement with classical economic theory was that it lacked the ability to deal with the *whole* range of social reality. He argued for the need for detailed descriptive work on past and present events, institutions, and social structures as the first step toward a genuine economic theory.[29] In this way Schmoller's work straddled the disciplines of history and the social sciences as much as economics. Such a disciplinary confluence was becoming more common in both Germany and the United States in the last two decades of the nineteenth century and was to find alignments with John Dewey's brand of pragmatism.[30]

It is clear from "The Renaissance of Ethics" that Du Bois already shared some of Schmoller's stress on the need to study the facts of everyday life and on the distinction between the Ought and the Is of actual events.[31] But the stress on the particulars of social experience in Schmoller's teaching was much more materialist, and the separation of what ought to be from what actually happens was much stronger and clearer than in the apprentice explorations of the thesis.

The developments in the social sciences represented by Schmoller were related to a similar radicalism then current in the arena of philosophy in Germany. Du Bois was in Berlin at a time when neo-idealism or neo-Kantianism, what is generally referred to as the "Back-to-Kant" movement, was at its height and had achieved "academic supremacy," particularly in the field of social and historical thought. The movement was an attempt by liberal intellectuals to apply Kant's ethics to social issues in order to "remedy the most serious deficiency of German liberalism—its narrowness and its inability to develop a broad social philosophy reaching beyond the confines of the professional, academic, and propertied middle class."[32] In the face of the new realities of mass industrial society and the rapid growth of radical socialism, the neo-idealists tried to overcome the middle classes' antipathy toward the enfranchisement of the working classes and toward social welfare through state intervention. The emphasis was on reform through the ballot and parliamentary debate or, at its most radical, through democratic socialism rather than revolutionary Marxism. But as the more radical neo-idealists were demonstrating, the road from a post-Hegelian critical idealism to Marx was a logical one for many intellectuals, and Du Bois's career was to follow this very path after the Depression. In the meantime, in the years following his return from Germany, Du Bois too was to argue for enfranchisement, social welfare, and state intervention on behalf of the black population of America.

The notebook for Philosophy 4 shows that Du Bois, while still an undergraduate at Harvard, had already encountered neo-Kantianism through the philosophies of Charles Bernard Renouvier, the leading French neo-Kantian, and Hermann Lotze, the founding figure of the Back-to-Kant movement. In his lectures on ethics, James had celebrated Renouvier as the philosopher who defended freedom in the phenomenal and not the noumenal world. James also referred his students to various works by Lotze, often to specific sections, and made his admiration for the German philosopher clear. Lotze is present again and again as a point of reference and comparison in Du Bois's notes. Furthermore, Royce had studied with Lotze and had supervised Santayana's doctoral dissertation on Lotze after Santayana's return from Germany.[33] Even Schmoller referred Du Bois to Lotze in his seminars on method and economics in 1893.[34]

The emphasis on ethical action that attracted Du Bois to Pragmatism must also have attracted him to the developments then taking place in Germany. What was important about neo-Kantianism for James as for Du Bois was not its transcendental method or its idealism, but its assumption of "the primacy of practical reason."[35] Neo-idealism grew out of the anti-Hegelianism that followed the political upheavals of the 1830s and 1840s and sought ultimately "to reassert the role of human consciousness in the historical process, to establish a methodology for humanistic studies different from that of the physical sciences, and to defend the efficacy of moral striving in the political arena against the claims of economic determinism."[36]

Neo-Kantianism, in other words, upheld a defense of voluntarism by means of a caricaturization of Hegel as a metaphysical monist in much the same way as James did. But some of the problems such a voluntarism is likely to encounter in its attempt to transform itself into a social ethics have already been described in the first chapter. They will be more clearly illustrated by Du Bois himself when, in *Souls*, he radically revises nineteenth-century readings of Hegel as a way of critiquing his own adoption of such a voluntarism. Prior to *Souls*, however, Du Bois seems to hold fast in his allegiance to a systematic social science that nods toward the freedom of will and distances itself from Hegelian historicism.

An unpublished article of Du Bois's on Schmoller demonstrates that he positioned himself in this way and that he grasped fairly well the nature of the developments then under way in the social sciences in Germany, particularly the relationship of the new social thought to neo-idealism.[37] Du Bois argued that the key to understanding Schmoller's social philosophy was to see it not so much as a protest against English economics but as a resistance to the German interpretation of it. Schmoller denied the title of science to a system of laws that applied only to a given place at a given time. He recognized the objectives and arguments of liberal economics without having to accept that "abstract school dogma" that believes in the unlimited harmony of all private interests, the unconditional right of economic egoism, and that overlooks the psychological, social, and moral prerequisites of every economic condition and deduces all economic life from abstract motives. But Schmoller's critique of the abstract deduction of economic motives does not appear to have extended to the supposed neutrality of the economic theorist or to his own theoretical logic. Du Bois places Schmoller's birth in the historical context of a post–French Revolution Germany surging toward the upheavals of 1848. At this time, Du Bois argues, Kantian philosophy had run its course through Fichte and Schelling, and the absolute idealism of Hegel had received its great realistic repulse from Johann Friedrich Herbart.[38] Schmoller himself is seen to be influenced by the systematizing dogmatism of Hegel to some extent but to have become, in the end, a Herbartian realist.

This narrative of Schmoller's move from a systematizing idealism to an empirical realism could easily be an account of Du Bois's own abandonment of the "sterile land of philosophic speculation" for James's "realist pragmatism." This parallelism also makes plain that the realisms of Schmoller and James were closely aligned for Du Bois. In "The Renaissance of Ethics" Du Bois had tried to transform James's so-called "realist" ethics into a science of human action. As James had pointed out to Du Bois in his marginal comments on the thesis, this was to misunderstand his argument about philosophy and voluntarism. In his lectures for Philosophy 4 James had used an attack on Hegelian metaphysics as a way of arguing the need to confine philosophy to a pragmatic stance that shared the realism of contemporary science. But James did not believe that this realism could lead to a systematic science of human action. For him such a project was an impossibility because human action was contingent and therefore not reducible to the workings of laws. However, Du Bois was not totally wrongheaded in trying to transform James's philosophy into a sociological science because, despite James's disclaimers, the possibility of such a transformation was already present in the logic of James's argument. James had, after all, retreated from his more radical formulations of voluntarism by making individual action subservient to the collective will. In doing so he had in fact both proposed and legitimated a law of conservative social process. Having first opposed voluntarism to determinism, he had reincorporated the former into the latter. It was exactly at this point of convergence that American pragmatism and American sociology were to find one of their most crucial common grounds.[39] What was only half visible in James's philosophy, and what Du Bois himself had only awkwardly articulated in "The Renaissance of Ethics," was clearly formulated by Schmoller's neo-idealist project of an empirical and historical methodology working up to the discovery of general laws of society. As the next two sections of this chapter demonstrate, Du Bois's practice of the scientific method led him to social critique, but also made him circle back to the accommodationist dilemmas of James's philosophical thought.

The Riddle of the American Sphinx: History, Sociology, and Exceptionalism

Both *The Suppression of the African Slave Trade* and *The Philadelphia Negro* adhere closely to the empirical realism of Schmoller's idea of the social sciences and of the methodological emphasis Du Bois had encountered through Hart and others at Harvard as well as by following contemporary sociological debates in America. Du Bois sees *Suppression* as a "contribution to the scientific study of slavery and the American Negro" based "mainly upon a study of the sources, i.e., national, State, and colonial statutes, Congressional documents, reports of societies, personal narratives, etc." (*SAST* 3). The Rankean characterization is more than justified. The last hundred and fifty pages of *Suppression* consist of an impressive and meticulous catalog of primary and secondary research materials, including a chronological conspectus of all relevant colonial and state legislation from 1641 to 1871, a detailed list of legal cases concerning vessels involved in the slave trade between 1619 and 1864, and a substantial bibliography of colonial laws, state documents, and more general materials, including works in French and German. It is this emphasis on the centrality of primary documentation and the rigorously localized focus that put Du Bois's work at the forefront of contemporary developments in American historiography rather than with the more outmoded literary tradition of nineteenth-century historiography represented by figures like

Macaulay (whom Du Bois had read with relish as a child and then at Fisk), Carlyle, or the American George Bancroft, whose *History of the United States from the Discovery of America* (1834–87) was informed by a nationalist mythology of heroic achievement and progress buoyed up with inflated liberal and nationalist sentiments.[40]

The Philadelphia Negro is equally positivist in its orientation and combines the theoretical frameworks offered by Schmoller and the American sociology of men like Small with the British empiricism of Charles Booth's *Life and Labor of the People of London* (1891–1903).[41] Like Booth's work, which is a meticulous gathering of statistical information on the London poor (with maps, as in Du Bois's work, used to plot the distribution of poverty and population), *The Philadelphia Negro* is a vast presentation (over five hundred pages long) of statistical data concerning various aspects of the life of African-Americans living in Philadelphia's Seventh Ward.[42] For the primary fieldwork that formed the core of his study, Du Bois, who was then living in the Seventh Ward, used no assistants but personally interviewed five thousand men and women, spending anywhere from ten minutes to an hour (an average of fifteen to twenty-five minutes) in each home (*A* 198, *PN* 62–63). Du Bois had devised a questionnaire designed to solicit a wide range of information, from the age, size, sex, and conjugal conditions of the black population, to detail regarding occupation, education and literacy, health, family life, crime, pauperism, alcoholism, and membership in religious, secret, and other social organizations. Du Bois supplemented the information so gathered with a historical account of the origins and development of the black population of Philadelphia. This account was based on additional fieldwork in the South and research in the public libraries of Philadelphia as well as in the private libraries of black residents of the city (*A* 198).

On the whole then, both *The Suppression of the African Slave Trade* and *The Philadelphia Negro* are contained within the positivist house practices of Du Bois's training. But the problem was that this method serving the cause of social amelioration and progress could be dependent upon an appeal to pseudo-objective reason at a time when America was virulently racist. Du Bois turns to a more positivist approach as a means of analyzing and improving African-American life at a time when this method is being used in American social science largely in support of a legitimation of progressive and exceptionalist accounts of American social process, as well as in defense of racist apologetics. As Peter Conn has accurately noted, Du Bois's faith in science revealed "his intellectual conformity with progressive assumptions." But "the history of science in these years was not to unfold along the path of accelerated liberation he foresaw. On the contrary, science inscribed a profoundly dialectical trajectory, a sustained contest between revolution and reaction."[43] Both science and pseudo-science provided alibis for white supremacy and support for the late-nineteenth-century and early-twentieth-century waves of xenophobia and racism. It is in the context of this racism and the social-scientific response to it, as well as to increased labor unrest, that Du Bois's *practice* of the scientific method must be understood.

According to Du Bois, as his ship sailed back from Germany into New York Harbor on a morning in June 1894, a little French girl on the deck said "Oh yes the Statue of Liberty! With its back toward America, and its face toward France" (*A* 182). During his two years in Europe Du Bois experienced a sense of escape from the culture of racism such as he had never experienced before. He traveled freely and extensively not only in Germany but throughout much of Western and Eastern Europe. He indulged to the full his taste for classical music and painting. And he came close to marrying a young German woman (see *DD* 585–89). The sense of confidence, freedom, and power is clearly noticeable in a diary entry made on the occasion of Du Bois's twenty-fifth birthday in Berlin. He describes an elaborate program of celebration that included dining out, listening to music, letter-writing, reflecting on the topics of "Parents" and "Home," and also a visit to "a pretty girl" (*AR* 27). But the birthday began with what he described as a "Sacrifice to the Zeitgeist" of "Mercy—God—work." The sacrifice apparently involved a "ceremony with candle, Greek wine, oil, song and prayer" conducted at midnight (*AR* 27). The ceremony initiated a day during which Du Bois seems to have been particularly preoccupied with thoughts of his future career. He concludes that his "plans" are "to make a name in science" or "to make a name in literature and thus to raise my race." But these definitions of "mercy" and "work" are immediately revised by the thought that "perhaps" he "can raise a visible empire in Africa" (*AR* 29). Du Bois would like to believe that "it is the silent call of the world spirit that makes me feel that I am royal and that beneath my sceptre a world of kings shall bow" (*AR* 28).

Vitalist projections continued to provide desperately needed models of self-esteem.[44] However, the democratic vistas opened up by Europe were sharply closed off as he "dropped suddenly back into 'nigger'-hating America" (*A* 183). Du Bois's nineteenth-century confidence in a progressive destiny that guarantees the just recognition and reward of talent was now threatened by a more characteristically modern sense of doubt and anxiety as he "began to realize how much of what I had called Will and Ability was sheer Luck!" (*A* 183). Du Bois saw that he could easily have been put to child labor or given training in crafts or industrial work rather than being sent to college, given a scholarship, and allowed to pursue graduate work (*A* 183). In terms that recall Ishmael's grim sense in *Moby Dick* that "those stage managers, the Fates," may have deluded him into believing that his actions were determined by "choice" and "unbiased freewill,"[45] Du Bois wondered, "Was I the masterful captain or the pawn of laughing sprites?" (*A* 183).

Du Bois notes in *Dusk of Dawn* that 1892 was the high tide of lynchings in America. Two hundred and thirty-five blacks were murdered that year (*DD* 593), and the violence continued throughout the 1890s. The second half of the decade saw the increasing disenfranchisement of blacks in the South, and in 1896 the Supreme Court decision in the *Plessy v. Ferguson* case upheld "separate but equal" existence for blacks and whites. The 1890s were also witness to unprecedented labor unrest. The middle years of the decade were marked by a severe depression and a series of major strikes, most notably Homestead in 1892 and Pullman in 1894. Continued labor unrest and union activity and the rise of the Populist movement set off antilabor and antiradical campaigns. With the defeat of Bryan and the victory of McKinley in the election of 1896, the widespread fear of a radical threat finally abated.

The response of white American social scientists to the new tide of racism and to the labor question was, on the whole, far from laudable. John David Smith has carefully documented the widespread development of proslavery ideology in the postbellum era in both academic historiography and popular polemic (Biblical, ethnological, educational, racial). Smith argues that "slavery provided a metaphor that explained and justified race relations in the postwar South" at precisely the time when black southerners "were ensnared in conditions of neoslavery—modified serfdom, economic peonage, enticement laws, emigrant agent restrictions, contract laws, vagrancy statutes, the criminal-surety and convict labor systems."[46] Though it was clearly identifiable from Reconstruction through the Gilded Age, the new proslavery school "surfaced most clearly in the 1890s. Slavery's new apologists filled scholarly monographs and journals, popular magazines and newspapers, with a historical rationale for the contemporary repression of blacks—mob terror, lynching, segregation, disfranchisement [*sic*]."[47]

Pseudo-science played its part in bolstering this reaction. Academic historians, seeking a reconciliation between North and South, and spurred on by the nationalism generated by America's growing imperial enterprise, used the scientific justifications of racial inferiority as well as their own "posture of impartiality, fairness, detachment, and objectivity" to attack the abolitionists, to soften the picture of slavery, and to reject theories of the "slave power conspiracy." Thus "a nationalist and racist consensus, which demonstrated historians' impartiality and objectivity, was achieved in the 'middle period' of the nineteenth century."[48] Even Hart, Du Bois's dissertation supervisor, proud of his abolitionist heritage and exceptionally active in his support of black advance, conceded in reviewing literature purporting to demonstrate black inferiority that "if provable, it is an argument that not only justifies slavery, but now justifies any degree of political and social dependence." Hart finally accepted that the argument was indeed provable and that blacks were inferior to even "poor white people, immigrants or natives."[49]

American professional social science's accommodation to racism was itself part of a more general acquiescence to an antiradical reaction that attempted to refurbish the nationalist ideology of exceptionalism and progress at a time when this ideology was under severe threat from growing social and political disunity. As Dorothy Ross has demonstrated in great detail, both the social sciences and the idea that "America occupies an exceptional place in history, based on her republican government and economic opportunity . . . emerged from the late eighteenth- and early nineteenth-century effort to understand the character and fate of modern society."

> The experience of civil war and rapid industrialization and the decline of religious assurance precipitated a national crisis and forced Americans to an understanding of history in the modern sense: history as a process of continuous, qualitative change, moved and ordered by forces that lay within itself. Under the impact of industrialization and the rise of class conflict, Americans confronted the possibility that the country would follow the same historic course that Europe did and that permanent classes, even socialism, might develop [in America]. As a result, many social scientists revised the idea of American exceptionalism. They argued that the realization of

American liberal and republican ideals depended on the same forces that were creating liberal modernity in Europe, on the development of capitalism, democratic politics, and science. America's unique condition did not block the full effects of modernity . . . but rather supported it.[50]

Among the early professional historians there was a commonly shared stance of what John Higham has called "conservative evolutionism." For these men, American history was the story of "freedom realized and stabilized through the achievement of national solidarity."[51] The younger generation of "Progressive Historians" who established themselves in the 1890s and the early twentieth century—men such as Frederick Jackson Turner, James Harvey Robinson, and Charles A. Beard—distanced themselves from the idealism of the previous generation and offered a more critical account of the past, but maintained a secular progressive belief "in the prospect of continuous amelioration 'within the system.'" This faith "kept their ideological heterodoxy from transgressing the limits of the accommodationist."[52]

The topic of Du Bois's own historiography was ideally suited to progressive treatment. An account of the efforts to stop the slave trade to the United States from 1638 to 1870, *The Suppression of the African Slave Trade* could have been a narrative of the triumph of liberty running parallel to the establishment of national identity and independence. But this was not the story Du Bois in fact told. The struggle against the slave trade is narrated as a series of failures, of the good intentions of the few perpetually undermined by the self-interest of the many and the incompetence and weakness of the government. Du Bois describes in detail the failure to enforce the 1808 act outlawing the importation of slaves, and the subsequent growth in the trade. Noting the late antebellum calls for the revival of the slave trade, Du Bois attacks America's continuous bargaining and compromising with slavery—a message that would have had obvious relevance in the 1890s, when proslavery arguments were once again rife. The eventual suppression of the trade is explained not as the triumph of the principles of the revolutionary fathers and the progressive forces of American society but as the outcome of chaotic chance and lucky coincidence.

At a time when accounts of American colonial and revolutionary history remained accounts of the rise of liberty and nationality,[53] Du Bois concluded his book with a very different "lesson for Americans" (*SAST* 196). He offered a remarkably critical and intensely eloquent survey of American history, from colonial days to the post–Civil War era, in which

what were usually regarded as the major historical moments marking
American progress were skillfully deflated by reference to the history of
slavery and the slave trade:

> No American can study the connection of slavery with United States his-
> tory, and not devoutly pray that this country may never have a similar
> social problem to solve, until it shows more capacity for such work than it
> has shown in the past. It is neither profitable nor in accordance with scien-
> tific truth to consider that whatever the constitutional fathers did was right,
> or that slavery was a plague sent from God and fated to be eliminated in
> due time. We must face the fact that this problem arose principally from
> the cupidity and carelessness of our ancestors. It was the plain duty of the
> colonies to crush the trade and the system in its infancy: they preferred to
> enrich themselves on its profits. It was the plain duty of a Revolution based
> upon "Liberty" to take steps toward the abolition of slavery: it preferred
> promises to straightforward action. It was the plain duty of the Constitu-
> tional Convention, in founding a new nation, to compromise with a threat-
> ening social evil only in case its settlement would thereby be postponed to
> a more favorable time: this was not the case in the slavery and the slave-trade
> compromises; there never was a time in the history of America when the
> system had a slighter economic, political, and moral justification than in
> 1787; and yet with this real, existent, growing evil before their eyes, a
> bargain largely of dollars and cents was allowed to open the highway that
> led straight to the Civil War. Moreover, it was due to no wisdom and
> foresight on the part of the fathers that fortuitous circumstances made the
> result of the war what it was, nor was it due to exceptional philanthropy
> on the part of their descendants that that result included the abolition of
> slavery. (*SAST* 196–97)

As the reference to "scientific truth" indicates, Du Bois is criticizing not
only the popular nationalist ideology of progress but also the none too
scientific support for this ideology from "scientific" historians. The critique of the conclusion leads Du Bois inevitably to exposing the ideology
of exceptionalism as a myth that America can no longer afford to believe
in the 1890s. Continuing the tour de force "lesson to Americans," Du
Bois writes:

> We have the somewhat inchoate idea that we are not destined to be harassed
> with great social questions, and that even if we are, and fail to answer them,
> the fault is with the question and not with us. Consequently we often

congratulate ourselves more on getting rid of a problem than on solving it. Such an attitude is dangerous; we have and shall have, as other peoples have had, critical, momentous, and pressing questions to answer. The riddle of the Sphinx may be postponed, it may be evasively answered now; sometime it must be fully answered. (*SAST* 197)

The Philadelphia Negro confronts just such a pressing social question and the attempts to evade it. Where *The Suppression of the African Slave Trade* describes the history of such an evasion in the past in relation to the question of slavery, Du Bois's sociological study offers an exemplary account of the persistence of the culture of racism and dispossession in the aftermath of slavery. *The Philadelphia Negro* is focused on the Seventh Ward of Philadelphia, the area in which the black population was concentrated. The black community of Philadelphia was the oldest and, in 1896, the largest Northern black community in the country, exceeded in size only by the three Southern black communities of New Orleans, Washington, D.C., and Baltimore (a border city).[54] The Seventh Ward was "a thickly populated district of varying character" that included some middle-class residential sections as well as the worst of the city's slums.[55] For Du Bois, the Seventh Ward represented "an epitome of nearly all the Negro problems," including "every class" and "varying conditions of life" (though Du Bois himself cautioned that "one must naturally be careful not to draw too broad conclusions from a single ward in one city") (*PN* 62).

After his return from Germany Du Bois had secured a teaching position at Wilberforce College in Ohio (where he had also married). Then, in 1896, he was invited by Philadelphia city officials and members of the University of Pennsylvania to undertake a study of the black population of their city. Du Bois was aware that he may have been invited to do this study for the wrong reasons. "The fact was," he wrote, "that the city of Philadelphia at that time had a theory; and that theory was that this great, rich, and famous municipality was going to the dogs because of the crime and venality of its Negro citizens, who lived largely in the slums at the lower end of the seventh ward." Philadelphia "wanted to prove this by figures," and thought that Du Bois "was the man to do it" (*DD* 596).

But where the city officials wanted an ahistorical account of their social world where their own prejudices were scientifically fixed into natural law, and the sustaining forces and ideologies of their world thereby validated, Du Bois actually offered them a critical and historical account. The historicized causality of Du Bois's study revealed, in fact, "the Negro group as a symptom, not a cause; as a striving, palpitating group, and not an inert, sick body of crime; as a long historic development and not a transient occurrence" (*DD* 596). Du Bois succeeded in deploying empirical practice against the alliance of pseudo-science, liberal optimism, and racism not only because his marginalized position fostered critical understanding, but also because he enlarged his scientific training to include a more historical assessment of the evidence in his work. This is in contrast to the models of the social world that dominated American social science at the turn of the century and have continued to dominate since then. These models "invite us to look through history to a presumably natural process beneath. Here the social world is composed of individual behaviors responding to natural stimuli, and the capitalist market and modern urban society are understood, in effect, as part of nature. We are led toward quantitative and technocratic manipulation of nature and an idealized liberal vision of American society."[56]

The Philadelphia Negro begins with a historical survey of the origins and growth of the black population of Philadelphia. As in *The Suppression of the African Slave Trade,* history appears as an ongoing struggle by black Americans for freedom and advancement. Du Bois describes how each period of advance has been pushed back by various factors, from the influx of white immigrants or poorly educated and poorly trained blacks from the South into the city to the continuing restrictions on black employment and political rights. The major part of *The Philadelphia Negro* is a survey of various aspects of continuing deprivation in the black community, including education, employment, health, freedom from crime, and family life.

If the city authorities wanted Du Bois to prove that the city's problems stemmed from its black population, Du Bois offered a more complex image of historical and social process. While he acknowledged various shortcomings in the black community, Du Bois not only exposed the myth of black criminality, but also laid a large part of the blame for the condition of the Seventh Ward at the doorstep of white prejudice and its enforcement in both overt and hidden ways. Du Bois argued that there could be no solution to the black "problem" until white racism was addressed, but also that the solving of the problems of the Seventh Ward was essential to the health of Philadelphia's society *as a whole*. Noting the antipathy of white "civilization" toward the "backward" blacks, Du Bois writes:

> It is right and proper to object to ignorance and consequently to ignorant men; but if by our actions we have been responsible for their ignorance and are still actively engaged in keeping them ignorant, the argument loses its moral force. So with the Negroes: men have a right to object to a race so poor and ignorant and inefficient as the mass of Negroes; but if their policy in the past is parent of much of this condition, and if to-day by shutting black boys and girls out of most avenues of decent employment they are increasing pauperism and vice, then they must hold themselves largely responsible for the deplorable results.
>
> There is no doubt that in Philadelphia the center and kernel of the Negro problem so far as the white people are concerned is the narrow opportunities afforded Negroes for earning a decent living. Such discrimination is morally wrong, politically dangerous, industrially wasteful, and socially silly. It is the duty of whites to stop it, and to do so primarily for their own sakes. Industrial freedom of opportunity has by long experience been proven to be generally best for all. Moreover the cost of crime and pauperism, the growth of slums, and the pernicious influence of idleness and lewdness, cost the public far more than would the hurt to the feelings of a carpenter to work beside a black man, or a shop girl to stand beside a darker mate. (*PN* 394–95)

This is from the conclusion of *The Philadelphia Negro,* and Du Bois is here using his historicized account to redefine the idea of interdependence. As industrial, technological, and social processes were thought to have become more and more complex in the second half of the nineteenth century, the idea of interdependence had come to play a central role in social analysis, particularly in the Gilded Age.[57] As Donald Bellomy notes, "the Progressive innovation was partly its broader understanding of interrelatedness, partly (and more momentously) its fresh response to the challenge of interdependence. In the problem lay its solution, for if the American people awoke to the mutuality of their lives, they could recreate the community ideal on a wider, national, ultimately international basis."[58] The guiding assumptions of *The Philadelphia Negro* and the goals that Du Bois outlines in the book are in complete harmony with the Progressive model. But in urging an awareness of mutuality and a new sense of community where interracial contacts are concerned, Du Bois is transgressing the liberal limits of Progressive reformism.

Du Bois's use of the political histories of race to delegitimate both exceptionalism and liberal programs for social harmonization places him outside the mainstream of American social science in the 1880s and 1890s. *The Suppression of the African Slave Trade* and *The Philadelphia Negro* belong with the work of a minority of social scientists whose work did include historicized and politicized accounts of contemporary capitalist society. Boas and Veblen provide useful points of comparison here.

Du Bois's conception of the scientific project is almost identical to Boas's or Veblen's, especially in its emphasis on historical particularity as against the type of historical reason associated with evolutionism and the comparative method. Boas's analysis of "The Limitations of the Comparative Method in Anthropology" makes plain that, in attempting "to explain customs and ideas of remarkable similarity which are found here and there," comparative studies also pursue "the more ambitious scheme of discovering the laws and the history of the evolution of human society."[59] But this amounts to "forcing phenomena into the strait-jacket of a theory" and "is opposed to the inductive process by which the actual history of definite phenomena may be derived."[60] Boas demands that the causes from which a phenomenon has developed "be investigated and that comparisons be restricted to those phenomena which have proved to be effects of the same causes."[61] Boas adds that what he is calling for "is no other than the much ridiculed historical method."[62] The transition Boas maps out is identical to the one signaled by Du Bois's rejection of Spencer and Giddings and a metaphysical science in favor of a more localized social science and historical research. Boas published his attack on the comparative method in 1896; the reader will recall this as the year in which Giddings published his *Principles of Sociology,* Spencer finished his Synthetic Philosophy, and Du Bois began his research for *The Philadelphia Negro.*[63]

Veblen also outlines and defends a more particularist historical method, and warns against the naturalizing tendencies of the ahistorical approach, in his review of Schmoller's work. He writes that the historical method "necessarily seeks to know and explain the structure and functions of economic society in terms of how and why they have come to be what they are, not, as so many economic writers have explained them, in terms of what they are good for and what they ought to be. It means, in other words, a deliberate attempt to substitute an inquiry into the efficient causes of economic life in the place of empirical generalizations, on the one hand, and speculations as to the eternal fitness of things, on the other hand."[64]

The Theory of the Leisure Class (1899), a trenchant exposé of values of the new bourgeois capitalist culture, and "The Place of Science in Modern Civilization" (1906), a warning about the technocratic drift of modern society, are just two examples of historicized and politicized critique from Veblen's work at the turn of the century. Boas's "Limitations of the Comparative Method" is less explicit in its politics, but its opening paragraph clearly suggests that the popularity of the comparative method may be due to its making social science available as a tool of social engineering. In proposing "that laws exist which govern the development of society, that they are applicable to our society as well as to those of past times and distant lands," the comparative method suggests "that, guided by this knowledge, we may hope to govern our actions so that the greatest benefit to mankind will accrue from them." It is this potential that has guaranteed anthropology the reception of "that liberal share of public interest which was withheld from it as long as it was believed that it could do no more than record the curious customs and beliefs of strange peoples; or, at best, trace their relationships, and thus elucidate the early migrations of the races of man and the affinities of peoples."[65] Boas is in fact pointing to the reactionary implication of assimilative programs that sought to engineer a normative conception of national character as a way of containing the disturbing effects of cultural, racial, and class difference. Himself a German Jew who had experienced anti-Semitism in his youth and had grown up in a "home in which the ideals of the revolution of 1848 were a living force,"[66] Boas had emigrated to America in 1886 believing that "America was politically an ideal country." But by the late 1890s he had come to feel that he "was emotionally through with America."[67]

Veblen's being the son of poor Norwegian peasants who emigrated to take up farming in Minnesota and Du Bois's being the son of a black domestic may also help explain the critical edge of their social commentaries. Unlike Du Bois, Veblen, and Boas, the majority of social scientists born between 1850 and 1870 were the "sons of the well-to-do, native born, Protestant middle class or recruits to that class from the poorer ranks of respectable Protestantism. They were Whig or Republican in culture if not in formal affiliation, and many of them sons or grandsons of ministers."[68]

But the issue of ideological conformity or nonconformity cannot be explained simply by class or ethnic origins. Du Bois's own ability to maintain a critical distance from liberal white society and at the same time to share in some of its key assumptions about society and history is a case in point. One way in which this paradox in Du Bois's thought can be described is by examining how his reliance on certain aspects of current social-scientific methods, the very tool of social delegitimation, can also lead him back to a position of consensus.

The Claims of "Thought and Feeling": Science, Literature, and Understanding

In his assessment of the work of Schmoller, Veblen qualified his praise for the German economist with a lengthy demonstration of the way in which Schmoller, when dealing with contemporary institutions, tends to abandon current scientific procedures for "appeal and admonition, urged on grounds of expediency, of morality, of good taste, of hygiene, of political ends, and even of religion."[69] Veblen's critique does not separate science and politics as such but demonstrates that in abandoning certain social-scientific assumptions Schmoller is led into an inadequate politics that can only accept the permanency of the status quo. For example, Schmoller rejects the idea of the equality of the sexes and fails to analyze the ways in which gender relations are historically constructed, something Veblen himself had done in *The Theory of the Leisure Class*. Schmoller's "discussion of the family and of the relation of the sexes, in modern culture, is [therefore] marked throughout by unwillingness or inability to penetrate behind the barrier of conventional finality."[70] The same process of "naturalization" characterizes Schmoller's discussion of business enterprise, another topic that Veblen had scrutinized in his *Theory of Business Enterprise* (1904). Veblen argues that in the economic realm "a dispassionate tracing-out of the sequence of cause and effect should be easier to undertake, because less readily blurred with sentiment, than in the case . . . of the family." But even here "the work of tracing the developmental sequence tapers off into advice and admonition proceeding on the assumption that the stage now reached is, or at least should be, final."[71]

Where race is concerned, Du Bois can use the historical method to challenge the assumptions of finality. Like Veblen, he argues for a scientific basis for advocacy. In "The Study of Negro Problems" (1898) he writes that "the frequent alliance of sociological research with various panaceas and particular schemes of reform, has resulted in closely connecting social investigation with a good deal of groundless assumption and humbug in the popular mind."[72] But there are also ways in which his very espousal of a scientific stance can lead Du Bois into an acceptance of the moralistic disguises of liberal capitalist society as ideal ends. In her account of the struggle between advocacy and science in American social science in the last two decades of the nineteenth century, Mary Furner has shown the extent to which this struggle was also a struggle between a largely nonacademic, reform-oriented social science and the new academic discipline of sociology seeking to establish an institutional and profession-alized hegemony.[73] Within this process of self-legitimation, any serious dissent from orthodoxy was likely to fail the test of objectivity.[74] Du Bois's adoption of the stance of objective observer and analyst in his historiography and sociology pushes him toward the centrist positions of liberal and professional consensus in the midst of his social critique.

In *The Philadelphia Negro,* for example, while Du Bois takes great pains to explain the present condition of the black community as the outcome of a historical process rather than of natural or innate characteris-tics, in projecting the ameliorative transformation of the present in the future he judges the present by the standards of liberal American "civiliza-tion." In describing the setbacks to the progress of black Philadelphians caused first by foreign immigration and then by an influx of freed slaves from the South, Du Bois writes: "Thus we see that twice the Philadelphia Negro has, with a fair measure of success, begun an interesting social development, and twice through the migration of barbarians a dark age has settled on his age of revival" (*PN* 11). It is not the workings of the capitalist economy but what prevents the successful integration of black Americans into that economy that is of primary interest to Du Bois. Therefore moralism tends to dominate political analysis. Du Bois can describe the disruption of African family structure by the system of slav-ery but also conclude that "the great weakness of the Negro family is still lack of respect for the marriage bond, inconsiderate entrance into it, and bad household economy and family government. Sexual looseness then arises as a secondary consequence, bringing adultery and prostitution in its train" (*PN* 72).

Moralism characterizes not only Du Bois's analysis of the black com-munity but also the reformist exhortations of the conclusions of both *The Philadelphia Negro* and *The Suppression of the African Slave Trade. The Philadelphia Negro* ends with a section on "The duty of the Negroes" and one on "The duty of the whites" in which both are urged to put their houses in order. Early on in *Suppression* Du Bois writes that "a feeble moral opposition [to the slave trade] was early aroused, but it was swept away by the immense economic advantages of the slave traffic. . . . This trade no moral suasion, not even the strong 'Liberty' cry of the Revolution, was able wholly to suppress" (*SAST* 44). *Suppression* presents overwhelming evidence for economic and political interests as the determining factors in the history of the slave trade, but still concludes with the suggestion that moral argument can effect social change. The last sentence of the book declares that "it behooves nations as well as men to do things at the very moment when they ought to be done" (*SAST* 198). "The paradox," as Joseph De Marco rightly notes, is "solved [by Du Bois] on the level of knowledge."[75]

When *Suppression* was reissued in 1954, Du Bois acknowledged in an "Apologia" that the moralism of the book revealed his early training "in the New England ethic of life as a series of conscious moral judgments" and that a knowledge of Marx and Freud would have radically shifted the study's conclusions.[76] The older Du Bois recognizes that his earlier voluntarism was an empty faith. Neither the appeal to a will to action nor the moralism of the critical judgments in Du Bois's social scientific works can offer an adequate account of social process or of the individual experience of history or of the process of referral between self and world. If Du Bois's social science is an outgrowth of James's "realist pragmatism," it must also be noted that it reproduces the inadequacies of that American ethics. Du Bois's positivist ideology and James's ethics overlap exactly in their potential acquiescence to the social process and in their inability to consider consciousness and reflection as potential sources of value and critical practice. Also, like James, Du Bois does not have a complex view of the distinctions between empirical ideology and empirical practice, between theories of validation and the role of hypothesis in science.

The issues can be developed further by looking in more detail at Gillian Rose's critical analysis of the neo-Kantian paradigms that underlie sociological thought. In her *Hegel contra Sociology* Rose argues that "the development of the idea of a scientific sociology was inseparable from the transformation of transcendental logic into *Geltungslogik,* the paradigm of validity and values." A "sociological interpretation of experience, like a psychological one, might be expected to address itself . . . to the history and genesis of experience, not to its justification and validity." But Rose notes that, in fact, the classical and positivist paradigms of sociology established by Durkheim and Weber "endorsed the neo-Kantian critique of psychologism, the derivation of validity from processes of consciousness. Like the neo-Kantians, Durkheim and Weber treated the question of validity as pertaining to a distinct *realm* of moral facts (Durkheim) or values (Weber) which is contrasted with the realm of individual sensations or perceptions (Durkheim) or from the psychology of the individual (Weber)." Rose rightly concludes that "when it is argued that it is society or culture which confers objective validity on social facts or values, then the argument acquires a metacritical or 'quasi-transcendental' structure," and "the status of the relation between the sociological precondition and the conditioned becomes . . . ambiguous."[77] It is precisely this ambiguity that troubles both determinism and indeterminism alike.

> Structural sociology is 'empty,' action theory is 'blind.' The former imposes abstract postulates on social reality and confirms by simplifying the contradictions of dominant law. The latter confirms social reality as a mass of random meanings in its immediate mode of representation. The lack in both cases of any reference to transformative activity, property relations, law and the corresponding media of representation results in absolutizing of the unconditioned actor on the one hand and of the totally conditioned agent on the other.
>
> If actuality is not thought, then thinking has no social import. The suppression of actuality results in sociologies which confirm dominant law and representation and which have no means of knowing or recognizing the real relations which determine that law and the media of representation.[78]

Gillian Rose's analysis helps to confirm that it is from within the intersection of Jamesian pragmatism and the neo-Kantian thought to which James is heavily indebted that Du Bois begins to move toward scientific method. Rose's critique of sociological methodologism and its debt to neo-Kantian logic is equally applicable to James's ethical theorizations of free will. It was seen in the previous chapter that James in fact tends to sacrifice individual freedom to habit and the collective will. Therefore, in James's pragmatism, as much as in the simplifications and unconsciousnesses of the theory and practice analyzed by Rose, an apparently particularist and historical account of experience can easily slip into a mere validation of experience. For all his resistance to the notion of a "science" of human action, James's own sacrifice of individual creativity to collective will means that his own theorization of the relationship of voluntarism and determinism is ideally suited to a sociology that used voluntaristic ethics only to temper its deterministic models of social process derived from the physical and natural sciences.

If Jamesian pragmatism and positivist social science share a "paradigm of validity and values" in which "the history and genesis of experience" are occluded, they also share an adherence to an instrumentalist logic. In this logic the relationship of reflection and praxis is also bypassed for a shallow definition of action. H. T. Wilson, in his account of the synthesis of the paradigms of classical sociology into what he calls "the American ideology," outlines the consequences of such a logic.

> The empirical view of explanation as a direct aid to prediction and control is linear in its emphasis on causes and effects, and . . . circular . . . when it argues "systematically" for a fit between structure and function. Social explanation limits itself to the observer role which emerged out of scientific rationalism in the seventeenth century, one which challenged *both* theorizing *and* common sense in its commitment to empirical truth through the discovery of lawlike behavior in nature. Such a posture sees no value in understanding at all, with the result that knowledge of social phenomena is viewed as inherently instrumental, desired for its control value *rather than* the contribution it might make as it stands to praxis.[79]

Praxis is here understood as Marx and Engels define it in *The German Ideology,* not only as the fabrication of use objects or the production of commodities for exchange, but also as the production of conceptions and ideas by "real, active men, as they are conditioned by a definite development of their productive forces and of the intercourse corresponding to these."[80] As Wilson notes, *The German Ideology* "presupposes a critical distinction later blurred by Engels between: experiencing and acting (life); observing and reporting on experience and activity; and theorizing or reflecting on the 'deep structures' of meaning to be found below and beyond self (and class) serving dichotomies of all sorts. Dialectics was clearly the vehicle of this excavation and understanding, yet this form of reasoning is not reducible to an empirical method."[81]

Souls offers just such an "excavation and understanding." Its meditations on "the 'deep structures' of meaning" dramatize a reflective consciousness that is ignored by positivist endorsement of "method" as well as by James's caricaturization of it as passive and self-absorbed introspection. The conjunction of positivism's refusal of subjectivism and the unconditioned action of James's voluntarism prevents critical perception that can emerge from the radical crisis of self-consciousness generated by the continual negation of freedom. That Du Bois is, unlike James, aware of these issues and potentialities is evident in what he writes at the turn of the century, not in what he says in his autobiographical commentaries later in life. Du Bois does not theorize a critique of positivist method or of James's voluntarism, but he does offer a radical dramatization of the limitations of both.

In *The Philadelphia Negro* Du Bois takes great pains to stress the incompatibility of psychological insight and the objective method. He is particularly concerned that subjective orientation and introspection may undermine the scientific authority of the sociological observer.

> The best available methods of sociological research [writes Du Bois] are at present so liable to inaccuracies that the careful student discloses the results of individual research with diffidence; he knows that they are liable to error from the seemingly ineradicable faults of the statistical method, to even greater error from the methods of general observation, and, *above all, he must ever tremble lest some personal bias, some moral conviction or some unconscious trend of thought due to previous training, has to a degree distorted the picture in his view*. Convictions on all great matters of human interest one must have to a greater or less [*sic*] degree, and they will enter to some extent into the most *cold-blooded scientific* research as a *disturbing* factor. (*PN* 2–3; emphases added)

Yet it is in the very midst of doing research for *The Philadelphia Negro* that Du Bois publishes his finest work of psychological understanding and autobiographical insight. "The Strivings of the Negro People" (1897), published in the *Atlantic Monthly* when Du Bois was exactly one year into his research for *The Philadelphia Negro*, and later to become "Of Our Spiritual Strivings," the first chapter of *Souls*, makes everything that the positivism of *The Philadelphia Negro* excludes the very basis for a true understanding of historical experience.[82] By contrast with the desire for a purity of discourse that drives *The Philadelphia Negro*, the opening chapter of *Souls* (like the book as a whole) is a generic hybrid, a moving and introspective poetic meditation blending autobiography, impressionistic historical survey, social critique, and an existential philosophical psychology in its description of historical experience. It dramatizes not only a critical perception born of the crisis of self-consciousness but also the ways in which this emergence can be transformed into a more complex and mediated model of self-realization and creativity than is offered by unconditioned voluntarism.

When the *Atlantic Monthly* essay became the first chapter of *Souls,* Du Bois explained at the end of the chapter that it was to be read as a preface to and a microcosm of the book as a whole. He has in "Strivings" "briefly sketched in large outline" what he will "on coming pages tell again in many ways, with loving emphasis and deeper detail" (*SBF* 371). The chapter opens with Du Bois's recollection of his earliest experience of racism in his childhood, goes on to his articulation of his educational and career ambitions, and then to a long section on the problem of "double aims" that is embodied in the adult Du Bois himself as the "black *savant.*" The ontogenic narrative is interwoven with a broader phylogenic one. The autobiographical narrative parallels the history of black political and social development after the Civil War and through the collapse of Reconstruction and the rise of Jim Crow, told as the journey of "the child of Emancipation to the youth with dawning self-consciousness, self-realization, self-respect" (*SBF* 368). The well-known passage on "double consciousness" lies at the heart of both the ontogenetic and phylogenetic narratives and gathers all the materials around itself to provide a penetrating dramatization of the contradictions experienced under historically specific circumstances of black life in late-nineteenth-century America.

In Du Bois's short story "A Vacation Unique," a politically and historically located autobiography is glimpsed as the testing ground for ethical action and the philosophy of history. Such an autobiography is developed into the major dramatic arena in *Souls.* This is not to suggest that Du Bois retreats into a confessional subjectivity. In *Dusk of Dawn* (1940), Du Bois defines his interest in autobiography in terms of the intersections of individual and collective history and not as a revelation of detached self-regard. In the "Apology" that prefaces the book, he writes that "midway in the writing," *Dusk of Dawn,* intended as a sequel to the commentaries on racial politics in *Souls* and *Darkwater* (1920), "threatened . . . to become mere autobiography." But Du Bois adds that

> in my own experience, autobiographies have had little lure; repeatedly they assume too much or too little: too much in dreaming that one's own life has greatly influenced the world; too little in the reticences, repressions and distortions which come because men do not dare to be absolutely frank. My life had its significance and its only deep significance because it was part of a Problem; but that problem was, as I continue to think, the central problem of the greatest of the world's democracies and so the Problem of the future world. The problem of the future world is the charting, by means

of intelligent reason, of a path not simply through the resistances of physical force, but through the vaster and far more intricate jungle of ideas conditioned on unconscious and subconscious reflexes of living things; on blind unreason and often irresistible urges of sensitive matter; of which the concept of race is today one of the most unyielding and threatening. I seem to see a way of elucidating the inner meaning and significance of that race problem by explaining it in terms of the one human life that I know best. (*DD* 551)

Du Bois then conceives of *Dusk of Dawn* as "not so much my autobiography as the autobiography of a concept of race, elucidated, magnified and doubtless distorted in the thoughts and deeds which were mine" (*DD* 551).

These comments from 1940 are, in some ways, even more appropriate as a description of *Souls*. In that work of a man in his early thirties the personal life is constantly evoked, but always as a quiet though firm counterpoint to the larger composition. Its presence is fleeting but never secondary, always weaving its way in and out of the cultural and political commentary in the foreground. Read as a narrative trajectory from its opening moment in Du Bois's Great Barrington childhood to its closing moment with the adult Du Bois at Atlanta University, *Souls* moves literally from Du Bois's childhood to his mid-thirties and from post-Emancipation America to the early twentieth century. Both "Strivings" and *Souls* as a whole represent the invention of a mode of cultural commentary that can best be described as a *Bildungsbiographie* in which personal, cultural, and philosophical narratives maintain a mutually transformative dialogue between the particulars of the individual life and the collective or social.

Du Bois's claim in *Dusk of Dawn* that the focus on the "one human life" that he knows best may be a productive way of "elucidating the inner meaning and significance of [the] race problem" cuts right across the attempt to safeguard scientific accuracy in *The Philadelphia Negro* by excluding psychology. In that earlier work Du Bois had written that the social scientist "must ever tremble lest some personal bias, some moral conviction or some unconscious trend of thought due to previous training, has to a degree distorted the picture in his view" (*PN* 3). In *Dusk of Dawn*, some forty years after *The Philadelphia Negro*, these very terms are used to justify the usefulness of the autobiographical project. Not only is the threat of autobiographical "distortion" now balanced out or indeed outweighed by the possibility of greater "elucidation" that self-investigation brings with it, but access to the very nature of the "race problem" has been shifted from the scientifically measurable realm of "physical force" to "the vaster and far more intricate jungle of ideas conditioned on unconscious and subconscious reflexes." Since it is "magnified" understanding that is the compensation for local distortions in *Dusk of Dawn*, Du Bois is clearly not arguing for the surrender of objectivity to unqualified relativism. Rather, *Souls* and *Dusk of Dawn* both recognize that only from the perspective of the particular can the universal be made intelligible. And this is so not because meaning has been absorbed into subjectivity (the dichotomization of objective and subjective is an unhelpful one in any case) but because Du Bois has come to understand that the universal itself is a multiplicity.

Du Bois is already groping toward an explicit articulation of this realization in the conclusion of *The Philadelphia Negro* itself. The opening of this conclusion is worth quoting at length because, seen in its entirety, it refers the reader to the opening passage of *Souls,* thereby suggesting that both texts are in some ways confronting the same problematic.

> Two sorts of answers are usually returned to the bewildered American who asks seriously: What is the Negro problem? The one is straightforward and clear: it is simply this, or simply that, and one simple remedy long enough applied will in time cause it to disappear. The other answer is apt to be hopelessly involved and complex—to indicate no simple panacea, and to end in a somewhat hopeless—There it is; what can we do? Both of these sorts of answers have something of truth in them: the Negro problem looked at in one way is but the old world questions of ignorance, poverty, crime, and the dislike of the stranger. On the other hand it is a mistake to think that attacking each of these questions single-handed without reference to the others will settle the matter: a combination of social problems is far more than a matter of mere addition,—the combination itself is a problem.
> (*PN* 385)

While Du Bois goes on to note that "the Negro problems are not more hopelessly complex than many others have been" (*PN* 385), what is important for the discussion here is Du Bois's conclusion that there can be no single answer to the question "What is the Negro problem?" As he comes to the close of his study the social scientist striving so hard for statistical and objective purity has understood that "a combination of social problems is far more than a matter of *mere addition*" because "the combination *itself* is a problem." The engagement of both diachronic and structural analyses in *The Philadelphia Negro* itself constitutes one attempt to explore the combination, though it is an attempt that is still constrained by the demands of a specialized discourse. However, by the time Du Bois writes the conclusion to *The Philadelphia Negro* he has already embarked on a more complex investigation of the problem of combination in "Strivings." The significance of the 1897 essay as a challenge to Du Bois's own positivism has already been commented on. That Du Bois himself sees "Strivings" as such, and so as an attempt to deal with the multiplicity of "the Negro problem," is further indicated by the opening passage of *The Philadelphia Negro*'s conclusion (quoted above), since the phrasings there allude directly to the opening of the earlier essay. Here is the opening of "Strivings":

> Between me and the other world there is ever an unasked question: unasked by some through feelings of delicacy; by others through the difficulty of rightly framing it. All, nevertheless, flutter round it. They approach me in a half-hesitant sort of way, eye me curiously or compassionately, and then, instead of saying directly, How does it feel to be a problem? they say, I know an excellent colored man in my town; or, I fought at Mechanicsville; or, Do not these Southern outrages make your blood boil? At these I smile, or am interested, or reduce the boiling to a simmer, as the occasion may require. To the real question, How does it feel to be a problem? I answer seldom a word. (*SBF* 363)[83]

Souls of course turns out to be Du Bois's reply. The investigations that eventually become *Souls* begin, then, exactly where *Philadelphia Negro* leaves off. Du Bois's need to write "Strivings" in the midst of his scientific research supports Wolf Lepenies's conclusion that the process of exclusion involved in the disciplinary purification undertaken by the social sciences is ultimately illusory.[84] But this is not to suggest that the utility and validity of Du Bois's sociological data and conclusions are negated or undermined in the same way or with the same conclusiveness as the fantasies of "The Renaissance of Ethics" are by "A Vacation Unique." "Strivings" grows out of the very same concrete existences that supply the data for Du Bois's study but offers a different order of reflection on these materials and so demarcates the limits and limitations of sociology's claims for itself as a science of the human.

In the first chapter of *Souls* Du Bois attacks not social science as such but the racist stereotypes perpetuated by an *unscientific* sociology. He laments that, when it comes to studying black life, sociologists are too preoccupied with "gleefully" counting "bastards and prostitutes" rather than investigating the "vast despair" that overshadows black life in America (*SBF* 368). In a similar vein later in the book Du Bois attacks "the car-window sociologist . . . who seeks to understand and know the South by devoting the few leisure hours of a holiday trip to unravelling the snarl of centuries" (*SBF* 469). It is in response to this reactionary dilettantism that Du Bois sets out, through most of *Souls*, "the physical, economic, and political relations of the Negroes and whites in the South" (*SBF* 487). To the extent that this kind of description is a crucial part of *Souls*, the book's literary and impressionistic social and cultural commentary shares a common base with Du Bois's historiographical and sociological work.

The first three chapters of *Souls* are preoccupied to differing extents with post-Emancipation political and legislative history. The first chapter ends on a rough and broad sketch of the history of black Americans since the Civil War. The next chapter, "Of the Dawn of Freedom," looks at this same history at greater length and with more specific legislative detail, focusing primarily on the history of the Freedman's Bureau as representative of larger developments. In "Of Mr. Booker T. Washington and Others," the third chapter, Du Bois uses the history of the eventual failure of the Freedman's Bureau as a context in which to analyze and criticize existing models of black political leadership and to propose new ones.

Concern with education is central to Du Bois's vision of leadership, and the next two chapters shift the focus from legislative and political history to the problem of education. "Of the Meaning of Progress" (chapter 4) deals with the educational handicaps suffered by the inhabitants of the Black Belt through a description of Du Bois's time as a schoolteacher in rural Tennessee, and "Of the Wings of Atlanta" (chapter 5) is a deeply felt warning to the pioneering black university against the sacrifice of its academic aims to the commercial culture of industrial capitalism. Chapter 6, "Of the Training of Black Men," is a moving indictment of the confinement of black education to industrial schools, such as Washington's Tuskegee Institute, as nothing short of racist. Du Bois insists that an education that "seeks as an end culture and character" and not just "breadwinning" must not remain "the privilege of white men" (*SBF* 428). Again Du Bois is careful to place himself within this debate, ending the chapter on the now famous passage in which he claims his right to sit in the company of the likes of Shakespeare, Aristotle, Balzac, and Dumas, and celebrates this dialogue as an assault upon the segregations of the color line (*SBF* 438).

In the two chapters that follow Du Bois shifts out of his discussion of the impact of commercial and industrial culture on education to focus fully on economics. Both "Of the Black Belt" (chapter 7) and "Of the Quest of the Golden Fleece" (chapter 8) expose the economic underdevelopment of the black South under the old plantation system and also under the postwar arrival of northern industrial capitalists. Du Bois is quite clear that, like the gains promised by legislative reform and an expanded education, freedom can be guaranteed only by economic and material independence.

This setting out of the concrete facts of black life is part of *Souls*'s project of taking its white reader behind what Du Bois, in his most oft-repeated conceit, refers to as the "veil" that hangs across the racial and political divide in America. But about two-thirds of the way through the book, in the ninth chapter ("Of the Sons of Masters and Man"), Du Bois acknowledges that

> after all that has been said on these more tangible matters of human contact, there still remains a part essential to a proper description of the South which it is difficult to describe or fix in terms easily understood by strangers. It is, in fine, the atmosphere of the land, the *thought and feeling,* the thousand and one little actions which go to make up life. In any community or nation it is these little things which are most elusive to the grasp and yet most essential to any clear conception of the group life taken as a whole. What is thus true of all communities is peculiarly true of the South, where, outside of written history and outside of printed law, there has been going on for a generation as deep a storm and stress of human souls, as intense a ferment of feeling, as intricate a writhing of spirit, as ever a people experienced. (*SBF* 487; emphasis added).

So as *Souls* progresses, Du Bois becomes increasingly involved with the problem of gaining access to this realm of historical experience, which, paradoxically, lies outside of history as the latter is defined in the historiography of a white America. Du Bois's attraction to world-historical figures and his turn to legislative and institutional history, both outlined earlier, belong very much within the mainstream of nineteenth-century conceptualizations of models of historical process, foregrounding a teleology that is propelled by heroic and individual historic agents or by major political events that engender rather than reflect major social and epistemic shifts. But the conception of unwritten history ("the thousand and one little actions which go to make up life") in the passage quoted above from the ninth chapter of *Souls* is quite different. Du Bois *here* is not asking for the inclusion of the history of slavery and its suppression in textbooks of national history, nor for the canonization of a Nat Turner or Toussaint L'Ouverture within the gallery of history-makers. He is concerned, instead, with uncovering those intricate structures of consciousness that are formed, broken, and re-formed under the slow and daily violence of actual historical process.

Such an uncovering requires not only the revelation of a new social and historical content but also a mode of understanding, a form of writing different from the kind of academic sociology or historiography Du Bois was using up to this time, even if these academic forms were in practice radical in their own right. In *Souls* one form taken by this other mode is Herderian organic history. This is most evident in the last third of the book, particularly in Du Bois's commentaries on African-American religious culture and the spirituals as a historical record of the human experience of slavery.

Du Bois himself signals the shift toward organic history by appealing repeatedly to sympathetic understanding in the final chapters of *Souls*. "Only by a union of intelligence and sympathy across the color-line in this critical period of the Republic," he writes, "shall justice and right triumph" (*SBF* 492). Sympathy, a key transcendentalist word, promises an initiation into that world of black "thought and feeling" (*SBF* 487) to which the "car-window sociologist" (*SBF* 469) is blind. Sympathy does not replace the scientific knowledge of "the physical, economic, and political relations of the Negroes and whites" (*SBF* 487), but seeks instead to discover for this knowledge its true human purpose and civic use.

The most extended comment on sympathy in *Souls* in fact fluctuates between the Herderian frameworks of Boas's anthropology and the less radical use of sympathy in the work of Adam Smith and James:[85]

> The nineteenth was the first century of human sympathy,—the age when half wonderingly we began to descry in others that transfigured spark of divinity which we call Myself; when clodhoppers and peasants, and tramps and thieves, and millionaires and—sometimes—Negroes, became throbbing souls whose warm pulsing life touched us so nearly that we half gasped with surprise, crying, "Thou too! Hast Thou seen Sorrow and the dull waters of Hopelessness? Hast Thou known Life?" And then all helplessly we peered into those Other-worlds, and wailed, "O World of Worlds, how shall man make you one?" (*SBF* 514)[86]

Where James's discussion of sympathy develops out of the numerous discussions of the idea in Anglo-American ethical discourse,[87] Boasian cultural relativism inherits the concept largely through the work of Johann Gottfried Herder.[88] Gerald Broce has provided a commentary on cultural relativism's debt to the eighteenth-century tradition of cultural analysis represented by Herder.[89] Broce notes that Herderian and Boasian relativism share "several related ideas," notably the insistence on the uniqueness of each genuine culture and critiques of the generalizing and comparative methods as violations of cultural authenticity, and therefore negations of intercultural understanding: "Only through the method of *Einfühlen,* therefore, only through a sympathetic and imaginative plunge into the 'national character' of a people, can its essence be grasped: fully to understand a culture one must come to think and feel as its members think and feel."[90] Du Bois's own desire to go beyond "the physical, economic, and political relations of Negroes and whites in the South" to the deep structures of "thought and feeling" (*SBF* 487), like the centrality of ideas of *soul* and *folk* in his work, places *Souls* very much in the Herderian tradition. Equally, the recognition of "Myself" in others and the desire to make the "World of Worlds" "one" (*SBF* 514) reproduces Herder's location of individual *Volk* within the broader pluralist harmony of universal *Humanität.* Du Bois acknowledges as much when he notes in the final chapter of *Souls* that "the same voice sings" in the slave songs "that sings in the German folk-song" (*SBF* 543).[91] This humanist tradition has remained a major support for the "message of broad ethical and political significance" that has underpinned the claims for a "laboratory" or scientific fieldwork in much of American cultural relativism since Boas's time.[92]

It is possible to read Du Bois's turn to sympathy as a resistance (albeit a liberal one from within a capitalist framework) to the white middle class's strategies for defining and defending its conception of national character in the last two decades of the nineteenth century. This period saw an unprecedented wave of black migration from the South to northern cities and the equally unparalleled influx of European (mainly Eastern European) immigrants in turn-of-the-century America. The middle class responded with strategies of both exclusion and the containment rhetoric of assimilation, which sought to disarm the threat of difference with behavioral engineering and found its most lasting embodiment in Israel Zangwill's hugely popular play *The Melting-Pot* (1908).[93] As already suggested, Boas's critique of the comparative method in anthropology was an oblique critique of these strategies.[94] Du Bois himself repeatedly noted the continuing violence against blacks and other minorities in America and, in *The Philadelphia Negro,* provided a detailed study of the exclusion of blacks from the political and civic life of the nation. But in Du Bois's program for an elite black leadership of the "talented tenth," as in James, sympathy offers a very limited sense of inclusion to the excluded. An openness to the lives of the other half does not lead to the emergence of the laboring classes as actors upon the political stage but promises them instead salvation at the hands of "great men" and the "college-bred," and strictly within normative structures defined by bourgeois values.[95]

In the passage on sympathy quoted above, Du Bois, like Adam Smith, constructs the sympathetic observer as clearly middle-class, white, and male (and, of course, northern), situated between "millionaires" on the one hand and "Negroes" and the white poor on the other. This is both appropriate and strategic since *Souls* is addressed primarily to a white middle-class audience and attempts partly to dislodge the universalist alibis on which white bourgeois cultural self-confidence is built. But Du Bois's own ethical and cultural attitudes came into direct alignment with the bourgeois and laissez-faire assumptions of Smith's ethical and economic programs because his early Puritan upbringing, and his New England belief in culture as the moral regulator of the excesses and exploitations of the commercial world, were mediated by his training in and acceptance of Ricardian economics at Harvard. This alignment is also acknowledged in the passage as Du Bois's repeated use of the first person plural places him in the company of the middle-class white observer. The sweep between "Negroes" and "millionaires" is close to James's spiritual unification of the "sick" and "ill-favored" with the "Vanderbilts and Hohenzollerns" (*PP* 1:313), and Du Bois's evocation of sympathy contains the same accommodationist potential as James's acceptance of "a wave of sympathy with the common life of common men."[96]

Du Bois's sense of a relativized black self, a self somehow separate from the black masses and fundamentally bourgeois in its outlook, is more than an effect of stylistic convention. It is integral to Du Bois's investigation of the dilemma of the black bourgeois artist and intellectual within "a critical period of the Republic." This investigation and Du Bois's use of organic history are examined in detail in the next part of this study. But before opening that discussion it is important to prepare the way for it by looking at one more text by Du Bois from the 1890s.

It has been suggested here that the struggle of discourses that is marked by the simultaneous composition of "Renaissance of Ethics" and "A Vacation Unique" earlier in Du Bois's career is, to some extent, reenacted by the publication of "Strivings of the Negro People" while Du

Bois is working on *The Philadelphia Negro*. The relationship of the two early texts was seen as the quest for both science and metaphysics confronted by satiric deconstruction. *The Philadelphia Negro* makes concrete the abstractions of the early formulations of a science of human action, and "Strivings" faces the particulars of African-American life with greater complexity than "A Vacation Unique." But this is not to say that Du Bois has abandoned his search for a philosophy of history. Although in his later years Du Bois wrote that James had turned him away from the sterilities of scholastic philosophy to realist pragmatism, the break between the undergraduate work in philosophy and the graduate work in history and the social sciences was by no means such a clean one. When Du Bois was first applying to do graduate work at Harvard he wavered between doing political science and political economy or philosophy and settled on social science only at a late stage.[97] The Du Bois who wants grand historical schemas reasserts himself in the 1890s with the publication of "The Conservation of Races" in the same year that "Strivings" is published (1897).

"The Conservation of Races" attempts once again in Du Bois's early career a synthesis of hero and universal law working toward teleological ascent. Du Bois argues that "all human striving must recognize the hard limits of natural law," and that "any striving, no matter how intense and earnest, which is against the constitution of the world, is vain."[98] The natural law of history that Du Bois proposes is "the law of race development" in which great men embody and enact the fateful unfolding of a racial essence.[99] The argument that "we see the Pharaohs, Caesars, Toussaints and Napoleons of history and forget the vast races of which they were but epitomized expressions" (CR 817) signals a dissent from Carlyle's idea of the great men of history. It is in this sense similar to Emerson's idea of representativeness. "The Conservation of Races" was delivered as a paper to the American Negro Academy and is in keeping with the program of the Academy. Founded by Alexander Crummell, the Academy was intended as a training ground for an elite African-American cultural leadership.[100] Du Bois supports this program and insists that only an "advanced guard of the Negro people" can fulfill the world-historical destiny of the race (CR 820).

That "The Conservation of Races" is in dialogue with both *The Philadelphia Negro* and "Strivings of the Negro People" is suggested by the textual overlaps between the three works. In "Conservation" Du Bois imagines "eight distinctly different races" on the "world's stage": "They are, the

Slavs of eastern Europe, the Teutons of middle Europe, the English of Great Britain and America, the Romance nations of Southern and Western Europe, the Negroes of Africa and America, the Semitic people of Western Asia and Northern Africa, the Hindoos of Central Asia and the Mongolians of Eastern Asia" (CR 817–18). In his conclusion to *The Philadelphia Negro* Du Bois laments that "we grant full citizenship in World Commonwealth to the 'Anglo-Saxon' (whatever that may mean), the Teuton and the Latin; then with just a shade of reluctance we extend it to the Celt and Slav. We half deny it to the yellow races of Asia, admit the brown Indians to an anteroom only on the strength of an undeniable past; but with the Negroes of Africa we come to a full stop, and in its heart the civilized world with one accord denies that these come within the pale of nineteenth-century Humanity" (*PN* 387). "Conservation" seeks to place the African-American and African peoples on the world stage, and *Souls*'s appeal to sympathy is a plea for their humanity. But if "Conservation" and "Strivings" participate in a common recuperative project, they come to it via very different conceptualizations of historical process and agency.

"Strivings" repeats the panoramic survey of races in the famous passage on the African-American as a "sort of seventh son" following after "the Egyptian and Indian, the Greek and Roman, the Teuton and Mongolian" (*SBF* 364). This passage is followed by the equally famous description of self-doubt and "the contradiction of double aims" experienced by blacks in America (*SBF* 365–67). In "Conservation" too the survey of races is followed by a meditation on the "incessant self-questioning and the hesitation" that arises from the denial of recognition (CR 821). However, where "Conservation" projects an abstract historical schema, "Strivings," like the rest of *Souls*, describes the concrete experience of an actual history which is hardly progressive. In these two essays from the 1890s the voices of the manifesto writer and the literary artist are opposed. Du Bois's simultaneous adoption of the roles of idealist philosopher, empirical scientist, and the poet who refuses generalization is made most evident in the publication of "Conservation," "Strivings," and *The Philadelphia Negro* within one year of each other. It is the most lasting achievement of the poet and analyst of self-consciousness that is examined in the chapters that follow.

Part II

The Souls

of

Black Folk

Four

"Double-Consciousness"

Locating the Self

This chapter examines Du Bois's dramatization of a divided self-consciousness in comparison with other nineteenth-century American accounts of consciousness. The discussion is anchored in a description of the ways in which Du Bois radically adapts Hegel's *Phenomenology of Mind* in order to describe the historical problematic that preoccupies him in the first chapter of *Souls*.[1] This problematic is the crisis of the black bourgeois leadership and intelligentsia generated by the clash between their political idealism and the history of race in the last two decades of the century.

Du Bois studied Hegel with George Santayana during 1889–90 in a course on modern French and German philosophy, at the same time that he was taking a course in psychology with William James, and during a period when European Romantic and idealist philosophy was widely taught at Harvard and when Hegelianism was widespread in American philosophy and social thought. The young Santayana was excited by his reading of the *Phenomenology*. It, in combination with his reading of Greek philosophy, had set him to planning his own literary psychology of consciousness, *The Life of Reason* (1905–6). All available evidence suggests that the Hegel text studied in Santayana's course was the *Phenomenology*.[2]

"Of Our Spiritual Strivings" constitutes itself as a narrative structure by reference to key sections of the narrative that dominates the central part of Hegel's *Phenomenology*, from the differentiation of self-consciousness from consciousness to the vision of the ethical state, or *Sittlichkeit*. The parallels between the narratives of the two texts are close and can be mapped quite precisely, although, as subsequent discussion will demonstrate, Du Bois's departures from the Hegelian narrative are crucial. What is referred to here as the central section of the *Phenomenology* begins at the moment when self-consciousness discovers its own self behind the world of appearance (the moment when Hegel uses the biblical conceit of the lifting of the curtain or veil). Self-consciousness goes on to greater self-realization through a struggle with another self-consciousness (the famous "Master and Slave" dialectic), and then to an internalization of this struggle in the form of the "unhappy consciousness." The first proper resolution of this divided self is achieved in the freedom promised by national culture, what Hegel calls *Sittlichkeit*.[3]

The opening scene of *Souls,* where the child Du Bois realizes the separations of the "color-line" for the first time in the rejecting "glance" (*SBF* 364) of a white playmate (the moment in Du Bois when the biblical veil *descends*), corresponds to the first stage of the Hegelian narrative outlined above. The meditation that follows on the struggle of blacks against racism in "the shades of the prison-house" (*SBF* 364) corresponds to the conflict between Master and Slave. The passage on "double-consciousness" corresponds to Hegel's commentary on the "unhappy consciousness." And Du Bois's recognition that "double-consciousness" can be overcome only when the black American can become "a co-worker in the kingdom of culture" (*SBF* 365) mirrors the state of *Sittlichkeit*.

An awareness of the parallels between "Strivings" and the *Phenomenology* aids a fuller understanding of the narrative structure of Du Bois's chapter. In doing so it also suggests that the description of "double-consciousness," which has so often been extracted from the chapter, can be properly understood only if it is read as part of the larger psychological and historical process narrated in "Strivings." Textual parallels are, of course, deceptive. There is not an identity of meaning between Hegel and Du Bois's critical reading of Hegel. Du Bois does not *adopt* Hegel but *adapts* him to his own ends. To understand Du Bois's investigation of historical consciousness out of Hegel it is as important to see how his reading differs from Hegel as it is to note the parallels.

By focusing on the middle chapters of the *Phenomenology* Du Bois cuts away the Hegelian concern with the development of consciousness toward the first stages of self-consciousness and also with the all-synthesizing idealistic monism of Absolute Spirit at the end of the *Phenomenology*. Du Bois's emphasis is not on the singular *Geist* but on *souls*. Du Bois's own projection of a possible resolution of historical division in a "kingdom of culture" may seem like a utopian negation of the tragic substance of historical particularity and multiplicity. But *Souls*, like *The Suppression of the African Slave Trade*, undermines exceptionalist and progressive versions of American history. Du Bois's reworking of Hegel includes a careful historical location of his own drama of alterity and entails precisely the critical testing of this cultural idealism, and so of Du Bois's own cultural and political programs of progressive reform, against the terrible facts of African-American history. Therefore, in using Hegel as a resource Du Bois neither psychologizes history nor reproduces a progressive and optimistic teleology of enlightenment. He moves instead toward a complex historicization of psychology.

Robert Gooding-Williams has argued that *Souls* is a kind of Hegelian philosophy of history and that Du Bois's turn to social science challenges his Hegelian idealism.[4] This may be true of the relationship of "The Conservation of Races" and Du Bois's work in sociology, but it is not true of *Souls*. *Souls* does not reproduce the grand idealist historical schema of the *Phenomenology;* instead it adapts to its own ends the micro-level sense of the negativity of historical experience that is embodied in Hegel's account of the "unhappy consciousness." As such *Souls* is a challenge not only to the idealism of "The Conservation of Races" but also to the positivism of Du Bois's sociology. The very sections of the *Phenomenology* that Du Bois takes as the platform for his psychological explorations (the sections narrating the development of consciousness into self-consciousness) were in fact intended by Hegel as a critique of positivism or commonsense philosophy. As Herbert Marcuse puts it in his examination of the relation of Hegel's thought to the development of social science, truth for Hegel resides not in "objective facts" but in "the living subject":

> The world is an estranged and untrue world so long as man does not destroy its dead objectivity and recognize himself and his own life "behind" the fixed form of things and laws. When he finally wins this *self-consciousness*, he is on his way not only to the truth of himself but also of his world. And with the recognition goes the doing. He will try to put this truth into action

and *make* the world what it *essentially* is, namely, the fulfillment of man's self-consciousness.[5]

Hegel's critique of positivism provides a link back to the discussions of the previous chapter (Gillian Rose's critique of positivist paradigms of validity works directly out of Hegel) and also an entrance into the examination of Du Bois's account of consciousness and of the critical function of this account in the present chapter.

Ideas of fragmented consciousness and the divided self were ubiquitous in the 1880s and 1890s not only in psychology but also in literature.[6] In his autobiography Henry Adams noted that in turn-of-the-century psychology "dualism seemed to have become as common as binary stars. Alternating personalities turned up constantly, even among one's friends" (*EHA* 433). It is this very omnipresence that makes it difficult to offer anything other than a generalized account of any particular deployment of the trope of double consciousness. Du Bois's own use of this figure remains one of the most frequently cited and quoted passages in African-American letters, yet the famous passage on the "two-ness" of the African-American has received little detailed commentary. Ironically it is precisely the wide currency of Du Bois's account of "double-consciousness" in African-American cultural discourse that indicates a fundamental misunderstanding of the specificity of that account.

The frequency with which Du Bois's description is used suggests that it is commonly accepted as a universally and transhistorically true analysis of a tragic aspect of African-American self-consciousness. But Du Bois's dramatization of "double-consciousness" is a historically specific and class-specific psychology. The account of "double-consciousness" in the first chapter of *Souls* represents the black middle-class elite facing the failure of its own progressive ideals in the late nineteenth century, in the aftermath of failed Reconstruction and under the gaze of a white America. "Of Our Spiritual Strivings" is intended as a psychology of the Talented Tenth in crisis, not of the "black folk" as a homogenized collectivity.[7]

The new psychology and American Romanticism, particularly the work of James and Emerson, have been cited as possible sources or contexts for Du Bois's psychology of "double-consciousness."[8] These comparisons are useful only inasmuch as they help map out a discursive field in which Du Bois's work can be critically differentiated. Unlike Du Bois, both James and Emerson tend to offer largely ahistorical and apolitical accounts of the self. James's discussions of double consciousness or of the divided self in the realms of hysteria or religious experience favor medicalized diagnoses and remedial strategies that naturalize society in their stress on the return to healthy equilibrium. Emerson too proposes to conquer double consciousness through a transcendence of the alienation of the divided self toward a spiritual union of the "Me" and the "Not-Me." Du Bois's psychology, by contrast, is committed to a political understanding of alienation and a social and historical location of the self.[9] Its sense of the self, therefore, is radically different from James's favoring presentist experience over consciousness and its relation to the past, his optimistic celebrations of future-oriented, heroic ethical activity, and his relative lack of interest in the political contexts of psychology.

The radical nature of Du Bois's reworking of the *Phenomenology* can be understood only if it is read against other nineteenth-century American interpretations of Hegel. With very few exceptions, when Hegel is used in nineteenth-century America he is used as a prophet of American exceptionalism. The American Hegel tends to be an upbeat Hegel, a theorist of an organic nation populated by wholistic selves. This was the Hegel that James dismissed as the metaphysical absolutist. But Du Bois's Hegel is much closer to the one that emerges from Marx's or Sartre's critical readings of the *Phenomenology*. At the same time it must understood that Du Bois's psychology of alterity works within idealist frameworks. Its primary concern is with recognition. Du Bois does not offer an adequately materialist critique of the failure of Reconstruction or his own program for the "Talented Tenth" until the publication of his Marxist historiography, *Black Reconstruction in America* (1935). What Hegel's idealist philosophy makes available to Du Bois is a complex model for thinking about the relationship of consciousness and history. Through Hegel Du Bois can conceptualize more clearly than before a sense of history and inheritance, of the pressure of the past on present action, though without any fatalistic submission to history as necessity. How is it then that Du Bois can read Hegel quite so critically, before he has begun to read Marx, without (as far as is known) a knowledge of Kierkegaard, well before Alexandre Kojève's and Sartre's commentaries on the *Phenomenology*, and very much against the grain of the readings of Hegel common in nineteenth-century America?

It is impossible to provide a fully comprehensive answer, either intentionalist or discursive, to this question, but it is possible to point to some enabling factors. The most important of these is Du Bois's historical and cultural position as a black intellectual, well trained in speculative thought, testing available philosophical models against the political realities of late-nineteenth-century America. To this must be added Du Bois's studies with James and Santayana. As already noted, Du Bois studied psychology with James and modern French and German philosophy, including Hegel, with Santayana simultaneously during the academic year 1889–90. *The Principles of Psychology* appeared in 1890 and, according to Santayana, James was teaching portions of his book in his classes during 1889, reading out sections and offering them for discussion.[10] At the same time it is relevant for the present discussion that the reading of Hegel had set Santayana to planning his own *Life of Reason* (1905–6),[11] itself a literary psychology that attempted a history of consciousness, of the imaginative life and its responses to the material conditions of its existence. James and Santayana would have made available to Du Bois both mutually supportive and also radically opposed conceptual models with which to think about consciousness and psychology in complex ways.

The foregrounding of the political and ideological context in the reading of "Strivings" in this chapter is meant as a reminder that the issue here is not, to adapt Louis Althusser's commentary on the young Marx's reading of German philosophy, one of an "ideal debate" between "characters" called Du Bois, Hegel, James, and so forth. It is more a matter of debate between "*concrete* ideological characters on whom the ideological context imposed *determinate features* which do not necessarily coincide with their literal historical identities." So "the Hegel who was the opponent of the Young Marx from the time of his doctoral dissertation was not the library Hegel we can meditate on in the solitude of 1960; it was *the Hegel of the neo-Hegelian movement,* a Hegel already summoned to provide German intellectuals of the 1840s with the means to think their own history and their own hopes." And at the same time the "literal historical identities" of Hegel and his followers were "much more extensive than the explicit representations Marx gave of them" in his critiques.[12] Similarly, Du Bois's dialogue with Hegel must be seen in the context of the nationalist invocations of Hegel in nineteenth-century America, of James's dismissals of Hegel's monistic system, and also of Santayana's more sympathetic and critical reading of Hegel. And the Hegel that emerges dialectically from Du Bois's own reading of the *Phenomenology* in the context of these other available readings must be differentiated from these Hegels and also the "literal" Hegel of 1807.

The precondition of such a rupture or differentiation is, as Althusser also notes, "the rediscovery of real history."[13] The transformation of the young, Hegelian Marx into the "Marxist" Marx is dependent upon "the discovery beneath the ideology which had deformed it of *the reality it had referred to*—and the discovery beyond contemporary ideology, *which knew it not,* of *a new reality.* Marx became himself by thinking this double reality in a rigorous theory, by changing elements—and by thinking the unity and reality of this new element."[14] The causality of such a transformation in thought cannot be posited, then, as simply a matter of "*ideological immanence*" (a logic of *ideas* alone), but must be stated as a moment of "*the irruption of real history in ideology itself.*"[15] Du Bois's critical Hegelian insights are also made possible by his becoming aware of the disjuncture between dominant ideology and the reality beneath. The gradual rise of this awareness in the thought of Du Bois is what is charted in this study. It is true that in the early part of his career Du Bois does not manage to think an alternative "rigorous theory." But *Souls* does represent a critical response complex in its exploration both of the implications of "the irruption of history" into Du Bois's ideological field and of a consciousness that can actively resist the threat of passivity and the abandonment of critical thought within such a rupture.

United Selves and United States: Hegel in America

As Henry Pochmann has commented, "it is noteworthy that at precisely the time when [the] process of winning intellectual maturity was at its height [in American thought], the acculturation of German philosophy was strongest."[16] The last twenty years of the nineteenth century marked "the highest point of Germanic influence in American philosophy. As idealism became dominant, even its opponents—including pragmatists, personalists, and realists—were profoundly influenced by the German classical and post-Hegelian philosophies."[17] Hegelianism became widespread in American philosophy and social thought in the 1870s, in large part a symptom of the resurgence of nationalist sentiment during and after the Civil War. Where the common sense school and Transcendentalism had prioritized the individual, Hegelianism stressed the group. "As a system of ethics it supplemented the individualism of Locke, and prepared the ground for collectivistic theories in politics, sociology, and economics." This trend was strengthened by and combined with the prevalence of Darwin's influence in American social thought.[18]

John Dewey's adoption of Hegelianism early in his career provides an exemplary instance of an optimistic reading of Hegel in which an idealist psychology is transformed into an organic doctrine of self and the nation-state.[19] The political context in which Dewey's organicism takes shape is important for understanding the thrust of his ideas. As Dorothy Ross stresses, Dewey "felt his 'disinheritance,' the strain between inherited dogmas and the world around him, as a profound separation of self and other, ideal and reality, which set him on a lifelong effort to abolish dualism. His early essays show clearly that the threat to the American political tradition in the Gilded Age [from Civil War, Reconstruction, and rapid industrialization] was one source of his unease and a principal dimension of his reconstructive efforts."[20]

The essays from the 1880s provide key statements. The heart of Dewey's defense of Hegelianism is a rejection of all formalistic logic that separates subject and object. In "Kant and Philosophic Method" (1884), Dewey argues that the logic of difference in analytic reason is transcended by the higher unity of synthetic reason. "Reason must be that which separates itself, which differentiates, goes forth into differences, that it may then grasp these differences into a unity of its own."[21] Both British empiricism and Kant are rejected as exemplars of analytic logic in favor of Hegel, since Hegel "offers us Reason affirmative *and* negative, and affirmative only in and through its own negations, as the solution."[22] Dialectic and negation are understood as affirmations of ultimate unity.

"The New Psychology" (1884) extends the critique of formal logic to psychology, aligning "the old psychology" with formalism and defining the new through an organic conceptualization of the self in which Hegel and biology, as well as the insights of the social and historical sciences, are joined together.[23] Dewey is trying to combine the scientific emphasis of the new psychology with a focus on the relation of the human mind and behavior to cultural life.[24] He can, therefore, in "The Psychological Standpoint" (1886), propose a synthesis of idealism and empiricism via psychology, just as Du Bois was to attempt to combine the two into a "science of Mind" in "The Renaissance of Ethics" only two years later.[25] It is understandable then that psychology becomes for Dewey the "philosophic method," and the denial of self-consciousness signals a denial of "the possibility of philosophy."[26]

What is potentially creative and radical in Dewey's Hegelian psychology, and what could align it to Du Bois's psychology, is its stress on difference, relationality, and self-consciousness, and its sense of the individual as a "transition" or "a process of becoming."[27] But unlike Du

Bois, Dewey always subsumes his particularist understandings into higher syntheses, his Hegelian sense of negativity into a Hegelian optimism of a unifying teleology. So finally "the individual consciousness is but the process of realization of the universal consciousness through itself. Looked at as process, as realizing, it is individual consciousness; looked at as produced or realized, as conscious of the process, that is, of itself, it is universal consciousness."[28]

Dewey's argument for a universal consciousness may be philosophically vague, but its social and political import becomes quite clear when Dewey transforms his psychology and his critique of formalistic logic into a defense of the American political system. In "The Ethics of Democracy" (1888) Dewey follows the arguments of George Sylvester Morris's *Hegel's Philosophy of the State and of History* (1887) and pits an organic theorization of democracy against those who see democracy as nothing but "a numerical aggregate, a conglomeration of units."[29] Dewey emphasizes that his organic conception of democracy "is as much an account of the individual as it is of the whole. One who has really adopted the notion can say not less, but more than anyone else, that society exists for and by individuals. But it is because he has given up the fiction of isolated unsocial units, and has realized that the individual embodies and realizes within himself the spirit and will of the whole organism."[30] The psycho-philosophical relation of the individual and the universal is here stated socially, and in this shift not Germany but America is made the Hegelian end of history. His organicism is for Dewey "the American theory, a doctrine which in grandeur has but one equal in history, and that its fellow, namely, that every man is a priest of God."[31] The radical puritan "priesthood of all believers" now legitimates the American state.

While Dewey's critique of atomistic social doctrine is valuable, his own Hegelian account of democracy drifts toward a centrist acceptance of the social process. As A. R. Buss has argued, the integrative nature of dialectical thought as it has developed from Hegel through Marx has been of central importance in the development of a humanistic psychology. But where Marx theorizes a transformation of the world and foregrounds the function of critique in this process, Hegel's philosophy can involve an incorporation of history "into the story of Reason's unfolding, hence a justification of everything that happens and an alibi for the status quo."[32] Dewey's subsuming of particularity within Reason's higher syntheses produces similar results. So, for example, Dewey sees the growth of industrialization and the consequent spread of wealth as adequate safeguards against the spread of socialism and communism. And while Dewey's theory of democracy lays great emphasis on individual choice and freedom, it also "admits that the full significance of personality can be learned by the individual only as it is already presented to him in objective form in society."[33] Society is for Dewey the sole criterion of the organic good. As Neil Coughlan notes, "the definition of virtue that seems eventually to have most satisfied [Dewey] was conduct that served society's end."[34]

Du Bois may or may not have known of the early work of Dewey, but a version of Hegel very close to Dewey's was available to him at Harvard in the work of Royce. Du Bois studied forensics with Royce in his junior year and met and talked with him at the Philosophical Club (*A* 143). He also studied Hegel with Santayana just a year after Santayana had read the *Phenomenology* with Royce as part of his graduate studies and during a year in which Royce was once again offering his graduate course on Hegel's system, focusing on the *Phenomenology,* in the philosophy department.[35]

Royce's interpretation of Hegel is available in his book *The Spirit of Modern Philosophy* (1892), published while Du Bois was still enrolled as a graduate student at Harvard. Like Dewey, Royce stresses that dialectical negativity is the process by which a higher harmonization and unity are achieved. "Consciousness . . . differentiates itself into various, into contrasted, forms and lives in their relationships, their conflicts, their contradictions, and in the triumph over these. . . . So, in short, everywhere in conscious life, consciousness is a union, an organization, of conflicting aims, purposes, thoughts, strivings." This is what Hegel calls "the law of universal *Negativität* of self-conscious life."[36] And like Dewey, Royce foregrounds relationality and organic collectivity in his reading of Hegel. So the self is seen as a "knot of relationships to other moments and to other people." In such an intersection, "I know myself only so far as I am known or may be known by another than my present or momentary self" and "I become myself by forsaking my isolation and by entering into community."[37]

The politics that are only implicit or half-visible in Dewey's and Royce's uses of Hegel are made more explicit in the writings of the St. Louis Hegelians, certainly the most important proponents of an American Hegelianism in the second half of the nineteenth century. Though largely forgotten now in considerations of thought in nineteenth-century America, the St. Louis movement was "the chief vehicle by which Hegel's ideas and those of virtually every other major post-Kantian German philosopher entered the mainstream of American thought."[38] The movement existed from about 1865 to the mid-1880s, during which time its members were unmatched in their publication record and the energetic dissemination of their ideas.[39] In 1867 William Torrey Harris, the leading light of the movement, founded the *Journal of Speculative Philosophy,* the first definitive and significant philosophical journal in the English language and unquestionably the most important philosophical publication in America at the time. It outlasted the group and continued publication until 1893 (past Du Bois's undergraduate work in philosophy), providing detailed and continuous coverage of German philosophy, particularly that of Kant and Hegel.[40] The uniqueness of the *Journal* made it an essential forum for both students and practitioners of philosophy, and rising American thinkers such as Royce and Dewey, as well as James, wrote for the *Journal.* As a recent assessment of the group's contribution to nineteenth-century American culture stresses, it "gave philosophy such a fresh sense of power and historicity that it was moved out of the genteel world of clerics and colleges into the realm of public affairs."[41]

Though centered in the Midwest, the movement had strong roots in New England Transcendentalism. Emerson had been an early and significant influence on Henry Brokmeyer, the leading theoretician and philosophic authority of the group. And Amos Bronson Alcott inspired Harris, who also maintained a long and continuous contact with Emerson. Both Alcott and Emerson visited the group in St. Louis, lectured there, and were auxiliary members.[42] After the breakup of the group in St. Louis, Harris and some of the other members moved to Concord around 1878 and joined Dean Alcott's Concord School. There, Harris was popular and Plato apparently was soon eclipsed by Hegel until the school closed in 1887, just a year before Du Bois entered Harvard.

Du Bois cannot have been ignorant of the history and ideas of the St. Louis Hegelians, given that the *Journal* was the major forum for philosophical debate at the time, that James and other philosophers known to Du Bois published therein, that a good part of James's animosity toward Hegelianism was, in fact, aimed at the St. Louis group,[43] and that members of the group had strong associations with the intellectual culture of New England and were active within this culture in the years just prior to Du Bois's arrival in Boston.[44] He may even have encountered the ideas of the group at Fisk through his New Englandized teachers from the Midwest. (Education was perhaps the area in which the St. Louis group was most influential.)[45]

The St. Louis movement applied Hegel's idea of Teutonic destiny and his theory of state to the conditions of contemporary America. The initial attraction was political more than metaphysical. The group, turning to Hegel as a reaction against what it saw as the flood of materialism and political chaos, was inspired by frontier expansion and saw St. Louis as the city of the future, playing its role in the fulfillment of the Teutonic destiny in America.[46] Hegel's political philosophy had itself grown as a response to a Germany in social and political disarray under Frederick William III. The volatile context of St. Louis provided "an urgent social *milieu*" in which Hegel could easily take root.[47] During the decades from 1858 to 1878, filled with the turmoil of the Civil War and its aftermath, "in a political, though not in a military sense, Missouri was at the center of the storm and St. Louis was at the center of Missouri." In the late 1850s, as the gateway to the West and Northwest, the city was also "the epitome of American frontier civilization."[48]

In *Lectures on the Philosophy of History*, Hegel himself had prophesied that America was "the land of the future, where, in the ages that lie before us, the burden of the World's History shall reveal itself." It was up to America "to abandon the ground on which hitherto the History of the World has developed itself."[49] Hegel provided the St. Louis Movement with a suitable postwar theory of the state, and the group elaborated its interpretation of Hegel's political philosophy in the pages of the *Journal* and in Denton J. Snider's *The American State*.[50] As early as 1848, Johan B. Stallo, in his *Principles of the Philosophy of Nature*, had outlined a Hegelian theory of organic, progressive, and rational society and had seen this as the true and inevitable fulfillment of the American Constitution.[51] So, despite the fact that many of the St. Louisans had fled from Prussian tyranny, they interpreted Hegel as the philosopher of liberty, not the theorist of the absolute state (a Hegel popularized by Heinrich von Treitschke's *History of Germany in the Nineteenth Century*), or the philosopher responsible for the events of 1848.[52] The faith in the destiny of American civilization was, of course, by no means confined to the St. Louis Hegelians, but was widespread in American philosophical and historical thought.[53] Snider, among the most prolific of the St. Louis group, was perfectly aware of the parallels between the group's and Emerson's American exceptionalism.[54]

The paradoxical use of Hegel as a legitimation of American exceptionalism was not unique to the St. Louis group. In 1881, dismissing Carlyle as "quite the legitimate European product to be expected," Walt Whitman proclaimed that the "formulas of Hegel are an essential and crowning justification of New World democracy in the creative realms of time and space." And in an unpublished lecture on Hegel the American poet insisted that "only Hegel is fit for America—is large enough and free enough." At the time that *Leaves of Grass* first appeared (1855), Whitman had access to Hegel and Hegelian ideas through several anthologies, translations, summaries, and adaptations, but he also corresponded with Harris, met him (and probably the other Hegelians) in St. Louis, and seems to have read, perhaps even subscribed to, their *Journal*.[55]

When the Civil War erupted, neither the St. Louis Hegelians nor Whitman abandoned the reassurances of an Americanized Hegel, though Whitman registered the shock-waves of doubt more clearly. The Hegelian historicism of both Whitman and the St. Louis Hegelians was also a flight from history, since it sought to reduce the concrete facts of history to an abstract schema of thesis, antithesis, and synthesis, an essentially static conceptualization of dialectic that Hegel himself had in fact rejected.[56] This schematization is nowhere more apparent than in the group's interpretation of the Civil War as a necessary part of the dialectic process of history in which America would assume its rightful and leading place in the onward movement of thought and culture. Hegel "was the prophet of a reunited nation after it had suffered the terrible 'dialectic' of civil war. The Southern position, Brokmeyer explained, was what Hegel termed 'abstract right'; the Northern, that of an equally 'abstract morality'; while the Union represented what Hegel called the 'ethical state.' "[57] So too the author of "Drum Taps" "can read or revise the Civil War symbolically and ahistorically as a negative moment in the destined arc of the Union."[58]

Snider wrote years later, in terms that, like Du Bois's "Renaissance of Ethics," appear to combine Hegel with Spencer, "the time was calling loudly for *First Principles*. The Civil War had just concluded, in which we all had in some way participated, and we were still overwhelmed, even dazed partially by the grand historic appearance. What does it all mean? was quite the universal question. . . . Naturally our set sought in philosophy the solution, that is, in Hegel as taught by our leaders."[59] This is much of a sameness with Du Bois's turn to Bismarck or to Spencerian theodicy in the context of the postwar and post-Reconstruction South, and confirms Adams's sense of the seductiveness of a predictable and uniform system in the aftermath of the war. But it is also likely that Du Bois's satires of Teutonic nationalism in "A Vacation Unique" and the "Jefferson Davis" commencement speech were aimed in part at the St.

Louis group. It will be remembered that Du Bois's experiences of racism in the Midwest, the home ground of the St. Louis group, provide the stage upon which the satire of Teutonic nationalism and of metaphysical historicism is dramatized in "A Vacation Unique." Similarly, the focus on Teutonism and on the Civil War as the latest manifestation of its destiny in "Jefferson Davis," and Du Bois's choice of the Confederate president as its representative, not only look toward Emerson but neatly invert the St. Louisans' support for the Union and so foreground the racist potentials of their metaphysical alibis for manifest destiny. The connection between the St. Louis group and Emerson would, of course, have been suggested to Du Bois by the Concord residence of Harris and others as well as by the philosophical links between Transcendentalism and St. Louis idealism. However, Du Bois's own continued attraction to heroic vitalism meant that he was to an important extent committed to the ideological form of this nationalism. Du Bois's dilemma, then, was somehow to critique a particular instance of the political deployment of historicism while still keeping the redemptive teleologies available for black Americans. The awkward attempt to synthesize Jamesian pragmatism, Hegelian historicism, and Spencerian evolutionism in "Renaissance of Ethics" was Du Bois's attempt to get himself out of this double bind. Where Hegelian historicism had, in America, become a powerful ideological support for both an expansionist and racist nationalism and an idealist exceptionalism inadequately aware of its own politics, Spencer's evolutionism offered a historicism anchored in alibis of scientific neutrality and objectivity and so free from the interference of political intentionalities and human volition. The "great laws" Du Bois dreamed of were guarantors of a universal teleology that unfolded without regard for the color line. "Renaissance of Ethics" sought, in effect, to rescue history from history itself, whereas "A Vacation Unique" insistently tethered these metaphysical flights of fancy to the contemporary social ground.

Nowhere does Du Bois refuse to subsume the negative particularity of African-American experience into historicist teleologies so clearly as he does in *Souls,* and it is this refusal that separates him from other American Hegelians. Whitman's Hegel, like the Hegel championed by the St. Louisans or by Dewey or Royce, "was an optimist" whose system "solved contradictions and enlarged the democratic self" rather than offering "the full logical and existential negativity of the dialectic" at the heart of the *Phenomenology.*[60] The American evasion of the "existential negativity" of Hegel's *Phenomenology,* and the political consequences of this evasion, are most startlingly apparent in the accounts of the master-and-slave dialectic given by the American Hegelians in the 1890s. These accounts consistently misrepresent Hegel's account of the struggle between master and slave by falsely attributing the myth of cowardly contract to Hegel, thereby providing philosophical alibis for the proslavery arguments of the 1890s whose prevalence in historiography and social commentary has already been noted in the previous chapter.

The St. Louis group's reading of the master-and-slave dialectic is outlined in *The Rebel's Daughter: A Story of Love, Politics and War* (1899), a historical romance about the Civil War published two years after the publication of "Strivings." The novel was written by John Gabriel Woerner, a judge, journalist, philosopher, legal scholar, and founding member of the St. Louis Hegelians. In the novel Professor Rauhenfels, a representation of Henry Brokmeyer, another founding member of the St. Louis group and one of their leading ideologues, explains, on the eve of the Civil War, the necessity for maintaining southern slavery in order to safeguard the freedom embodied in the constitutionally elected American government:

> Under the present condition of things it is of far greater importance to humanity—to the cause of freedom—that our government remain intact, than the normal condition of the slaves be changed. As Doctor Taylor [a cipher for Denton Snider, another member of the group] once neatly expressed it—
>
> " 'Tis not the outward bond that makes the slave—but the base craven thought within the man."
>
> Slaves are such upon their own compliance. No freeman, loving liberty above life or ease, was yet ever made a slave. To the slave, then, manumission is of no benefit.[61]

In the *Phenomenology* Hegel himself never says that "slaves are such upon their own compliance." His theorization of the master-and-slave relationship stresses the interdependence of two self-consciousnesses caught in "a life-and-death struggle" (*PM* 232). Hegel is concerned with the exercise and experienced mediations of power, not the justification of mastery through a theory of innate acquiescence. The *Phenomenology* in fact describes a complex dialectical process whereby the master is ultimately forced to recognize his dependence on the slave and the slave is able to realize his independence through his own labor. The cowardly contract theory of slavery simplifies this complexity and makes the servitude and subjection of the slave a means toward the absolute freedom of the master, a freedom that Hegel sees as an empty form of independence.

Royce outstrips the St. Louis Hegelians here. In *The Spirit of Modern Philosophy* he understands the master-and-slave dialectic not philogenetically but ontogenetically. That is to say, he takes Hegel's account to be a description not of actual slavery but of inner struggles of self-consciousness with its own contradictions. But Royce's reading of Hegel nevertheless presents the logic of mastery in its purest form.

> The more of a self I am, the more contradictions there are in my nature and the completer my conquest over these contradictions. The absolute self with which I am seeking to raise my soul, and which erelong I find to be a genuine self, yes, the only self, exists by the very might of its control over all these contradictions, whose infinite variety furnishes the very heart and content of its life.
>
> Hegel, as we see, makes his Absolute, the Lord, most decidedly a man of war. Consciousness is paradoxical, restless, struggling. Weak souls get weary of the fight, and give up trying to get wisdom, skill, virtue, because all these are won only in the presence of the enemy. But the absolute self is simply the absolutely strong spirit who bears the contradictions of life, and wins the eternal victory.[62]

This is not an accurate account of Hegel. It is rather an imposition onto a distorted Hegel of an ethics of self-realization that is identical to the conceptualization of ethical means and ends as a matter of the "victorious" and the "vanquished" by James, Royce's colleague at Harvard.

Woerner's dramatization of the St. Louisans' Hegelian interpretation of slavery is a little less absolute in its celebration of mastery. While insisting on the willingness of the slave to be made a slave, Rauhenfels (Brokmeyer) also paradoxically acknowledges the humanity of the slave, but does so only to temporarily trouble the master's ethics. Immediately after arguing that manumission is of no use to the slave, he goes on to say that

> the vice of slavery consists in the degradation of the master, because slavery is incompatible with his own freedom. Its recognition in the constitution is a monstrous contradiction of the principle of our government, and of the solemn declaration upon which we achieved independence. In depriving a human being of his liberty (for though this cannot be done without the

slave's consent, neither can it be done without the master's act) he destroys the divine quality wherein man is the image of God. This is the sin that will bring upon us retributive punishment as surely as effect follows cause. (*RD* 332)

But if this sounds like the resounding declamation of an abolitionist (despite the troubling parenthesis), an immediate change of direction follows as Rauhenfels goes on to argue, according to a "higher" logic, that some nevertheless have the right to be more equal than others. He insists that "the forcible abolition of slavery would be no remedy" for the possibility of imminent "retributive punishment": "It would be a new crime. Not only sinning against the constitutional rights of the slave-owner, but adding the base perfidy of violating our own solemn covenant" (*RD* 333). It does not matter if one abhors slavery or not; it is more important that one abhor "the treachery involved in robbing the South of the property solemnly guaranteed to them by the constitution" (*RD* 333). When someone points out to Rauhenfels that his position implies "that under the constitution human freedom is at a discount,—good only for one class, wicked in another," he replies that such sentiments reflect only the "nursery-room morality" inculcated in the American public by Stowe's *Uncle Tom's Cabin*. This sentimental morality seeks to impose "conscience as law," to falsely violate "the law of the land" in the name of "a higher law of God" (*RD* 333; 334). "Romantic sentiment [Rauhenfels argues] makes short work of problems . . . that sorely try the wit of the anxious statesmen, philanthropists and philosophers. It is so easy to follow the dictates of the heart if you can only stifle the skeptical protests of the head,—most easy to those who are least oppressed with brains" (*RD* 333).

The triumph of "the head" over "the dictates of the heart" in Rauhenfels's speech negates any sense that the meaning of history resides above all in the lived experience of human beings, and not in the sacrificing of this experience to the abstracted idols of so-called historical and institutional "laws" and "principles." The (albeit momentary and indirect) acknowledgment of the humanity of the slave is also evasive, since its implied notion of recognition is moralistic and idealist. The master is degraded because his act of conquest is an act against the divinity in Man. This suggests that the supremacy of the master can be destabilized if the humanness of the slave is recognized. But this is, once again, a gross distortion of Hegel's account of recognition, and it is a distortion perpetuated by modern critics of Hegel's theorization of the master-and-slave relationship.

Frantz Fanon, for example, insists that "the black man has no ontological resistance in the eyes of the white man."[63] For Fanon, unlike for Hegel, the master "laughs at the consciousness of the slave. What he wants from the slave is not recognition but work."[64] Orlando Patterson reinforces Fanon's conclusion in his study *Slavery and Social Death* when he argues against Hegel that slavery did *not* create "an existential impasse for the master" since "the master could and usually did achieve the recognition he needed from other free persons, including other masters."[65]

Others have repeated these criticisms, but neither Fanon nor Patterson does justice to Hegel's model of recognition in the *Phenomenology*.[66] In the *Phenomenology* the master does not seek recognition *from* the slave. Rather, he comes to recognize that his own freedom is dependent *on* the slave *and his labor* and is therefore a determined freedom and not an absolute and indeterminate one as he had thought: "for, just where the master has effectively achieved lordship, he really finds that something has come about quite different from an independent consciousness. It is not an independent, but rather a dependent consciousness that he has achieved. He is thus not assured of self-existence as his truth; he finds that his truth is rather the unessential consciousness [of the dependent slave], and the fortuitous unessential action of that consciousness" (*PM* 236–37). The master is brought to "an existential impasse" not by acknowledging the humanity of the slave and then seeking mutual recognition, but by recognizing that he himself is materialized through the property made by the slave. And just as the master comes to discover his dependency through the labor of the slave, so the slave discovers therein the possibility of his own consciousness passing "into real and true independence" (*PM* 237). Hegel is quite clear that "for recognition proper there is needed the moment that what the master does to the other he should also do to himself, and what the bondsman does to himself, he should do to the other also." Without this mutual labor, recognition remains "one sided and unequal" (*PM* 236). It is something like this mutuality that Du Bois will imagine in the first chapter of *Souls* when he writes that "the end" of the "striving" of the divided African-American is "to be a co-worker in the kingdom of culture" (*SBF* 365).

It was Marx who realized that "the outstanding achievement of Hegel's *Phänomenologie* and of its final outcome, the dialectic of negativity as the moving and generating principle, is thus first that Hegel conceives the self-creation of man as a process, conceives objectification as loss of the object, as alienation and transcendence of this alienation; that he thus grasps the essence of *labour* and comprehends objective man—true, because real man—as the outcome of man's *own labour*."[67] The 1890s interpretations of Hegel in America acknowledge neither the process by which the positions of the master and slave are made interdependent and reversed, nor the centrality of the concept of labor in the *Phenomenology*. As a consequence these interpretations either ignore the political meaning of mastery and slavery, reducing self-realization to the imperial assertion of will rather than a process of alienation and transcendence through work (Royce), or they justify actual slavery (Brokmeyer). They also equate wage labor with slavery as an alibi for industrial capitalism's exploitation of workers.

In *Hegel's Logic* (1890), William Torrey Harris, the leading figure of the St. Louis Group, repeats the myth of the cowardly contract and uses Hegel as a justificatory masking for the alienation of labor within the capitalist mode of production and so for the economic status quo in the rapidly expanding industrial and commercial culture of contemporary America, the very opposite of what Marx had done with Hegel's master-and-slave dialectic almost fifty years earlier in *The Economic and Philosophic Manuscripts of 1844*. Harris argues that if self-consciousness "prefers life to independence, then it becomes a slave":

> One reflects on the fact that in savage tribes this is the characteristic condition. This is the lowest stadium of human history, but it has its uses in preparation for further developments. Hegel makes some interesting and valuable suggestions on this head, showing how the fact that the slave does not gratify his wants immediately from what is before him, but receives his food, clothing, and shelter as gifts from his master, although he, by his own labor, produces those things, develops ethical insight. The slave mediates his will through another, and begins the discipline which may lift him above a worse servitude to his passions and appetites. Even in modern civilization this discipline is retained as essential, and the system of industry demands of each man that he labor at some occupation which produces an article for the market of the world and not for his own consumption. He shall receive for his own consumption, for the most part, the products of the labor of his fellow-men. This mediation is necessary. But there can be

a higher freedom attained in stoicism, and the slave who withdraws into the depths of his soul away from the actual, and renounces his finite interests, realizes this higher freedom.[68]

The extraordinary transition from the legitimated enslavement of "savage tribes" to the necessity of a slavish working class within a capitalist economy projects a seamless continuity between the antebellum agrarian South and the turn-of-the-century industrialized North and industrializing South. Across this seamless and social Darwinist transition each half of the proposition acts as an alibi for the other half, with freedom for the slave relegated to a "higher" realm "away from the actual." Harris's argument here reproduces in essential ways the ubiquitous nineteenth-century defense of the paternalism of plantation slavery projected against an alarmist vision of northern capitalism's urban poor turned into unruly masses (perhaps best known through George Fitzhugh's much earlier conflation of black slaves and the industrial working class in his *Cannibals All! or, Slaves without Masters* [1857]).

Du Bois's sense in *Souls* that the encroachments of northern capitalism into the South after the War have only instituted a system of peonage in place of plantation slavery also explores the intersections of plantation and industrial economies, but from a position of critical denunciation, not legitimation. But neither this denunciation nor Du Bois's vision of blacks and whites laboring together as "co-workers" should be taken as a suggestion that *Souls* presents a full materialist or Marxist account of alienation. Marx, who understood the radical achievement of the *Phenomenology,* also argued for the limitations of its radicalism. "For Hegel," Marx writes, "the *human being—man*—equals *self-consciousness.* All estrangement of the human being is therefore *nothing* but *estrangement of self-consciousness.* The estrangement of self-consciousness is not regarded as an *expression*—reflected in the realm of knowledge and thought—of the *real* estrangement of the human being. Instead, the *actual* estrangement—that which appears real—is according to its *innermost,* hidden nature (which is only brought to light by philosophy) nothing but the *manifestation* of the estrangement of the real human essence, of *self-consciousness.*"[69] Du Bois's own psychology of the crisis of self-consciousness works somewhere between idealist and materialist critique. The awareness of the economic and political contexts of "double-consciousness" in *Souls* does not translate itself into a radical critique of capitalist political economy. By focusing on the relationship of the black middle-class intelligentsia to the black "folk," *Souls* also tends to evade the issue of this group's relationship to the black urban working class. By appealing to white liberal sympathetic understanding, Du Bois also circles back to an idealist conception of recognition. But *Souls* does offer a highly politicized account of "double-consciousness." It is an account in which the class bases of Du Bois's own progressive idealist political programs and the evasions of historical reality in liberal American exceptionalism are simultaneously exposed to critical dramatizations. It is on the ground cleared by this critique that Du Bois goes on, in the final chapter of *Souls,* to offer a politicized account of black folk culture and to extend the insights of his psychology of alienation toward a fuller dramatization of creative self-realization. It is to Du Bois's own use of Hegel in his dramatization of "double-consciousness" that the discussion now turns.

"The Contradiction of Double Aims" and "The Talented Tenth"

After outlining his psychology of divided self-consciousness in the first part of "Of Our Spiritual Strivings," Du Bois locates this psychology as the product of a specific history, a history presenting a view of the American republic very different from the one presented by the American Hegelians. The second part of Du Bois's chapter offers a sketch of black American history, from "the days of bondage," when emancipation seemed like "the key to a promised land" (*SBF* 366), through the failure of Reconstruction and the rise of Jim Crow, to the time of the publication of *Souls* (and this is a history that is then delineated in greater detail throughout the remainder of *Souls*).[70] Despite the promise of emancipation, the first decade of Reconstruction was, writes Du Bois, "only a prolongation of the vain search for freedom. . . . The holocaust of war, the terrors of the Ku Klux Klan, the lies of carpet-baggers, the disorganization of industry, and the contradictory advice of friends and foes, left the bewildered serf with no new watchword beyond the old cry for freedom" (*SBF* 367). Despite the winning of the ballot, the black American remained a "half-free serf weary, wondering," though "inspired" (*SBF* 367).

Throughout his historical sketch Du Bois is mapping the failure of Reconstruction and the constitution of a new kind of slavery, a system of peonage and indentured labor reinforced by a revived culture of racist violence in the form of Black Codes.[71] Du Bois is concerned with the meaning of the persistence of the black struggle for freedom within this history and, like Fanon after him, with the psychological effects of "the inevitable self-questioning, self-disparagement, and lowering of ideals which ever accompany repression and breed in an atmosphere of contempt and hate" (*SBF* 369). Given this history it is appropriate that Du Bois should turn to Hegel. The Hegelian dialectics of mastery, servitude, and alienation in the *Phenomenology* were themselves grounded in the socio-historical setting of a Germany dominated by a "protracted feudal system" at a time when, for German idealists, the French Revolution and industrialization "not only abolished feudal absolutism, replacing it with the economic and political system of the middle class, but . . . completed what the German Reformation had begun, emancipating the individual as a self-reliant master of his life."[72]

Du Bois goes on to talk of the dawning of a new ideal after the winning of the vote, the ideal of education as the path of progress toward true freedom. The struggle for education remains, however, an unfulfilled quest in Du Bois's own time, and this period of "reflection and self-examination" confirms the Pauline denial of the possibility of revelation and true understanding in the fallen world: "In those somber forests of his striving his own soul rose before [the African-American], and he saw himself,—darkly as through a veil" (*SBF* 368). This is "the time of *Sturm und Drang*" (*SBF* 369) in which "double-consciousness" becomes the description of the black self as it is shaped by history but also by its struggles and resistances within history.

It is from within this drama that the concreteness of Du Bois's description of self-consciousness's experience of fragmentation and otherness emerges. But, given the terrible violence and disgracefulness of this history and the tragic depth of its psychological impact, it is curious that Du Bois chooses as the point of departure for his psychology an incident from his childhood that, by comparison with the experiences of most black Americans at that time, must appear as potentially trivial and certainly unrepresentative. However, as so often in *Souls,* the choice is well calculated, and it is worth examining the incident in some detail.

It is in the early days of rollicking boyhood that the revelation first burst upon one, all in a day, as it were. I remember well when the shadow swept across me. I was a little thing, away up in the hills of New England, where the dark Housatonic winds between Hoosac and Taghkanic to the sea. In a wee wooden schoolhouse, something put it into the boys' and girls' heads to buy gorgeous visiting cards—ten cents a package—and exchange. The exchange was merry, till one girl, a tall newcomer, refused my card,— refused it peremptorily, *with a glance*. Then it dawned upon me with a certain suddenness that I was different from the others; or like, mayhap, in heart and life and longing, but shut out from their world by a vast *veil*. (*SBF* 363–64; emphases added)

Here two distinct moments from the narrative of Hegel's *Phenomenology* are collapsed together: the transition of consciousness into self-consciousness and the master-and-slave (or lordship-and-bondage) struggle that follows it a little later. In the first of these moments Hegel, like Du Bois, uses the biblical conceit of the veil or curtain to mark the instance of transition and transformation. In Exodus the veil hides the holy of holies, the sanctuary for "the ark of the testimony" (26:33). In Hebrews it marks the transformation of "those who were once enlightened and tasted of the heavenly gift" into those who "fell away" (6:4–19). Most important, the rending of the veil marks the conversion of the Roman centurion at the crucifixion:

And Jesus cried again with a loud voice, and yielded up his spirit.

And behold, the veil of the temple was rent in twain from the top to the bottom; and the earth did quake; and the rocks were rent;

And the tombs were opened; and many bodies of the saints that had fallen asleep were raised;

And coming forth out of the tombs after his resurrection they entered into the holy city and appeared unto many.

Now the centurion, and they that were with him watching Jesus, when they saw the earthquake, and the things that were done, feared exceedingly, saying, Truly this was the Son of God. (Matthew 27:50–54)[73]

In Hegel, at the moment that self-consciousness discovers itself behind natural appearance, the curtain is drawn aside and the veil lifted. "What is for understanding an object in a covering veil of sense," writes Hegel, "now comes before us in its essential form as a pure notion":[74]

This curtain [of appearance], therefore, hanging before the inner world is withdrawn, and we have here the inner being [the ego] gazing into the inner realm. . . . What we have here is Self-consciousness. It is manifest that behind the so-called curtain, which is to hide the inner world, there is nothing to be seen unless we ourselves go behind there, as much in order that we may thereby see, as that there may be something behind there which can be seen.[75]

Where the veil is lifted in Hegel, it descends in Du Bois, and what is primarily a natural history of consciousness in the *Phenomenology* is transformed into a social history in *Souls*. In attempting to lift the veil that hangs across the color line and in using the veil as a psychological metaphor Du Bois will, like Hegel, transform this prophetic allegory of revelation and conversion into a psychologistic account of consciousness. Throughout *Souls* this account is simultaneously a revelation of a history of racial oppression. As far as Du Bois's dramatization of his own consciousness is concerned, the veil is lifted not to reveal him as martyr but to reveal to him a vision of terror and failure. From this vision there emerges a sense of prophetic imagination that is not transcendent but that is engaged in the direct confrontation of the actual and present world.

In the first chapter of *Souls* the moment of radical self-awareness comes through the confrontation between two self-consciousnesses, a moment that, in Hegel, belongs properly within the social and political drama of the master-and-slave dialectic. By collapsing together the two moments in Hegel, Du Bois suggests that the development of black American self-consciousness is always a political history scarred from the very start by the experience of rejection and subjection, though at this early stage of *Souls* the exact nature of Du Bois's understanding of subjection and power is at best only hinted at. Where Hegel, even at his most concrete and political, works through abstractions, Du Bois is careful to specify historical and social contexts for his commentary. In particular, in the visiting-card episode there is a clear sense of the audience being addressed and, more important, of Du Bois's own peculiar positioning somewhere between this audience and the "black folk." This social placing of both audience and self and Du Bois's reworking of the master-and-slave dialectic in terms of a quotidian drama of seeing and being seen are two aspects of the opening scene of *Souls* that deserve special attention.

In this scene the New England children are involved in a playful imitation of the social rituals of the adult and white bourgeois world in a mythical landscape resonant with New England self-idealization. Du Bois's New England hills, like his descriptions of southern landscape, recall Washington Irving's world of the Catskill Mountains and Sleepy Hollow, and, as in "A Vacation Unique," the boy Du Bois is shocked into new awareness of the violence of social transformation. Du Bois rehearses the clash of nostalgic retreat and history, a recurring preoccupation of American romance. He evokes the dreamy landscape "where the dark Housatonic winds between Hoosac and Taghkanic to the sea" in order to quickly shatter the dream, much like Irving.

Du Bois's opening scene is a calculated class- and culture-specific enlistment, through appeal to sentiment, of the sympathy of northern white liberal readers—before, that is, Du Bois sets this very sentiment of moral support adrift in a sea of a more violent history and tragic self-division than is revealed in the opening scene itself. At a time when the vast majority of African-Americans were illiterate or barely literate, and when the majority of literate southern whites were hardly interested in a book like *Souls,* Du Bois's audience was made up largely of northern middle-class and probably liberal whites. As has already been pointed out, "Of Our Spiritual Strivings" was first published in a slightly different form in the *Atlantic Monthly* in 1897. The *Atlantic Monthly,* founded in 1857, was a Boston-based, middle-class publication with a substantial circulation, supporting the antislavery cause and good literature, and, after the appointment of Walter Himes Page as editor in 1896, increasingly interested in current social issues, including issues of race and the New South.[76] The childhood world evoked at the start of *Souls* is a world that most of the readers of the *Atlantic Monthly* would have recognized.

It is the tourist curiosity of these northern readers that Du Bois mocks at the very start of "Of Our Spiritual Strivings." "Between me and the other world," he writes, "there is ever an unasked question: . . . How does it feel to be a problem?" But the question is never asked directly. Instead, the whites say, "I know an excellent colored man in my town; or, I fought at Mechanicsville; or, Do not these Southern outrages make your blood boil?" Du Bois's first response is stoic restraint and silence: "At these I smile, or am interested, or reduce the boiling to a simmer, as the occasion may require. To the real question, How does it feel to be a problem? I answer seldom a word" (*SBF* 363).

With the very next paragraph of *Souls,* however, Du Bois finally does begin to answer, but he does not turn for illustration to the dramatic possibilities of "Southern outrages," or incidents from the Civil War or from slavery. Du Bois could have begun *Souls* with such illustrations, but this not only would have been untrue to his own experience, the necessary starting point for a response to the question "How does it feel to be a problem?" but also would have permitted his northern audience the luxury of historical, geographical, and cultural distance. More clearly than in the "Jefferson Davis" speech, Du Bois forestalls this possibility. By opening with the childhood incident in New England and then moving to a fuller exposé of the conditions of black life in the post-Reconstruction South, Du Bois forges a small but effective link between North and South.

It is, however, a very small link, and it is worth asking why Du Bois chose such an incident with which to anchor his account of black life during one of the darkest periods of African-American history. It could be argued that a more explicit example of *northern* "outrages" would have alienated his audience, whereas the visiting-card episode allows Du Bois to implicate his audience without losing its sympathy. Most likely there is some truth in this. But the main reason for Du Bois's choice lies elsewhere. It has to do with his location of himself in *Souls*.

The boy Du Bois's rude awakening does more than unravel the Edenic idealization of New England. His own stance of shocked innocence aligns him with this idealized world and its values. The "newcomer's" rejecting look is both the source of Du Bois's first experience of racism and also a revelation of his commitment to the bourgeois culture of New England. The refusal of the visiting card disrupts the decorum of the children's game and so threatens the genteel values embodied in the social ritual being imitated, values the child Du Bois clearly shares. In fact, by making the origin of disruption a "newcomer" Du Bois effectively puts the source of racism outside this culture and so manages to safeguard, at least in part, its values and his own allegiance to them.

As David Levering Lewis has demonstrated, in *Souls* and in his autobiographies Du Bois tends to present a very idealized picture of Great Barrington, his childhood hometown in Massachusetts.[77] Some of what he leaves out of the picture in *Souls* is a reflection of his political leanings at the time of writing, but other omissions invite critical reflection on Du Bois's cultural position. For instance, his failure to mention that there was industrial development in the hills around Great Barrington or that there was increasing racial and class tension in the town due largely to the influx of new white European immigrants is in keeping with Du Bois's faith in capitalism and his unease about the working class and the more radical side of socialism. On the other hand, Du Bois's silences about his own experience of poverty in his childhood, about living on Railroad Street, a particularly wretched part of town, or about his having had a broader knowledge of black life in his childhood than he admits in later life are, in *Souls* at least, aids to an unmasking rather than a masking of certain aspects of his politics. As has already been pointed out in the introduction, for all their hardships, Du Bois's childhood and upbringing were, by comparison with the lives of the vast majority of black Americans at the time, highly privileged. Du Bois's silences highlight this separation between himself and the "black folk" rather than disguise it. In doing so Du Bois, right from the very start of *Souls,* problematizes his own status as guide to the black world for the white reader and incorporates the exploration of the difference between himself and the vast majority of blacks as part of the central drama of *Souls.* If *Souls* is a journey into the world behind the veil for the white reader, it is also presented as a journey into unknown or half-known aspects of black life for Du Bois himself. As the child Du Bois of the first chapter of *Souls* becomes the adult Du Bois of the last chapter, he also moves from the experience of the rejected visiting card to a direct confrontation of the conditions of rural black life in the South and to the truths about black historical experience voiced in the "sorrow songs."

Many of these songs remember slavery, but Du Bois's own biographical narrative does not move up from slavery. It begins rather with an infant version of the encounter between a white female and a black male that is so charged a part of the mythology of black-white relations in America. In a country where a black boy could be murdered for so much as looking in the direction of a white woman, it is the white girl who stares down the black boy at the start of *Souls,* an experience that appears to have been a source of deep bitterness for Du Bois.[78] The Hegelian master-slave struggle is here refigured in terms of the operation of power within the subjecting gaze. Du Bois's description of otherness is dominated by the sense of the transformation of black self-consciousness within the "glance" or "eyes of others" (*SBF* 364). These terms do not so much recall Hegel as prefigure *aspects* of Sartre's descriptions in his commentary on Hegel in *Being and Nothingness* (1953). The gaze of the other is in Du Bois, as in Sartre, the *"original fall"*[79] that fixes the freedom of activity into passivity. The appearance of the other is the disintegration of the self's world and a plunge into a state of vulnerability. By opening *Souls* at the moment when he is contemptuously rejected by the "glance" of the "tall newcomer" and so forced into a new sense of self, Du Bois, like Sartre, acknowledges that the disintegration of the self's world is also partly its negative structure or coherence:

Thus suddenly an object has appeared which has stolen the world from me. Everything is in place; everything still exists for me; but everything is traversed by an invisible flight and fixed in the direction of a new object. The appearance of the Other in the world corresponds therefore to a fixed sliding of the whole universe, to a decentralization of the world which undermines the centralization which I am simultaneously effecting.

But *the Other* is still an object *for me.* He belongs to *my distances;* the man is there, twenty paces from me, he is turning his back on *me.* As such he is again two yards, twenty inches from the lawn, six yards from the statue; hence the disintegration of my universe is contained within the limits of this same universe; we are not dealing here with a flight of the world toward nothingness or outside itself. Rather it appears that the world has a kind of drain hole in the middle of its being and that it is perpetually flowing off through this hole. The universe, the flow, and the object. All this is there *for me* as a partial structure of the world, even though the total disintegration of the universe is involved. (*BN* 255–56)

This experience is what R. D. Laing calls a state of "ontological insecurity."[80] In Sartre this moment is characterized by the experience of shame as the self discovers itself to be "in suspense," fallen into the midst of objects as an object and requiring the mediations of the Other in order to be what it is: "Pure shame is not a feeling of being this or that guilty object but in general of being *an* object; that is, of *recognizing myself* in this degraded, fixed, and dependent being which I am for the Other" (*BN* 288).

The episode of the visiting card and the moment of rejection described by Du Bois is similar to Fanon's recollection, in his *Black Skin, White Masks* (1952), of a French child pointing to him in the street with the exclamation "Look, a Negro!" Thus the adult Fanon finds that he, like the child Du Bois, is "an object in the midst of other objects." The issue is one of "a slow composition of my *self* as a body in the middle of a spatial and temporal world." The aim of Fanon's book, like that of *Souls,* is to describe how "the fragments" can be "put together again by another self."[81]

The moment of negativity described by Du Bois and Fanon must be overcome through struggle and creative activity. But in *Souls* there is as yet only the *thought* of an active self-realization and transformation of the world. The dramatizations of "Of Our Spiritual Strivings" are concerned with posing the question of how such activity can be conceived and put into practice inside a culture and history where it is repeatedly thwarted. In the moment immediately following the visiting-card episode (in the same paragraph), Du Bois begins to elaborate this dilemma and in doing so moves from the master-and-slave dialectic to Hegel's description of skepticism.

Du Bois now describes his reaction to the descent of the veil:

> I had thereafter no desire to tear down that veil, to creep through; I held all beyond it in common contempt, and lived above it in a region of blue sky and great wandering shadows. That sky was bluest when I could beat my mates at examination-time, or beat them at a foot-race, or even beat their stringy heads. Alas, with the years all this fine contempt began to fade; for the worlds I longed for, and all their dazzling opportunities, were theirs, not mine. But they should not keep these prizes, I said; some, all, I would wrest from them. Just how I would do it I could never decide: by reading law, by healing the sick, by telling the wonderful tales that swam in my head,—some way. With other black boys the strife was not so fiercely sunny: their youth shrunk into tasteless sycophancy, or into silent hatred of the pale world about them and mocking distrust of everything white; or wasted itself in a bitter cry, Why did God make me an outcast and a stranger in mine own house? The shades of the prison-house closed round about us all: walls strait and stubborn to the whitest, but relentlessly narrow, tall and unscalable to sons of night who must plod darkly on in resignation, or beat unavailing palms against the stone, or steadily, half hopelessly, watch the streak of blue above. (*SBF* 364)

Du Bois is caught here between a transcendence of and a simultaneous entrapment in concrete existence. He holds the world that fixes his freedom into an object state in "common contempt," choosing to live "above it in a region of blue sky." But this very transcendent contempt ties Du Bois to the world he wishes to rise above: the sky is "bluest" when Du Bois is defeating the white world at its own game and by its own rules, beating his mates "at examination-time, or . . . at a foot-race, or even . . . their stringy heads." However, Du Bois goes on to note that, with the passage of time, "this fine contempt began to fade." There is now a more realistic return to the world and also a more meaningful sense of challenging this world through creative labor. The plans to read law, to become a doctor or a writer, are intended to "wrest" the "prizes" from the white world, but to do so in the service of the black community and not just a resentful ego.

The transition is something like the move from pride to arrogance in Sartre. Pride is for Sartre "a reaction of flight" and a mode of "bad faith"

(*BN* 290) because, as Joseph Catalano explains in his commentary on Sartre, "when I am proud, or vain, because of some personal quality or accomplishment, I recognize that I need the Other to constitute my qualities and accomplishments as being objectively mine. . . . But then I attempt to have the Other freely acknowledge that these qualities are intrinsically mine and that I do not need him for the objectivity, or 'objectiveness,' of my accomplishments."[82] Arrogance is an authentic attitude because through arrogance "I apprehend myself as the free object by which the Other gets his being-other." It is "the affirmation of my freedom confronting the Other-as-object" (*BN* 290)—it is, in other words, the direct confrontation of the other's freedom.

Neither in his declaration of his plan to wrest the prizes from the white world nor in his reworking of the master-and-slave struggle does Du Bois confront, as Hegel and Sartre do, the dependence of the master on the slave. *Souls* is, for the most part, concerned primarily with the self-consciousness of the "slave" or objectified self, though, as the next chapter tries to demonstrate, there is a displacement of the white reader by the end of the book. And also, as already noted, the idea of "direct confrontation" is still only a notion for Du Bois. As this notion develops from "common contempt" to a more complex idea of activity, the sense of the barriers to freedom also becomes more intense in Du Bois's writing. Just as the pose of transcendent disregard is juxtaposed to the "glance" of the "tall newcomer," so the plans for serving the black community are now placed against the "shades of the prison-house." The evocation of the prison-house that "closed round about us *all*" is the first moment in *Souls* in which Du Bois moves out of a largely autobiographical focus into a more broadly collective concern.

At first Du Bois seems to be introducing an invidious hierarchization. Where he can conceive of transformative activity that will lead to genuine freedom, "other black boys" seem "shrunk into tasteless sycophancy, or into silent hatred of the pale world," unable to rise above the "bitter cry" of hopeless resignation. But Du Bois posits this difference not as one of innate superior ability but rather as a product of class privilege guaranteed by lighter skin color. The "walls" of the prison are "strait and stubborn to the *whitest*, but relentlessly narrow, tall, and unscalable to *sons of night*." Those African-Americans who can be seen to possess white blood in their veins have tended to form a privileged social group or class among the African-American community, and Du Bois is fully aware that there are many doors in the white world that will be more easily opened for a mulatto like himself than for those with darker skins. The hierarchy of this relationship will be reversed in the final chapter of *Souls,* but in its statement here, as in the reversal, Du Bois is again making clear that there is an important separation between himself and the "black folk."

The movement of self-consciousness between an absolute freedom negating its bonds and life within these bonds that characterizes the passage from Du Bois quoted above is what Hegel calls skepticism. In the *Phenomenology* self-consciousness develops from the master-and-slave stage to the unhappy consciousness by passing through the stages of stoicism and skepticism. This transition also marks the movement from labor to thought, and the relationship of the master and the slave is mirrored on the level of thought in the relationship of stoicism to skepticism. So stoicism is the notion of an absolute and independent freedom free of any determining mediations. "The essence of this consciousness," writes Hegel, "is to maintain that solid lifeless unconcern which persistently withdraws from the movement of existence, from effective activity as well as from passive endurance, into the simple essentiality of thought" (*PM* 244). Skepticism is the realization in thought of the idea of freedom of which stoicism is merely the empty form. In skepticism thought "wholly annihilates the being of the world with its manifold determinateness" (*PM* 246). In other words, in skepticism the "negative process" of the dialectic becomes "a moment of self-consciousness" itself (*PM* 248). The dilemma of skepticism is that in the very act of negation it is tied to that which it wishes to negate. Hence skepticism is a doubled or dualized consciousness caught in a recurring transition, like Du Bois's self-consciousness, between transcendence and determinateness, "the instability of going to and fro, hither and thither, from one extreme of self-same self-consciousness, to the other contingent, confused and confusing consciousness" (*PM* 249). It is a consciousness which at times "places the world in parentheses and rises above all the forms of the being that it constitutes; at other times it is itself caught in this world of which it is only a contingent fragment."[83]

The skeptical consciousness becomes the unhappy consciousness when it brings the two separate modes together and realizes that they are, in fact, part of a single consciousness and not outside it. Just as Hegel in the *Phenomenology* moves immediately from his description of the skeptical consciousness and its limits to his description of the unhappy consciousness, so too Du Bois in *Souls* now proceeds to his famous account of "double-consciousness" and "the contradiction of double aims." As

Jean Hyppolite notes, "unhappy consciousness is the fundamental theme of the *Phenomenology*."[84] Du Bois's idea of a doubled self bears the same relationship to the overall narrative of *Souls* as that of "unhappy consciousness" to the plot of Hegel's *Phenomenology*. In both Du Bois and Hegel the idea of "double-consciousness" is central to the conceptualization of the negativity of historical experience. Here is Du Bois's well-known passage:

> After the Egyptian and Indian, the Greek and Roman, the Teuton and Mongolian, the Negro is a sort of seventh son, born with a veil, and gifted with second-sight in this American world,—a world which yields him no true self-consciousness, but only lets him see himself through the revelation of the other world. It is a peculiar sensation, this double-consciousness, this sense of always looking at one's self through the eyes of others, of measuring one's soul by the tape of a world that looks on in amused contempt and pity. One ever feels his twoness,—an American, a Negro; two souls, two thoughts, two unreconciled strivings; two warring ideals in one dark body, whose dogged strength alone keeps it from being torn asunder.
>
> The history of the American Negro is the history of this strife,—this longing to attain self-conscious manhood, to merge his double self into a better and truer self. In this merging he wishes neither of the older selves to be lost. He would not Africanize America, for America has too much to teach the world and Africa. He would not bleach his Negro soul in a flood of white Americanism, for he knows that Negro blood has a message for the world. He simply wishes to make it possible for a man to be both a Negro and an American, without being cursed and spit upon by his fellows, without having the doors of Opportunity closed roughly in his face. (*SBF* 364–65)

While the linking of self-consciousness to seeing and being seen is, as already suggested, very much Du Bois's own, the vocabulary of this passage, like the vocabulary of the ensuing discussion of the "contradiction of double aims" or "double-aimed struggle" that plagues "black artisan" and "black *savant*" alike (*SBF* 365), is very close to the terminology of Hegel's formulation of the "unhappy consciousness" and its struggle with disunity and for unity. It is most likely that Du Bois read his Hegel in the original German, since Santayana preferred teaching texts in the original language and since Du Bois's German was good enough to do doctoral-level work in Berlin. So the German text is given here after J. B. Baillie's translation of the passage on the unhappy consciousness

(Baillie's arguably being the closest to Hegel's original among the currently available translations).

In describing the transition from the skeptical to the "unhappy consciousness," Hegel writes that

the duplication, which previously was divided between two individuals, the lord and the bondsman, is concentrated into one. Thus we have here that dualizing of self-consciousness within itself, which lies essentially in the notion of mind; but the unity of the two elements is not yet present. Hence the *Unhappy Consciousness,* the Alienated Soul which is the consciousness of self as a divided nature, a *doubled* and merely *contradictory* being.

This unhappy consciousness, divided and at variance within itself, must, because this contradiction of its essential nature is felt to be a single consciousness, always have in the one consciousness the other also; and thus must be straightaway driven out of each in turn, when it thinks it has therein attained to the victory, and rest of unity. Its true return to itself, or reconciliation with itself, will, however, display the notion of mind endowed with a life and existence of its own, because it implicitly involves the fact that, while being an undivided consciousness, it is a *double-consciousness.*[85]

die Verdopplung, welche früher an zwei einzelne, an den Herrn und den Knecht sich verteilte, in eines eingekehrt; die Verdoppelung des Selbstbewußtseins in sich selbst, welche in Begriffe des Geistes wesentlich ist, ist hiemit vorhanden, aber noch nicht ihre Einheit [,—] und das *unglückliche Bewußtsein* ist das Bewußtsein seiner als des gedoppelten [,] nur widersprechenden Wesens.

Dieses *unglückliche, in sich entzweite* Bewußtsein muß also, weil dieser Widerspruch seines Wesens sich *Ein* Bewußtsein ist, in dem einen Bewußtsein immer auch das andere haben, und so aus jedem unmittelbar, indem es zum Siege und zur Ruhe der Einheit gekommen zu sein meint, wieder daraus ausgetrieben werden. Seine wahre Rückkehr aber in sich selbst oder seine Versöhnung mit sich wird den Begriff des lebendig gewordenen und in die Existenz getretenen Geistes darstellen, weil an ihm schon dies ist, daß es als Ein ungeteiltes Bewußtsein ein gedoppeltes ist.[86]

The state of perpetual transition between unity and disunity is a state of terror that is also the ground upon which the transformation of existence can take place. Du Bois's "double-consciousness," like Hegel's "unhappy consciousness," is the internalization of the dialectics of struggle and confrontation. In the "unhappy consciousness," the master-slave dialectic, "which arises in the midst of externality transposes itself to the interior of self-consciousness itself," so that the "unhappy consciousness" "is always divided within itself, a consciousness both of absolute self-certainty and of the nothingness of that certainty."[87] In Hegel the slave is the one who achieves a more complex level of self-awareness and understanding than the master, and the unhappy consciousness represents a higher level of self-awareness than the skeptical consciousness. So too in Du Bois black self-consciousness is "gifted with second-sight." This "second-sight" is a sign of this self-consciousness's sense of alienation from self and exclusion from the white world. But it also signals a higher understanding, born of this alienation, of political and social realities.[88] The process by which an external struggle is internalized in Du Bois is also identical to that in Hegel. The existential drama of being with which *Souls* opens, where the boy Du Bois, like the "seventh son," sees himself "through the revelation of the other world," finally becomes the struggle of "two warring ideals in one dark body." The opening moment of "ontological insecurity" is, in fact, transmuted into a drama of cultural relativism. The white girl who rejects the black boy is now internalized in the abstract as the cultural ideals of the world to which she belongs and is now placed in opposition to a black self newly aware of its own cultural and racial status as "a Negro" distinct from being "an American," and with a unique "message for the world." Here, as on several other occasions in *Souls*, a radical sense that self-consciousness is the product of a "history" of "strife" is tinged with a more reactionary and essentialist sense of self-identity secured in "blood."

The two paragraphs on the "two-ness" of the African-American and his desire "to merge his double self into a better and truer self" are the most generalized of the passages on self-consciousness in the first chapter of *Souls*. As has already been demonstrated, the account of self-consciousness that precedes these two paragraphs is strongly anchored in autobiography, with Du Bois only gradually and with qualification moving out toward claiming some sort of representative status for his own experiences. What follows Du Bois's famous account of double-consciousness is a return from the universal to the particular. The ensuing passages describe how the dream of a more unified black self laboring as "a co-worker in the kingdom of culture" (*SBF* 365) alongside white Americans has been shattered in post-Emancipation America. In outlining the effects of this failure on the consciousness of African-Americans Du

Bois continues to frame his account with references to "the black man" or "ten thousand thousand people" whose "unreconciled ideals" have sent them "wooing false gods and invoking false means of salvation" (*SBF* 366), but he focuses in detail on the particular dilemma of the black elite, what he elsewhere calls "the Talented Tenth."

Du Bois begins by placing African-American "striving" within a broader world historical narrative in which the "Negro's" "latent genius" and "powers of body and mind" are perceived to have been "strangely wasted, dispersed or forgotten": "The shadow of a mighty Negro past flits through the tale of Ethiopia the Shadowy and of Egypt the Sphinx. Throughout history, the powers of single black men flash here and there like falling stars, and die sometimes before the world has rightly gauged their brightness" (*SBF* 365). This historical meta-narrative, combining a metaphysics of racial destiny and the deeds of exceptional men, so characteristic of Du Bois's thought at this time, is given as the framework in which "the black man's turning hither and thither in hesitant and doubtful striving" "in the few days since Emancipation" is to be understood. Du Bois stresses that what seems "like absence of power, like weakness" is in fact "the contradiction of double aims" (*SBF* 365), and by the specific examples he gives Du Bois also makes it clear that he believes that this contradiction is experienced most acutely by "the Talented Tenth":

> The double-aimed struggle of the black artisan—on the one hand to escape white contempt for a nation of mere hewers of wood and drawers of water, and on the other hand to plough and nail and dig for a poverty-stricken horde—could only result in making him a poor craftsman, for he had but half a heart in either cause. By the poverty and ignorance of his people, the Negro minister or doctor was tempted toward quackery and demagogy; and by the criticism of the other world, toward ideals that made him ashamed of his lowly tasks. The would-be black *savant* was confronted by the paradox that the knowledge his people needed was a twice-told tale to his white neighbors, while the knowledge which would teach the white world was Greek to his own flesh and blood. The innate love of harmony and beauty that set the ruder souls of his people a-dancing and a-singing raised but confusion and doubt in the soul of the black artist; for the beauty revealed to him was the soul-beauty which his larger audience despised, and he could not articulate the message of another people. (*SBF* 365–66)

The skilled artisan, minister, doctor, teacher, and artist are representatives of an African-American social and professional elite. Du Bois's own survey of the occupational stratification and distribution of the African-American population of Philadelphia reveals that those involved in "conducting business on their own account," "in learned professions" (including "clergymen," "physicians," and "teachers"), "in skilled trades" (including "carpenters," though not, given the urban context, farmers), and those employed as "clerks, semi-professional and responsible workers" constitute about the top 15 percent among those over twenty-one years of age.[89]

In *The Philadelphia Negro* Du Bois explains why he thinks it so important to understand the social stratification of the black community and the role of the social elite within this community. First of all, such an understanding counteracts the "strong tendency . . . to consider the Negroes as composing one practically homogeneous mass." Du Bois accepts that black Americans "have had a common history, suffer today common disabilities, and contribute to one general set of social problems." But he also adds that the statistics he has gathered plainly show "that wide variations in antecedents, wealth, intelligence and general efficiency have already been differentiated within this group" (*PN* 309). The social problems confronting African-Americans cannot be understood until this differentiation is recognized (*PN* 310). Most whites never reach such an understanding because "it is hard for the average white American to lay aside his patronizing way toward a Negro, and to talk of aught to him but the Negro question; the lack, therefore, of common ground even for conversation makes such meetings rather stiff and not often repeated" (*PN* 318). It is such an encounter that forms the point of departure for *Souls,* and Du Bois's commentary from *The Philadelphia Negro* helps explain why within his more general commentary on "the Negro question" in *Souls* he feels it necessary to remind his reader of the class specificity of his account. And Du Bois's underscoring of the simultaneity of a "common history" and "wide variation" among African-Americans also indicates a perspective from which the recurring tension between particularization and universalization in the account of self-consciousness in *Souls* can be approached.

Along with the challenge to racist stereotypes that fail to distinguish between the "better class of Negroes" and the "thugs and whoremongers and gamblers" (*PN* 310), Du Bois wants also to defend his own program of social leadership for African-Americans. In *The Philadelphia Negro* he accepts that "it is natural" for the 90 percent of black Americans not in the top 10 percent to resent this elite and "just as natural for the well-

educated and well-to-do Negroes to feel themselves far above the criminals and prostitutes . . . and even above the servant girls and porters of
the middle class of workers" (*PN* 317). But Du Bois adds a warning to
the "better class of Negroes" who "make their mistake in failing to recognize that, however laudable an ambition to rise may be, the first duty of
an upper class is to serve the lowest classes. The aristocracies of all people
have been slow in learning this and perhaps the Negro is no slower than
the rest, but his peculiar situation demands that in his case this lesson be
learned sooner" (*PN* 317).

The functions of the aristocracy are outlined with greater force in the
well-known essay "The Talented Tenth" in 1903. Here Du Bois proposes
that "the Negro race, like all races, is going to be saved by its exceptional
men." Educational reform among black Americans must, therefore, focus
on the training of an elite vanguard, on "developing the Best of this race
that they may guide the Mass away from the contamination and death of
the Worst, in their own and other races" (TT 842).

> Can the masses of the Negro people be in any possible way more quickly
> raised than by the effort and example of this aristocracy of talent and charac-
> ter? Was there ever a nation on God's fair earth civilized from the bottom
> upward? Never; it is, ever was and ever will be from the top downward
> that culture filters. The Talented Tenth rises and pulls all that are worth the
> saving up to their vantage ground. This is the history of human progress;
> and the two historic mistakes which have hindered that progress were the
> thinking first that no more could ever rise save the few already risen; or
> second, that it would better the unrisen to pull the risen down. (TT 847)

Du Bois's evaluation of class differences within the black community
is tied to a qualitative differentiation of northern and southern African-
Americans within his political programs. The terms in which Du Bois
constructs this differentiation are also worth noting in some detail, since
Souls is focused almost entirely on the South, despite the fact that Du Bois
begins to write it when working in a northern urban ghetto, Philadelphia's
Seventh Ward.

Du Bois explains that, in the case of the Philadelphia community, the
Talented Tenth class is "largely Philadelphia born," "descended from the
house-servant class," and contains "many mulattoes" (*PN* 318), three
facts that, along with his education, align Du Bois himself with this
group. By contrast with Philadelphia's black upper class, more than two-
thirds of the city's black population was born outside the city, largely in

the South, and out of these "less than a quarter have been resident in the city twenty years or more." Du Bois concludes from these facts that "half the Negro population can not in any sense be said to be a product of the city, but rather represents raw material, whose transformation forms a pressing series of social problems" (*PN* 80).

In a series of articles on black communities in northern cities written in 1901 Du Bois elaborates on the political implications of the regional differentiation of the black population. He argues that the waves of black migrants from the South entering northern cities at the turn of the century pose a potential threat to the efforts of a northern bourgeois leadership.[90] Where the free blacks of the North have fought against segregation and claimed a full American identity, the newly arrived southerners have concentrated in enclosed black communities and effectively redrawn a color line for self-protection. "They made a negro world and then in turn taunted the free negroes with wishing to escape from themselves, and being ashamed of their race and lineage. Here stood the paradox, and here it stands to puzzle the best negro thought."[91] Du Bois offers no direct solutions but notes that the waves of migration and the growth of ghettos have "estranged the older free negro element, and deprived the whole group of its best natural leadership."[92] He concludes that "social distinctions should be observed. A rising race must be aristocratic; the good cannot consort with the bad—nor even the best with the less good."[93]

Du Bois's defense of an elite leadership is part of an increasing faith in an intellectual elite as cultural guides and saviors that was a major current of the Progressive Era from the late nineteenth century to the early twentieth and became aligned with a pragmatist sociology as a reaction to the conservatism of social Darwinism.[94] But Du Bois's recurrent recourse to a rhetoric of the survival of the fittest also legitimates social Darwinism from within a deeply reactionary aristocratic vitalism.

Neither this aristocratic vitalism nor the hierarchical differentiation of North and South are sustained with confidence in *Souls*. In *The Philadelphia Negro* Du Bois attempts to further his defense of the elite by adding that "this class is itself an answer to the question of the ability of the Negro to assimilate American culture" (*PN* 318). In *Souls*, however, this very process of assimilating "American culture" is placed at the heart of the dilemma of "double aims" confronting the Talented Tenth. In the passage from *The Philadelphia Negro* Du Bois is seeking legitimation for the black elite among white Americans. In *Souls* this elite is forced to address itself to the "black folk" as much as to the inquisitive white interlocutor at the start of the book. In both *The Philadelphia Negro* and "The Talented Tenth" there is a pervasive sense of the "black folk" as raw material that must be molded and lifted up out of ignorance and passivity by the elite into an acceptance of cultural values that are more or less identical to those of the white aristocracy. In "Of Our Spiritual Strivings," however, there are "two warring ideals" that appear to be equally matched. And where the conclusions of Du Bois's sociology and reformist program are propelled by a progressive teleology whose agent is the black elite, the conclusion of the first chapter of *Souls*, with its outline of the disasters of post-Emancipation history, leaves this agency in historical suspense.

Alexandre Kojève's commentary on Hegel's conception of the bourgeois intellectual provides a useful gloss on this state of suspension. The comparison with Du Bois is appropriate not only because the *Phenomenology* is an essential resource for the first chapter of *Souls* but also because, in illustrating "the contradiction of double aims," Du Bois himself lavishes more attention on "the black *savant*" and "the black artist" than on the "artisan" and the "minister or doctor." Kojève notes that in his *Phenomenology* Hegel "takes a great interest in the phenomenon of the Christian or bourgeois intellectual" who lives in society and in a state but perceives himself to be alienated from the world. "Being neither Master nor Slave," such an intellectual "is able—in this *nothingness*, in this absence of all given *determination*—to 'realize' in some way the desired synthesis of Mastery and Slavery: he can *conceive* it. However, being *neither* Master *nor* Slave—that is, abstaining from all Work and from all Fighting—he cannot truly *realize* the synthesis that he discovers: without Fighting and without Work, this synthesis conceived by the Intellectual remains purely *verbal*."[95] Kojève's sense, part Hegelian and part Marxist, that the "ideal process" must be connected up to the "real process" of the transformation of "social and historical conditions"[96] implies the return of philosophical speculation to the realm of material existence. Kojève's dichotomies are a little simplistic, but Du Bois himself does not fully escape such oppositions in his struggle between activism and contemplation. While this struggle is more clearly played out in Du Bois's career in the terms defined by Kojève when he becomes a Marxist, it is also the problematic that dominates "Of Our Spiritual Strivings": how to realize "the kingdom of culture" and to end the fragmentation of the self, how to turn the thought of self-realization and freedom into actuality.

James's ethical philosophy would dismiss the dilemma of the Hegelian as well as the African-American intellectual as "pessimistic fatalism, depth within depth of impotence and indifference" (OSH 298), what in "The Dilemma of Determinism" James calls "subjectivism" and "sniveling complaint" (DoD 165, 172). As Ross Posnock argues, James, in his critique of Hegel, attempts to preserve the stress on the concrete and on becoming and to dispense with the absolutism that threatens to swamp the particular into a totalizing metaphysical system. But Posnock concludes rightly that "James neglects the lesson of Hegel's dialectical logic for man in society. In James's quest for the 'immediate experience of life,' a quest that forsakes his pragmatism's suspicion of metaphysics, he jettisons Hegel's emphasis on the power of psychological, cultural, and historical mediations to constitute the individual and enmesh him in a web of dependent relations."[97] If James did not grasp this side of Hegel, he appears also to have missed it in his reading of *Souls*. He read the book the year it was published and sent a copy to his brother Henry. He called *Souls* "a decidedly moving book," but told Henry to "read Chapters VIII and XI for local color, etc."[98]

That Du Bois himself espouses the vitalist program of an elite political leadership indicates the extent to which he, like James, wishes to escape from the "feverish dream" of troubled thought into the "sacred coolness" of doing and right conduct (DoD 174). *Souls,* however, resolutely refuses such an escape. "Of Our Spiritual Strivings" offers a deeply mediated sense of the self, and it is because Du Bois can locate the self in this way that he can also offer a more complex idea of activity than is available in James. Du Bois shares Hegel's sense that genuine self-realization and independence can begin only when the fear experienced in bondage is transformed by labor. "In the master, the bondsman feels self-existence to be something external, an objective fact," and "in fear self-existence is present within himself." But in labor, writes Hegel, "self-existence comes to be felt explicitly as his own proper being, and he attains the consciousness that he himself exists in its own right and on its own account" (*PM* 239). The first chapter of *Souls* moves through these same stages as the struggle of the "prison-house" succeeds the insecurity of the object state and leads to a vision, however threatened and compromised, of an ethical culture in which black self-consciousness finds self-fulfillment.

The differences between *Souls* and Du Bois's turn-of-the-century sociological and political pronouncements are more fully dramatized in the final chapters of *Souls,* particularly in "Of the Sorrow Songs." These chapters expand Du Bois's location of the self and move toward a more complex understanding of the relationship of critical thought and agency than is offered by vitalism or pragmatism. These developments will be examined in the following chapter of this study. The present chapter concludes by comparing Du Bois's account of self-consciousness and the self with that given by James and, more briefly, with Emerson's.

The Unlocated Self: James, Santayana, Emerson

Piotr Hoffmann argues that the paradox of activity and passivity in idealist thought can be resolved by the adoption of naturalist frameworks. For Hoffmann, naturalism includes not only Marx, but also American Prag-matism.[99] But it is arguable whether James actually overcomes this dual-ism in any satisfactory way. In a cogent critique of *The Principles of Psychology*, Bruce Wilshire demonstrates that James's project for a natural scientific psychology founders precisely because he is unable to resolve the dualism of the mental and the physical.[100] What James's psychology *does* provide (in terms of ideas useful to Du Bois's psychology) is a sense of the self plunged into the world, an awareness of the centrality of the body, an idea of the self as it is formed through its being in the eyes of others, and some conceptualization of the self as multiple (what James calls the "material," "social," and "spiritual" selves).[101] However, the transition between experience and action is weakly theorized in James, and the function of consciousness is largely passive and noncreative. San-tayana, on the other hand, offers a more positive evaluation of conscious-ness's reflective function. Given his "Old World" and Catholic back-ground, Santayana is more open to the traditions of European idealist and speculative thought than James, and also more deeply aware of the relation of consciousness to memory and the past—though always tending toward the aristocratic in his assessment of the political implications of these un-derstandings. Marx may not have been taught at Harvard, but Du Bois studied Hegel with Santayana at a time when European idealist philoso-phy dominated the philosophy curriculum.[102] Hegel would have received a fuller and much more sympathetic hearing from Santayana than he received from James in, for instance, the course on ethics that Du Bois took with James during 1888–89. Du Bois seems to have been engaged enough with the texts of modern French and German philosophy to pur-sue private tutorials with Santayana.[103]

Arnold Rampersad has noted that Du Bois "drew on the psychology of his time" for his conceptualization of "double-consciousness":

The term "soul" was used synonymously with consciousness both by ideal-istic psychologists and by the religiously orthodox James McCosh, whose philosophy Du Bois had studied at Fisk. His favorite professor, William James, posited in 1890 that the structure of the brain allowed "one system [to] give rise to one consciousness, and those of another system to another *simultaneously* existing consciousness." The psychologist Oswald Kulpe wrote in 1893 of "the phenomenon of double consciousness or the divided self . . . characterized by the existence of a more or less complete separation of two aggregates of conscious process . . . ofttimes of entirely opposite character."[104]

Ideas of double consciousness, of the divided self shaping itself inside the dialectics of disunity and reintegration, are of course commonplaces of much of "Romantic" and "post-Romantic" or "Modern" thought.[105] But to put the issues this way is not to anchor Du Bois in his historical context but to set his work adrift in a sea of possible contexts, all of which appear as equally true, even if mutually contradictory. Henry Adams's sense of the ubiquity of dualism in turn-of-the-century psychology is worth remembering. Rampersad's choice of points of comparison is to some extent arbitrary and largely uncritical and unanalytic. To point to various notions of consciousness and the divided self without a critical assessment of their differences, and of the ways in which these differences may aid a clearer understanding of Du Bois's work, is to abandon analysis to an uncritical pluralism. To note that both Hegel and James have some idea of a divided self tells us nothing about their respective theories, and even less about Du Bois's relation to these theories. The sketching of a general-ized field of "influence" must be put in the service of a more detailed investigation of Du Bois's critical reading of some of the relevant materials available to him. A closer look at the passage Rampersad quotes from James's *Principles of Psychology* will help elaborate the differences between Du Bois and James.

James's remarks on "simultaneously existing" systems of conscious-ness occur during a discussion of "the mutations of the self," which James divides into "alterations of memory" and "alterations in the present bodily and spiritual selves."[106] The latter he divides into "insane delu-sions," "alternating selves" (or schizophrenia), and "mediumships or pos-sessions" (*PP* 1:375). James has little to say on the first set of "alterations." He offers brief remarks on "losses" of memory or "false recollections" as forms of changes in the self (*PP* 1:373). The other set of "alterations in the present self" he sees as "abnormal" (*PP* 1:375). The discussion of the possibility of simultaneous consciousnesses unfolds during James's consideration of hysteria and the phenomenon of automatic writing in mediumship as particular forms of what he calls collectively "perversions of personality."

> If we speculate on the brain-condition during all these different perversions of personality, we see that it must be supposed capable of successively changing all its modes of action, and abandoning the use for the time being of whole sets of well organized association-paths. In no other way can we explain the loss of memory in passing from one alternating condition to another. And not only this, but we must admit that organized systems of paths can be thrown out of gear with others, so that the processes in one system give rise to one consciousness, and those of another system to an-other *simultaneously* existing consciousness. . . . But just what sort of dissociation the phrase 'thrown out of gear' may stand for, we cannot even conjecture; only I think we ought not to talk of the doubling of the self as if it consisted in the failure to combine on the part of certain systems of *ideas* which usually do so. It is better to talk of *objects* usually combined, and which are now divided between the two 'selves,' in the hysteric and auto-matic cases in question. Each of the selves is due to a system of cerebral paths acting by itself. If the brain acted normally, and the dissociated sys-tems came together again, we should get a new affection of consciousness in the form of a third 'Self' different from the other two, but knowing their objects together, as the result. (*PP* 1:399)

As far as the second set of "abnormal alterations in the present self" is concerned, then, the issues are never stated politically or socially. Ab-normality and normalcy are pitted against each other in a medical para-digm that favors a return to homeostasis as a sign of "health." The politi-cal implications of such a paradigm of the self are disguised by the apparently apolitical vocabulary of organic equilibrium and disequilib-rium.[107] The paradoxical combination of the organic and the mechanical (the metaphor of the "gear") also suggests the extent to which conscious-ness can be reduced in James to passive response to a world of "objects."

The politics of James's medicalization of self-consciousness has no-where been better exposed than in Clive Bush's recent critical commen-tary on James and his legacy in American thought. As Bush notes, "one of the problems with a medical professional model is the notion of social health. Health . . . is itself based on the notion of the self-regulation of an organism tending towards replication and stability. It invites normative and centrist versions of social truth."[108]

This is a point that is elaborated and reinforced by Dorothy Ross's demonstration of the ways in which the adaptive model mind of James's functionalist psychology provided crucial support for social-scientific theory seeking to legitimate the status quo. Functionalist psychology proposed that "the mind was an active purposive agent in its transactions with the environment" and that it "sought always to adjust to a changing social environment": "From the first proposition psychologists and social scientists could construct an active individual, possessor of a unique will and capable of changing the surrounding environment to rational specifications. From the second proposition they could construct a socialized individual, habituated to the social environment and drawn toward the rational consensus adjustment enforced."[109]

As Daniel Robinson notes, the theory of will in *The Principles of Psychology* is an ideomotor theory based on the hypothesis that "all original stimulus-response sequences are involuntary, grounded in the instinctive and reflexive machinery of neonatal life." The stored memory of these is the basis for "ideas of possible action." But such an ideomotor theory "would seem to confine all volitional aspects of consciousness to the realm of possible behaviors." The theory "seems to require that every genuinely voluntary action either be composed of previously stored elements of possible action or be original in a merely statistical sense."[110] It is hardly surprising then that *The Principles of Psychology* psychologizes Darwinian natural selection and self-interest as primary definitions of the self. In the chapter on "consciousness of self," for instance, James argues that "all minds have come . . . to take an intense interest in the bodies to which they are yoked" "by the way of the survival of the fittest," and that altruism is really an outgrowth of self-interest working within "natural selection" (*PP* 1:324).[111]

There is a direct alignment between James's medicalized and Darwinian conceptualization of the self and his theorizations of religious experience and the will to believe. In the chapter on "The Divided Self" in *The Varieties of Religious Experience* (1902), James noted that "to find religion is only one out of many ways of reaching unity; and the process of remedying inner incompleteness and reducing inner discord is a general psychological process, which may take place with any sort of mental material." And he went on to propose that "in all of these instances we have precisely the same psychological form of event,—a firmness, stability, and equilibrium succeeding a period of storm and stress and inconsistency."[112] But neither in *The Varieties of Religious Experience* nor elsewhere does James have much to say about these other, nonreligious modes of crisis management. Health is in James ultimately a matter of faith and a will to faith, not an issue of a creative response to the world. It is faith that ultimately mediates between "the sick soul" and "healthy-mindedness."[113] Religion, however secularized, offers the divided self a reassurance of transcendence through optimistic acquiescence in a future determined by reasonable natural selection. Within this "doctrine of the new American realists," as Santayana observed, "it will suffice to live on, to live forward, in order to see everything as it really is."[114]

Santayana understood better than anyone else that this "doctrine" was symptomatic of a larger American refusal of consciousness in favor of an absolutism of experience: "To deny consciousness is to deny a prerequisite to the obvious, and to leave the obvious standing alone. That is a relief to an overtaxed and self-impeded generation; it seems a blessed simplification. It gets rid of the undemocratic notion that by being very reflective, circumspect, and subtle you might discover something most people do not see."[115] It is not necessary to accept Santayana's implied aristocratic politics in order to appreciate the truth of his critique of an unreflective populism. The elimination of consciousness that leaves "the obvious standing alone" fails to theorize any process of referral between experience and mind. Consciousness is turned from a creative faculty, "what Descartes called thought or cognition,"[116] to a passive faculty, receiving the world as experience. James notes that "in the function of knowing there is a multiplicity to be connected, and Kant brings this multiplicity inside the mind." Against this equation of "Reality" with "Noumenon" James puts "the Multiplicity with the Reality outside" and so hopes to "leave the mind simple" (*PP* 1:363). But this reduces consciousness to a passive experience of objects. Santayana is right in arguing that "when consciousness is disregarded, in the proper sense of cogitation, the name of consciousness can be transferred to the stream of objects immediately present to consciousness; so that consciousness comes to signify the evolving field of appearances unrolled before any person."[117] In light of this remark it is telling that James begins his chapter titled "The Consciousness of Self" with a definition of self as a structure of commodity fetishism. "*In its widest possible sense*," he writes, "*a man's Self is the sum total of all that he CAN call his,* not only his body and his psychic powers, but his clothes and his house, his wife and children [!], his ancestors and friends, his reputation and works, his lands and horses, and yacht and bank-account" (*PP* 1:291).[118]

Despite his radical opposition to Jamesian Pragmatism, Santayana wrote that he remained "a disciple of [James's] earlier unsophisticated self." Santayana meant the James who was "a master in the art of recording or divining the lyric quality of experience as it actually came to him" and not the James who "renounced" his "gift of literary psychology" for a Darwinian abolition of creative consciousness.[119] In defending his own literary psychology in *The Life of Reason,* a study of the "adaptation of fancy and habit to material facts and opportunities," Santayana defined its aims precisely against the Darwinian bias of James's psychology. James, wrote Santayana,

> insisted passionately on the efficacy of consciousness, and invoked Darwinian arguments for its utility—arguments which assumed that consciousness was a material engine absorbing and transmitting energy: so that it was no wonder that presently he doubted whether consciousness existed at all. He suggested a new physics or metaphysics in which the essences given in immediate experience should be deployed and hypostatised into the constituents of nature: but this pictorial cosmology had the disadvantage of abolishing the human imagination, with all the pathos and poetry of its animal status.[120]

For Santayana, by contrast, consciousness was characterized by the creativity of metaphor and the synthetic imagination. Building on the Cartesian concept of cognition, Santayana insisted that consciousness "colors events with memories and facts with emotions, and adds images to words. This synthetic and transitive function of consciousness is a positive fact about it, to be discovered by study, like any other somewhat recondite fact."[121] "Literary psychology, with its dramatic plausibilities, was, [therefore,] indispensable to [Santayana] in composing *The Life of Reason.*"[122]

The literary form that Santayana gave to his epic of human consciousness was, in large part and in keeping with the influence of the *Phenomenology,* one of *Bildungsbiographie.* As one critic noted of the first volume of *The Life of Reason,* "sometimes the description is in terms of the mental history of the individual mind, at other times it refers to the general dawning of knowledge in the collective consciousness of the race."[123] Josiah Royce, the man who taught Santayana Hegel, once remarked that the *Phenomenology* was akin to the contemporary *Bildungsroman.* M. H.

Abrams rightly argues that the work is better conceived of as a fusion of the individual and collective spiritual history of *Bildungsbiographie* with systematic philosophy (*Wissenschaft*) and the contemporary form *Universalgeschichte,* the universal history of humankind emplotted as the correlative to *Bildungsbiographie.*[124] Abrams's description of the "narrative traps" of the *Phenomenology* accurately captures the reader's experience of transitions through multiple perspectives:

> For example, the spirit, the protagonist of the story, maintains no one phenomenal identity, but passes through bewildering metamorphoses in the form of outer objects and phenomenal events, or "shapes of consciousness" [*Gestalten des Bewußtseins*], as well as multiple human personae, or particular "spirits"—"a slow procession and sequence of *Geister,* a gallery of pictures, each of which is endowed with the entire abundance of the *Geist.*" This protagonist, the spirit, is also its own antagonist, who appears in a correlative multitude of altering disguises, so that the one actor plays all the roles in the drama; as Hegel says of one stage of the evolution, "the I is We, and the We is I." . . . For the reader, no less than the author and the subject matter of the *Phenomenology,* is one of the *Geister* in which the spirit continues to manifest itself. The *Bildungsbiographie* thus turns out to have been a concealed first-person narrative—in the fullest possible sense of the term, an autobiography—and one that is told, explicitly, in the mode of a double consciousness. For the spirit at the end of the process narrated in the *Phenomenology* has experienced a rebirth into a new identity [*das neue Dasein*], which "preserves" its former identity as a "sublimated identity" [*dies aufgehobene Dasein*]—it is its "former identity, but new-born out of knowledge."[125]

If the structure of the *Phenomenology* suggested the form of *Bildungsbiographie* to Santayana for his own history of consciousness, it may have done the same for Du Bois. In the intermingling of ontogeny and phylogeny in *Souls,* Du Bois's soul-protagonist also "passes through bewildering metamorphoses in the form of outer objects and phenomenal events, or 'shapes of consciousness'": the strangely moving and cathected journeys across the history-laden geography of the South (chaps. 4 and 7); the failure of the struggle to achieve true freedom after emancipation narrated as a history of political disasters (chaps. 1 and 2); the loss of a newborn son experienced as the dark night of the soul out of which no true religious resurrection comes (chaps. 10 and 11); the "sorrow songs," those ten great African-American spirituals meditatively explored in the final chapter of the book, as the most consummate aesthetic embodiments of the double-consciousness. And just as Hegel's *Geist* appears as "multiple human personae" as well as its own antagonist, so too does the soul in Du Bois: it appears not only in the form of the author, but also as Josie and the other poor blacks who cluster around the school-house in Tennessee (chap. 4); as the son in whom the promise of life remains unfulfilled; as the anonymous singers of the sorrow songs; as Alexander Crummell (chap. 12) and John (chap. 13), historical and fictional representatives of Du Bois's cultural ideals, and of their successes and failures; and as Booker T. Washington (chap. 3), the living antithesis of these ideals. This ebb and flow of dramatic reversals and counterpoints, itself tied to various discourses and genres, shifts as *Souls* ranges from psychology, philosophy, history, and sociology to autobiography, public mourning, fiction, and a socio-anthropology of aesthetics. And at the end of *Souls* Du Bois too will emerge with a transfigured identity, "new-born out of knowledge."[126]

However, what is important is not only the literary form of *The Life of Reason* and *Souls* but the ideas of consciousness that are embodied in the use of this form by Santayana and Du Bois respectively. In assessing the usefulness of the differences between Santayana and James in understanding Du Bois, it is important to remember that what set Santayana to planning his *Life of Reason* was his reading of Hegel's *Phenomenology* just a year before Du Bois studied the *Phenomenology* with him.[127] It is true that the five volumes of *The Life of Reason* were published between 1905 and 1906, sixteen years after Du Bois studied with Santayana. But Santayana's early Catholic and European disaffiliation from the doctrines of the American philosophers who were his teachers and colleagues at Harvard and the high degree of continuity in his aesthetic, ethical, and philosophical ideas throughout his life suggest that many of the attitudes that inform *The Life of Reason* were already well in the process of formation by 1889–90 when he taught Du Bois. The crucial difference between the dramatizations of consciousness in Santayana and Du Bois on the one hand and James and the "new American realists" on the other is dependent on their respective understandings of the relationship of consciousness to history. What the Du Bois who has seen the serfdom of the post-Emancipation South and the slums of Philadelphia shares with the Spanish Catholic Santayana, and with the Hegel of the early parts of the *Phenomenology,* is a deep sense of the negativity of history that cannot be anesthetized by the American belief in history as moral progressivism.

Something of what attracted Santayana to the *Phenomenology* may be gauged from the fact that, as preparation for *The Life of Reason,* subtitled

The Phases of Human Progress, he offered in later years a course on the "philosophy of history." Santayana noted in his autobiography that the title "philosophy of history" attracted large numbers, "perhaps thirty men, many of them Jews."[128] Santayana here registers the obvious appeal of such a course for the historically dispossessed or the culturally marginalized. But despite the subtitle of *The Life of Reason,* Santayana, "from earliest youth," was deeply opposed to the "then popular notion that historical sequence is equivalent to moral progress." This "was precisely the taint that [Santayana] wished to wash out from Hegel's phenomenology of spirit."[129] Despite its debt to Hegel's *Phenomenology, The Life of Reason* did not present linear or dialectical progress. "Rather it was a picture of man's perennial condition, the nature of the processes that go on within him, the sober attempt to hold together in a coherent pattern the forces that would propel him in different and disruptive directions if pursued in isolation, all seen as they appear in human consciousness which reflects these variegated tendencies and in the form in which they were projected in the history of thought. The focus on consciousness is central."[130]

This is a fairly accurate description of Du Bois's historicized dramatization of "the contradiction of double aims" and of the dilemma of choice and activity that it presents to the "black *savant.*" When Du Bois studied with Santayana, *The Life of Reason* may have been only the germ of an idea in Santayana's mind, but his resistance to the harmonization of ethics and natural law in the works of James, Royce, and George Herbert Palmer was already well entrenched.[131] It is unlikely, therefore, that Santayana would have taught the *Phenomenology* without subjecting its historical teleology to some critique. What Santayana would have positively valued then in Hegel's work would have been the same "historical and critical lights that appear by the way" that he praised in later life, and not "the dialectical sophistry" of Hegel ("dialectical sophistry" meaning for Santayana not so much dialectical thought per se but the alignment of dialectics with progressive teleologies).[132]

James, reacting in large part to contemporary American and British appropriations of Hegelian philosophy, offers a less sympathetic and considerably more reductive account of Hegel than the ones suggested in the writings of Santayana and Du Bois. James offers a marvelous satire of "the silly Hegelian all-or-nothing insatiateness," arguing that the outcome of this totalizing urge is a moral "*indifferentism*" (OSH 292, 298). The charge is one of solipsistic nihilism: "the identification of contradictories,

so far from being the self-developing process which Hegel supposes, is,"
for James, "really a self-consuming process, passing from the less to the
more abstract, and terminating either in a laugh at the ultimate nothingness, or in a mood of vertiginous amazement at a meaningless infinity"
(OSH 298). James even gestures toward politicizing his critique. Where
Bonaparte and Philip II are called "monsters," he notes, "an *intellect* . . .
found insatiate enough to declare that all existence must bend the knee to
its requirements" is hailed as "a philosophic prophet" (OSH 272). Posnock points out that the terms of James's philosophic critique are carried
over into an attack on imperialism when, in 1899, James denounces Roo-
sevelt as an "arch abstractionist" and accuses him of practicing what
amounts to a Hegelian absolutist politics that "swamps everything together in one flood of abstract bellicose emotion."[133] The politics of Hegelian logic are similarly parodied when James remarks that "the inmate of
the penitentiary" is "foolish" to ignore "his blessings": he, being a bad
Hegelian, does not realize that the prison walls are unreal, since according
to Hegelian logic "to know a limit is already to be beyond it" (OSH
283–84).

Given the account of American Hegelianism earlier in this chapter,
the accuracy of much of James's satire should be obvious. But in the light
of Du Bois's reading of Hegel, the one-dimensionality of this account
should also be self-evident. What is most glaring in James's critique is
that his own location of the subject, offered as an alternative to Hegel, is
as inadequate and shallow as the straw Hegel that is set up as the target.

In place of the Hegelian process of contradiction and dialectical negation
James offers a vision of a simple and voluntaristic subject comfortable in a
benign and cosmic flow of life around him. Shouting "Either—or!" against
the Hegelian "both-and," James insists that "while many possibilities are
called, the few that are chosen are chosen in all their sudden completeness"
(OSH 269). James is here repeating the same argument that he makes in
"Great Men and Their Environment" and elsewhere, that the mind responds to plurality by retreating, "by *picking out* what to attend to, and ig-
noring everything else" (GM 219). This is the hope of leaving the mind
"simple" (*PP* 1:363). The source of this confidence appears to lie in James's
ability to transform what Hegel sees as "strife" into "that law of sharing
under whose sacred keeping, like a strain of music, like an odor of incense
(as Emerson says), the dance of the atoms goes forward still" (OSH 290).
This is "the great, the sacred law of partaking" in which "elements mutually
contingent are not in conflict so long as they partake of the continua of time,

space, etc." (OSH 289, 294). The logic of this religious consolation, yet another Jamesian flight into "sacred coolness" out of the terror of a "feverish dream" (DoD 174), is identical to the politics of the social essays of the 1890s in which James pronounces that "if the poor and the rich could look at each other" with sympathetic understanding, "how gentle would grow their disputes! What tolerance and good humor, what willingness to live and let live, would come into the world!"[134]

James's invocation of Emerson suggests that his own sacred reverie can be placed alongside other American refusals of dialectical thought. It is precisely through a refusal of dialectical thought that the American tradition that includes James and American Transcendentalism attempts to overcome the dilemma of alterity and to recenter the subject, even though it is this very refusal that underlies the crisis of the location of the subject. James, as heir of Transcendentalism, shares Emerson's anxieties about the dualism of subject and object, and his failure to theorize a process of referral between world and mind leads, as it does in Emerson, toward a transcendence of otherness through a will to power. This includes the definition of freedom against memory and through possession, with James and Emerson both sharing vocabularies of commodification and market economics.[135] In contrast to James or Emerson, Du Bois is able to *locate* the subject in relation to the world, particularly the political and social realms, more concretely and with greater specificity than either James or Emerson, precisely through a literary psychology of a radically *de*centered subject and through his refusal of *non*dialectical transcendence.

In his essay "The Transcendentalist" (1841), Emerson had employed "double consciousness," the very phrase that Du Bois uses, to describe his idealist division between understanding and soul, or understanding and Reason: "The worst feature of this double consciousness is, that the two lives, of the understanding and of the soul, which we lead, really show very little relation to each other; never meet and measure each other; one prevails now, all buzz and din; and the other prevails then, all infinitude and paradise; and, with the progress of life, the two discover no greater disposition to reconcile themselves."[136] Emerson's strategy for overcoming the divided state of the self was to become "nothing" by seeing "all." The moment of this transcendence is the moment in *Nature* (1836) when Emerson becomes "a transparent eyeball":

Standing on the bare ground—my head bathed by the blithe air and uplifted into infinite space—all mean egotism vanishes. I become a transparent eyeball; I am nothing; I see all; the currents of the Universal Being circulate through me; I am part or parcel of God. The name of the nearest friend sounds then foreign and accidental: to be brothers, to be acquaintances, master or servant, is then a trifle and a disturbance. I am the lover of uncontained and immortal beauty. In the wilderness, I find something more dear and connate than in the streets or villages. In the tranquil landscape, and especially in the distant line of the horizon, man beholds somewhat as beautiful as his own nature.[137]

Here the division between the "Me" and the "Not-Me" is overcome through an imperial visionary possession of the "Not-Me" by the "Me." Society is bypassed for an immersion of the "I" into the cosmos. R. Jackson Wilson is right that Emerson had no usable or satisfying concept of society, and so society "could not function for him as a mediating term between man and Nature. Any notion of society as mediation was dropped out of the analysis of experience, and man was lured into solitude in a state of social undress to be summarily ravished of identity."[138]

The dialectics of thought is, in Emerson, reduced to a merely aesthetic dialectics, a dialectics of style only. On the level of thought, dialectics is transcended, and so too otherness is abolished.[139] There is a strangely passive sense of the self within this willed transcendence, since the autonomy of the self is dependent upon a possessive receptivity to the "Not-Me" and not an active or transformative relation. As Stephen Whicher, one of Emerson's most perceptive and sympathetic readers, comments, "Emerson's whole dream of practical power through self-reliance is just that—a dream." It is not "a genuine program of action" but "what he afterwards called it, romance."[140]

Harold Bloom notes that Emerson's famous image of the transparent eyeball is "an image impatient with the possibility of loss, indeed less an image than a promise of perpetual repetition."[141] For Bloom this repetition (or doubling) marks Emerson's transcendence of dialectical thought, something that elicits admiration from Bloom even though, within his Oedipal vision of literary history, such transcendence is ultimately doomed. Without accepting Bloom's vision of the negativity of history as a "family romance,"[142] it is still useful to quote his commentary on Emerson and dialectics because it offers an accurate definition of a *verbal* concept of the self in American thought, and also because Bloom's formulations are more sophisticated than those readings that reductively impose the mechanical trinity of thesis, antithesis, and synthesis on Emerson:[143]

> Emerson, in *Nominalist and Realist*, . . . simply says: "No sentence will hold the whole truth, and the only way in which we can be just, is by giving ourselves the lie. . . ." That is a wilder variety of dialectical thinking than most post-Hegelian Europeans attempt. . . . For, in Emerson, dialectical thought does not fulfill the primary function of fighting off the idealistic drive of an expanding consciousness. . . . Emerson doesn't worry about ending in solipsism; he is only too happy to reach the transparency of solipsism whenever he can. . . . Dialectical thinking in Emerson does not attempt to bring us back to the world of things and of other selves, but only to a world of language, and so its purpose is never to *negate* what is directly before us.[144]

Bloom goes on to add that "from a European perspective, probably, Emersonian thinking is not so much dialectical as it is plain crazy." However, he also notes that Nietzsche at least "understood that Emerson had come to prophesy not a de-centering, as Nietzsche had, and as Derrida and de Man are brilliantly accomplishing, but a peculiarly American *re-centering*."[145] Bloom paraphrases accurately but seems himself to be "only too happy to reach the transparency of solipsism whenever he can." If this is what constitutes an "American *re-centering*" then the issues need to be formulated more critically than in Bloom's account.

Emerson fails to reconcile thought and action in his critical perceptions and so also does not grasp the relationship of self and society in material and historical terms. Quentin Anderson's critique of the "absolutism of the self" in Emerson is useful here (though without Anderson's time-scaling of the differences between Europe and America). For Anderson "[American] Transcendentalism, which Emerson described as 'the Saturnalis or excess of Faith' in individual powers and individual sufficiency, simply attempted to supplant society," whereas "[European] romanticism was laggard, anachronistically involved in the dialectic of self and society."[146] Sacvan Bercovitch moves toward a similar differentiation in his distinction between "Romantic autobiography" and "auto-American-biography." In the latter, specifics of a personal and historical condition are bypassed and society is subsumed into the self; the self becomes synonymous with and a prophecy of the fate of the nation.[147] This "secular incarnation . . . may be construed as the act not of identifying oneself with the fathers, but of catching up all their powers into the self, asserting that there need be no more generations, no more history, but simply the swelling diaspon of the expanding self."[148] Emerson's transcendentalism is, of course, even more radical than is suggested by Anderson and Bercovitch, because, in immersing the self in the "Universal Being," Emerson not only abolishes society and history, but the self itself.[149]

It may appear that in this excursion into the thought of Emerson the argument has drifted away from its primary concern with James and Du Bois. But it is important to establish the links between the ideas of James and Emerson, not in the name of an ahistorical genealogy of ideas, but because James and Emerson *are* brought together in the social criticism of the 1890s in order to defend an exceptionalist dream of American subjectivity against the threats of a new social and industrial order. The confluence takes place in *Essays on Nature and Culture* (1896), a book by Hamilton Wright Mabie, one of the leading genteel cultural critics of the time, in a passage that historian John Higham takes to be an exemplary statement of the spirit of the age:

> Nothing breeds doubt and despair so quickly as a constant and feverish self-consciousness, with inability to look at life and the world apart from our own interests, emotions, and temperament. This is, in an exceptional degree, an epoch of morbid egoism, of exaggerated and excessive self-consciousness; an egoism which does not always breed vanity, but which confirms the tendency to measure everything by its value to us, and to decide every question on the basis of our personal relation to it. It is always unwise to generalize too broadly and freely about contemporary conditions, but there are many facts to bear out the statement that at no previous period in the history of the world have so many men and women been keenly and painfully self-conscious; never a time when it has been so difficult to look at things broadly and objectively. . . .
>
> From this heated atmosphere and from these representations of disease, put forth as reproductions of normal life, we fly to Nature, and are led away from all thought of ourselves. We escape out of individual into universal life; we bathe in the healing waters of an illimitable ocean of vitality. . . . To drain into ourselves the rivulets of power which flow through Nature, art, experience, we must hold ourselves open on all sides; we must empty ourselves of ourselves in order to make room for the truth and power which come to us through knowledge and action; we must lose our abnormal

self-consciousness in rich and free relations with the universal life around us.[150]

The terms appear to be taken straight out of James and Emerson as Mabie moves from recapitulation of the simplistic dichotomy of pessimistic and unhealthy subjectivism and healthy, unself-conscious action in James's "Dilemma of Determinism" to the scene of the "transparent eyeball's" escape from society and history in Emerson's *Nature*. Jackson Wilson's proposition that the period between 1860 and 1920 in America is witness to a crisis of "the transcendental individual" (along with the account of James given in the first chapter of this study) can provide a context for reading Mabie.[151] Jamesian mind-cure and Emersonian transcendence combine to engineer a retreat from the entrapment of the individual in the social complexities of a corporate capitalist industrial society. The political function of speculative thought and introspection is made invisible. The aim is not to think, not even to act (a desire that continues in Frederick Turner's contemporaneous nostalgia for the closing of the frontier), but only to partake of the sacred coolness in cosmic oblivion.

In mapping the plight of the transcendental individual at this time, Wilson argues that, after the Civil War, an idea of individualism that stressed subservience to society and was drawn largely from a southern tradition embodied in the writings of men like George Fitzhugh gradually triumphed in American social thought.[152] Neither the false transcendence of history and society nor a subservience to it is entertained as an option by the African-American Du Bois in a Jim Crow America. Du Bois offers a different model for the transformation of the self in which self-consciousness confronts and resists the claims of society and history—and, after "Of Our Spiritual Strivings," he does so by dramatizing African-American life and his own relationship to it almost entirely in the theater of the South.

But in stressing Du Bois's achievement, it is also important to acknowledge some of the limitations of his account of consciousness. In "Strivings" Du Bois dramatizes black consciousness as it actively struggles within political confinement toward a transformation of the self and its world. Such activity is neither Nietzsche's reactive *ressentiment* nor his active transcendence of history. So the real difference between "Strivings" and "The Talented Tenth" is not one of passivity pitted against activity, but the difference between two different notions of the active life. Both the activity of the contemplative life and action in the outer world are political notions of activity, but they are political in very different ways and in different realms of experience. The full political import of such an understanding can, of course, emerge only if its insights can be articulated with a model through which it is possible to conceive of the transformation of the material world without a utopian negation of the past, and also without an idealist faith in future salvation and transcendence. The contradictions between "The Talented Tenth" and "Strivings" indicate that Du Bois has not, by 1903, discovered the means by which to make this transition or leap. In its faith in the reformative power of education at the hands of an elite, "The Talented Tenth" repeats a liberal progressivism that can only offer an ethical critique of political and economic issues.

The next chapter examines how "Of the Sorrow Songs," the last chapter of *Souls,* extends the historical and social placing of the self begun in the book's first chapter, and how it brings the Hegelian emergence of consciousness toward a more critical self-understanding and a more creative self-realization.

Five

A "Prosody of Those Dark Voices"

The Transformation of Consciousness

In an address titled "The Need for New Ideas and New Aims," Alexander Crummell, founder of the American Negro Academy, urged African-Americans to forget the past in order to successfully enter modernity. According to Crummell, "memory . . . is a passive act of mind . . . the necessary and unavoidable entrance, storage and recurrence of facts and ideas to consciousness. Recollection . . . is the actual seeking of the facts, the endeavor of the mind to bring them back to consciousness. The natural recurrence of the idea or the fact of slavery is that which cannot be faulted. What I object to is the unnecessary recollection of it."[1] Crummell's influence on the early thought of Du Bois has been well documented.[2] The American Negro Academy's program to promote an interest in literature, science, and art among African-Americans as a way of developing a scholarly and refined elite was adopted with little modification by Du Bois in "The Talented Tenth." But Frank Kirkland, in a discussion of the problem of modernity and the past in the thought of African-American intellectuals, demonstrates that if Crummell's refusal of history and of active recollection leads anywhere, it leads to Booker T. Washington, not to Du Bois. Focusing his discussion of Du Bois on "Of the Sorrow Songs," the final chapter of *Souls,* Kirkland argues that

Du Bois firmly ties the present and the future to the past and accepts the creative and critical function of recollection.

> For Du Bois, recollection pries loose from the continuum of past horrors fleeting revelations of enslaved Africans punctuating it with forms of expression that rendered their hopes and expectations of what counted as good and just reflectively transparent albeit constantly unfulfilled. It enables African-Americans to highlight fragments torn from the past and define them as motives for rending "the Veil"; it enables them to conceive themselves as breaking the repetition of unfulfilled expectations regarding what counts as good and just in their future-oriented present. Without it, they fall victim to the "irreverence toward Time" and to the "ignorance of the deeds of men," succumbing to a complacency of mind regarding a past that goes unredeemed and a future-oriented present that lends itself to being forgotten.[3]

Crummell's refusal of recollection ties his programmatics to American exceptionalism, a problematic alignment that persists, so the conclusion to this study argues, in contemporary African-American critical thought. Several forms of this exceptionalism have already been encountered, from the social sciences to the work of Emerson and James. Max Horkheimer's critique of Pragmatism's refusal of the past is pertinent here because it offers a reminder that the failure of active remembering leads to the sacrifice of creative contemplation and truth:

> Pragmatism reflects a society that has no time to remember and meditate. . . . Like science, philosophy itself "becomes not a contemplative survey of existence nor an analysis of what is past and done with, but an outlook upon future possibilities with a reference to attaining the better and averting the worst." Probability or, better, calculability replaces truth, and the historical process that in society tends to make of truth an empty phrase receives its blessing, as it were, from pragmatism, which makes an empty phrase of it in philosophy.[4]

This chapter examines not so much the way in which Du Bois recovers the facts of the past in his encounters with the acts of recollection already embodied in the great African-American spirituals as how these encounters lead Du Bois toward a transformation of consciousness. This transformation is described in part through a shifting ratio of the senses. Between the first and last chapters of *Souls* Du Bois moves from being seen by the "tall newcomer" to *hearing* the voices of the "black folk" as they sing the "sorrow songs." The sense of both distance and connection between the Harvard-trained black New Englander and the southern singers and their songs is captured with precision by the poet Jay Wright:

> All night, again, all night,
> you've been at your
> fledgling history,
> passing through the old songs,
> through the old laments.
> But here, in Harvard Square,
> the prosody of those dark voices
> is your connection.[5]

But at the close of *Souls* Du Bois is not immersed in solitary study at Harvard; instead he is seen as a teacher at Atlanta University, listening to the music rising up through his window. In opening himself up to "those dark voices" that sing the spirituals, Du Bois finds himself and his political program for black leadership in the midst of another challenge. Confronted by the articulate knowledge of suffering embodied in the songs, Du Bois cannot sustain either the detached observational stance of the social scientist or the political narrative of a superior leadership pulling the primitive black masses into modernity. At the very moment that he is forced to acknowledge that the Talented Tenth may have something to learn from those they would lead, Du Bois is also pushed into involvement and response by the interactions of speech and hearing, interactions that undermine the sensuous detachment of the silent, observing scientist. The response is the writing of the book called *Souls of Black Folk,* imaged in its own closing moments as the labors of the "weary traveller" and as the text sent out into the world in the book's "Afterthought." Du Bois's foregrounding of listening, speech, and writing ties consciousness to the production of language and to the relationship of self to others (though here as elsewhere in *Souls* Du Bois never slips into romantic notions of collective identity). Consciousness cannot, therefore, be conceived of reductively as simply a content that can be "expressed" or "represented."[6] The foregrounding of the production of language from within human contact also means that Du Bois's sense of consciousness and its activities is also more social and certainly more creative than the sense of it in either James's or Emerson's accounts. But at the same time it must also be stressed that while Du Bois places his own consciousness in relationship to the folk with accuracy and detail, the destabilizations of the self resulting from the social and historical placing in *Souls* do not lead to a position from which Du Bois can begin to imagine the possibility of political action in collective and populist terms.

Souls's final chapter can be read as an attempt to resolve the "contradiction of double aims" that traps the "black *savant*" and black artist alike. In "Of Our Spiritual Strivings" the black educator is caught in the double awareness that the knowledge needed to educate the black masses is a "twice-told tale" to most whites, and the knowledge needed to educate the whites is "Greek" to most blacks. Similarly, the black artist tries to work in a world where the whites despise the "soul-beauty" of black culture, but he cannot bring himself to abandon that culture in order to "articulate the message of another people" (*SBF* 365–66). These dichotomies are dissolved into greater complexity in "Of the Sorrow Songs."

Du Bois's commentary on the spirituals focuses on the political and sociological meaning of the lyrics, not on the romantic and primitivist notion of some innate "soul-beauty." By adopting Herderian organic history, which makes folk culture central to national identity, as a frame for his commentary, Du Bois suggests that the spirituals and their political content must be made central to any national self-definition in America. The destabilization of white self-confidence also troubles the confidence of the black bourgeoisie because the insistence on the spirituals as an embodiment of historical knowledge also reverses the flow of knowledge and power between the Talented Tenth and the black masses. As in the first chapter of *Souls*, the crisis of the leadership elite is dramatized through a reworking of a key Western philosophic text, this time the allegory of the cave from Plato's *Republic*.[7] The allegorical reworking is the culmination of a series of dramatizations of the crisis of leadership, dramatizations that dominate the last five chapters of *Souls*, and it is a reworking to which Du Bois returns years later in *Dusk of Dawn*.

This chapter examines Du Bois's treatment of this crisis, the ways in which he anchors his descriptions within a dramatization of his own relationship to the spirituals and the revisions of the Platonic allegory, and how the account of consciousness suggested above arises out of these materials. In the final section the account of consciousness and of the relationship of self and the African-American masses in *Souls* is compared to Du Bois's later autobiographical writings. The chapter begins with a brief look at Du Bois's commentary on the political content of the sorrow songs in the context of other nineteenth-century American accounts of folk culture and the spirituals.

The Sorrow Songs: Using an Unusable Past

In his essay "Negro Spirituals" (1867), Thomas Wentworth Higginson, the white commander of the First South Carolina Volunteers, the first African-American regiment in the Civil War, wrote that by the singing of these songs the black soldiers

> could sing themselves, as had their fathers before them, out of the contemplation of their own estate, into the sublime scenery of the Apocalypse. I remember that this minor-keyed pathos used to seem to me almost too sad to dwell upon, while slavery seemed destined to last for generations; but now that their patience has had its perfect work, history cannot afford to lose this portion of its record. There is no parallel instance of an oppressed race thus sustained by the religious sentiment alone. These songs are but the vocal expression of the simplicity of their faith and the sublimity of their long resignation.[8]

Throughout his essay Higginson offers a sympathetic account of African-American music, remarking on the beauty of the songs, suggesting the syncretism of African and non-African materials, and commenting on the social and historical content of the songs. But in the passage quoted above, while he acknowledges that the spirituals speak of suffering, Higginson nostalgically stresses their spiritual transcendence of material conditions, and at the same time—writing with the postwar confidence of the victor—relegates racist oppression to the past. The spirituals must now be preserved as museum artifacts precisely because their existence is in doubt; the history upon which they have fed has now come to an end.

Higginson's "Negro Spirituals" was, along with William F. Allen, Charles P. Ware, and Lucy McKim Garrison's *Slave Songs of the United States* (also 1867),[9] the most notable early commentary on African-American music.[10] Higginson's attitudes are worth noting because they are representative of the analytic and valuative frameworks of studies of folk culture within which—and also against which—Du Bois's own commentary on the spirituals takes shape.

The late nineteenth century saw the full development of a search for a usable past in American folklore studies. These studies sought in folk culture a set of values to place in opposition to the materialism and technological rationality the folklorists took to be the dominant spirit of their age. Though these studies were critical of contemporary social transformations, their organicist nostalgia also confirmed and validated contemporary progressive evolutionism.[11] Du Bois was in touch with these developments not only through his reading of the work of Higginson and other early commentators on African-American music,[12] but also via the work on the Scottish and English folk ballads undertaken by the Harvard communalists. Francis James Child, Francis Barton Gummere, and George Lyman Kitteredge were all active during the years when Du Bois was a student at Harvard, and were working within a tradition of Herderian theorizations of national culture and literature that went back in America at least as far as Emerson and Whitman.[13] The communalists held to a group theory of folk poetry, seeing it as the expression of a collective consciousness generated by a peasant or classless society that predated the atomization of the modern state, and as antithetical to the poetry of high art.

To some extent Du Bois was also invested in the reactionary (and potentially accommodationist) baggage of the organicist primitivism of late-nineteenth-century American studies of folk culture. He insists too often that "like all primitive folk, the slave stood near to Nature's heart" (*SBF* 541), or that black Americans are "the sole oasis of simple faith and reverence in a dusty desert of dollars and smartness" (*SBF* 370).[14] Nor is Du Bois always able to sustain a cultural and linguistic definition of the *Volk,* as Herder did.[15] He slips easily from the spiritual essentialism of his celebrations of the "*latent* genius" (*SBF* 365) and "*innate* love of harmony and beauty" (*SBF* 366) into at least a rhetoric of biological racial definition in his claim that "Negro *blood* has a message for the world" (*SBF* 365; all emphases added).[16] But in the end Du Bois's commentary on the spirituals proves to be more politicized than the studies that precede it. Certainly, like Higginson, Du Bois accepts the songs as a record of the past. But unlike Higginson, he understands the songs not as a dead record but as a living recollection that continues to speak to the disgraces of a present that has by no means severed its links with the antebellum era.

The very opening of "Of the Sorrow Songs" announces a shift in cultural emphasis different from the rest of the book. All the chapters in *Souls* are prefaced by a quotation, usually from a well-known white poet identified by name,[17] and some bars of music taken from the great and anonymous spirituals, with the source of the music always left unidentified (until Du Bois names the songs in the final chapter [*SBF* 539–40]). In the last chapter, bars from "Wrestlin' Jacob, the day is a-breaking" are juxtaposed not to the words of one of the well-known poets but to lyrics taken from one of the spirituals.[18] At the start of the chapter on the spirituals Du Bois writes:

> Little of beauty has America given the world save the rude grandeur God himself stamped on her bosom; the human spirit in this new world has expressed itself in vigor and ingenuity rather than in beauty. And so by fateful chance the Negro folk-song—the rhythmic cry of the slave—stands today not simply as the *sole* American music, but as the *most beautiful expression of human experience born this side of the seas.* It has been neglected, it has been, and is, despised, and above all it has been persistently mistaken and misunderstood; but notwithstanding it still remains as the *singular spiritual heritage of the nation* and the greatest gift of the Negro people. (*SBF* 536–37; emphases added)

The implications of this exaggerated centralization are radical within the frameworks of Herderian organic history that Du Bois employs. For Herder, folk music is a basis for national self-definition. "Music," he argues, "is the first of the fine arts" among "the uncultivated nations," and in its rough and popular folk form it "displays the internal character of the peoples."[19] When the above passage from *Souls* is read in this light, Du Bois appears to be doing more than offering his white reader a glimpse into the heart of black life behind the veil: he is suggesting that black experience, as it is embodied and voiced in the spirituals, must stand at the very center of any American national self-fashioning.

The shifting of black music to the center stage of national culture has two effects. First, by replacing high art's claims for representing the health of national culture with the counterclaims for the higher authenticity of black *folk* art, Du Bois is able to relativize the criteria by which racist evolutionary theories provided alibis for Anglo-Saxon superiority and for the assimilation or exclusion of minority groups:

> The silently growing assumption of this age is that the probation of races is past, and that the backward races of to-day are of proven inefficiency and not worth the saving. Such an assumption is the arrogance of peoples irreverent toward Time and ignorant of the deeds of men. A thousand years ago such an assumption, easily possible, would have made it difficult for the Teuton to prove his right to life. Two thousand years ago such dogmatism, readily welcome, would have scouted the idea of blond races ever leading civilization. So woefully unorganized is sociological knowledge that the meaning of progress,

the meaning of "swift" and "slow" in human doing, and the limits of human perfectibility, are veiled, unanswered sphinxes on the shores of science. Why should Aeschylus have sung two thousand years before Shakespeare was born? Why has civilization flourished in Europe, and flickered, flamed, and died in Africa? So long as the world stands meekly dumb before these questions, shall this nation proclaim its ignorance and unhallowed prejudices by denying freedom of opportunity to those who brought the Sorrow Songs to the Seats of the Mighty? (*SBF* 544–45)

This passage comes near the end of the chapter on the spirituals, itself the last chapter of *Souls*. Du Bois is trying to draw out the broader implications of his discussion of the slave songs. He is himself unable to let go of the idea of civilization and to make the move to *society,* though he *has* reached the middle ground of a new and broader definition of culture. From this vantage point, and against the grain of his own dichotomization of primitive and civilized, he is at least able to grope his way to the idea that once the criterion for judging the "progress" or "backwardness" of a people is shifted from technological or imperial achievement to poetry, the hierarchy between "civilized" and "primitive" becomes unstable.[20] The shift is from the spatio-temporal distancing of the knower and the known in conventional sociological and anthropological discourse toward what Johannes Fabian calls "coevalness" or "contemporality."[21]

It is on this basis that Du Bois asks admittance for "those who brought the Sorrow Songs to the Seats of the Mighty." But if this, like the suppression of economic and political causality from the historical process in the passage, is another example of Du Bois's ethical idealism, the next paragraph of *Souls* asks abruptly, "Your country? How came it yours?" continuing, "Before the Pilgrims landed we were here" (*SBF* 545). The asking of this question and Du Bois's reply, coming as they do in the midst of his summing-up of the meaning of the slave songs, suggest that this meaning is inseparable from the history of slavery and conquest upon which the nation is built. This is the second effect of Du Bois's centralization of black music within the national culture. The "message" of the songs, "veiled and half articulate" and buried "beneath conventional theology" (*SBF* 541), turns out to be a revelation of their social and historical content:

These songs are the articulate message of the slave to the world. They tell us in these eager days that life was joyous to the black slave, careless and happy. I can easily believe this of some, of many. But not all the past

South, though it rose from the dead, can gainsay the heart-touching witness of these songs. They are the music of an unhappy people, of the children of disappointment; they tell of death and suffering and unvoiced longing toward a truer world, of misty wanderings and hidden ways. (*SBF* 538)

Du Bois's sentiments here recall those of Frederick Douglass before him, who was "utterly astonished" upon his arrival in the free North "to find persons who could speak of the singing, among slaves, as evidence of their contentment and happiness."[22] Douglass's discussion of the slave songs in his first autobiography in fact prefigures something of Du Bois's drift away from metaphysics and social science to a recognition of poetry as a different and powerful mode of understanding in *Souls*. Recalling the days when he had escaped to the North and was asked by the abolitionists to write his slave narrative, Douglass remembered that one leading abolitionist told him, "Give us the facts, we will take care of the philosophy."[23] Douglass gave more than facts and something other than philosophizing in his first narrative when he asserted his conviction that "the mere hearing" of the slave songs "would do more to impress some minds with the horrible character of slavery, than the reading of whole volumes of philosophy on the subject could."[24]

If the moving romanticism of Du Bois's writing on the sorrow songs, like his tempting language of secrecy and revelation, promises the white reader an encounter with the exotic, the subtlety with which Du Bois nudges the organicism into political history at key moments checks the predatorism of the cultural tourist and cuts short that same nostalgic flight that sentimentally primitivized the North American Indians in the midst of genocide. The progress of the sympathetic imagination in *Souls* is not without its hazards. It cannot rest on the leisurely self-confidence that seems to underlie James's expansive openness to the "laboring classes." It must be aware of its own complicity in the condition of the Other. What the white American reader finds behind the veil of the color line is, finally, a mirror. But if Du Bois destabilizes the position of the reader in the final chapter of *Souls*, his account of the songs leads to a simultaneous problematization of the assumption of privileged cultural access implicit in his own position as interpretive mediator between the songs and the reader. Within the organic history of the final chapter of *Souls*, Du Bois's dramatization of his own relationship to black culture is as important as his displacements of the white reader.

Voices from the Caverns and the Guardians of the Folk

To recall Jay Wright's poem on Du Bois, "the prosody of those dark voices" that sing the "old songs" *is* Du Bois's "connection" to his "fledgling history," but it is a connection that cannot be taken for granted. Du Bois's dramatization of his relationship to the songs is marked by a representational hesitancy that is symptomatic of the fact that his own understanding of the songs is itself partly grounded in sympathetic imagination (though different in kind from the white reader's). Du Bois's commentary is not based in an *exactly* shared history between his post-Emancipation northern self and the roots of the songs in a long history of southern violence and slavery, and therefore does not have the legitimation of absolute commonality. These differences, determined by factors of geography, class, and education, emerge only very allusively and elliptically in the final chapter of *Souls* because Du Bois appears to be caught between wanting, on the one hand, to disguise them in order to strengthen the political challenge to the white reader, and on the other hand, to acknowledge them within a nondogmatic art. A more immediate and concrete sense of the differences and the strategic hesitancies can be given by comparing Du Bois's accounts of his encounters with the "sorrow songs" in the chapter with his quite different accounts of these same encounters in his later autobiographical writings and, in one instance, also in an earlier part of *Souls*.[25]

"Of the Sorrow Songs" opens with Du Bois's earliest recollection of hearing the spirituals and describes the powerful sense of recognition experienced by the young Du Bois:

> Ever since I was a child these songs have stirred me strangely. They came out of the South unknown to me, one by one, and yet at once I knew them as of me and of mine. Then in after years when I came to Nashville I saw the great temple builded of these songs towering over the pale city. To me Jubilee Hall seemed ever made of the songs themselves, and its bricks were red with the blood and dust of toil. Out of them rose for me morning, noon and night, bursts of wonderful melody, full of the voices of my brothers and sisters, full of the voices of the past. (*SBF* 536)

Although there is here just sense enough of the distance and difference between North and South, as the shadow of strangeness and the "unknown" momentarily passes across the transparent meaning of the songs, the overwhelming sense of the passage is one of an intensely felt cultural identity experienced as an almost familial bond. When Du Bois returns to the memories of his earliest encounters with the spirituals at the end of his life, there is a much more inflected sense of cultural difference in his account. He remembers in his *Autobiography* (1968) that he "heard the Negro folksong first in Great Barrington, sung by the Hampton Singers. But that was *second-hand, sung by youth who never knew slavery*" (*A* 120, emphasis added). The songs were, then, an importation into the New England (and predominantly white) culture of Du Bois's hometown. And an importation weakened for Du Bois by divorce from its historic and geographic roots, a divorce that reflects the situation of Du Bois as listener as much as that of the singers. Du Bois goes on to describe how he "heard the Negro songs by those who made them and in the land of their American birth" (*A* 120) when he first went South as an undergraduate and taught school in rural Tennessee. There he attended his first revival meeting. As Du Bois details his sense of curiosity and excitement at the novelty of the situation, the sense is very much that of an ethnographic participant-observer reporting from the field. After the "quiet and sub-dued" church meetings in Berkshire, Du Bois finds himself in the midst of "a pythian madness, a demoniac possession" that reveals "a scene of human passion such as I had never conceived before" (*A* 120). This same passage occurs in chapter 10 of *Souls* (*SBF* 493) and provides a point of contrast within *Souls* for the descriptions that follow it in the book's final chapter. The feelings of the young Du Bois tend toward reproducing the exoticism that led the white middle-class reading public to seek out works that revealed how the other half lived at the turn of the century, but he registers the deeply disturbing effects of the passionate scene with a force that moves beyond exoticism.

Du Bois's recourse to images of the irrational aligns him with his mentor Crummell's dislike for black folk culture. For Crummell, African-American folk and proletarian culture had to be purged of its rudeness and heathen retentions. When most African-Americans were Baptists or Methodists, Crummell was an Episcopalian. The Episcopal church was associated with the black bourgeoisie and the upper classes.

> The church had dignified rituals and was far removed from the plantation culture that he identified with barbarism, depravity, and weakness. Episco-palianism, with its principles of "submission to authority, respect for rules, quietness and order," was congenial to Crummell's conservative tempera-

ment. The American Episcopal church brought him into contact with Anglicanism and nurtured his sense of participating in the literary and intellectual traditions of England. The Anglican music and architecture appealed to him, as did the Anglican liturgy. His religious sentiments were closely linked to aesthetic preferences that were uncommon among black Americans.[26]

Du Bois's own self-fashioning in his first description in *Souls* of his earliest encounter with plantation culture is very much in the image of Crummell's Episcopalianism. But in Du Bois's account, what the young Du Bois sees as irrational is balanced by a mature evaluation of the cultural achievement of the spirituals. Out of this contrast Du Bois can generate gentle self-mockery. As he notes with restrained humor, "To be sure, we in Berkshire were not perhaps as stiff and formal as they in Suffolk of olden time; yet we were very quiet and subdued, and I know not what would have happened those clear Sabbath mornings had some one punctuated the sermon with a wild scream, or interrupted the long prayer with a loud Amen!" (*SBF* 493).[27]

Du Bois's recollections of an African song that had been handed down in his own family and his tracing of the genealogy of the song provide another useful point of comparison between *Souls* and later autobiographical writings. In the middle part of the final chapter of *Souls* he writes:

> My grandfather's grandmother was seized by an evil Dutch trader two centuries ago; and coming to the valleys of the Hudson and Housatonic, black, little, and lithe, she shivered and shrank in the harsh north winds, looked longingly at the hills, and often crooned a heathen melody to the child between her knees, thus:
>
>   Do bana coba, gene me, gene me!
>   Do bana coba, gene me, gene me!
>   Ben d' nuli, nuli, nuli, nuli, ben d' le.
>
> The child sang it to his children and they to their children's children, and so two hundred years it has travelled down to us and we sing it to our children, *knowing as little as our fathers what its words may mean, but knowing well the meaning of its music.* (*SBF* 538, emphasis added)[28]

Again, the overriding sense here is of a transcendent bond. But at the same time the ambivalent wavering between not knowing the meaning of the words to the song (the lyrics appear to be from no known African language)[29] and a fundamental understanding of the meaning of the music hints at the fact that although the historical continuity of black culture in America is hardly in doubt, it is nevertheless fractured enough to require a sympathetic leap.

Du Bois's later autobiographical writing presents a less transcendent vision. In *Dusk of Dawn* (1940) Du Bois writes that he is, in fact, not sure if his great-great-grandmother was born in Africa or in America and does not know where she learned the song (*DD* 636–37). This acknowledgment comes at the close of a long section of the autobiography in which Du Bois traces his very mixed and very complicated family genealogy back to its French Huguenot, Dutch, African, and even Native American roots (*DD* 630–37). The song sung by his great-great-grandmother becomes then his "only one direct cultural connection" with Africa (*DD* 636). After quoting the passage on the African song from *Souls* at length, Du Bois adds that "living with my mother's people I absorbed their culture patterns and these were not African so much as Dutch and New England" (*DD* 638). The "African racial feeling was then purely a matter of . . . later learning and reaction," of Du Bois's "recoil from the assumptions of the whites" and his "experience in the South at Fisk," though "it was none the less real and a large determinant of my life and character" (*DD* 638).

The passages from the final chapter of *Souls* quoted above signal certain hesitancies, but these hesitancies are more than securely contained within Du Bois's impassioned acceptance of a common history of oppression. However, Du Bois's dramatization of his own relationship to the songs in *Souls* is more subtle than this. It manages finally to suggest the extent of both separation and identity and so resists the alibi of an essentialized idea of *communitas*. The scene that closes *Souls,* the climax of the final chapter, presents a tableau in which Du Bois's relationship to the songs is represented with greater self-reflexivity and complexity:

> If somewhere in this whirl and chaos of things there dwells Eternal Good, pitiful yet masterful, then anon in His good time America shall rend the Veil and the prisoned shall go free. Free, free as the sunshine trickling down the morning into these high windows of mine, free as yonder fresh young voices welling up from the caverns of brick and mortar below—swelling with song, instinct with life, tremulous treble and darkening bass. My children, my little children, are singing to the sunshine, and thus they sing:
>
> Let us cheer the weary traveller,
> Cheer the weary traveller,

Let us cheer the weary traveller,
Along the heavenly way
And the traveller girds himself, and sets his face toward the Morning, and
goes his way. (*SBF* 545–46)

This curious scene is a careful revision of both Du Bois's own description of his hearing the spirituals at Nashville's Jubilee Hall that opens the chapter on the spirituals and of Plato's well-known allegory of the cave in his *Republic,* with Du Bois as Plato's enlightened man caught between the light of the sun and the darkness of the caverns. This double revision embodies a plural intentionality on Du Bois's part. Du Bois tries to dramatize simultaneously the independence and artistic integrity of the collective voice that sings through the songs and his own relationship to this voice as a bourgeois intellectual. Such a representational strategy comes as no surprise within the framework of organic history and, to some extent, Du Bois is inevitably trapped within this historical model's paradox of desired immersion and identity and the distance of interpretive authority. Nevertheless, to ignore Du Bois's own openness to displacement by the songs would be to misrepresent his writing.

Du Bois's treatment of the spirituals seems at first to be marked by a pronounced sense of cultural elitism or hierarchization that reinforces pastoral nostalgias. Nashville's Jubilee Hall, "towering over the pale city" at the opening of the chapter on the spirituals, has by the end become the academic tower of Atlanta University, where Du Bois taught from 1897 to 1910, and where he sits listening to the songs drifting up from below through the "high windows" of the university building.[30] Where the young Du Bois, an undergraduate in his late teens, had been overwhelmed by his first hearing of the songs and an initial sense of community promised by "the voices of my *brothers and sisters,*" the older professor sits alone in his office, a little more removed and reflective in his attention to the singing of "my *children,* my little children." This "older" Du Bois was, in fact, only in his mid-thirties at the time he wrote the last chapter of *Souls,*[31] but the kindly (and grating) paternalism of the closing scene belies this fact and offers the reader a self-image that artificially stresses a greater sense of age and therefore a more pronounced sense of distanced contemplation.

There is, then, submerged beneath the sociological and aesthetic meditations on black music in the final chapter, an authorial self-fashioning and an autobiographical narrative of Du Bois's development from infancy (when the African song is first heard) to youthful immersion (in Tennessee) and to mature self-consciousness (at Atlanta University). This narrative is told as an ongoing dialectical engagement between Du Bois and the "sorrow songs" that unfolds primarily across the historically charged landscape of the South, from Nashville, Tennessee, to Atlanta, Georgia. Du Bois's commentary on the songs is itself a product of the older self and represents a discourse of a different, more self-conscious, nature than the songs themselves, the organicism of the latter being, within Du Bois's Herderian communalism, by definition unself-reflexive. Du Bois's particular interpretive access to the content at the heart of the songs is therefore guaranteed not simply by his fraternal or paternal bonds with the culture and history of the songs but also by those perspectives available to him as a trained academic, intellectual, and writer. The unveiling of the songs seems to be dependent upon their mediation by and incorporation into the different order of reflection and art represented by Du Bois's writing. This seems to shift the axis of articulation away from the songs themselves toward Du Bois's written synthesizing.[32]

This self-fashioning on Du Bois's part pushes his dramatization of his relationship to the songs toward what James Clifford has described as the allegorical structure of "salvage, or redemptive, ethnography," where "the recorder and interpreter . . . is custodian of an essence, unimpeachable witness to an authenticity." As Clifford accurately notes, this structure "is appropriately located within a long Western tradition of pastoral."[33] Within such an allegoric narrative, "the self, cut loose from viable collective ties, is an identity in search of wholeness, having internalized loss and embarked on an endless search for authenticity. Wholeness by definition becomes a thing of the past (rural, primitive, childlike) accessible only as a fiction, grasped from a stance of incomplete involvement."[34] Clifford is describing what Frederic Jameson, in a discussion of historicism, has called "historical and cultural aestheticism," a stance in which "*historicity* as such is manifested by means of the contact between the historian's mind in the present and a given synchronic cultural complex from the past."[35]

Nostalgic contemplation is never fully abandoned in Du Bois's commentary, and Clifford's ethnographic commentary does help describe the radical desire that is the content of Du Bois's or Higginson's critical nostalgia. Higginson's account of the spirituals offers a clearer example than *Souls* of what Clifford means by "salvage ethnography." Calling himself "a faithful student of the Scottish ballads," Higginson describes hearing and writing down the songs around the campfire as a gathering "on their own soil [of] these strange plants, which I had before seen as in museums alone": "Writing down in the darkness, as I best could,—perhaps with my hand in the safe covert of my pocket,—the words of the song, I have afterwards carried it to my tent, like some captured bird or insect, and then, after examination, put it by."[36] But in Du Bois the sense of salvage ethnography does consistently give way. For one thing, Du Bois's account of the spirituals lays stress not on the recuperation of an essentialized wholeness from the past, but instead on an art that is responsive to historical change. Submerged in the commentary of the final chapter of *Souls* is a narrative of the gradual transformation of the slave songs. This narrative traces the development of the songs from their original African forms, first through their early American form in the music encountered by the young Du Bois in the rural South and by whites during the Civil War at Port Royal in "the Sea Islands of the Carolinas" (*SBF* 537), then through the subsequent and greater hybridization of elements "both Negro and Caucasian" (*SBF* 540), to the contemporary form of the songs heard in Atlanta at the end. It is true that for Du Bois the early forms of the songs are somehow more authentic than some of the later hybridizations. But his stress on the political content of the songs is also dependent on an acceptance of the transformation of the songs in response to a changing political history. In keeping with the *Bildungsbiographie* structure of *Souls,* the history of the songs runs alongside an autobiographical narrative in which the stages of personal development are in fact linked to specific encounters with the slave songs. To describe these moments of contact as "historical and cultural aestheticism" is to give only half the truth, because Du Bois is also responsive to the songs and can move from detachment to an openness to self-transformation.

The moment of response and change is most fully dramatized in Du Bois's revision of the opening scene of the "Sorrow Song" chapter (the encounter with the songs at Nashville) found at the chapter's end (with Du Bois hearing the songs at Atlanta). This revision unfolds within a rewriting of Plato's allegory of the cave and must be read through this other revision.

Plato's allegory is designed "to illustrate the degrees in which our nature may be enlightened or unenlightened."[37] In a cave there are prisoners, chained and immobile since birth. Behind them there is a wall, and behind that a fire. Men carrying various objects pass between the wall and the fire. As these objects extend above the height of the wall, they cast shadows on the cave wall in front of the prisoners. The prisoners know nothing of reality other than these shadows, which they take to be reality. One prisoner becomes free and finds true enlightenment when he leaves the cave and walks out into the sunshine. The allegory is concerned with the dilemma facing this one individual, who is fully aware of a higher, transcendent reality but derided as a fool and rejected by the other unenlightened prisoners. Du Bois's location within the academic tower at the end of *Souls* appears at first simply to reproduce this dilemma. He is caught between, on the one hand, the vision of freedom promised by the transcendental "Eternal Good" and the "free . . . sunshine trickling down the morning into these high windows," and on the other hand the "prisoned" blacks and the "voices welling up . . . from the caverns of brick and mortar below." Du Bois's implied self-identification with Alexander Crummell, and the theories of education and progress that undergird that identification, suggests the obvious appropriateness of the allusion to the Platonic parable. Plato too is advocating the leadership of a cultured elite as a guarantee of "the welfare of the commonwealth."[38] The allegory suggests that the guardians of the Republic must give up the contemplation of higher ideals and triumph over individualism by returning to the cave to help the prisoners. The thinker who leaves the cave *is* the enlightened one, who then takes the others toward enlightenment.[39]

However, at *Atlanta* not only are the voices from below singing "to the sunshine" and urging on the "weary traveller" in his quest (where in Plato the prisoners have no conception of freedom), the voices from the caverns are themselves "instinct with life" and as "free" as the sunshine that represents higher enlightenment. If the University of Atlanta is supposed to represent the institutional embodiment of the program of educational reform outlined in "The Talented Tenth," then it is also important to note that Du Bois spends some time in "Of the Sorrow Songs" explaining that Fisk University, where he himself had studied, was founded on $150,000 raised by the Fisk Singers on their national and international tour begun in 1871 (*SBF* 266–67). And if Plato's cave represents the senses and his outside an ideal enlightenment in an allegory that is concerned with justice and morality rather than optics,[40] then it is also worth noting that it is the sensuous interaction of the singing voices and Du Bois's hearing that brings Du Bois to new understanding. There is here, in fact, also a reversal of the genealogy that marks the transmission across the generations of the African song handed down in Du Bois's family. Whereas that song was sung by the parents of each generation to their children, but with its meaning obscure to the "children" and their "fathers" alike, here the children sing to their father, who struggles to read the meaning of their songs. The evocation of the rending of the Veil at Christ's crucifixion most clearly indicates Du Bois's relation to the singers of the song. The Christian allegory is superimposed on the Platonic allegory. Du Bois occupies the same structural position in relation to the "prisoned" as the Roman centurion to Christ in St. Matthew's account of the crucifixion. He, like the centurion, experiences a moment of visionary perception.

Du Bois is not trapped between enlightenment and ignorance but poised between different forms of insight and understanding. "Beneath the conventional theology and unmeaning rhapsody" of the songs there is a hard and bitter knowledge of historical experience that challenges the transcendental cultural universalism championed in the progressive reformism of "The Talented Tenth." The slaves who created the spirituals and the voices that sing at the end of *Souls* have, unlike Plato's prisoners, suffered actual, not metaphorical, enslavement and oppression, and their music vocalizes a poetry of experiential truths, not unwitting falsehood. The poised tableau at the end of *Souls,* then, is not so much an *allegorical* rewriting of Plato as a momentary breaking of the allegorical spell, because, in the midst of Du Bois's "historical and cultural aestheticism," it manages to acknowledge that the "prisoned" may be more than just symbols in support of an idealist political program. In opening himself up in sympathetic understanding to "the souls of black folk," Du Bois, like his projected white reader, finds a mirror behind the veil. The image at the close of *Souls* of the "weary traveller" who "girds himself" and "goes his way," cheered on by his "children," is not an image of a false collectivity parasitically recuperated into the promise of messianic leadership but a genuinely tragic and political vision that returns Du Bois for strength to the grounds of solitude.

The moment in which the voices of the prisoners singing to the sunshine urges the traveler to renew his journey recasts the moment in the first chapter of *Souls* in which "the shades of the prison-house closed round about us all: walls strait and stubborn to the whitest, but relentlessly narrow, tall and unscalable to sons of night who must plod darkly on in resignation, or beat unavailing palms against the stone, or steadily, half hopelessly, watch the streak of blue above" (*SBF* 364). It is this earlier moment that introduces the famous passages on the "two-ness" of the African-American and on the "contradiction of double aims" experienced by the black middle class. In the final chapter the trope of the sunshine and the prisoners reintroduces the crisis of the "black *savant*" and "black artist," but, as the next section argues, also moves it toward different conclusions.

The Platonic revisions through which Du Bois dramatizes an ambivalence of cultural authority between the songs and himself as interpreter come as the conclusion to a series of chapters that are meditations on the role of religious leadership among African-Americans. After the survey in the first nine chapters of the political, economic, and educational issues that affect black American life, the last five chapters of *Souls* are concerned primarily with religious culture—particularly with the political and social function of the religious leader and with the jeremiad of the preacher-prophet as the dominant model of leadership rhetoric available to African-Americans. As in "Of the Sorrow Songs," Du Bois manages to establish both a historical and a contemporary understanding of African-American religious culture by combining anthropological and sociopolitical commentaries. However, acute assessments of the centrality of religion in African-American culture are juxtaposed to dramatizations of the fracture of faith. It is this fracture that underlies Du Bois's distinction between the political and historical content of the songs and the apparently "conventional theology" of their lyrics. The redemptive biblical typologies of religious prophecy are repeatedly qualified by personal experiences of loss and violence. Du Bois inverts the prophetic models of ascent and uplift. It is within the space cleared by these qualifications that Du Bois's model of his own insight and understanding can be properly described.

The terms in which Du Bois describes himself listening to the sorrow songs at the close of *Souls* refigure the description of Alexander Crummell's growth into enlightenment and leadership earlier in the book. In the twelfth chapter Du Bois argues that the education of Crummell at the hands of white abolitionists proved to be a process of mutual transformation. The white schoolboys discovered a realm "of thought and longing beneath one black skin, of which they had not dreamed before. And to the lonely boy came a new dawn of sympathy and inspiration" (*SBF* 514). It is through the sympathy awakened by education that Crummell is able to overcome his hatred for the white world and to see for the first time "the sun-swept road that ran 'twixt heaven and earth" (*SBF* 514), a vision of higher cultural ideals offered by the white world. But it is also because of this newly inspired sympathy that Crummell himself can hear "the bronzed hosts of a nation calling" and "the hateful clank of their

chains" from "behind the forests," and can respond with a career of "protest" and "prophecy" as "a priest—a seer to lead the uncalled out of the
house of bondage" (*SBF* 514). Educational training and the revelation of
higher goals necessarily entail a distancing from the repeated cycles of
despair in the dark forest, and while sympathy promises a return to roots,
it is a return in which both identity and difference must be acknowledged.
Crummell answers the call of his fellow blacks, but as the priestly head
of "the headless host" (*SBF* 514).

The scene where Du Bois listens to the spirituals "welling up from
the caverns of brick and mortar below" as the "free . . . sunshine," the
enlightening embodiment of the "Eternal Good," trickles through the
"high windows" (*SBF* 545–46) refigures the dialectic of Crummell's sympathetic imagination moving between the "sun-swept road" and the "forest." Just as Crummell "girded himself to walk down the world" (*SBF*
514), so too Du Bois as the "weary traveller" at the very end of the book
"girds himself, and sets his face toward the Morning, and goes his way"
(*SBF* 546). Du Bois's placing of this allusive self-fashioning at the end of
Souls seems at first to suggest that the autobiographical narrative of the
book should be read as a teleological ascent. There is a way in which the
book's double ontogenetic and phylogenetic narrative seems to suggest an
optimistic reading as the most appropriate one for the book. The narrative
seems, after all, to move from racist alienation to personal enlightenment,
from continued social discrimination and exclusion to the fulfillment of
educational ideals at the universities of Fisk and Atlanta as the "advanced
guard" toils "slowly, heavily, doggedly" up the "mountain path to Ca-
naan" (*SBF* 367). This would align *Souls* with the redemptive biblical
typologies and rhetoric of the "American Jeremiad" inherited by the slave
narratives and with the uplift message of Booker T. Washington's autobiography, *Up from Slavery* (1901), a contemporary version of the slave
narrative combined with the Horatio Alger myth.[41] But, as Arnold Rampersad has suggested, *Souls* can also be read as an inverted slave narrative
that reverses the plot of enlightenment and attained freedom.[42] From this
perspective, the narrative of *Souls* moves from Emancipation to the slave
songs and their reassertion of continued oppression and violence, from a
prelapsarian infancy to a repeated return to the condition of the divided
self.

There is little in the actual chapter on Crummell to suggest that Du
Bois is in any way critical of or ambivalent about Crummell's political and
cultural programs. However, he carefully places the unqualified eulogy to

Crummell between the threnody for the loss of his infant son in chapter 11 and the fictionalized dramatization of the negation of his own adult ideals by racist violence and prejudice in chapter 13. The closing moments of "Of the Coming of John" (chapter 13), where John faces the sea as the lynch mob thunders toward him, refer the reader back to the closing moments of the chapter on Crummell, where, on the morning before his death and at the end of a life of solitary struggle and hardship, Crummell sits "gazing toward the sea" (*SBF* 520). If the tragic end of "Of the Coming of John" cuts short the visionary projections of the eulogy for Crummell, these projected trajectories are already threatened by the Gothic omen of the death of the "first-born" in the previous chapter.

"Of the Passing of the First-Born" opens with biblical resonance: "Unto you a child is born" (*SBF* 506). Du Bois sees "the strength of my own arm stretched onward through the ages through the newer strength" of the child's, and hears in "the baby voice" of his son "the voice of the Prophet that was to rise within the Veil." But the "hot winds" that roll into Atlanta from the "fetid Gulf" strangle this redemptive hope almost at birth (*SBF* 508). This sense of loss and personal grief is, however, mixed with a sense of relief. "All that day and all that night there sat an awful gladness in my heart,—nay, blame me not if I see the world thus darkly through the Veil,—and my soul whispers ever to me, saying, 'Not dead, not dead, but escaped; not bond, but free.' No bitter meanness now shall sicken his baby heart till it die a living death, no taunt shall madden his happy boyhood. Fool that I was to think or wish that this little soul should grow choked and deformed within the Veil!" (*SBF* 510). This is perhaps Du Bois's most ironic and bitter condemnation of American racism. As Arnold Rampersad notes, "Of the Passing of the First-Born" is, in certain respects, "an almost classical elegy, in impassioned yet formal language. But it is one in which the central mourner, as a black, can find no consolation. Thus it is in truth anti-Christian, a bitter parody of the Christian elegy."[43] John, the educated black hero who returns to the South to teach in the thirteenth chapter of *Souls,* is the embodiment of what Du Bois's infant son could have become. But John's death at the hands of a lynch mob also represents the life that the son has escaped through his untimely death. Du Bois only reinforces the anticonsolatory thrust of his mourning by placing its antireligious reversals after the chapter titled "On the Faith of the Fathers."

For the most part, Du Bois keeps personal life out of *Souls.* The autobiographical narrative is always woven along the edges of the cultural and political commentaries of the book. It reinforces or counterpoints, but is never the primary or sole site of exploration. Those denunciations of racism that draw upon autobiographical experience penetrate because their articulation is always so overly restrained. This is precisely why the impassioned grief of the elegy for the dead son is so unexpected and overwhelming. Suddenly, a personal loss that has little to do with the history or politics of racism occupies center stage, and stoic reticence gives way to melodramatic public mourning. Throughout *Souls* Du Bois has struggled to build a refuge of reason against both racism and the irrationality of "the vein of vague superstition" among African-Americans themselves. But the death of his son seems to unhouse the faith in rationality and providence alike, even if only for a moment. It is as if the seat of arbitrary violence and irrationality is discovered at the very heart of nature itself.

Comparison with Adams is again useful. Du Bois was thirty-one years old when his son died of dysentery. Adams was thirty-two when his sister died of a tetanus infection:

> The last lesson—the sum and term of education—began then. He had passed through thirty years of rather varied experience without having once felt the shell of custom broken. He had never seen Nature—only her surface—the sugar-coating that she shows to youth. Flung suddenly in his face, with the harsh brutality of chance, the terror of the blow stayed by him thenceforth for life. . . . He found his sister, a woman of forty, as gay and brilliant in the terrors of lockjaw as she had been in the careless fun of 1859, lying in bed in consequence of a miserable cab-accident that had bruised her foot. Hour by hour the muscles grew rigid, while the mind remained bright, until after ten days of fiendish torture she died in convulsions. (*EHA* 287)

Adams's reaction to death is more immediately violent than Du Bois's. Du Bois's deep and paradoxical sense of loss and relief is contained within a highly formalized language that parodies Christian elegy by using the very language of messianic hopes and salvation. Adams's language reveals both the horror of the drop into chaos and the inability of language to hold that experience:

> Impressions like these are not reasoned or catalogued in the mind; they are felt as part of violent emotion; and the mind that feels them is different from the one which reasons; it is thought of a different power and of a different person. . . . For the first time, the stage-scenery of the senses

collapsed; the human mind felt stripped naked, vibrating in a void of shape-less energies, with resistless mass, colliding, crushing, wasting, and destroy-ing what these same energies had created and labored from eternity to perfect. . . . For pure blasphemy, it made pure atheism a comfort. God might be, as the Church said, a Substance, but He could not be a Person. (*EHA* 288–89)

In the end, the literary imagination of *Souls* is not able to propose a model of political leadership that will answer the doubts of the book's deeply negative historical consciousness. The late nineteenth century and the early twentieth century are, for the African-American, "a time of intense ethical ferment, of religious heart-searching and intellectual un-rest." Such a time of radical doubt "must give rise to double worlds and double ideals, and tempt the mind to pretence or to revolt, to hypocrisy or to radicalism" (*SBF* 502), a division that Du Bois charts along the North-South axis (*SBF* 503). But if the polarization of dangerous "anar-chy" (*SBF* 504) and "hypocritical compromise" (*SBF* 505) suggests a defense of the liberal center, Du Bois only reveals a middle ground occu-pied by assimilation or fatalistic acquiescence:

> Between the two extreme types of ethical attitude which I have thus sought to make clear wavers the mass of the millions of Negroes, North and South; and their religious life and activity partake of this social conflict within their ranks. Their churches are differentiating,—now into groups of cold, fashionable devotees, in no way distinguishable from similar white groups save in color of skin; now into large social and business institutions catering to the desire for information and amusement of their members, warily avoiding unpleasant questions both within and without the black world, and preaching in effect if not in word: *Dum vivimus, vivamus.* (*SBF* 504–5)

Du Bois adds that "back of this still broods silently the deep religious feeling of the real Negro heart, the stirring, unguided might of powerful human souls who have lost the guiding star of the past and are seeking in the great night a new religious ideal" (*SBF* 505). Crummell is the "guiding star" that promises the incarnation of this ideal, and it is an ideal that Du Bois fully endorses in "The Talented Tenth." But it is also an ideal whose horizon of possibility perpetually recedes in the face of the political and cultural history charted by *Souls*. At the end of *Souls* Du Bois himself appears not as a Moses guiding "his" people out of the wilderness but as "the weary traveller." In the romantic trope of the weary traveler Du Bois attempts to put alongside the vitalist and messianic ideas of activity another notion of action in which the value of the work of meditative and creative consciousness is recognized.

Thoughtful Deed: The Senses of Prophetic Imagination

In the brief "Afterthought" that concludes *Souls*, Du Bois asks the reader to "vouchsafe that this my book fall not still-born into the world-wilderness," and hopes that from it will "spring . . . vigor of *thought* and *thoughtful deed*" (*SBF* 447, emphases added). The possibility here that thinking may constitute meaningful action or that action needs to be informed by meditative intelligence challenges the equation of contemplation with passivity or detachment. In his analysis of the ways in which anthropology structures its knowledge of its object, Johannes Fabian uses this equation as a point of departure for his critique. "We need," argues Fabian, "to overcome the contemplative stance (in Marx's sense) and dismantle the edifices of spatiotemporal distancing that characterize the contemplative view."[44] Fabian is right to suggest that such distancing tends, "first, to detemporalize the process of knowledge and, second, to promote ideological temporalization of relations between the Knower and the Known."[45] Against this separation Fabian proposes that, as paradoxical as it may sound, "consciousness, individual and collective," be considered the "starting point" of any "materialist theory of knowledge." The definition of consciousness given is closely matched by Du Bois's dramatizations in "Of the Sorrow Songs." Fabian means "not disembodied consciousness . . . but 'consciousness with a body,'" inextricably bound up with language":

> A fundamental role for language must be postulated, not because consciousness is conceived as a state internal to an individual organism which would then need to be "expressed" or "represented" through language (taking that term in the widest sense, including gestures, postures, attitudes, and so forth). Rather, the only way to think of consciousness without separating it from the organism or banning it to some kind of *forum internum* is to insist on its sensuous nature; and one way to conceive of that sensuous nature (above the level of motor activities) is to tie it to the production of meaningful sound. Inasmuch as the production of meaningful sound involves the labor of transforming, shaping matter, it may still be possible to

distinguish form and content, but the relationship between the two will then be *constitutive* of consciousness. Only in a secondary, derived sense (one in which the conscious organism is presupposed rather than accounted for) can that relationship be called representational (significative, symbolic), or informative in the sense of being a tool or carrier of information.[46]

In "Of the Sorrow Songs" the emphasis on hearing and response, on the interaction of self and others, on the coevalness of the Other, all support a model of consciousness that is closely aligned with the one Fabian describes. Furthermore, while Du Bois is not exactly offering a *theory* of knowledge in *Souls,* the distance between *Souls* and *The Philadelphia Negro* again suggests the validity of Fabian's distinctions between different conceptualizations of consciousness and different structures of knowledge. One need only compare the scene in which Du Bois listens to the spirituals at Atlanta in *Souls* with the panopticon gaze of the Victorian sociologist and moralist as he surveys the Seventh Ward in *The Philadelphia Negro* to grasp the distinctions:

Starting at Seventh street and walking along Lombard, let us glance at the general character of the ward. Pausing a moment at the corner of Seventh and Lombard, we can at a glance view the worst Negro slums of the city. The houses are mostly brick, some wood, not very old, and in general uncared for rather than dilapidated. The blocks between Eighth, Pine, Sixth and South have for many decades been the center of the Negro population. Here the riots of the thirties took place, and here once was a depth of poverty and degradation almost unbelievable. Even to-day there are many evidences of degradation, although the signs of idleness, shiftlessness, dissoluteness and crime are more conspicuous than those of poverty. The alleys near, as Ratcliffe street, Middle alley, Brown's court, Barclay street, etc., are haunts of noted criminals, male and female, of gamblers and prostitutes, and at the same time of many poverty-stricken people, decent but not energetic. There is an abundance of political clubs, and nearly all the houses are practically lodging houses, with a miscellaneous and shifting population. The corners, night and day, are filled with Negro loafers—able-bodied young men and women, all cheerful, some with good-natured, open faces, some with traces of crime and excess, a few pinched with poverty. . . . Some are stevedores, porters, laborers and laundresses. On the face of it this slum is noisy and dissipated, but not brutal, although now and then highway robberies and murderous assaults in other parts of the city are traced to its denizens. (*PN* 58–60)

It could be argued that Fabian's linking of consciousness to the sensuous body could be taken as a description of James's account of consciousness too. But Fabian's linking of consciousness and the production of language offers the possibility of conceiving of consciousness as a *praxis*, an activity of creative transformation, which James's stress on consciousness as passive selection and crisis management toward equilibrium never gets to. Du Bois's transition (discussed a little later) from hearing the songs to leaving his academic tower as the "weary traveller" and offering the world his book in response in the "Afterthought" does move toward conceiving the work of consciousness as potentially creative and transformative.

While Fabian's account of sensuous consciousness helps describe the processes of transformation in the final chapter of *Souls,* his separation of contemplation and consciousness is less useful in that it tends toward a false dichotomy. If Fabian means by contemplation nothing more than positivist myths of detachment and objectivity, then his argument finds obvious alignments with the critiques of sociological positivism discussed in chapter 3. But in her critique of methodologism Gillian Rose insists that the theoretical and meditative functions of consciousness have their own value and should not be ignored by social science. Similarly, in H. T. Wilson's critical account of sociological paradigms that he calls "the American ideology," a defense of speculative thought leads to the conclusion that "contemplation unrelated to mastery, far from violating true openness to possibility and change, encompasses both as the real subject of its concerns."[47] Rose's critique works out of Hegel, and Wilson's out of Marx. The two philosophers come together in the thought of Max Horkheimer, whose defense of contemplation against its refusal in American Pragmatism is pertinent here. For Horkheimer,

> pragmatism, like technocracy, has certainly contributed a great deal toward the fashionable disrepute of that "stationary contemplation" which was once the highest aspiration of man. Any idea of truth, even a dialectical whole of thought, as it occurs in a living mind, might be called "stationary contemplation," in so far as it is pursued for its own sake instead of as a means to "consistency, stability, and flowing intercourse." Both the attack on contemplation and the praise of the craftsman express the triumph of means over ends.[48]

Horkheimer is quoting from James's *Some Problems of Philosophy* (1924), but the attitudes critiqued should be familiar from the discussion in chapter 1 of earlier texts by James. Also, Horkheimer's alignment of Pragmatism and technocracy reinforces the parallels drawn earlier in this study between James's ethical thought and what Wilson calls technocratic rationality and what Rose refers to as the positivist logic of validity.

Du Bois's departure from academia as the "weary traveller" and the production of his book at the end of *Souls* arise out of a simultaneity of contemplation and the work of sensuous consciousness. Du Bois is moved to action by opening his ears to the music and by his solitary meditation on the songs in his university office. The complexity of Du Bois's dramatizations of consciousness can be more fully grasped by adding to the comparisons with social-scientific and philosophical discourse an examination of the way in which Du Bois's account also suggests a revision of a model of prophetic imagination in American poetry.

Linking ethnographic writing to traditions of travel literature, Fabian argues that "the image of the 'philosophical traveler' whose roaming in space leads to the discovery of 'ages' " is a classic embodiment of the spatiotemporal distancing of Knower and Known.[49] But Du Bois as the "weary traveller" is neither a salvage ethnographer nor a reincarnated priest-prophet in the image of Crummell or Moses. He is the companion of Blake's "Mental Traveller." In *The Mental Traveller* the "Babe" liberty is "begotten in woe" and "born in joy." But the child is "given to a Woman Old," society, "who nails him down upon a rock."[50] As Foster Damon explains, Blake's poem "is the formula of the history of the idea of Liberty, showing how it is born, how it triumphs, how in its age its opposite is born, how it is cast out, how it then rejuvenates, until it becomes a babe again, and the cycle recurs."[51] *Souls* too dramatizes the recurring struggles of the consciousness of freedom and of bondage. As in Blake, it is from a knowledge of this struggle that prophetic vision is created in *Souls*.

Prophecy is understood here not in a predictive or futuristic sense but as Northrop Frye describes it in his remarkable study of Blake: "an honest man is not quite the noblest work of God until the faith by which the just live develops into full imaginative vision. The fully imaginative man is therefore a visionary whose imaginative activity is prophecy and whose perception produces art. These two are the same thing, perception being an act. . . . It is the superior clarity and accuracy of the prophet's vision that makes him an artist, and that makes the great artist prophetic.[52]

In American Transcendentalism, as in European Romanticism, poetic prophecy is preoccupied with the dialectics of passivity and activity. On the American side, the primary mode of transcending passivity is through a voluntaristic act of *seeing*. A brief examination of Emerson and Whitman, particularly of the triumph in their work of sight over the other senses and of a self defined by seeing, will provide a context in which the poetics of *Souls*'s structuring can be more clearly understood.

In *Nature* (1836), his first major work, Emerson seeks to reverse the Pauline relegation of prophetic vision to a future world in which the Fall is recovered. For St. Paul, "now we see in a mirror, darkly," but "when that which is perfect is come," then we shall see "face to face" (1 Cor. 13:10, 12). Emerson, however, argues that "the foregoing generations beheld God and nature face to face; we through their eyes," and asks "Why should not we also enjoy an original relation to the universe?"[53] The prophet of the New World restores his vision by becoming "a transparent eyeball" whose Platonic insight transcends society. By contrast with *Nature, Souls* opens not with a seeing subject but with a moment of being seen. Where Emerson seeks solitude in nature, the boy Du Bois is seeking the company of his white and black playmates when he is repulsed by the gaze of the "tall newcomer." The black body and not the "tranquil landscape" becomes the field of the "Not Me" in which the white subject unfolds its freedom. The moment in which the gaze penetrates is the moment in which the biblical veil descends and obscures vision in *Souls*. But if the penetrating gaze sets off a process of objectification and the division of consciousness, it also makes possible a "second sight." The look of Du Bois's new playmate is like that "certain Slant of light" that is both "An imperial affliction" and a source of tragic understanding in Emily Dickinson:

> Heavenly Hurt, it gives us—
> We can find no scar,
> But internal difference,
> Where the Meanings, are—[54]

Not only does *Souls* open with being seen, it closes with Du Bois *listening* to the voices singing the spirituals, a more social act than seeing, and sending out into the world his *written* work. This presents a very different ratio of the senses than the one that dominates in Emerson, or even the more "amative" Whitman, and also a very different conceptualization of visionary action. Emerson's attempts to defend the mind as active in "The American Scholar" (1837) and Whitman's poetic self-fashioning in "Song of Myself" (1855) can help illustrate the differences between Du Bois's formulations and American Transcendentalism.

"The American Scholar" is a program for the cultivation of the life of the mind in the new nation. In it Emerson writes that "the so-called 'practical men' sneer at speculative men, as if, because they speculate or *see,* they could do nothing." Emerson takes this to be a false accusation:

> Action is with the scholar subordinate, but it is essential. Without it he is not yet man. Without it thought can never ripen into truth. . . . The preamble of thought, the transition through which it passes from the unconscious to the conscious, is action. Only so much do I know, as I have lived. Instantly we know whose words are loaded with life, and whose not.
>
> This world,—this shadow of the soul, or *other* me,—lies wide around. Its attractions are the keys which unlock my thoughts and make me acquainted with myself. I run eagerly into this tumult. I grasp the hands of those next me, and take my place in the ring to suffer and to work, taught by an instinct that so shall the dumb abyss be vocal with speech.[55]

Despite this last image of collective toiling, Emerson's formulations of the activity of visionary understanding and cultural leadership describe, for the most part, a solitary and passive process. The sense of self-reliance and mastery in the face of the "Not Me" is, after all, dependent upon the passivity of seeing.[56] In the passage from "The American Scholar" quoted above, the transition from seeing to saying involves no process of *hearing.* Notwithstanding the image of the ring of clasped hands, the scholar does not work from a social location. What is vocalized is, in fact, not a social or historical knowledge, but the passive emergence of preexisting Platonic forms that are autonomous of consciousness. In Du Bois's revision of Plato, however, the bright revelation of pure and transcendent forms in the light outside the caves is eschewed in favor of the knowledge embodied in the voices of those imprisoned inside the cave. As Denis Donoghue observes,

> the site of [Emerson's] poetry and his sageness is the history of voluntarism. The more we read *Nature,* the more clearly it appears that the whole essay is predicated upon the capacity of Will. Not knowledge but power is its aim; not truth but command. . . . So if we go back to the transparent eyeball passage and read it as a voluntaristic act rather than an instance of the Sublime, we find that the eyeball becomes transparent because a light higher than its own sensory light is made to shine through it. . . . We have

access to [Emerson's work] only by recourse to the vocabulary of Will and to its social form, a pragmatics of the future.[57]

The interactions of the senses and the social politics in Whitman's "Song of Myself" are closer to those in Du Bois than to those in Emerson, but they are still marked by a fundamental difference that is useful in describing *Souls*. Whitman, like the author of *Souls*, is "attesting sympathy" ("Shall I make my list of things in the house and skip the house that supports them?" he asks).[58] He shouts "Hurrah for positive science!" but also tells the scientist and the mathematician, "Your facts are useful, and yet they are not my dwelling, / I but enter by them to an area of my dwelling" (*LG* 51). This dwelling is what Du Bois, in turning away from social-scientific description in *Souls*, calls the realm of "thought and feeling." In exploring this realm, the poet of the "Song of Myself" touches and feels in his democratic openness in a way Emerson never does (and with a corporeal candor that is also alien to the Victorian Du Bois): "I believe in the flesh and the appetites, / Seeing, hearing, feeling" (*LG* 53). And the poet's "voice goes after what [his] eyes cannot reach" (*LG* 55). In his social openness, Whitman is led to make vocal not just "the threads that connect the stars," but political outrage on behalf of the oppressed and socially excluded:

> Through me many long dumb voices,
>   Voices of the interminable generations of prisoners and slaves,
>   Voices of the diseas'd and despairing and of thieves and dwarfs,
>
>   . . .
>
>   Through me forbidden voices
>   Voices of sexes and lusts, voices veil'd and I remove the veil,
>   Voices indecent by me clarified and transfigured. (*LG* 52–53)

It is the poet's transfiguration of the voices that lifts the veil. This is closer to Du Bois, but the transfiguration dramatized in the last chapter of *Souls* is somewhat different.

As Larzer Ziff demonstrates, sight ultimately triumphs over the other senses even in Whitman, because the other senses are a threat to prophetic stability and self-confidence. With the appearance of the other senses, Whitman's prophetic power of digesting good and evil, ugliness and beauty, into the incorporative self on equal terms "becomes entangled in self-doubt."

The doubtings, of course, are plotted. It is through a marvelous series of sights that he arrives at the middle point of *Song of Myself*, where he can stand up and, after naming so much else, name himself: "Walt Whitman, an American, one of the roughs, a kosmos." As he compiles those sights he brushes aside the opposition to his gathering strength that comes from sound and touch: "Trippers and askers surround me." But they are not the "Me myself," and when he affirms, "Apart from the pulling and hauling stands what I am," he does so by showing that he "looks."[59]

Unlike Whitman, Du Bois does not attempt to recuperate a threatened self-confidence or a stable self and its powers of incorporation. In the final moments of "Of the Sorrow Songs" Du Bois is left listening. He does not master the songs but is sent out into the world by them. Tragedy and evil are not assimilated. It is true that, like Whitman, Du Bois transfigures the voices he hears. But he does not incorporate them into the imperial command of his own voice. Through his "Afterthought," he foregrounds the *writtenness* of his transfiguration and the separation between the spirituals and the "book" that is *Souls.* If the weary traveler is urged into a renewal of his exploratory journeying by the voices singing the spirituals, the creation of the book called *Souls of Black Folk* is a direct product of this responsive displacement.

The dislocation of Du Bois's representative bourgeois consciousness takes place of course not just in the final chapter of *Souls* but, in one way or another, throughout the book, and the sending of the book out into the world in the "Afterthought" suggests that the text is a culminative synthesis of all that has gone before. Du Bois's fear that the book might fall "still born" into the world metaphorically gathers up the dialogues of fathers and sons, of parents and children, that dominate the last five chapters of *Souls,* from the faith of the fathers and the death of the newborn son to Crummell as father and John as defeated son, and finally to Du Bois as the father listening to the singing of his children. The plea to the reader that he or she "vouchsafe" the survival of the book is an invitation to sustain this gathering in a continued act of recollection and imaginative meditation in which the contemplation of what Horkheimer calls truth and the historical process is not sacrificed to an instrumentalist or exceptionalist future.

Missing the End: Toward Revolution

In *Dusk of Dawn,* the autobiography from 1940, the allegory of the cave and other moments from "Of Our Spiritual Strivings" are reworked toward more radical social transformations than are imagined in *Souls*. In a chapter titled "The Concept of Race," the lifelong struggle to define and explore the concept is described against the background of the early career (a biography already encountered in *Souls*) seen from the vantage point of Du Bois's trip to Liberia in the mid-1920s. At the end of the chapter Du Bois returns to the Platonic allegory and shifts the emphases of the earlier reworking in *Souls* in significant ways:

> It is difficult to let others see the full psychological meaning of caste segregation. It is as though one, looking out from a dark cave in a side of an impending mountain, sees the world passing and speaks to it; speaks courteously and persuasively, showing them how these entombed souls are hindered in their natural movement, expression, and development; and how their loosening from prison would be a matter not simply of courtesy, sympathy, and help to them, but aid to all the world. One talks on evenly and logically in this way, but notices that the passing throng does not even turn its head, or if it does, glances curiously and walks on. It gradually penetrates the mind of the prisoners that the people passing do not hear; that some thick sheet of invisible but horribly tangible plate glass is between them and the world. They get excited; they talk louder; they gesticulate. Some of the passing world stop in curiosity; these gesticulations seem so pointless; they laugh and pass on. They still either do not hear at all, or hear but dimly, and even what they hear, they do not understand. Then the people within may become hysterical. They may scream and hurl themselves against the barriers, hardly realizing in their bewilderment that they are screaming in a vacuum unheard and that their antics may actually seem funny to those outside looking in. They may even, here and there, break through in blood and disfigurement, and find themselves faced by a horrified, implacable, and quite overwhelming mob of people frightened for their own very existence. (*DD* 649–50)

In *Souls* the reworking of the allegory focused on a set of doubts about the relationship of a member of the Talented Tenth to the black folk. Here the concern is with the relationship of the white world to the black world, with the figure of the black spokesman mediating between the two. The relationship of the two worlds is again presented through a differentiation of hearing and sight. The failure of hearing leads to a distortion of sight so that the "entombed" begin to appear in their frustration either as laughable or as a savage threat that can be contained only through mob violence. The source of enlightenment is not so much reversed as made reciprocal. Freedom lies outside the cave, but there is also a truth the white world needs to learn from the imprisoned.

The treatment of the black leader figure is more equivocal. The passage begins with attention focused on the "one" who has to speak on behalf of the prisoners to the outside world. (Here at least Plato's guardian seeks to bring knowledge out of the cave and not into it.) Later in the passage, attention shifts from the one to the many as the prisoners themselves become speaking subjects. Earlier in *Dusk of Dawn,* describing the impact of racist mob violence on his own stance of scientific objectivity and progress, Du Bois writes that "one could not be a calm, cool, and detached scientist while Negroes were lynched, murdered and starved" (*DD* 603). In the passage quoted above from the later "Concept of Race" chapter, it is when the spokesman's talking "evenly and logically" leads to nothing that the prisoners become collectively vocal. But if the reasoned arguments of the "one" fall on deaf ears, the efforts of the many can be seen only within the racist stereotypes of farce and savagery as long as their true meaning is silenced by the "plate glass" barrier between the two worlds.

With the failure of both individual and collective effort, Du Bois does not at first offer any alternatives. He circles back to a description of divided consciousness caught between two worlds, once again presented with intelligence within the limits of a radical conservatism. The "freeing and making articulate" of the "submerged caste" is imagined as the function of the spokesman's ethical address to the white world (*DD* 651). The danger is that in the process of such advocacy the leader himself becomes an outsider to the group, and Du Bois recognizes that "outside leadership will continually misinterpret and compromise and complicate matters, even with the best of will" (*DD* 651). But to remain only within the group is to risk becoming "provincial and centered upon the problems of his particular group" (*DD* 651). In order to become "a group man, a 'race' man," the individual may have to sacrifice "the wider aspects of national life and human existence" (*DD* 651).

Much of this is familiar from the analysis of the "contradiction of double aims" from the first chapter of *Souls*. But the conclusion of *Dusk of Dawn* takes the autobiographical commentary in a direction quite different from the conclusion of the earlier book. The final chapter of *Dusk of Dawn* is called "Revolution." The chapter charts Du Bois's move "beyond my conception of ignorance and deliberate ill-will as causes of race prejudice" toward an understanding of other "hidden and partially concealed causes of race hate" (*DD* 761). These other causes are succinctly summarized as capitalism's planned perpetuation of material *and* spiritual and intellectual deprivation. The summary is itself placed between two visions of collective political action, one from the past, leading Du Bois toward a radical reformulation of his ideas, and the other a promise of future revolution. Consciousness and materialist understanding, self and collectivity, now begin to move toward a new synthesis:

> I think it was the Russian Revolution which first illuminated and made clear [the] change in my basic thought. It was not that I at any time conceived of Bolshevik Russia as ushering in any present millennium. I was painfully sensitive to all its failures, to all the difficulties which it faced; but the clear and basic thing which appeared to me in unquestioned brightness, was that in the year 1917 and then, after a struggle with the world and famine ten years later, one of the largest nations of the world made up its mind frankly to face a set of problems which no nation at that time was willing to face, and which many nations including our own are unwilling fully to face even to this day.
>
>  Those questions involved the problem of the poverty of the mass of men in an age when an abundance of goods and technical efficiency of work seemed able to provide a sufficiency for all men, so that the mass of men could be fed and clothed and sheltered, live in health and have their intellectual faculties trained. Russia was trying to accomplish this by eventually putting into the hands of those people who do the world's work the power to guide and rule the state for the best welfare of the masses. It made the assumption, long disputed, that out of the downtrodden mass of people, ability and character, sufficient to do this task effectively, could and would be found. I believed this dictum passionately. It was, in fact, the foundation stone of my fight for black folk; it explained me. (*DD* 761–62)

By the time *Dusk of Dawn* appeared in print Du Bois had already published his Marxist historiography, *Black Reconstruction in America, 1860–1880* (1935). In *Dusk of Dawn* twentieth-century liberalism's failure to "realize the fundamental change brought about by the world-wide organization of work and trade and commerce" (*DD* 765) is placed against the Marxist recognition that "economic foundations . . . are the determining factors in the development of civilization, in literature, religion, and the basic pattern of culture" (*DD* 775).

The base-superstructure argument is rudimentary in its statement. But the stress on political economy shifts the bewilderment of the Talented Tenth in the face of historical disaster in *Souls* toward greater understanding of the causes of the disaster. At the end of *Dusk of Dawn* Du Bois still endorses the Talented Tenth, but in a very modified manner. In the chapter titled "Revolution" Du Bois prints the "Basic American Negro Creed," a political manifesto for African-Americans he had drafted in 1936. The third item of the Creed states that the function of the Talented Tenth is to determine "by study and measurement the present field and demand for racial action and the method by which the masses may be guided along this path" (*DD* 788). But the social Darwinistic rhetoric and moralistic idealism of the original "Talented Tenth" essay has now given way to a sense of the function of the elite within a broader political process. Economics dominates the concerns of the Creed. Du Bois proposes the establishment of "a co-operative Negro industrial system in America . . . in the midst of and in conjunction with the surrounding national industrial organization and in intelligent accord with the reconstruction of the economic basis of the nation which must sooner or later be accomplished" (*DD* 788). The next two items of the Creed urge the "Negro workers" to join forces with the "labor movement," and Du Bois asserts his belief "in the ultimate triumph of some form of Socialism the world over; that is, common ownership and control of the means of production and equality of income" (*DD* 789).

Du Bois had appended the draft of his credo to a paper titled "The Negro and the New Deal" commissioned by the Associates in Negro Folk Education, working under the American Association for Adult Education, for a series edited by Alain Locke. The manuscript was rejected (*DD* 787; 789). *Dusk of Dawn* itself was completed just as the world was plunged into the Second World War. But the disaster of the war and its aftermath did not dull Du Bois's radical hopes. When in the late 1950s Du Bois turned to the writing of another autobiography, he rearranged the chronology of his life so that the *Autobiography* began not with his childhood but with an extended account of his travels in the Soviet Union and communist China. Between this account, which formed part 1 of the book, and the rest of the *Autobiography* there was an "Interlude" titled "Communism." In *Dusk of Dawn* Du Bois had imagined the possibilities of socialism within a capitalist system and declared "I . . . am not a communist" (*DD* 775). In the "Interlude" in the *Autobiography*, Du Bois stated bluntly that he now believed in communism, meaning by communism "a planned way of life in the production of wealth and work designed for building a state whose object is the highest welfare of its people and not merely the profit of a part" (*A* 57). There follows a radical denunciation of the myths of the free market and the American political system:

> Once I thought these ends could be attained under capitalism, means of production privately owned, and used in accord with free individual initiative. . . . I now believe that private ownership of capital and free enterprise are leading the world to disaster. I do not believe that so-called "people's capitalism" has in the United States or anywhere replaced the ills of private capitalism and shown an answer to socialism. The corporation is but the legal mask behind which the individual owner of wealth hides. Democratic government in the United States has almost ceased to function. A fourth of the adults are disfranchised [*sic*], half the legal voters do not go to the polls. We are ruled by those who control wealth and who by that power buy or coerce public opinion. (*A* 57)

The last part of the *Autobiography* frames the account of the middle years of Du Bois's life with an account of his trial, indictment, and acquittal at the start of the 1950s on the charge of being an "unregistered foreign agent" (under the Foreign Agents Registration Act of 1938) in connection with his leadership of the Peace Information Center. In 1961, at the age of ninety-three and only two years before his death, Du Bois joined the Communist Party of the United States and that same year took up residence in Ghana at the invitation of President Nkrumah.

To give Du Bois's own descriptions of his turn to socialism in his later autobiographies as a coda to a study of his early writings is not meant to suggest that the meaning of those early writings can be grasped only teleologically, as if a logic immanent in the early works were somehow fulfilled in the later ones. The brief review of the later socialism is meant, in fact, to lead to quite the opposite argument. To argue for a teleological logic by which the young Du Bois becomes the older Du Bois would be to reproduce that Hegelian reading of Marx's thought by which the young Hegelian Marx becomes the old Marxist Marx by means of the immanent potential of the idealist logic of his early Hegelian works. But as Joachim Hoeppner argues in a discussion of the relation of Hegel to Marx, "history must not be studied from the front backwards, searching for the heights of Marxist knowledge its ideal germs in the past. The evolution of philosophical thought must be traced on the basis of the real evolution of society." Hoeppner adds that as far as the relation of Hegel and Marx goes, "it is not a question of knowing what Marxist content a Marxist investigator might today be able to read into . . . passages [from

Hegel], but rather of knowing what social content they had for Hegel himself."[60] Quoting this passage, Louis Althusser argues that Hoeppner's position on Hegel "*is also unreservedly true for Marx himself* when his early works are being read from the standpoint of his mature works."[61]

> Of course, we now know that the Young Marx *did* become Marx, but we should not want to live faster than he did, we should not want to live in his place, reject for him or discover for him. We shall not be waiting for him at the end of the course to throw around him as around a runner the mantle of repose, for at last it is over, he has arrived. Rousseau remarked that with children and adolescents the whole art of education consists of knowing how to *lose time*. The art of historical criticism also consists of knowing how to lose time so that young authors can grow up. This lost time is simply the time we give them to live. We *scan* the necessity of their lives in our understanding of its nodal points, its reversals and mutations.[62]

In investigating the thought and writings of Du Bois at the turn of the century, this study has sought to understand that moment as what Althusser calls a "nodal point" and to respect the complexity of its "reversals and mutations." It has tried not to hurry Du Bois, nor to "reject" or "discover" for him. The meaning and value of the early achievements are not derived from their contribution to a totalizing account of the whole life. The later socialism and the earlier dramas of Hegelian negativity are juxtaposed; the latter are not given as the germ that is fulfilled in the former. Du Bois's own autobiographical writings offer his readers a conceptualization of his life not so much as a linear trajectory but as a palimpsest in visible and continuous process. For the middle part of the *Autobiography,* dealing with the years from his childhood to the late 1940s, Du Bois drew almost entirely on previously published works. The results are not as impressive as some of the earlier works. But the framing of this middle section of the autobiography between an account of the trip to the Soviet Union and China, as well as the declaration of communist sympathy, and an account of his trial in the 1950s does create a formal structure of awkward tonal overlayering in which the different moments of the life are curiously available in simultaneous contrast. The last sentence of *Dusk of Dawn* offers a more self-conscious sense of the life as a continual process in which the telos of both biography and historical process is deferred. "I like a good novel," writes Du Bois, "and in healthful length of days, there is infinite joy in seeing the World, the most interesting of continuing stories, unfold, even though one misses THE END" (*DD* 792–93). The final lines of Du Bois's *Autobiography,* written in the last decade of his long life, tie the imagination of future achievement firmly to a living sense of the past in such a way that the recollective and contemplative model of consciousness from *Souls* is joined to the imagination of revolution, not superseded by it:

> This is a wonderful America, which the founding fathers dreamed until their sons drowned it in the blood of slavery and devoured it in greed. Our children must rebuild it. Let then the Dreams of the Dead rebuke the Blind who think that what is will be forever and teach them that what was worth living for must live again and that which merited death must stay dead. Teach us, Forever Dead, there is no Dream but Deed, there is no Deed but Memory. (*A* 422–23)

The sense of the last sentence is not only that the dream is an activity in its own right, but also that there can be no meaningful action unless it is also an act of remembering feeding the dream.

Six

Conclusion

This study has sought to describe how Du Bois is led by his reflections on the relationship of the black and white worlds to develop a complex model of the location of the self alongside an equally complex literary practice. In *Souls* it is clear that these models are very much part of a single imaginative process and are anchored in a conceptualization of consciousness's experience of historical process that is adapted out of a Hegelian psychology of alienation. This conclusion considers briefly the continued value of Du Bois's Hegelian account of consciousness. In order to highlight this potential Du Bois's work is compared to Fanon's oscillation between Hegelian and Nietzschean models of action in *Black Skin, White Masks* and to the attempt to bypass altogether dialectical thought and process in those contemporary African-American literary theorizations that take the trickster as their key critical trope.

The opposition between Hegel and Nietzsche has become a commonplace of poststructuralism. But in discussions of race and colonialism its locus classicus remains Fanon's *Black Skin, White Masks*, though, unlike the poststructuralists, Fanon grounds his use of Nietzsche in an existential notion of subjectivity. Some points of similarity in the descriptions of racial alterity in Du Bois and Fanon have already been noted. The differ-

ences in their views of historical consciousness are, however, more fundamental. Though this comparison takes the discussion of Du Bois out of
the American context, it should still be apparent that it is a continuation
of the comparison between Du Bois's dialectical sense of consciousness
and the will to transcendence in Emerson and James.

In *Black Skin, White Masks*, Fanon's critique of Hegel goes beyond
the criticisms of the model of reciprocity in the master-slave dialectic. At
times it appears to extend to a Nietzschean rejection of dialectical thought
altogether and a divorcing of action from historical contingency.[1] Toward
the end of his book, Fanon refers to Nietzsche's *Will to Power* in support
of his own critique of reactional behavior, what Nietzsche calls *ressentiment*. "To educate man to be actional," argues Fanon, "preserving in all
his relations his respect for the basic values that constitute a human world,
is the prime task of him who, having taken thought, prepares to act."[2]
Thought is included as part of action, and the revolutionary affirmation
at the heart of Fanon's book is that "the real *leap* consists in introducing
invention into existence" (*BS,WM* 229). But this invention appears to
unfold in a historic vacuum, since Fanon insists that "the body of history
does not determine a single one of my actions" (*BS,WM* 231).

Something of the problem in Fanon's conceptualization of free action
can be gauged from his use of Richard Wright's Bigger Thomas as exem-
plum. For Fanon, "in the end Bigger Thomas acts. To put an end to his
tension, he acts, he responds to the world's anticipation" (*BS,WM* 139).
Bigger is, however, an ambiguous model of action in the Nietzschean
sense. He kills accidentally when he is trapped in a corner, like the hunted
rat with which *Native Son* (1940) opens. It is also well known that the
dramatization of human behavior in Wright's novel is indebted to the
theories of environmental determinism of the Chicago school of sociology. Fanon's own vocabulary here fluctuates between action and reaction,
since Bigger "responds" because he has internalized the image of himself
in the white world's eyes. There is, finally and most important, no acknowledgment in Fanon that Bigger's actions may be quite different in
kind from those of Richard Wright the writer.[3]

The ambivalence of Fanon's vocabulary for human action also characterizes the larger refusal of dialectical thought in *Black Skin, White Masks*,
particularly in its theorization of literature and the historicity of literary
practice. Fanon's most detailed critique of Hegelian and dialectical thought
is given in his attack on Sartre's commentary on "negritude." In "Orphée

Noire," his introduction to the *Anthologie de la nouvelle poésie nègre et malgache* (1948), Sartre wrote that

> negritude appears as the minor term of a dialectical progression: The theoretical and practical assertion of the supremacy of the white man is its thesis; the position of negritude as an antithetical value is the moment of negativity. But this negative moment is insufficient by itself, and the Negroes who employ it know this very well; they know that it is intended to prepare the synthesis or realisation of the human in a society without races. Thus negritude is the root of its own destruction, it is a transition and not a conclusion, a means and not an ultimate end. (Quoted in *BS,WM* 133)

Fanon writes that when he read this, "I felt that I had been robbed of my last chance. . . . For once, that born Hegelian had forgotten that consciousness has to lose itself in the night of the absolute, the only condition to attain to consciousness of self" (*BS,WM* 133–34). Fanon does characterize negritude as an "unhappy romanticism," but also insists that "I needed to lose myself completely in negritude. . . . I *needed* not to know" (*BS,WM* 135).

Sartre may be too schematic, but Fanon's positing of a local and immediate historical necessity does not negate Sartre's larger dialectical thesis; in fact, it validates it. Having criticized Sartre's view of the historical transitoriness of negritude, Fanon goes on to adopt exactly Sartre's position. In the conclusion to *Black Skin, White Masks,* Fanon rejects the very "unhappy romanticism" that he saw as a necessity earlier in the book. The final affirmation of Fanon's book is that "the discovery of the existence of a Negro civilization in the fifteenth century confers no patent of humanity on me. Like it or not, the past can in no way guide me in the present moment" (*BS,WM* 225).

Black Skin, White Masks presents history as a choice between the fatalistic overdeterminations of an inherited oppression and the romanticism of a mystical past within a false polarization of human activity between reaction (or the passive determinations of consciousness) and action (the willed transcendence of this passivity). *Souls* refuses such polarities. Something of the extent of this refusal has already been suggested by the comparison of Du Bois with James and Emerson. If, like Fanon, Du Bois challenges the acceptance of the legacy of a racist history as fate, he does not see this history as the only form in which white culture is available to a black American. *Souls* as much as *Dusk of Dawn* acknowledges that there are materials in the Euro-American tradition (be it a certain type of

education or the work of a Hegel or Shakespeare) that offer aids to critical reflection and creative survival. And while Du Bois shares Fanon's
eventual suspicion of anthropological romanticism, his examination of
African-American music offers a sociology of a black art that does not
fall into the traps of negritude's nostalgias. Contra Emerson's manifesto
for an American art untethered to the "sepulchers of the fathers," the
"sorrow songs" embody a deeply historical consciousness. In examining
these songs Du Bois is inevitably led to examine his own relationship to
them and through them to black American folk culture. Here too Du
Bois avoids the nostalgias of collectivity that inform the romanticism of
negritude (or its American equivalents).

The tension between the claims of historical process and the requirements of revolutionary action faced by Fanon is comically evaded in
Henry Louis Gates's book *The Signifying Monkey* (1988).[4] Gates's work
offers itself as "a theory of African-American literary criticism" that takes
as its central critical trope the African and African-American trickster,
from Eshu Elegbara of West African religious systems, to Legba of
the Haitian Vodoun pantheon and Brer Rabbit and other tricksters in
African-American folklore. Though only one among many critical works
that have turned to the supposedly trangressive function of tricksters
or of carnivalization, Gates's has been the single most influential book in
African-American criticism in the past decade. The book began life as an
essay on Ishmael Reed's novel *Mumbo Jumbo* (1972), a novel in which
Papa Labas, a figure based on Legba, is a central character in a plot that
speaks in obvious ways to certain postmodern concerns.[5]

Gates's conclusion about Reed's novel is that "it is indeterminacy, the
sheer plurality of meaning, the very play of the signifier, which *Mumbo
Jumbo* celebrates" (*SM* 235). The source of this indeterminacy, its motor
as it were, is to be found largely in the figure of the trickster conceived
as "a figure of doubled duality, of unreconciled opposites" (*SM* 30). It is,
argues Gates, through procedures of parodic doubling that *Mumbo Jumbo*
and Reed's other work undertake a satiric critique not only of the Western
tradition but also of the African-American literary tradition. Gates first
argues that *Mumbo Jumbo* is, "salient point for salient point," a parodic
deflation of Plato's *Phaedrus*. He then goes on to read Reed's poem "Dualism: in ralph ellison's invisible man" as a satire (through parodic doubling)
of the idea of duality in African-American literature, particularly of Du
Bois's original formulation of the idea as "double-consciousness" and
Ellison's use of it in *Invisible Man* (*SM* 237–38).

The concern of the present discussion is not to endorse or critique Gates's commentary on Reed but to examine his attempt to theorize out of his reading of *Mumbo Jumbo* an alternative to what he takes to be the meaning of double consciousness. In the introduction to *The Signifying Monkey* Gates insists that his desire has been "to allow the black tradition to speak for itself about its nature and various functions, rather than to read it, or analyze it, in terms of literary theories borrowed whole from other traditions, appropriated from without" (*SM* xix). But Gates's theoretical formulations are in fact deeply indebted on the one hand to the ahistorical religio-mystical interpretations of the trickster by a Catholic priest, Robert Pelton, and on the other hand to Jacques Derrida's account of the Egyptian trickster Thoth and his discussion of Plato's *Phaedrus* in his long essay "Plato's Pharmacy" in *Dissemination* (1972). The silent elision of the "black tradition" with poststructuralism and a trans-cultural mysticism that is inattentive to social and historical particularities, leads Gates to a position where Du Bois's Hegelian sense of consciousness is replaced by an African-American version of American exceptionalism in which a largely verbal self seeks a kind of religious transcendence.

In his study of the West African trickster, Robert Pelton quotes a Yoruba poem for Eshu which is recited as part of the divinatory sacrifice:

> The world is broken into pieces;
> The world is split wide open,
> The world is broken without anybody to mend it;
> The world is split open without anybody to sew it.
>
> . . .
>
> If the sacrifice of Eshu is not made,
> It will not be acceptable [in heaven].[6]

Gates quotes a similar poem, also from the Yoruba, in which Eshu is imagined as the

> Swift footed one!
> Agile and restless one!
> One who scatters himself abroad
> One who, scattered, cannot be put together again. (*SM* 30)

It is Eshu's mastery of divinatory grammar and the sacrifice to Eshu that put the world back together. Throughout Pelton's study, as throughout *The Signifying Monkey,* we are told that Eshu and the other tricksters are liminal figures, creating passages "out of a structure cut off somehow from the real shape of things, into a time and a space capable of showing forth this shape, and finally back into a structure renewed and enlarged by the act of sacrifice."[7] However, Pelton never explains how a social system designed to maintain its conservative order is constantly "renewed and enlarged." The trickster in West Africa is, to a great extent, a figure of permission ensuring the continued and fundamentally unaltered survival of the social hierarchies and codes. The transitional and initiating passages are from one highly encoded stage in the life cycle to another. The trickster-divination interaction is primarily *sociotherapeutic,* an analysis geared toward the goals of social equilibrium, toward reintegrating the individual into society rather than providing bases for politicized critique or challenge.[8]

Pelton's own euphoric mobilization of Victor Turner's descriptions of ritual process in terms of "structure," "anti-structure," and "liminality" here reveals his and Turner's schematizations as a vertiginous encounter with the sacred. And Gates fully shares Pelton's sustained religio-poetic vocabulary of epiphanies, transformations, and initiations. For Gates, "Eshu's two sides 'disclose a hidden wholeness'; rather than closing off unity, through the opposition, they signify the passage from one to the other as sections of a subsumed whole." Gates goes on to note that "Eshu stands as the sign of this wholeness" and quotes "Pelton's explanation of this doubleness" as "especially cogent" proof (*SM* 30). The contradictions between "duality" and "wholeness" are mystically resolved, religiously transcended. This is James's escape from "feverish dream" into "sacred coolness" all over again.

The failure to historicize is also evident in Gates's appropriation of Derrida. Gates's preoccupations with parodic doubling, the nature of signification and indeterminacy, trickster figures, and the relationships of the oral and the written, both in his discussion of Reed and in *The Signifying Monkey* as a whole, are indebted to classic Derridean insights and obsessions. Pursuing his preoccupation with notions of supplementarity and *différance* in relation to the history of the ideas of speech and writing (represented in Plato by Ra and Thoth respectively), Derrida asserts that Thoth is "precisely the god of non-identity. . . . Sly, slippery, and masked, an intriguer and a card, like Hermes, he is neither king nor jack, but rather a sort of *joker,* a floating signifier, a wild card, one who puts play into play. . . . He would be the mediating movement of dialectics if he did not also mimic it, indefinitely preventing it, through his ironic doubling, from reaching some final fulfillment or eschatological reappropriation."[9] The validity of Derrida's reading of *Phaedrus* or the accuracy of his account of Egyptian mythology is not of primary concern here. What is at issue is the effect of Gates's use of a vocabulary and of frameworks derived from Pelton and Derrida to analyze various distinct mythologies from Africa and the New World.

The figures through which Gates formulates the religious and deconstructive turns of his theory align him firmly with the Transcendentalist refusal of history and the simultaneous relegation of action to the realm of language alone.[10] Gates's conceptualization of Du Bois's idea of "double-consciousness" as a "repeated trope of dualism," and his celebration of Reed's deconstruction of this trope through the epiphanous repetitions of parodic doubling, reenacts, in postmodern or Derridean guise, the drama of the divided self and of the transcendence of division through liberatory verbal gesture so central in Emerson. Gates's confusion of doubling and dialectics signals in the direction of such an alignment. Gates refers to Eshu as a figure of both "doubled duality" and the "dialectical principle" (*SM* 30, 31), but doubling and dialectics are quite different things. Gates's suggestion that the idea of "double-consciousness" in Du Bois is a "trope of dualism" is equally a misrepresentation. Du Bois does not propose a static structure of the divided self, as Emerson does in "The Transcendentalist." In *Souls* Du Bois in fact dramatizes a historical consciousness that conceives of historical process dialectically and insists on multiple social and historical contexts as the arena in which the self both creates itself and is created.

To speak of Du Bois's Hegelianism as a possible model for conceptualizing ideas of identity and difference in the context of black and white relations in America is not to argue for an ahistoric "return to Hegel." It is simply to recognize that the Hegelian tradition that includes Marx, Alexandre Kojève, and Sartre, and indeed Du Bois himself, provides models of historical consciousness that are still, for all their problems, more capable of offering sophisticated and complex descriptions of the nature of historical process than the kinds of models that underlie the thought of James or Emerson—and this notwithstanding either the arguments against the utility of using Hegel to think about issues of race, power, and psychology[11] or the current, poststructuralist critiques of dialectical thought.[12] As Judith Butler notes, "when the dialectic no longer denotes the ontological unity of opposites or the logical principle of dialectical reversal, it no longer maintains its conventional meanings." It can open onto what Sartre calls "concrete and individual being" or what Butler refers to as "an occasion in which the loss of metaphysical moorings clears the way for a poetic affirmation of what is."[13]

Hegel links the epistemological process of self-consciousness with the historical process of the transcendence of bondage and the attainment of freedom. To some extent Du Bois appears to reproduce this idealist homology, but he is more interested finally in historicizing psychology than in psychologizing history. *Souls*'s focus on the concrete individual, its insistence in its sociopolitical analyses on the materialist conditions prerequisite to a definition of freedom (rather than the relegation of freedom to beyond these conditions), and its refusal to transcend the dialectics of estrangement, of identity and difference within a dramatization of the multiplicity of life, all push against the subsuming of the realm of being (ontology) into the realm of knowing (epistemology) in Hegel in ways that recall Marx's and Sartre's critiques of the *Phenomenology* (and indeed Kierkegaard's too).

Marx states the issues clearly in *The Economic and Philosophic Manuscripts of 1844*. While acknowledging the radicalness of Hegel's depiction of alienation and self-actualization, he also points to the problem of Hegel's restriction of these to mind alone rather than the realm of material existence.[14] Marx's commentary can be placed next to Sartre's critique of what he refers to as Hegel's epistemological and ontological optimism. *Being and Nothingness* refuses metaphysics in favor of a description of the structures of being in the real world. Sartre opposes Kierkegaard's representation of "the claims of the individual as such" to Hegel: it is "concrete and individual being which flows into [the] universal and fills it. . . . The particular is here the support and foundation of the universal; the universal . . . could have no meaning if it did not exist for the purpose of the individual" (*BN* 239–40). Against Hegel's monism Sartre insists that "no logical or epistemological optimism can cover the scandal of the plurality of consciousnesses. If Hegel believed that it could, this is because he never grasped the nature of that particular dimension of being which is self-consciousness. The task which an ontology can lay down for itself is to describe this scandal and to found it in the very nature of being" (*BN* 244). To say that *Souls* offers something like this description or to point to some of its materialist tendencies is not to argue that it is a work of Marxist humanism or of mid-twentieth-century existentialism. It is only to give a better sense of the originality of the book's insights and procedures.

Du Bois recognizes that the self is culturally constructed within the parameters of a given historic and social context within which it can resist and create. This is what is understood here by negativity and activity. In *Souls* the desire that seeks to overcome "double-consciousness" is, as in Hegel, a desire for recognition. The desiring I's transformation of the world to the point where it will recognize it is the definition of activity. As Kojève explains, the being of this desiring I is not "identity" or "equality to itself" but "negating negativity." Which is to say that "the very being of this I will be becoming, and the universal for this being will not be space, but time."[15] The transformation of desire out of the repetitive cycles of biological nature into activity is, then, the "fall" into history.

Slavoj Žižek's gloss on the Marxist idea of "the negation of the negation" offers a description of what the present discussion is trying to outline here:

> this double, self-referential logic of the negation does not entail any kind of return to positive identity, any kind of abolition, of cancellation of the disruptive force of negativity, of reducing it to a passing moment in the self-mediating process of identity; in the "negation of the negation," the negativity preserves all its disruptive power; the whole point is that we come to experience how this negative, disruptive power, menacing our identity is simultaneously a positive condition of it. The "negation of the negation" does not in any way abolish the antagonism, it consists only in the experience of the fact that this immanent limit which is preventing me from achieving my full identity with myself simultaneously enables me to achieve a minimum of positive consistency, however mutilated it is.
>
> This, then, is the "negation of the negation": not a kind of "superseding" of negativity but the experience of the fact that *the negativity as such has a positive function,* enables and structures our positive consistency. In simple negation, there is still the pre-given positive identity which is being negated, the movement of negativity is still conceived as the limitation of some pre-given positivity; while in the "negation of the negation," negativity is in a way *prior to what is being negated,* it is a negative moment which opens the very place where every positive identity can be situated.[16]

As already demonstrated in the introduction, in *Dusk of Dawn* Du Bois himself formulates a sense of the struggle for identity through mediation and negativity that is very close to this. This is the meaning of Du Bois's feeling both "imprisoned, conditioned, depressed" and also "exalted and inspired" in "the folds of this European civilization." It is from this vantage point that he has "made vocal to many, a single whirlpool of social entanglement and inner psychological paradox" (*DD* 555). It is from a position of such ambiguous possibilities that Du Bois can insist that he can "sit with Shakespeare" and "summon Aristotle" in a realm "above the Veil" (*SBF* 438), and also insist that the African-American spirituals are among the finest creations of American culture.

Alluding to the "clothes philosophy" of Carlyle's *Sartor Resartus,* Henry Adams writes in the preface of his *Education* that "the tailor's object, in this volume, is to fit young men, in universities or elsewhere, to be men of the world, equipped for any emergency; and the garment offered to them is meant to show the faults of the patchwork fitted on their fathers" (*EHA* xxx). But if this seems to promise a seamless epistemology for the age of multiplicity, by the end of his autobiography Adams, as has already been noted, concludes that "the new American" must "think in contradictions," and that the ever accelerating transformation of society requires "a new social mind" (*EHA* 497–98). Adams neither refuses to engage with the challenge posed by multiplicity, as James ultimately does, nor submits uncritically to his culture's trajectories of development. Adams equips the young "in universities and elsewhere" for emergency by demonstrating that a set of crises underlies the self-confidence of his age, that these crises can be described, and that analysis and intelligence need not be set adrift when they are separated from the totalizations of law. Discussions of Du Bois's educational theories tend to concentrate almost exclusively on his defense of humanistic studies against Booker T. Washington's prioritization of manual and technical training. The curriculum offered by *Souls* cannot be contained within these polarities; it is closer to Adams's sense of education and, like Adams's autobiography, it continues to demonstrate survival within states of emergency.

rest of the manuscript. According to Linda Sideman, the chief archivist of the Du Bois papers, the hand is that of the older Du Bois. So it would seem that Du Bois had gone back to the story in later life and had unfortunately decided against the profitability of pursuing the fictional possibilities opened up by the youthful story. Given this attitude on the part of the older Du Bois, it might be that he sorted through his notes and chose to preserve only the lecture notes on the economic development of railways that appear on the other side of the pages on which the story is written.

It is Broderick who titles the story "A Vacation Unique," and that title has been adopted here. Broderick also dates the story June 1889. The accuracy of this dating seems to be borne out by the version of the story among the Du Bois papers. The academic notes written on the loose leaves from the notebook include notes on American railways. Du Bois took Political Economy 9, a course on the "Management and Ownership of Railways," during the second half of the 1888–89 academic year, at a time when he was also completing the second half of his course on ethics (Philosophy 4) with James. In Du Bois's version of the story there is a reference to registering at Harvard in September 1889. This would also place the events of the story in the preceding summer of that year.

"A Vacation Unique's" fantastic, almost science-fictional plot is reminiscent of works such as Swift's or Voltaire's or even, in some sense, Edward Bellamy's *Looking Backwards* (1888), and its startling shifts of modes and tonalities, its meandering meditations blending autobiographical introspection and fiction, may owe a debt to Carlyle's *Sartor Resartus.* The story anticipates much of *Souls,* particularly its treatment of "double-consciousness" in the first chapter and its descriptive insights into black life behind the veil of the color line. More significantly, perhaps, Du Bois's extraordinary and stilted combination of realism, romance, and a kind of grotesque—a combination whose effect is almost surreal and generates a radical satire—prefigures certain developments in twentieth-century American literature. The story looks ahead not only to Ellison's surreal investigations of invisibility in *Invisible Man* (1952), but also to Nathanael West (particularly Balso Snell's intestinal journey through history), George S. Schuyler's science fiction satire *Black No More* (1931), in which a drug transforms all blacks into whites, and of course Ishmael Reed's *Free-Lance Pallbearers* (1967), an alimentary voyage through the cannibalistic insides of Uncle Sam. At the same time, the treatment of passing—albeit white passing for black—offers a very early example of a theme that preoccupies both black and white writers, from James Weldon Johnson's *Autobiography of an Ex–*

Colored Man (1912) and Nella Larsen's *Passing* (1929) to Griffin Howard's
Black Like Me (1961), the journalistic report of a white man passing for black
that more than reconfirms Du Bois's vision of the "intestines of the fourth
civilization." Written at a time when both white and black American fiction
was dominated by realism, Du Bois's "A Vacation Unique," even in its
incomplete form, opens unexpected perspectives onto a more hybrid and
complex literary history.

A Note on the Transcriptions

In the first transcription, which is the version of the story in the Du Bois
papers, square brackets ([]) indicate additions I have made, a question
mark ([?]) after a word indicates a word that is unclear in the manuscript,
and curly brackets ({}) indicate words or phrases that Du Bois inserted
above a line. The lines of plus signs (+ + +) used to separate different
sections in this version of the story appear in Du Bois's original manuscript and are not editorial additions.

In the transcription of the Broderick version, square brackets ([])
indicate Broderick's comments. Broderick tends to abbreviate certain
words (e.g., "Neg" for Negro and "A-Sax" for Anglo-Saxon). These are
given in full in the transcription below.

Some sections of both versions appear to be confused. No attempt
has been made to impose order on these sections.

First Version:
Du Bois's Hand-Written Manuscript

[The story begins in medias res.]
Now here I have a very choice article, something unique and entirely
new; warranted not to cloy, bracing, refreshing, healthy, safe, remunera-
tive and dangerous—you are interested? Of course you are. For particulars
you may call at my room at any time during study hours when you [are]
presumably least engaged, hm! My card[:]

Cuffy Johnsing [*sic*],
199 Arlworthy.

Good day I must leave you here.

Ah! to get a little fresh air on the common. There now lies Epicurus
flat on his back with a "good hit! steal your second! foul out" and a pipe;
and here's your John Stuart Mill with a Hurry! Babylon's falling. Sic vita,

the Night is coming, O I die Horatio—what lubber-heads. The Crispus Attucks monument—you think then, sir, the commemoration inappropriate? My dear fellow you are just years behind the time—at which date according to J. Homer, DD. LLD., the Greeks erected a young pile to Mr. Achilles {in commemoration of a certain brawl}—how tall was Alexander Pa? Now I'm constitutionally opposed to parks, commons, and the like: they are nuisances—like the rest of the world—but I must hasten home to my fool—this car is going and I go.

+ +

This then is the plan: after a painless operation performed by one of my friends you will appear as a Negro, a full-fledged darky; we will then set out through the land of the Free and Home of the Brave as two readers giving 40 or 50 entertainments during the vacation; now mark you the advantages: by becoming a Nigger you step into a new and, to most people, entirely unknown region of the universe—you break the bounds of humanity and become a—er—colored man. Again you will not only be a Negro but a Negro in an un-thought of and astoundingly incongruous role. Having in this manner reached an entirely unique and strange position you will be in [a] position to solve in a measure the problems of Introspection and [the] Fourth Dimension, for you will have an opportunity of beholding yourself in your seaside and mountain {resort} [?] and beholding too parts of character invisible to {the general run of} men, and your view of mankind in general will have a striking resemblance to the view which Mr. Field [?] of Flatland had of Mr. Drelic [?] of Lineland intestines. I might mention many other striking advantages in this vacation-tide [?] lark—but I'll not. I will merely say that I have chosen you for the trip because in most particulars you fill the bill surprisingly well—you are old enough, you are tall enough, you are fool enough—I am sorry you have a distinguished ancestry—other things being equal I prefer a man with no ancestry at all not even a father—I should have been pleased to make the acquaintance of Adam.

+ +

You are now sir a Negro and let me say my friend did a remarkably good job—your {Anglo-Saxon} lips, of the Sir Walter Scott pretty red pouting variety have gained thickness with color, your hair with becoming modesty has slunk back, cringing [?], ashamed either of the owner or its owner's owners and your countenance which before the application of prepared lampblack was open and winning has suddenly become to the last degree repulsive. You don't feel! Pish! Hold your tongue—your feelings have played but small part in history. Now, sir, this veneer will last just three {mos} [*sic*] at which date without further ado like this one-horse [?] shay [?] it will all drop off just in time for you to register, "Harvard '90" Sept '26, 1889. Presto! Away now to the street, to the world, the [?] world that gaping—gapes.

+ +

You have your letters of recommendation? Ah that's good boy know you my fool your ordinary jackass may go through the world gates by your jackass with the fourth dimension of color why bless you—it's "What do [?] it? [?] Why so? I'm afraid I can't" keep you overnight or give you a peacable [*sic*] [?] meal of victuals or refrain from telling how much I did for your People!

+ +

To the Berkshire [?] Hills! we are sitting and the world is flying past. O I love this grimly unconscious old world this conservative old Widower whose son persists in setting yesternight just as it did 6000 years ago & who has never added an extra tint to the rainbow. It is a beautiful day: the rain {does not come} down in a raging flood as if angry with its task it sought to choke the Earth—but it comes lovingly in a drizzle and the parched forests drink slowly and thankfully and only Man is discontented—see now in the West it is breaking away—grey, pink, red, blue—back! [?] now comes your sun to dazzle and glare—see my Fool this is life in a nut-shell

+ +

Good afternoon: I am {one of two} students of Harvard College (now you needn't start and look surprised and say with your eyebrows "what Niggers in *Harvard!*) who are giving a series of readings this summer to help pay our expenses next year.

UNPROPHETABLE

Second Version: Broderick's Transcription

Just "endured my first class-day at Fair Harvard." One attended in new swallow-tail coat wrinkled in back, another ate for three hours, 256 mammys and papas did not enjoy the prize fight "around the Tree but nevertheless lied about it thereafter; Donkey '91 met Miss De Skit, he bowed prettily." Now for vacation—rest, rest, but pick up $243 in three months among men of straw than in street car crowd: "O such gelatinous dignity, such ludicrous repose, such shocked propriety when a little human nature escapes—luckless prisoner."

Another '92 appears. ". . . as you doubtless suspect I have long been aware that I am a Negro—it isn't necessary for you to remind me of the fact by asking me for the race's statistics at Harvard." 275/300 visitors last year asked, so I have it printed up on a card. ". . . take it and read it at your leisure." ["God bless you" penciled in above "read it." Learned references to Epicurus, Johnathan (sic!) Edwards, Achilles, Bible.]

"Have you heard of the Fourth Dimension, Fool?" Spend summer in that portion of space, viewing world's intestines from new point of view. Not impossible: merely disguise self as Negro and travel around and see the world from the Negro point of view. "A Darky of the most approved type (you will pardon me for capitalizing the words.)" Pose as college students giving readings to help defray expenses. A new unexplored area. From this experience, you can solve the intricate problems of introspection and the fourth dimension: "Outside of mind you may study mind, and outside of matter by reason of the fourth dimension of color you may have a striking view of the intestines of the fourth great civilization." Done, your whole complexion has suddenly become so repulsive—but your feelings no longer count, they are not a part of history. Away to the streets and let the gaping gape.

Seated at decent dinner. Don't notice the stares, it's ill bred to notice them. Don't yell at the waiter in that manner, or I'll knock you down. I'm a former waiter myself, and "if there is one foul and festering sore on civilization which most characteristically shows the rottenness beneath it is your American Hotel. Teuton loves his belly better than his Christ. Enters, tells headwaiter: I, I only am able to pay your wages—I shall be served. Yells after waiter, "Hey, darky." Or John, when waiter's Mother called him Edward. Tells waiter that he will supplement miserable pay if the waiter steals enough to satisfy hunger of guest: cheat and steal from anybody. I know about waiters: they're devilishly sly and are able to steal food for themselves, and are expected to do so. Negroes "he hired, he bought he's sold to cringe . . ." "O your Anglo-Saxon civilization built upon the Eternal I. . . ."

There will be grades as long as heaven is not level with earth. Not it should not be at caste level. A student waiter can eventually command enough cash to sit at the same level with guest, but not the nigger. Here John! "O there is where the Heart aches: not that I is above You but that I despises You he is above him: that is the little worm that gnawing at the vitals of the World Soul shall . . . [one word not clear] drown him in the Deep Sea."

Anglo-Saxon's "high Episcopal Nicene creed" to put heel on neck of man down. When inequality is in posse only and not in esse, then the fine American lady will stop at no level of ignominy to taunt him while she sings love of the creator in sweet religious carols. America tried by sleight of hand to decree that there were no inequalities: "why there were more glaring legally unalterable, despicable inequalities under Tom Jefferson's venerable nose when he penned that line than he could flutter a club at."

Back to the waiter: others will leave their mother's knee to fight the world, but the world fights him. Alas, thou copper-colored, "well mayst thou look dismayed better wert thou between the devil and the wild and raging sea for thou art worse than that thou are between man & nigger."

Brief satire of academic philosophizing and distinctions: several professors differ on a multiplication table with result 6930, arrived at by different factors. "Which now is the truth? Argue. Argue. Argue. Why my fool the truth is there is no truth . . . but, oho my audience sleeps. Well, rah rah rah! rah rah rah! rah rah rah! Harvard. I sleep too."

Instead of dreaming, I must get down to rector of ——— church. On way, everyone stares but you do not mind; God-given right of American ladies to eye a social inferior from head to foot and still retain their self-respect. Domestic is astonished to see Negro calling. Hostess is cordial: letting you know how nice she can be to colored people; she mentions casually the vast debt owed to Anglo-Saxon race because of great interest her people had in your people and pile of clothes sent to Tuskegee last winter. If she mentions these things, and she surely will, you are supposed to look grateful. Then rector will come. You give an account of the extraordinary fact that you are at Harvard, and "a verbal census of all other such past present and future anomalies of your race." Wants to do reading for some church group, to share profits with church and with students (Negro) at Harvard. Some excuse found for every organization. I am sorry. "Mind not, little heart, if the world were you I could love it. And so we have spent a sample day. We are disappointed. And yet I have spent the happiest hours of my life when I have come home in the twilight with a life plan in my bosom smashed—and alone—sturdy man, foresooth: laid my head on my table, and wept."

Seeing Sir Joshua's portrait of Jared Sparks in Gore Hall in toga, he looks for Socrates in wig and top boots, or Minerva in corsets.

Back on math equation again: you must get away from simple multiplication as measure. "You must have an indefinite or as I should prefer to say infinite if you would escape a tiresome insipid farce & gain true life." Humanity has nothing to do with math: if 6930 is brute fact, what difference how you reach it? ". . . I seriously doubt if there is any truth after all your blatant world-search. Truth is not the object of knowledge nor even consistency. It is the best workable hypothesis." "The moral equation with its Indefinite is the only equation that will make 6930 worth living." No matter whether it is consistent or not, true or false; important thing is a world etc. [Breaks off thus]

I don't deny Anglo-Saxon civilization has done much; I just deny that it has done all. Only the self forgetful Quakers still remember God. Among rest, "not that I is above Thee but that I despises thee—there is the death warrant of Teutonic civilization."

Notes

One

1. Trans. Bernard Frechtman (London: Methuen, 1967), pp. 23–24.

2. Most critics, approaching Du Bois as a political activist and social commentator, have confined their discussions of *Souls* either to the book's third chapter's critique of Booker T. Washington or to fragmentary summaries of the book. This approach has tended to relegate *Souls* to the periphery of Du Bois's social and political thought. See Francis L. Broderick, *W. E. B. Du Bois: Negro Leader in a Time of Crisis* (Stanford: Stanford University Press, 1959), pp. 46–48; Elliot M. Rudwick, *W. E. B. Du Bois: A Study in Minority Group Leadership* (Philadelphia: University of Pennsylvania Press, 1960), pp. 68–69. Joseph De Marco, *The Social Thought of W. E. B. Du Bois* (Lanham: University Press of America, 1983), chooses not to discuss *Souls,* classifying it as a literary work. There is a passing discussion in Manning Marable, *W. E. B. Du Bois: Black Radical Democrat* (Boston: Twayne, 1986), pp. 48–50, 189–99. David Levering Lewis's biography, *W. E. B. Du Bois: Biography of a Race, 1868–1919* (New York: Henry Holt, 1993), pp. 277–91, does not add greatly to existing discussions.

Those who have come to *Souls* from a literary perspective either have offered inadequate discussions of the relationship of the book to the intellectual history of the times and to Du Bois's previous writings or have sidestepped these contexts. Arnold Rampersad's *The Art and Imagination of W. E. B. Du Bois* (Cambridge, Mass.: Harvard University Press, 1976), is an important contribution to Du Bois studies, but its discussion of *Souls* is thin and fragmented (see chapter 4). Chapter 3 of Robert Stepto's *From Behind the Veil: A Study of Afro-American Narrative*

(Urbana: University of Illinois Press, 1979) is almost certainly the most careful literary reading of the book, but it is essentially formalist in its attention to ritual topography and literary revisionism; Jack B. Moore, *W. E. B. Du Bois* (Boston: Twayne, 1981), pp. 63–81, adds little to previous criticism. Other aspects of critical writing on Du Bois are discussed in chapter 4.

3. As Althusser notes, "to say that an ideology constitutes an (organic) totality is only valid *descriptively*—not *theoretically,* for this description converted into a theory exposes us to the danger of thinking nothing but the empty unity of the described whole" ("the Hegelian ambiguities of '*totality*' "). To approach an "ideological thought" as a problematic, however, is to see it within the full ideological field and the historical conditions that are its proper context. To do so is not only to examine the answers given by an ideology but to investigate "the system of *questions* commanding the *answers* given," to resist the empty totalizing of ideological description, and to read the ruptures and contradictions of ideological formulations as these are exposed by the mediation of history. See Louis Althusser, "On the Young Marx: Theoretical Questions" (1961), in Althusser, *For Marx,* trans. Ben Brewster (1965; London: Verso, 1990), pp. 66–67.

4. Peter Conn, *The Divided Mind: Ideology and Imagination in America, 1898–1917* (Cambridge: Cambridge University Press, 1983), p. 1.

5. Henry Adams, *The Education of Henry Adams,* ed. Ernest Samuel (1907; Boston: Houghton Mifflin, 1973), p. 12. Hereafter cited as *EHA.*

6. Donald C. Bellomy, "Two Generations: Modernists and Progressives, 1870–1920," *Perspectives in American History,* New Series 3 (1987), p. 293.

7. Ibid.

8. The phrase is taken from Eric Mottram, "Henry Adams: Index of the Twentieth Century," in Y. Hakutani and L. Fried, eds., *American Literary Naturalism: A Reassessment* (Heidelberg: Carl Winter Universitätsverlag, 1975), pp. 90–105.

9. On the publication history of *Souls,* see Herbert Aptheker, "*The Souls of Black Folk:* A Comparison of the 1903 and 1952 Editions," *Negro History Bulletin* 34, no. 1 (1971): 15–17.

10. August Meier, *Negro Thought in America 1880–1915* (1963; Ann Arbor: University of Michigan Press, 1991). Other useful accounts of Afro-American thought at this time include Rayford W. Logan, *The Negro in American Life and Thought: The Nadir, 1877–1901* (New York: Dial Press, 1954), Joel Williamson, *The Crucible of Race: Black-White Relations in the American South since Emancipation* (New York: Oxford University Press, 1984), the second half of Hazel V. Carby's *Reconstructing Womanhood: The Emergence of the Afro-American Woman Novelist* (New York: Oxford University Press, 1987), and Howard Brotz, ed., *African-American Social and Political Thought 1850–1920,* new ed. (New Brunswick: Transaction Publishers, 1992).

11. Meier, *Negro Thought in America,* pp. 47, 184.

12. Ibid., p. 196. In later life Du Bois himself argued that the differences between his own early thought and that of Washington had been exaggerated. See *Dusk of Dawn,* pp. 604–5. Meier provides the most detailed account of the Du Bois–Washington debate, though most of the major works on Du Bois cited

earlier discuss the relationship of the thought of the two men. See also chapter 5 of Conn, *The Divided Mind*.

13. See note 2 above for a survey of previous scholarship on Du Bois.

14. Cornel West, *The American Evasion of Philosophy: A Genealogy of Pragmatism* (Madison: University of Wisconsin Press, 1989), p. 142.

15. West's alignment of Du Bois with James has gained some currency. Nancy Ladd Muller, "Du Boisian Pragmatism and 'The Problem of the Twentieth Century,'" *Critique of Anthropology* 12, no. 3 (1992): 319–37, offers a very confused elaboration of West's position. Giles Gunn, *Thinking Across the American Grain: Ideology, Intellect, and New Pragmatism* (Chicago: University of Chicago Press, 1992), pp. 2–3, accepts West's genealogy uncritically. See also Larry C. Miller, "William James and Twentieth-Century Ethnic Thought," *American Quarterly* 31, no. 4 (1979): 533–34.

16. Lewis, *W. E. B. Du Bois*, passim.

17. Robert Gooding-Williams, "Evading Narrative Myth, Evading Pragmatism: Cornel West's *The American Evasion of Philosophy*," *Massachusetts Review* (Winter 1991–92): 517–42. For further differentiation from Gooding-Williams's argument, see chapter 4.

18. William James, *The Principles of Psychology*, vol. 1 (1890; New York: Dover, 1950), p. 363.

19. Ross Posnock, *The Trial of Curiosity: Henry James, William James, and the Challenge of Modernity* (New York: Oxford University Press, 1991), pp. 35, 64.

20. Other commentaries on Du Bois's relation to Hegel and the ways in which the present account differs from them are examined in detail in chapter 4.

21. See the essays "The Dilemma of Determinism" (1884) and "On Some Hegelisms" (1882), both collected in *The Will to Believe* (1897; New York: Dover, 1956), pp. 145–83, 263–98. Both essays are discussed later in this study.

22. These commentaries are discussed in chapter 4.

23. Posnock, *The Trial of Curiosity*, pp. 110–11.

24. Dorothy Ross, *The Origins of American Social Science* (Cambridge: Cambridge University Press, 1991), p. xv.

25. Ibid., p. xiv. For a thorough survey on the debate about American exceptionalism, see Michael Kammen, "The Problem of American Exceptionalism: A Reconsideration," *American Quarterly* 45, no. 1 (1993): 1–43.

26. Ross, *The Origins of American Social Science*, pp. xii–xiv.

27. West, *American Evasion of Philosophy*, p. 5.

28. Ralph Waldo Emerson, *Nature*, in Stephen E. Whicher, ed., *Selections from Ralph Waldo Emerson* (Boston: Houghton Mifflin, 1957), pp. 21, 24.

29. The imagery of health and sickness is derived from chapters 6 and 7 of *The Varieties of Religious Experience* (1902). For James's application of the medical polarity to America and Europe, see his "Dilemma of Determinism."

30. Louis Hartz, *The Liberal Tradition in America: An Interpretation of American Political Thought since the Revolution* (New York: Harcourt, Brace and World, 1955), pp. 285, 309. Cf. also Richard Hofstadter, *Anti-Intellectualism in American*

Life (Boston: Beacon Press, 1964), for another well-known critique of the particular attitude Hartz analyzed.

31. For a critique of Rorty, see Ian Shapiro, *Political Criticism* (Berkeley: University of California Press, 1990), pp. 8–9. In terms that recall Hartz, Shapiro critiques Rorty's failure to theorize the relation of self to society and the Jamesian "atomistic liberal outcomes" of his work.

32. Clive Bush, *Halfway to Revolution: Investigation and Crisis in the Works of Henry Adams, William James and Gertrude Stein* (New Haven: Yale University Press, 1991), p. 444.

33. Kenneth W. Warren, "Delimiting America: The Legacy of Du Bois," *American Literary History* (Spring 1989): 178–79. Warren is reviewing Bernard W. Bell, *The Afro-American Novel and Its Tradition* (Amherst: University of Massachusetts Press, 1987); Henry Louis Gates, Jr., *Figures in Black: Words, Signs, and the "Racial" Self* (New York: Oxford University Press, 1987); and Melvin Dixon, *Ride Out the Wilderness: Geography and Identity in Afro-American Literature* (Urbana: University of Illinois Press, 1987). However, his comments are equally applicable to the tradition of African-American literary criticism that has tried to define a theory of African-American literature by isolating a series of scenes of literary revision within that literature. Essentially formalist in its procedures, this criticism has become perhaps the most dominant model of African-American literary criticism since the late 1970s. Its development can be traced from Stepto's *From Behind the Veil* to Henry Louis Gates, Jr.'s, *The Signifying Monkey: A Theory of African-American Literary Criticism* (New York: Oxford University Press, 1988). Alongside Warren's qualifications, see also Houston A. Baker, "Generational Shifts and Recent Criticism of Afro-American Literature," *Black American Literature Forum* 15, no. 1 (1981): 3–21; Hazel Carby, "The Canon: Civil War and Reconstruction," *Michigan Quarterly Review* 28, no. 1 (1989): 29–40; Theodore O. Mason, "Between the Populist and the Scientist: Ideology and Power in Recent Afro-American Literary Criticism, or 'The Dozens' as Scholarship," *Callaloo* 11, no. 3 (1988): 606–15; and Werner Sollors, "A Critique of Pure Pluralism," in Sacvan Bercovitch, ed., *Reconstructing American Literary History* (Cambridge, Mass.: Harvard University Press, 1986), pp. 250–79.

34. Warren, "Delimiting America," p. 184.

35. Søren Kierkegaard, *Concluding Unscientific Postscript*, trans. David F. Swenson and Walter Lowrie (Princeton: Princeton University Press, 1941), p. 35n.

36. Carby, *Reconstructing Womanhood*, p. 91, notes that Francis Harper also outlined a program for a black leadership that has close parallels with Du Bois's notion of the Talented Tenth.

37. Raymond Williams, *Culture and Society: 1780–1950* (1958; New York: Columbia University Press, 1983), p. 71.

38. George Oppen, "Of Being Numerous" (1967), in Oppen, *Collected Poems* (London: Fulcrum, 1972), p. 117.

Two

1. Du Bois completed his degree at Fisk between 1885 and 1888 and joined Harvard as a junior.

2. See W. E. B. Du Bois, *The Black North in 1901: A Social Study. A Series of Articles Originally Appearing in the New York Times, November–December 1901* (New York: Arno Press and the New York Times, 1969), p. 31, for Du Bois's account of Boston in the second half of the nineteenth century.

3. Seymour Martin Lipset, in Lipset and David Reisman, *Education and Politics at Harvard* (New York: McGraw-Hill, 1975), pp. 105–6.

4. David Levering Lewis, *W. E. B. Du Bois: Biography of a Race, 1868–1919* (New York: Henry Holt, 1993), pp. 15–17. For further details of Du Bois's family background and boyhood, see chapter 2 of *Dusk of Dawn* and chapters 6 and 7 of the *Autobiography*. Two articles by Robert Paynter also provide some useful information on Great Barrington and its surroundings: "Afro-Americans in the Massachusetts Historical Landscape," in P. Gathercole and D. Lowenthal, eds., *The Politics of the Past* (London: Unwin Hynaman, 1990), pp. 49–62, and "W. E. B. Du Bois and the Material World of African-Americans in Great Barrington, Massachusetts," *Critique of Anthropology* 12, no. 3 (1992): 277–91.

5. On the use of the South to critique national myths in the Gilded Age, see the last three chapters of C. Vann Woodward's *The Burden of Southern History*, 2d ed. (Baton Rouge: Louisiana State University Press, 1968).

6. See Eric Bentley, *The Cult of the Superman: A Study of the Idea of Heroism in Carlyle and Nietzsche, with Notes on Other Hero-Worshippers of Modern Times* (Gloucester, Mass.: Peter Smith, 1969), p. 18. Originally published as *A Century of Hero Worship* (1944).

7. The literature on the history of race relations in postbellum America is too vast to rehearse here. Two studies provide useful overviews of the period: C. Vann Woodward's *The Strange Career of Jim Crow*, 3d ed. (New York: Oxford University Press, 1974); and Joel Williamson, *The Crucible of Race: Black-White Relations in the American South since Emancipation* (New York: Oxford University Press, 1984).

8. Arnold Rampersad, *The Art and Imagination of W. E. B. Du Bois* (Cambridge, Mass.: Harvard University Press, 1976), p. 45.

9. Henry Steele Commager, *The American Mind: An Interpretation of American Thought and Character since the 1880s* (New Haven, Conn.: Yale University Press, 1950), p. 47.

10. The first reference to Carlyle in Du Bois's work dates from the same year as the "Bismarck" speech, and Du Bois's admiration for the Prussian leader clearly reflects his approval of Carlyle's admiration for Frederick of Prussia, Bismarck, and German Nationalism as well as of Carlyle's belief that Prussia offered the solution for the future in the face of the imminent collapse of democracy. Du Bois mentions Carlyle in an editorial for the *Fisk Herald* 5 (January 1888): 8. Cited in Rampersad, *Art and Imagination of W. E. B. Du Bois*, pp. 66 and 303, n. 64. For Carlyle's attitude to Prussia and Bismarck, see Bentley, *The Cult of the Superman*, pp. 30–35.

11. Harold Kaplan, *Power and Order: Henry Adams and the Naturalist Tradition in American Fiction* (Chicago: University of Chicago Press, 1981), pp. 68–69.

12. For an account of the student days, see chapter 9 of the *Autobiography* and chapter 3 of *Dusk of Dawn*.

13. For a history of philosophy at Harvard, see Bruce Kucklick, *The Rise of American Philosophy: Cambridge, Massachusetts, 1860–1930* (New Haven: Yale University Press, 1979). Members of faculties other than the philosophy faculty included "Shaler in geology and Hart in history; there were Francis Child, Charles Eliot Norton, Justin Winsor, and John Towbridge; Goodwin, Taussig and Kitteridge. The president was . . . Charles William Eliot, while Oliver Wendell Holmes and James Russell Lowell were still alive and emeriti" (*DD* 581).

14. Harvard University Catalogue, 1888–1892, Harvard University Archives. According to a listing of Du Bois's library made in 1952, and now in the Du Bois papers at Amherst, Du Bois owned both works of Martineau's in their entirety. Du Bois's library is housed in Ghana and I have not had access to it. All subsequent information regarding Du Bois's library is derived from this list.

15. Du Bois's surviving notebook covers the second half of the course that centered on Martineau's *Study of Religion,* but the notes begin with a summary of the discussion of ethics from the first half of the year. The Philosophy 4 notebook is among the Du Bois papers at the University of Massachusetts at Amherst. Since this notebook is used frequently in the discussions that follow, the abbreviation "P4" follows all quotations taken from it or any summary of its arguments in order to avoid any confusion about the source of the quotations. Although I have not yet been able to consult the smaller collections of Du Bois papers at Fisk University and at Atlanta University, the librarians there have not been able to locate any other notebooks or material relevant to the Harvard years.

16. William James, *Manuscript Lectures* (Cambridge: Harvard University Press, 1988).

17. The two volumes of the *Principles of Psychology* appeared in 1890, *The Will to Believe* in 1897, and *The Varieties of Religious Experience* in 1902. Of the essays in *The Will to Believe,* several had seen publication prior to Du Bois's studies with James: portions of "The Sentiment of Rationality" appeared in 1879 and 1882, "Great Men and Their Environment" in 1880, "Reflex Action and Theism" in 1881, "On Some Hegelisms" in 1882, and "The Dilemma of Determinism" in 1884. Other important essays from *The Will to Believe* appeared at the end of Du Bois's studies with James or a few years after: "The Importance of Individuals" (1890), "What Physical Research Has Accomplished" (1890–1896), "The Moral Philosopher and the Moral Life" (1891), "Is Life Worth Living?" (1895), and "The Will to Believe" (1896).

18. Many of these concerns from the lectures also dominate James's published essays from this period. These works are listed in note 17 above. Almost all of them cover matters that are, in one way or another, important for Du Bois's intellectual development.

19. It is usually clear in the notes when it is James speaking and when Du Bois. Du Bois's own thoughts seem to intervene rarely, and usually in parentheses.

20. The relevance of the alignment between James's Pragmatism and the European neo-Kantian movement for Du Bois's development is considered in chapter 3.

21. James, *Manuscript Lectures,* p. 185.

22. Herbert Spencer, *The Data of Ethics* (London: Williams and Norgate, 1879), p. iii.

23. William James, "Great Men and Their Environment" (1880), hereafter abbreviated GM, in James, *The Will to Believe and Other Essays in Popular Philosophy* (1897; New York: Dover Press, 1956), pp. 244, 253. Spencer's system is, in fact, an uneasy attempt to mediate nineteenth-century naturalistic and metaphysical historicism. Darwin's evolutionary theories made nature a part of history. As a result, the post-Herderian natural sciences were able to challenge Hegelian idealism's claim to hold the key to historical understanding. The radical new sense of historical process and change led to a profound crisis of historicism that also enveloped ethics into relativism. For a succinct account of these developments, see Hayden White, "On History and Historicism," his introduction to Carlo Antoni's *From History to Sociology: The Transition in German Historical Thought,* trans. Hayden White (1940; London: Merlin, 1962), pp. xv–xxviii. While he admired Spencer's empiricism, James understood that "the evolutionary *philosophy* is monism" or "pure subjective Idealism—tho't [*sic*] fatally obeying destiny—with no real object" (James, *Manuscript Lectures,* pp. 158, 134). The first quote is from an 1878–79 course on psychology and the second from a course on the philosophy of evolution taught from 1879 to 1885. Du Bois's notes for Philosophy 4 also indicate that James moved easily and logically from discussions of causality in Spencer's work to critiques of idealist notions of Universal Mind, Oversoul, and Roycean philosophy.

24. Ralph Barton Perry, *The Thought and Character of William James,* briefer version (1948; New York: Harper and Row, 1964), p. 221.

25. The commentary here on the potential conservatism of environment in James's Great Man theory and its social-Darwinistic implications draws on Daniel N. Robinson, *Toward a Science of Human Nature: Essays on the Psychologies of Mill, Hegel, Wundt and James* (New York: Columbia University Press, 1982), pp. 196–98, 206–7, and 572, and Clive Bush, *Halfway to Revolution: Investigation and Crisis in the Work of Henry Adams, William James, and Gertrude Stein* (New Haven: Yale University Press, 1991), pp. 200–201.

26. James, *Manuscript Lectures,* p. 184.

27. William James, "The Dilemma of Determinism," in James, *Will to Believe,* p. 164. Hereafter cited in the text as DoD.

28. The relevance of the arguments of *The Economic and Philosophic Manuscripts of 1844* and of *Being and Nothingness* for comparing Du Bois and James is fully elaborated in chapter 4.

29. John Higham, "The Reorientation of American Culture in the 1890s," in Higham, *Writing American History: Essays on Modern Scholarship* (Bloomington: Indiana University Press, 1970), p. 93.

30. Ibid., p. 100.

31. See T. J. Jackson Lears, *No Place of Grace: Antimodernisim and the Transformation of American Culture, 1880–1920* (New York: Pantheon Books, 1981), pp. 47–58. My own account is derived from Lears's. *American Nervousness* is the title of a book by Beard.

32. See, for instance, chapter 13 of Perry, *The Thought and Character of William James,* briefer version.

33. Henry Childs Merwin, quoted in Lears, *No Place of Grace,* p. 47.

34. Ibid., p. 53.

35. Ibid., p. 54.

36. William James, *The Varieties of Religious Experience: A Study in Human Nature* (1904; New York: Macmillan, 1961), p. 110.

37. Max Horkheimer, *The Eclipse of Reason* (1947; New York: Seabury Press, 1974), p. 51.

38. Ibid., p. 19.

39. Ibid., p. 51.

40. Ross Posnock, by contrast, sees Horkheimer's critique as ultimately "lopsided," a distortion produced by the bleakness of the war, but this is not a fair assessment. Posnock, *The Trial of Curiosity: Henry James, William James and the Challenge of Modernity* (New York: Oxford University Press, 1991), p. 123.

41. Randolph Bourne, "Twilight of Idols," *Seven Arts* 2 (October 1917): 691.

42. Ibid., p. 698.

43. For an outline of James's social and political statements during this period, see Perry, *Thought and Character of William James,* chaps. 25 and 26.

44. See, for example, Larry C. Miller, "William James and Twentieth-Century Ethnic Thought," *American Quarterly* 31, no. 4 (1979): 533–55.

45. William James, *Talks to Teachers on Psychology; and to Students on Some of Life's Ideals* (Boston: Henry Holt, 1899), p. v.

46. William James, *The Principles of Psychology* (1890; New York: Dover Publications, 1950), vol. 1, p. 312. Hereafter cited in the text as *PP.*

47. For a brief comment on the relation of sympathy to James's ethics of the "strenuous" life, see Don S. Browning, *Pluralism and Personality: William James and Some Contemporary Cultures of Psychology* (Lewisburg: Bucknell University Press, 1980), pp. 103–4. James often refers to his own radical descriptive techniques for depicting the flux and process of this life as "sympathetic imagination." For comments on James's idea of the "sympathetic imagination," see John Wild, *The Radical Empiricism of William James* (Garden City: Doubleday, 1969), pp. 155–56, 159.

48. James, *Talks to Teachers,* pp. 273–74.

49. Alan Trachtenberg, *The Incorporation of America: Culture and Society in the Gilded Age* (New York: Hill and Wang, 1982), pp. 140–42.

50. Ibid., p. 145.

51. Ibid., p. 144.

52. James, *Talks to Teachers,* pp. 298–99.

53. Ibid., p. 299.

54. See Sydney Kaplan, "Taussig, James, Peabody: A 'Harvard School' in 1900?" *American Quarterly* 7, no. 4 (1955): 320.

55. For Giddings's place in the history of American sociology, see Thomas L. Haskell, *The Emergence of Professional Social Science: The American Social Science Association and the Nineteenth-Century Crisis of Authority* (Urbana: University of Illinois Press, 1977), pp. 203–4.

56. The first edition of Smith's book appeared in 1759. He worked on the book in the succeeding decades and had made significant revisions and additions by the time the sixth edition came out in 1790. All references are to the later edition.

57. Smith argued that only by means of imagination is it possible to move "beyond our own person" to an understanding of the sensations and sufferings of others: "By the imagination we place ourselves in [the other's] situation, we conceive ourselves enduring all the same torments, we enter as it were into his body, and become in some measure the same person with him, and thence form some idea of his sensations, and even feel something which, though weaker in degree, is not altogether unlike them." This sense of "fellow-feeling" Smith terms "sympathy." In Smith the moral faculty of sympathy works with least hindrance inside the gaze of the "impartial spectator," who forms the polished "looking-glass" of the conscience. This spectator is a white bourgeois consciousness offered ahistorically and apolitically as a universal mean. Smith's ethical theory was, of course, a justificatory program for his defense of a naturally self-regulative capitalist economics. Smith, *The Theory of Moral Sentiments* (1790, 6th ed.), ed. D. D. Raphael and A. L. Macfie (1979; Indianapolis: Liberty Classics, 1982), pp. 9, 10, 112.

58. Frank Henry Giddings, *The Principles of Sociology: An Analysis of the Phenomena of Association and Social Organization* (New York: Macmillan, 1896), p. 17.

59. After citing Smith's *The Theory of Moral Sentiments* as the best conceptualization of the importance of sympathy and imitation in the social process, Giddings writes: "Association . . . moulds the natures of individuals, and adapts them to social life. It creates a social nature. The true social nature is so far susceptible to suggestion and so far imitative in respect of all matters of material well-being, that its possessor desires and endeavors to live at least as well as the average, fairly successful, fairly well-to-do members of the community. The desire to enjoy what others enjoy, and the imitative tendency to act as others act, are strong enough in the social individual to impel him to pursue his material interests as diligently as most other individuals pursue their interests. This combination of desire and diligence is the basis of what economists call a standard of living. It is the foundation of wealth and of all individual advancement" (ibid., p. 123).

60. Dorothy Ross, *The Origins of American Social Science* (Cambridge: Cambridge University Press, 1991), p. 130. C. Van Woodward has also argued that Giddings, along with sociologists like William Graham Sumner, fixed the patterns of racial segregation and conflict into permanence. See Woodward, *The Strange Career of Jim Crow*, pp. 103–4.

61. Like Du Bois, James takes not only Bismarck but also Carlyle as a representative figure in support of his argument. Du Bois could have read the essay before he came to Harvard or during the time that he was at Harvard.

62. According to Broderick Du Bois did give readings in church, but Broderick takes large sections of the story as "diary" entries, a reading not warranted by the text itself. See Francis L. Broderick, *W. E. B. Du Bois: Negro Leader in a Time of Crisis* (Stanford: Stanford University Press, 1959), p. 23.

63. See Lewis, *W. E. B. Du Bois*, pp. 82–83.

64. W. E. B. Du Bois, *Darkwater: Voices from within the Veil* (New York: Harcourt Brace, 1920), pp. 112–13.

65. On theories of Teutonic origins and their relation to historiography, see Edward N. Saveth, *American Historians and European Immigrants, 1875–1925* (New York: Columbia University Press, 1948), chap. 1, and Jurgen Herbst, *The German Historical School in American Scholarship: A Study in the Transfer of Culture* (New York: Cornell University Press, 1965), pp. 115–22.

66. C. H. Hinton, "What Is the Fourth Dimension?" (1884), in Hinton, *Scientific Romances* (London: Sonnenschein, 1884), pp. 4–5. For a fuller exposition of Hinton's ideas on the fourth dimension, see his *The Fourth Dimension* (London: Sonnenschein, 1904).

67. Hinton, "What Is the Fourth Dimension?" p. 31.

68. Edwin A. Abbott, *Flatland: A Romance of Many Dimensions,* 2d ed. (1884; New York: Dover, 1952), p. 32. Hereafter cited in the text as *F*.

69. Thomas Dixon's fiction is exemplary here, as are Charles Caroll's *"The Negro a Beast"; or, "In the Image of God"* (1900), William P. Calhoun's *The Caucasian and the Negro in the United States* (1902), William B. Smith's *The Color Line: A Brief in Behalf of the Unborn* (1905), and Robert W. Shufeldt's *The Negro, A Menace to American Civilization* (1907). For a survey of this and earlier literature, see George M. Fredrickson, *The Black Image in the White Mind: The Debate on Afro-American Character and Destiny, 1817–1914* (New York: Harper and Row, 1971).

70. The full title of the thesis is "The Renaissance of Ethics: A Critical Comparison of Scholastic and Modern Ethics." The manuscript of the thesis is in the James Weldon Johnson Collection in the Beinecke Library at Yale University. Rampersad, *The Art and Imagination of W. E. B. Du Bois,* pp. 25–27, offers a very different reading of this text than the one that follows here. Rampersad focuses much more on the earlier sections of the thesis in the light of James's ideas. The final version, or at least a draft close to the finished thesis, appears to have been completed by June 1889. The manuscript of the thesis is in loose leaves and contained in a hard folder. The dating on the outside of the folder is given as both 1890 and 1889. The dating on the inside, on the actual manuscript, is 1890. One possible explanation for the discrepancy, other than a possible misdating by Du Bois himself when he donated the manuscript to the Beinecke Library at Yale, is that a first draft of the thesis was completed by the end of James's course in June 1889 and that Du Bois then spent some time revising the work and handed it in very late in the next academic year. If this is the case then it means the final version of the thesis was completed while Du Bois was reading Kant and Hegel with Santayana, a fact that may account for some of the idealist strain in the thesis. For the studies with Santayana, see chapter 4. However, the close parallels between "A Vacation Unique" and "Renaissance of Ethics," and the close ties of the fiction with James's course, suggest that both the story and the thesis were written sometime in the summer of 1889.

71. Herbert Spencer, *First Principles* (1862; 5th ed., London: Williams and Norgate, 1890), 553. For Spencer's definition of synthetic philosophy, see pp. 131–33.

72. J. D. Y. Peel, *Herbert Spencer: The Evolution of a Sociologist* (London: Heineman, 1971), p. 245.

73. Daniel J. Wilson, *Science, Community, and the Transformation of American Philosophy, 1860–1930* (Chicago: University of Chicago Press, 1990); see esp. introduction and chap. 4.

74. Peter Allan Dale, *The Victorian Critic and the Idea of History: Carlyle, Arnold, Pater* (Cambridge, Mass.: Harvard University Press, 1977), p. 5.

75. For a full list of courses Du Bois took at Fisk, see *Against Racism*, pp. 6 and 10–12. See also Francis Broderick, "W. E. B. Du Bois: The Trail of His Ideas," Ph.D. diss., Harvard University, 1955, pp. 11–14.

76. Rampersad, *The Art and Imagination of W. E. B. Du Bois,* p. 22.

77. Du Bois also objected to being told by the local church at Fisk that dancing was a "sin" (*DD* 578).

78. Rampersad, *The Art and Imagination of W. E. B. Du Bois,* p. 22.

79. Ibid. See also James McCosh, *Herbert Spencer's Philosophy as Culminated in His Ethics* (New York: Charles Scribner's Sons, 1885), for McCosh's religious attack on Spencer.

80. Rampersad, *The Art and Imagination of W. E. B. Du Bois,* p. 22.

81. Lorraine J. Daston, "The Theory of Will versus the Science of Mind," in William R. Woodward and Mitchell G. Ash, eds., *The Problematic Science: Psychology in Nineteenth Century Thought* (New York: Praeger, 1982), p. 110.

82. Du Bois, "Bismarck," MS in the Du Bois papers at the University of Massachusetts at Amherst. The papers also contain an undated essay from the Fisk years written in German and titled "Das Neue Vaterland."

83. Du Bois had studied English and American literature at Fisk (see *AR* 6) and had taken courses in the English Department at Harvard.

84. If there were any African-Americans in the audience, they would have been a very small minority indeed. I have not been able to obtain more detailed information on the composition of the audience.

85. See Robert D. Richardson, Jr., "Emerson on History," in Joel Porte, ed., *Emerson: Prospect and Retrospect,* Harvard English Studies 10 (Cambridge: Harvard University Press, 1982), p. 63, for the more simplistic distinction between Carlyle and Emerson. Kenneth Marc Harris, *Carlyle and Emerson: Their Long Debate* (Cambridge: Harvard University Press, 1978), p. 70, offers a more nuanced discussion.

86. Robert A. Hume, *Runaway Star: An Appreciation of Henry Adams* (Ithaca: Cornell University Press, 1951), p. 118.

87. It is of course unlikely, given the occasion and his own status as an undergraduate seeking to go on to graduate work, that Du Bois could have flaunted the ironies of his speech any more than he did.

88. See the chapters on "The Everlasting No" and "The Everlasting Yea" in *Sartor Resartus.*

89. "Carlyle," MS in the Du Bois papers at the University of Massachusetts at Amherst. The speech appears to date from about 1890; a more exact dating is not possible.

90. Du Bois's program for the "Talented Tenth" is discussed in greater detail later.

91. Du Bois himself recognized that, during his boyhood years, he became "in general thought and conduct . . . quite thoroughly New England" (*DD* 566). And while the move from Great Barrington to Nashville marked a radical cultural and social dislocation, the New England intellectual traditions continued to provide the theoretical framework in which the new realities were interpreted: "All of [Fisk's] teachers but one were white, from New England or from the New Englandized Middle West." Du Bois's "own culture background thus suffered no change or hiatus. Its application only was new" (*A* 108). The subjects of some of the other commencement speeches at Fisk in 1888 may indicate the strength of New England influence there: these included "Anglo-Saxon Influence" and "Thought as the Prime Condition of Progress" (*A* 126).

92. See Bentley, *The Cult of the Superman*, pp. 19–20.

Three

1. As J. D. Y. Peel notes, "At the end of the [nineteenth] century evolutionary theories, Spencer's above all, lost their power to convince very suddenly because history played them false: their predictions, stages and continua just did not fit events any more. Sociology's inability to function as theodicy permitted it to be of use for limited prediction in order to control. This use had already been envisaged by Comte ('*Savoir pour prévoir, prévoir pour pouvoir*'), but it is difficult for the evolutionary sanctification of desired ends to be combined with the open-ended assessment of feasible means. The latter requires that the ends be considered as contingent and that theory have the role of effecting change, not reconciling men to it. The end of the century saw therefore a revived discussion of the place of ends or values in sociology." Peel, *Herbert Spencer: The Evolution of a Sociologist* (London: Heineman, 1971), p. 245. In the American context this reorientation of sociological theory understandably aligned sociology with the traditions of pragmatism.

2. Dorothy Ross, *The Origins of American Social Science* (Cambridge: Cambridge University Press, 1991), p. 132. For an outline of the debate between Giddings and Small, see pp. 130–32.

3. In an essay titled "Sociology Hesitant," apparently written just after the turn of the century, Du Bois criticized Comte for "steering curiously by the deeds of men as objects of scientific study," and was unimpressed by Spencer's "verbal juggery," which he said would lead to troublesome vagueness of Giddings's "consciousness of kind." Quoted in Dan S. Green and Edwin D. Driver, "W. E. B. Du Bois: A Case in the Sociology of Sociological Negation," *Phylon* 37, no. 4 (1976): 312. Passages from this essay, along with some from the published "Atlanta Conferences" (*Voice of the Negro* 1 [March 1904]), were clearly reworked by Du Bois when he came to write his comments on sociological method in *Dusk of Dawn*. These essays indicate that Du Bois had, by the turn of the century, a clear idea of what he meant by a scientific sociology, and that the recollections of *Dusk of Dawn* are accurate. Green and Driver discuss both in their article.

4. Du Bois, "The Atlanta Conferences," quoted in Green and Driver, "Du Bois: The Sociology of Sociological Negation," p. 315.

5. Ibid., p. 311.

6. Peter Allan Dale, *The Victorian Critic and the Idea of History: Carlyle, Arnold, Pater* (Cambridge: Harvard University Press, 1977), p. 6.

7. The most thorough account of this neglect in terms of the history of sociology is Green and Driver, "Du Bois: The Sociology of Sociological Negation." See also Elliot M. Rudwick, "Notes on a Forgotten Sociologist: W. E. B. Du Bois and the Sociological Profession," *American Sociologist* 4 (November 1969): 303–6, and Rudwick's later (and fairly uneven) "W. E. B. Du Bois as Sociologist," in James E. Blackwell and Morris Janowitz, eds., *Black Sociologists: Historical and Contemporary Perspectives* (Chicago: University of Chicago Press, 1974), pp. 25–55. R. Charles Key's "Society and Sociology: The Dynamics of Black Sociological Negation," *Phylon* 39, no. 1 (1978): 35–48, deals with Du Bois in a broad discussion of the negation of black sociology by the sociological profession, but the discussion is thin and many of the insights regarding Du Bois are borrowed from Green and Driver. There is also Werner Lange, "W. E. B. Du Bois and the First Scientific Study of Afro-America," *Phylon* 44, no. 2 (1983): 135–46. For a brief sketch of the place of *The Philadelphia Negro* in the history of urban sociology and anthropology, see Council Taylor, "Clues for the Future: Black Urban Anthropology Reconsidered," in Peter Orleans and William Russell Ellis, Jr., eds., *Race, Change and Urban Society* (Beverly Hills: Sage, 1971), pp. 605–11, as well as E. Digby Blatzell's introduction to the 1967 edition (used throughout this study) of *The Philadelphia Negro*. While the criticism of the neglect of Du Bois's work in all these articles and essays is fully justified, almost all of them fail to offer sufficiently thorough histories of the development of social science or sufficiently detailed comparisons with other sociologists. Without this framework it is difficult to assess properly the claims for Du Bois's importance in the history of American social science. I know of no substantial account of the place of Du Bois's work in historiography in the history of the American historical profession.

8. Du Bois, "Sociology Hesitant," quoted in Green and Driver, "Du Bois: The Sociology of Sociological Negation," p. 313. For a dating of the manuscript, see p. 312.

9. Ibid., p. 313.

10. Haskell, *Emergence of Professional Social Science: The American Social Science Association and the Nineteenth-Century Crisis of Authority* (Urbana: University of Illinois Press, 1977), chap. 1. Haskell is drawing on Parsons's *The Structure of Social Action: A Study in Social Theory with Special Reference to a Group of Recent European Writers* (New York: McGraw-Hill, 1937). Another useful account of the epistemological and methodological issues in the sociology of this period is Roscoe C. Hinckle's *Founding Theory of American Sociology, 1881–1915* (London: Routledge and Kegan Paul, 1980).

11. Haskell, *Emergence of Professional Social Science,* p. 5.

12. Green and Driver, "Du Bois: The Sociology of Sociological Negation," p. 313.

13. The pragmatist accounts of Du Bois's thought, given by Cornel West and others and discussed in the introduction, tend to support this kind of organicism. This is what West means by "a genealogy of pragmatism."

14. Du Bois studied physics, physiology, astronomy, botany, zoology, geology, and chemistry at Fisk, and he took further courses in geology and chemistry at Harvard.

15. Du Bois studied political economy with Taussig in his second year at Harvard. The course was Political Economy 1. According to details in the Harvard course catalog for the academic year 1889–90 (p. 119), the first half of the course focused on "Mill's Principles of Political Economy" and "Dunbar's Chapters on Banking." The second half of the year was split into two elective divisions, the first theoretical (continuing the focus on Mill and also looking at "Cairne's Leading Principles of Political Economy") and the second descriptive (examining "topics in Money, Finance, Labor and Capital, Cooperation, and Railways"). It is not possible to tell from Du Bois's transcripts which division he took, but the previous year he had done Political Economy 9, a course on the "Management and Ownership of Railways," and he may have extended that focus by taking the second elective division.

16. See Mary O. Furner, *Advocacy and Objectivity: A Crisis in the Professionalization of American Social Science, 1865–1905* (Lexington: University Press of Kentucky, 1975), pp. 98–100; Sydney Kaplan, "Taussig, James and Peabody: A 'Harvard School' in 1900?" *American Quarterly* 7, no. 4 (1955): passim; and Dorothy Ross, *The Origins of American Social Science* (Cambridge: Cambridge University Press, 1991), pp. 104–5, 115.

17. Description in the Harvard course catalog for 1889–90. The course was Philosophy 11, "The Ethics of Social Reform." As with Taussig's course, this was taken by Du Bois in his second year.

18. Peabody, quoted in L. L. Bernard and Jessie Bernard, *Origins of American Sociology: The Social Science Movement in the United States* (1943; New York: Russell & Russell, 1963), p. 616. Here too Peabody lists "Charity, Divorce, the Indians, the Labor Question, [and] Intemperance" as the "great moral movements."

19. Peabody, quoted in Kaplan, "Taussig, James, Peabody," p. 323.

20. Ibid., pp. 315–31.

21. Ibid., p. 319.

22. Hart, "Imagination in History" (1910), quoted in Peter Novick, *That Noble Dream: The "Objectivity Question" and the American Historical Profession* (Cambridge: Cambridge University Press, 1988), p. 38. As John Higham and Peter Novick have shown, American historians had only a partial knowledge of Ranke and adopted his positivism without understanding his debt to Hegelian idealism and Romantic historicism. For the American historians, Ranke resisted reading history through abstract schemas, attempting instead to read the global from the concrete. His primary impact on historiography came through his positivist insistence on a realist, documentary approach to historical research that would establish history as a truly scientific discipline in its own right. Graduate studies in history at Harvard were established in the Rankean mold by Henry Adams, and Hart continued this tradition in his stress on documentary research and the

seminar method. On Ranke, see John Higham, with Leonard Krieger and Felix Gilbert, *History* (Englewood Cliffs, N.J.: Prentice-Hall, 1965), pp. 97–99, 92–93, and Novick, *That Noble Dream,* pp. 24–30. For an introduction to Ranke's work in English, see Leopold von Ranke, *The Theory and Practice of History,* ed. Georg G. Iggers and Konrad von Moltke, with new translations by Wilma A. Iggers and Konrad von Moltke (New York: Bobbs-Merrill, 1973). On Adams as historian, see W. H. Jordy, *Henry Adams: Scientific Historian* (New Haven: Yale University Press, 1952), and J. C. Levenson, *The Mind and Art of Henry Adams* (Boston: Houghton Mifflin, 1957). On the seminar method, see Herbst, *The German Historical School,* pp. 34–38.

23. In the preface to *The Suppression of the African Slave Trade* Du Bois noted his "obligation" to Hart and also thanked "the trustees of the John F. Slater Fund, whose appointment made it possible to test the conclusions of this study by the general principles laid down in German universities" (*SAST* 3).

24. For an account of Americans studying in Germany and of German historical influence in America, see Herbst, *The German Historical School.* Herbst points out that the 1880s and 1890s were key decades for the influence of German scholarship in American universities because many American academics trained in Germany then became influential in American academia (p. 15). He also notes that in 1893, when Du Bois was in Berlin, there were 200 American students at the university there while there were only 30 registered at the Sorbonne (pp. 8–9).

25. Francis Broderick, "German Influence on the Scholarship of W. E. B. Du Bois," *Phylon* 19, no. 4 (1958): 368.

26. See chapter 10 of Du Bois's *Autobiography* and Manning Marable, *W. E. B. Du Bois: Black Radical Democrat* (Boston: Twayne Publishers, 1986), pp. 17–18.

27. This characterization of the new German school in economics is based on Herbst, *The German Historical School,* pp. 145–46.

28. Broderick, "German Influence," pp. 368–69. For a complementary account of Schmoller and Wagner, see Furner, *Advocacy and Objectivity,* p. 48. Veblen also wrote a lengthy review of Schmoller's work, praising him for his combination of historical methodology with theoretical concerns. See Veblen, "Gustav Schmoller's Economics" (1901), in Veblen's *The Place of Science in Modern Civilization and Other Essays* (1919; New York: Russell and Russell, 1961), pp. 252–78. For a comparison of Wagner and Schmoller, particularly for Wagner's criticisms of what he saw as the unrigorous nature of Schmoller's historical and theoretical work, see Gerhard Meyer, "Adolf Wagner," in *International Encyclopedia of the Social Sciences,* ed. David L. Sills (New York: Macmillan and Free Press, 1968), vol. 16, pp. 421–32.

29. See Wolfram Fischer, "Gustav Schmoller," in *International Encyclopedia of the Social Sciences,* vol. 14, p. 61.

30. See Herbst, *The German Historical School,* pp. 151–52, 158, 161–62.

31. Du Bois himself had rounded off the Hegelian-Jamesian plot of his thesis with a neo-Kantian flourish, claiming as the teleologic goal "first the What, then the Why—underneath the everlasting Ought."

32. Thomas E. Willey, *Back to Kant: The Revival of Kantianism in German Social*

and Historical Thought, 1860–1914 (Detroit: Wayne State University Press, 1978), p. 21. While in Berlin Du Bois also heard Max Weber lecture (*A* 162) at a time when Weber was very much under the influence of the neo-Idealist movement (see Willey, *Back to Kant,* pp. 156–57; 161ff.). Weber later showed interest in Du Bois's work and met him on a visit to the United States in 1904. See Faye V. Harrison, "The Du Boisian Legacy in Anthropology," *Critique of Anthropology* 12, no. 3 (1992): 242.

33. Santayana, unlike James, found Lotze "still-born" (see Santayana, *Persons and Places: Fragments of Autobiography,* ed. William G. Holzberger and Herman J. Saatkamp [Cambridge: MIT Press, 1986], p. 389). For a detailed account of Lotze's influence on James and American philosophy, see Paul Grimley Kuntz's introduction, "Rudolph Hermann Lotze, Philosopher and Critic," in George Santayana, *Lotze's System of Philosophy,* ed. Kuntz (Bloomington: Indiana University Press, 1971), pp. 48–68. See also Henry A. Pochmann, *German Culture in America, 1600–1900: Philosophical and Literary Influence* (Madison: University of Wisconsin Press, 1957), pp. 312, 318, 672.

34. See Du Bois's economics notebooks from 1893–94 in the Du Bois papers at the University of Massachusetts.

35. Willey, *Back to Kant,* p. 37

36. Ibid., p. 9.

37. The following discussion relies on the paraphrase, with some direct quotation, of this article in the research notes taken by Francis Broderick for his Ph.D. thesis of 1955 on Du Bois, now at the Schomburg Institute in New York. As with the sketches for the story made by Du Bois as an undergraduate, this manuscript is not in the Du Bois papers at Amherst. For fuller details of Broderick's notes and their relationship to Du Bois's papers, see the discussion in the previous chapter and in the appendix. I have followed Broderick's paraphrase as closely as possible.

38. Schmoller frequently referred to Herbart in his seminars. See Du Bois's economic notebooks from 1893–94. Herbart, the Göttingen philosopher who was also Kant's successor at Königsberg from 1809 to 1833, posited a plurality of "reals," or objects that possess in themselves an absolute existence apart from apperception by the mind.

39. On the relationship of sociology and pragmatism, see C. Wright Mills, *Sociology and Pragmatism: The Higher Learning in America,* ed. with intro. by Irving Louis Horowitz (New York: Paine-Whitman, 1964), and J. David Lewis and Richard L. Smith, *American Sociology and Pragmatism: Mead, Chicago Sociology, and Symbolic Interaction* (Chicago: University of Chicago Press, 1980).

40. Higham, *History* (esp. pp. 6–25, 92–103, 147–70), and Novick, *That Noble Dream* (chaps. 1–4), offer the best accounts of American historiography in the late nineteenth century. Chapter 5 of Herbst, *The German Historical School,* provides a more focused survey of the relationship of American historiography and German methodology. See also Michael Kraus, *The Writing of American History* (Norman: University of Oklahoma Press, 1953), esp. chap. 8 on the "Scientific School," and the brief survey of the late nineteenth and early twentieth centuries in chap. 2 of Susan L. Mizruchi, *The Power of Historical Knowledge: Narrating the Past in Hawthorne, James and Dreiser* (Princeton: Princeton University Press, 1988). Other

useful sources include James Westfall Thompson, *A History of Historical Writing* (1942; Gloucester, Mass.: Peter Smith, 1967), vol. 2, and G. P. Gooch, *History and Historians in the Nineteenth Century* (1913; 2d ed., London: Longmans, 1952). Chapter 2 of Arthur Marwick's *The Nature of History* (London: Macmillan, 1970) provides a lucid summary of main trends. Ross's *The Origins of American Social Science* also includes very useful discussions of the historical profession (see esp. chap. 8).

41. Booth's work was inspired by Frederic Le Play's *Les Ouvriers Européens* (1855, 6 vols.) and in turn inspired the American Jane Addams's Chicago study *Hull-House Maps and Papers* (1895), published only a year before Du Bois began his research, but much more widely known and acknowledged than *The Philadelphia Negro*. Addams's work is rightly seen as one of the sources of urban sociology, but Du Bois's work has equal claim to a central place in any such history. On the relationship of Du Bois's work to that of Booth and Addams and to the Settlement House movement in America and England in the late nineteenth century, see Baltzell's introduction to *The Philadelphia Negro,* pp. xvi–xviii. On the centrality of empiricism, especially British (as much as the grand theories of Spencer and Comte), to the rise of sociology, see Nathan Glazer, "The Rise of Social Research in Europe," in Daniel Lerner, ed., *The Human Meaning of the Social Sciences* (Cleveland: Meridian Books, 1959), pp. 43–72, and also Alan Swingewood, *A Short History of Sociological Thought* (London: Macmillan, 1984), p. 51. On the mixture of reformism and empiricism as characteristic of the mainstream of the social sciences in America, see Elliott Rudwick, "W. E. B. Du Bois as Sociologist," in James E. Blackwell and Morris Janowitz, eds., *Black Sociologists: Historical and Contemporary Perspectives* (Chicago: University of Chicago Press, 1974), p. 48.

42. Schmoller argued that statistics were to be used as an auxiliary way of handling historical materials. Wagner, however, strongly supported the use of statistics for studying social and natural phenomena in a uniform quantitative manner in order to yield laws explaining causal relations. This statistical emphasis was reinforced by British empiricism. On the German economic school's views of statistics, see Herbst, *The German Historical School,* pp. 138–41.

43. Peter Conn, *The Divided Mind: Ideology and Imagination in America, 1898–1917* (Cambridge: Cambridge University Press, 1983), pp. 138–39.

44. Another instance of these continuities would be Du Bois's admiration for the Hegelian nationalist historian Heinrich von Treitschke during his time in Berlin, despite the fact that Treitschke spoke of the inferiority of mulattoes in a class that Du Bois took with him (*A* 165). For Du Bois, Treitschke was "the very embodiment of united monarchical, armed Germany" and had the outlook "of the born aristocrat who has something of the Carlyle contempt of levelling democracy" (*A* 164; 165). The comments on Treitschke were written while Du Bois was in Berlin and were later incorporated into the *Autobiography* (*A* 162).

45. Herman Melville, *Moby Dick, or, The Whale* (1851; Harmondsworth, Mddx.: Penguin, 1972), p. 98.

46. John David Smith, *An Old Creed for the New South: Proslavery Ideology and Historiography, 1865–1918* (1985; Athens: University of Georgia Press, 1991), pp. 5, 286.

47. Ibid., p. 10.

48. Novick, *That Noble Dream,* pp. 76–77.

49. Hart, quoted in ibid., p. 75.

50. Ross, *Origins of American Social Science,* pp. xiv, xv.

51. Higham, *History,* pp. 95–96, 159–60. For a discussion of the ways in which theories of evolution could be tied to progressivism, see also William F. Fine, *Progressive Evolutionism and American Sociology, 1890–1920* (n.p.: UNI Research Press, 1979), esp. chap. 4. Possible alignments between German historical thought and the progressive narratives of American exceptionalism are also suggested by Brook Thomas, "The New Historicism and Other Old-fashioned Topics," in H. Aram Veeser, ed., *The New Historicism* (New York: Routledge, 1989), pp. 189, 193–94.

52. Novick, *That Noble Dream,* p. 97. The appellation "Progressive Historians" is taken from Richard Hofstadter, *The Progressive Historians: Turner, Beard, Parrington* (New York: 1968). On the American historical profession's continued commitment to the ideology of exceptionalism, see also David D. van Tassel, *Recording America's Past: An Interpretation of the Development of Historical Studies in America, 1607–1884* (Chicago: University of Chicago Press, 1960), and David W. Noble's *Historians against History: The Frontier Thesis and the National Covenant in American Historical Writing since 1830* (Minneapolis: University of Minnesota Press, 1965) and his *The End of American History: Democracy, Capitalism, and the Metaphor of Two Worlds in Anglo-American Historical Writing, 1880–1890* (Minneapolis: University of Minnesota Press, 1985).

53. See Ross, *Origins of American Social Science,* pp. 266–70.

54. See Baltzell's introduction to *The Philadelphia Negro,* p. xxviii.

55. "The Seventh Ward starts from the historic center of Negro settlement in the city, South Seventh street and Lombard, and includes the long narrow strip, beginning at South Seventh and extending West, with South and Spruce streets as boundaries, as far as the Schuylkill River" (*PN* 58).

56. Ross, *Origins of American Social Science,* pp. xiii–xiv.

57. For an account of the importance of the idea of interdependence in American social science in the 1880s and 1890s, see Haskell, *Emergence of Professional Social Science,* chap. 2.

58. Donald C. Bellomy, "Two Generations: Modernists and Progressives, 1870–1920," *Perspectives in American History* (new series) 3 (1987): 299.

59. Franz Boas, "The Limitations of the Comparative Method of Anthropology" (1896), in Boas, *Race, Language and Culture* (1940; Chicago: University of Chicago Press, 1982), p. 275.

60. Ibid., p. 277. When Boas republished this article in *Race, Language and Culture* in 1940 he changed "actual *history* of definite phenomena" to "actual *relations* of definite phenomena." I have retained the original version. For comment on the revision, see George W. Stocking, Jr., ed., *A Franz Boas Reader: The Shaping of American Anthropology, 1883–1911* (Chicago: University of Chicago Press, 1974), p. 13.

61. Boas, "Limitations of the Comparative Method," p. 275.

62. Ibid., p. 277.

63. It is uncertain whether Du Bois was aware of the parallel developments in Boas's work at this time. Du Bois was certainly interested in Boas's work by 1906 when he invited Boas to participate in a conference and to give the commencement speech at Atlanta University, where Du Bois was then working. But neither Du Bois's autobiographical writings nor studies of Du Bois indicate when Du Bois first became acquainted with Boas's work. See *Dusk of Dawn*, 602, and Boas, "The Outlook for the American Negro," in Stocking, Jr., ed., *A Franz Boas Reader*, pp. 310–16.

64. Veblen, *Place of Science in Modern Civilization*, pp. 267–68.

65. Boas, "Limitations of the Comparative Method," p. 270.

66. From Boas, "An Anthropologist's Credo" (1938), in Stocking, Jr., ed., *A Franz Boas Reader*, p. 41.

67. Boas in a letter of December 8, 1930. See *The Ethnography of Franz Boas*, ed. Ronald P. Rohner (Chicago: University of Chicago Press, 1969), pp. 295–96. Boas had first visited the United States in 1884, settling there when he was offered a job in 1886. See Melville J. Herskovits, *Franz Boas: The Science of Man in the Making* (New York: Charles Scribner's Sons, 1953), p. 12.

68. Ross, *Origins of American Social Science*, p. 101. See also Novick, *That Noble Dream*, p. 68.

69. Veblen, *Place of Science in Modern Civilization*, p. 269.

70. Ibid., p. 273.

71. Ibid., p. 277.

72. Du Bois, quoted in Green and Driver, "Du Bois: Sociology of Sociological Negation," p. 313.

73. See Furner, *Advocacy and Objectivity*, passim.

74. See Novick, *That Noble Dream*, pp. 68, 105.

75. Joseph De Marco, *The Social Thought of W. E. B. Du Bois* (Lanham, Md.: University Press of America, 1983), p. 18. Manning Marable notes that "Du Bois's emphasis on moral factors in the evolution of slavery was largely in keeping with the state of American historiography of that period." Marable, *W. E. B. Du Bois*, p. 23.

76. W. E. B. Du Bois, *Writings*, p. 1315.

77. Gillian Rose, *Hegel contra Sociology* (London: Athlone Press, 1981), pp. 13–14.

78. Ibid., p. 214.

79. H. T. Wilson, *The American Ideology: Science, Technology and Organization as Modes of Rationality in Advanced Industrial Societies* (London: Routledge and Kegan Paul, 1977), pp. 13–14.

80. Marx and Engels, quoted in ibid., p. 11.

81. Ibid., p. 12.

82. The research for *The Philadelphia Negro* lasted from August 1, 1896, to December 31, 1897 (*PN* 1). Du Bois finished writing in the spring of 1898, and the study was published in 1899 (*A* 198). "Strivings of the Negro People" was published in the *Atlantic Monthly* 80 (August 1897): 194–98. There are some differ-

ences between the original version of "Strivings" and the version that appears in *Souls,* but these differences have no bearing on the discussions of the present study. Therefore no distinction between the two is made here.

83. As far as I know the relationship of *The Philadelphia Negro* to the first chapter of *Souls* has never been examined. In the conclusion to *The Philadelphia Negro* Du Bois goes on to discuss the place of the "Negroes of Africa" in the "World Commonwealth" that consists of the "Anglo-Saxon," "the Teuton and the Latin," "the Celt and the Slav," and even "the low races of Asia" and "the brown Indian" (*PN* 387). This is a reworking of the famous passage on "the Negro [as] a sort of seventh son, born with a veil" in *Souls* (*SBF* 364). Equally, the call for a black American cultural elite that will provide leadership (*PN* 387–88) is close to much of the argument of *Souls* and, of course, to "The Talented Tenth."

84. Wolf Lepenies, *Between Literature and Science: The Rise of Sociology,* trans. R. J. Hollingdale (1985; Cambridge: Cambridge University Press, 1988), p. 7. Lepenies's book is a study of the relationship of the rise of sociology in the nineteenth century to the struggle between literature and science.

85. For Smith's and James's use of sympathy, see chap. 2.

86. Du Bois returns to the idea of sympathy again and again in the book. See, for example, *Souls,* pp. 479, 480, 481.

87. In the second volume of *Principles of Psychology* (p. 411), James suggests that his discussion of sympathy is indebted to a vast amount of writing on sympathy in "books on Ethics."

88. In their introduction to Smith's *Theory of Moral Sentiments,* D. D. Raphael and A. L. Macfie point out that there are several references to Smith's work in Herder's writings. See Adam Smith, *The Theory of Moral Sentiments* (1790, 6th ed.), ed. D. D. Raphael and A. L. Macfie (1979; Indianapolis: Liberty Classics, 1982), pp. 30–31.

89. Gerald Broce, "Discontent and Cultural Relativism: Herder and Boasian Anthropology," *Annals of Scholarship* 2, no. 1 (1981): 1–13.

90. Ibid., pp. 2–3.

91. Du Bois wrote in *Dusk of Dawn* that, while traveling in Germany, he "stopped in a little German 'Dorf' in the Rheinpfalz, where I had an excellent opportunity to study the peasant life closely and compare it with country life in the South. We visited perhaps twenty different families, talked, ate, drank with them; listened to their gossip, attended their assemblies, etc." (*DD* 588).

92. James Clifford, "On Ethnographic Allegory," in James Clifford and George E. Marcus, eds., *Writing Culture: The Poetics and Politics of Ethnography* (Berkeley: University of California Press, 1986), p. 102. As Clifford has pointed out, "the ethnographic stories [Margaret] Mead and [Ruth] Benedict told [in works like *Coming of Age in Samoa* (1923) and *Patterns of Culture* (1934) after World War I] were manifestly linked to the situation of a culture struggling with diverse values, with an apparent breakdown of established traditions, with utopian visions of human malleability and fears of disaggregation" (p. 102).

93. On the reception and influence of Zangwill's play, see Werner Sollors, *Beyond Ethnicity: Consent and Descent in American Culture* (New York: Oxford University Press, 1986), pp. 67–71.

94. Boas's "The Limitations of the Comparative Method of Anthropology" was published in 1896, three years before James's "What Makes a Life Significant?"

95. James's faith in heroic vitalism as the motor of history has already been examined. For his arguments for the centrality of an academic elite in social reform, see his essay "The Social Value of the College-Bred" (1908) in *Memories and Studies* (London: Longmans, Green, 1911), pp. 307–25.

96. William James, "What Makes a Life Significant?" in James, *Talks to Teachers on Psychology; and to Students on Some of Life's Ideals* (Boston: Henry Holt, 1899), pp. 273–74.

97. See Nancy Ladd Muller, "Du Boisian Pragmatism and 'The Problem of the Twentieth Century,'" *Critique of Anthropology* 12, no. 3 (1992): 322–23.

98. W. E. B. Du Bois, "The Conservation of Races," in Du Bois, *Writings* (New York: Library of America, 1986), p. 815. Hereafter cited in the text as CR.

99. Du Bois's thinking on race at this time moves between essentialist and non-essentialist, cultural-historical, and biological definitions. It has already received a detailed examination and the discussion is not repeated here. See Anthony Appiah, "The Uncompleted Argument: Du Bois and the Illusion of Race," *Critical Inquiry* 12, no. 1 (Autumn 1985): 21–37, and Tommy L. Lott, "Du Bois on the Invention of Race," *Philosophical Forum* 24, nos. 1–3 (1992–93): 166–87. For Du Bois's own comments, see *Dusk of Dawn,* pp. 625–28.

100. For more on Crummell and the Academy, see chap. 5.

Four

1. Only Robert Gooding-Williams has previously noted a possible connection between *Souls* and Hegel's *Phenomenology* ("Philosophy of History and Social Critique in *The Souls of Black Folk,*" *Social Science Information* 26, no. 1 [1987]: 99–106). Gooding-Williams reads *Souls* as a philosophy of history that embodies a "vision of unified historical process" (p. 103). He also argues that Josiah Royce's account of the *Phenomenology,* rather than the *Phenomenology* itself, is the more likely source for Du Bois. The reading of the first chapter of *Souls* that follows in the present chapter argues that the negativity of Du Bois's psychology dramatizes the failure of a unified philosophy of history, and that it cannot be aligned with Royce's reading of Hegel, but must be seen to be in direct and close dialogue with the *Phenomenology.*

Apart from one or two other scholars who have referred in general terms to the Hegelianism of Du Bois's thought, nothing has been written on Du Bois and Hegel. There is a brief discussion of the Hegelianism of Du Bois in Joel Williamson's *The Crucible of Race: Black-White Relations in the American South since Emancipation* (New York: Oxford University Press, 1984), pp. 399–413. Williamson draws some general parallels between *The Philosophy of History* and Du Bois's ideas. While noting echoes of Hegelian vocabulary, Williamson concludes that the first chapter of *Souls* is vague and emotive and that there are no one-to-one parallels between Du Bois's work and Hegel's (p. 403). This is not so. And while Williamson is right to point out the Hegelian resonances of the *volk* ideology of *Souls* and of Du Bois's theories of racial progress, these ideas were common currency at the time and came to Du Bois through multiple sources, one of which may have been a direct or indirect knowledge of *The Philosophy of History*. In his "The Veil Transcended: Form and Meaning in W. E. B. Du Bois' *The Souls of Black Folk*" (*Journal of Black Studies* 2 [March 1972]: 303–21), Stanley Brodwin refers in passing to the "Neo-Hegelian" form of the book, but he is more concerned with a crude reduction of *Souls* to a mechanical "dialectical" structure of thesis-antithesis-synthesis (pp. 306, 310). Kendall Thomas refers to Du Bois's passage on "double-consciousness" at the end of a discussion of Hegel's master-slave dialectic, but only as an unconnected verification of Hegel's idea of the inverted world ("A House Divided against Itself: A Comment on 'Mastery, Slavery, and Emancipation,'" *Cardozo Law Review* 10, nos. 5–6 [March–April 1989], part 2: 1513–14). There is also a very brief and undeveloped suggestion of a connection between Du Bois and Hegel in Robert C. Williams, "W. E. B. Du Bois: Afro-American Philosopher of Social Reality," in Leonard Harris, ed., *Philosophy Born of Struggle: An Anthology of Afro-American Philosophy from 1917* (Dubuque: Kendall-Hunt, 1983), pp. 11–19. The title of Jesse N. McDade's "The Significance of Hegel's *das unglückliche Bewußtsein* and Du Bois' 'Double Consciousness'" [(1976) *A Luta Continua*] suggests that its concerns are closely related to those of the present study, but I have not been able to obtain a copy of this piece. The article is cited by Gooding-Williams (p. 114), though he too has been unable to obtain it.

2. According to Du Bois's course transcripts in the Harvard University archives and the course catalog for 1889–90, Du Bois that year took an introductory course in logic and psychology with James (Philosophy 2) and at the same time an advanced course on modern German and French philosophy with Santayana. Santayana's course (Philosophy 6) covered "French Philosophy from Descartes to Leibnitz, and German Philosophy, from Kant to Hegel" (see the Harvard College Course Catalogue, 1889–90, p. 118). The course had been taught by Professor Bowen the previous year. Although the catalog for 1888–89 states that Bowen's course was omitted for that year, an annotation inserted in handwriting on August 26, 1980, indicates that the course was in fact given (p. 112). The fact is confirmed by Santayana's autobiography (see below). The course catalog for 1889–90 does not list the Hegel text studied, but all available evidence points in the direction of the *Phenomenology*. The latter year, 1889–90, was Santayana's first year as instructor. The previous academic year he had taken a graduate course on Hegel's system, concentrating on the *Phenomenology*, with Josiah Royce (while also taking graduate seminars in psychology with James). Santayana was very excited by the *Phenomenology* and disliked the abstracted sophistry of Hegel's other works. The *Phenomenology* proved much more interesting than the work of Lotze, on which Santayana was writing his dissertation, and the reading of the *Phenomenology* in fact set Santayana to planning his own *Life of Reason* (see George Santayana, *Persons and Places: Fragments of an Autobiography*, ed. William G. Holzenberger and Herman J. Saatkamp [1944–53; Cambridge: MIT Press, 1986], pp. 389–90. The relationship of *The Life of Reason* to Hegel's text is discussed in more detail later). It is also worth noting that Royce was again teaching his course on Hegel during the year that Du Bois studied with Santayana. The description in the Harvard course catalog for 1889–90 reads: "The Development of the Hegelian System—Hegel's

Phaenomenologie des Geistes" (p. 119). Santayana preferred teaching texts in the original language (*Persons and Places,* pp. 389–94), and Du Bois's German was good enough for him to do extensive graduate work in Berlin. Du Bois received extensive training in both French and German at Fisk (see *AR,* pp. 6 and 10).

3. The key points of reference in the *Phenomenology* are the closing pages of chapter 3, titled "Force and Understanding; Appearance and the Supersensible World"; the sections titled "Independence and Dependence of Self-Consciousness: Lordship and Bondage" and "Freedom of Self-Consciousness: Stoicism, Scepticism, and the Unhappy Consciousness" in chapter 4 ("The True Nature of Self-Certainty"); and the opening section of chapter 6 ("Spirit"), titled "Objective Spirit: The Ethical Order." See G. W. F. Hegel, *The Phenomenology of Mind,* trans. J. B. Baillie (1807, trans. 1910; New York: Harper Torchbooks, 1967), pp. 212–506.

4. Gooding-Williams, "Philosophy of History and Social Critique in *The Souls of Black Folk,"* pp. 99, 101, 113.

5. Herbert Marcuse, *Reason and Revolution: Hegel and the Rise of Social Theory* (2d ed. 1954; Atlantic Highlands, N.J.: Humanities Press, 1983), p. 113.

6. Numerous discussions of this area in literature and intellectual history are available. A useful recent example is Judith Ryan, *The Vanishing Subject: Early Psychology and Literary Modernism* (Chicago: University of Chicago Press, 1991).

7. For a passing acknowledgment of the class specificity of Du Bois's psychology, see Ernest Allen, Jr., "Ever Feeling One's Twoness: 'Double Ideals' and 'Double Consciousness' in *The Souls of Black Folk,"* *Critique of Anthropology* 12, no. 3 (1992): 267.

8. See Arnold Rampersad, *The Art and Imagination of W. E. B. Du Bois* (Cambridge: Harvard University Press, 1976), p. 74; Dickson D. Bruce, Jr., "W. E. B. Du Bois and the Idea of Double Consciousness," *American Literature* 64, no. 2 (1992): 299–304; and Eric Sundquist, *To Wake the Nations: Race in the Making of American Literature* (Cambridge, Mass.: Harvard University Press, 1993), p. 571.

9. For Du Bois's sense of the political understanding that can be derived from the experience of alienation, see Thomas C. Holt, "The Political Uses of Alienation: W. E. B. Du Bois on Politics, Race, and Culture, 1903–1940," *American Quarterly* 42, no. 2 (1990): 301–23. Frank M. Kirkland, "Modernity and Intellectual Life in Black," *Philosophical Forum* 24, nos. 1–3 (1992–93): 151, also provides a brief reading of the positive and negative meaning of "double-consciousness" in the first chapter of *Souls.*

10. George Santayana, "A General Confession," in Paul Arthur Schilpp, ed., *The Philosophy of George Santayana* (New York: Tudor, 1951), p. 15. Originally published as "A Brief History of My Opinions" (1930). According to a catalog of books in Du Bois's library in the Du Bois archives at the University of Massachusetts at Amherst, Du Bois owned a copy of the two-volume, complete edition of the *Principles of Psychology.* The catalog, however, lists neither the date of publication nor the date of acquisition. The library is housed in Ghana and it has not been possible to examine its contents.

11. See note 2.

12. Louis Althusser, "On the Young Marx: Theoretical Questions" (1960), in Althusser, *For Marx,* trans. Ben Brewster (1965; London: Verso, 1990), p. 65.

13. Ibid., p. 76.

14. Ibid., p. 81.

15. Ibid., p. 82.

16. Henry A. Pochmann, *German Culture in America, 1600–1900: Philosophical and Literary Influences* (Madison: University of Wisconsin Press, 1957), p. 321. See also p. 302 on the increased influence of Hegel in American philosophy departments.

17. Ibid., p. 313.

18. Jurgen Herbst, *The German Historical School in American Scholarship: A Study in the Transfer of Culture* (New York: Cornell University Press, 1965), pp. 66–67.

19. Dewey's attempt to combine Hegelianism with the new psychology and the transformation of his Hegelianism into instrumentalism via Darwin have been well documented in two studies: Morton White's *The Origin of Dewey's Instrumentalism* (1943; New York: Octagon Press, 1964) and Neil Coughlan's *Young John Dewey: An Essay in American Intellectual History* (Chicago: University of Chicago Press, 1975).

20. Dorothy Ross, *The Origins of American Social Science* (Cambridge: Cambridge University Press, 1991), p. 163.

21. John Dewey, "Kant and Philosophic Method," in Dewey, *The Early Works of John Dewey, 1882–1898,* vol. 1 (Carbondale: Southern Illinois University Press, 1969), p. 44.

22. Ibid., p. 45.

23. Dewey, "The New Psychology," in Dewey, *The Early Works,* vol. 1, pp. 55–58.

24. On the development of the cultural emphasis in nineteenth-century psychology, see Emily D. Cahan and Sheldon H. White, "Proposals for a Second Psychology," *American Psychologist* 47, no. 2 (1992): 224–35.

25. Dewey, "The Psychological Standpoint," in Dewey, *The Early Works,* vol. 1, p. 123.

26. Dewey, "Psychology as Philosophic Method" (1886), in Dewey, *The Early Works,* vol. 1, p. 152.

27. Dewey, "The Psychological Standpoint," p. 142.

28. Ibid., p. 142.

29. Dewey, "The Ethics of Democracy," in Dewey, *The Early Works,* vol. 1, p. 229. On the relationship between Dewey and Morris (who was Dewey's Hegelian teacher and colleague), see the second chapters of White's *Origins of Dewey's Instrumentalism* and Coughlan's *Young John Dewey* (esp. pp. 29–30).

30. Dewey, "The Ethics of Democracy," p. 236.

31. Ibid., p. 237.

32. A. R. Buss, "Development of Dialectics and Development of Humanistic Psychology," *Human Development* 19, no. 4 (1976): 253.

33. Dewey, "The Ethics of Democracy," pp. 246, 244.

34. Coughlan, *Young John Dewey,* p. 85. Compare the discussion of conduct in James's thought in chapter 2.

35. For details, see note 2 above on Du Bois's studies with Santayana.

36. Josiah Royce, *The Spirit of Modern Philosophy* (Boston: Houghton Mifflin, 1892), pp. 212, 213.

37. Ibid., pp. 210, 207, 210.

38. William H. Goetzmann, "Introduction," in Goetzmann, ed., *The American Hegelians: An Intellectual Episode in the History of Western America* (New York: Alfred Knopf, 1973), p. 4. In the same volume, see Dewey's concurring assessment (p. 383). And Jacques Denton Snider, one of the leading members of the movement, recalls that the movement was remembered and talked about as late as 1920 (p. 24).

39. Pochmann, *German Culture in America*, pp. 257–94, provides a general history of the St. Louis movement. For a more lengthy history by one of the actual group members, see Denton J. Snider's *The St. Louis Movement in Philosophy, Literature, Education, Psychology, with Chapters of Autobiography* (St. Louis: Sigma, 1920). For a more up-to-date history of the group see Elizabeth Flower and Murray G. Murphey, *A History of Philosophy in America* (New York: Capricorn Books & G. P. Putnam & Sons, 1977), chap. 8. See also Herbert W. Schneider, *A History of American Philosophy* (1946; 2d ed., New York: Columbia University Press, 1963), pp. 161–68.

40. On the importance of the *Journal* in both America and Europe, see Edward L. Schaub, "Harris and the Journal of Speculative Philosophy," in Schaub, ed., *William Torrey Harris, 1835–1935* (Chicago: Open Court, 1936), pp. 51–55.

41. Flower and Murphey, *History of Philosophy in America*, p. 463.

42. See Henry A. Pochmann, *New England Transcendentalism and St. Louis Hegelianism: Phases in the History of American Idealism* (Philadelphia: Carl Schurz Memorial Foundation, 1948), pp. 8–11, 15, 34–63, 112–13; and Goetzmann, ed., *The American Hegelians*, pp. 6–7, 9, 32, 71–75, 118–28, 149–53.

43. When, in 1882, James attacked the growing trend toward "Hegelism" in American thought, he seems, in part, to have had the St. Louis group in mind. In December 1880, James had written to Renouvier that he had spent the winter "resisting the inroads of Hegelism in our University." In a letter of February 1880, addressed to Royce, James had made it clear that his target was the St. Louis group of Hegelians. He was angry at Harris for rejecting an essay he had submitted to the *Journal* and was apprehensive about Harris's plans to move to the East Coast. "My ignorant prejudice against all Hegelians, except Hegel himself," he explained to Royce, "grows wusser and wusser. Their sacerdotal airs! and their sterility! Contemplating their navels and the syllable *oum!*" For the 1882 attack, see "On Some Hegelisms," in *The Will to Believe and Other Essays in Popular Philosophy* (1897; New York: Dover, 1956), pp. 263–98 (hereafter cited in the text as OSH). James also believed that, in 1882, Hegelianism could "be reckoned one of the most powerful influences of the time in the higher walks of thought" (263). See also note 16 above. For the letters, see Elizabeth Hardwick, ed., *The Selected Letters of William James* (New York: Farrar, Straus, and Cudahy, 1961), pp. 110–13.

44. The programs and lectures of the Concord school were regularly published in the *Journal*. James and Royce, as mentioned above, had lectured at the school,

and James had even studied and discussed the manuscript of Brokmeyer's translation of Hegel's *Logic*, the unpublished bible of the St. Louis Movement, when Samuel H. Emery, a Hegelian from Quincy, Indiana, had brought a copy to Boston in 1879. See Pochmann, *New England Transcendentalism*, pp. 112–13, 104, 76–77, 72–73.

45. The St. Louis group had a significant impact on educational theory and administration throughout the country. Harris made major contributions to educational theory and administration. He was head of the Bureau of Education for seventeen years and Commissioner of Education of the United States from 1889 to 1906 and internationally recognized. See Henry Ridgely Evans, "William Torrey Harris: An Appreciation," in Schaub, ed., *William Torrey Harris*, pp. 1, 7. See also Goetzmann, ed., *American Hegelians*, section 6, "Education and Democracy," pp. 269–324. As far as the issue of Du Bois's possible knowledge of the St. Louis Hegelians is concerned, it is also worth noting that after the stay at the hotel the group traveled to Minneapolis, St. Paul, Madison, Milwaukee, and Chicago. Du Bois remembers meeting many "ministers, heads of Christian associations, and literary groups" (*A* 129). It was through this trip that he "received an impression of American civilization in the Middle West at the age of 20" (*A* 128).

46. Pochmann, *German Culture in America*, pp. 259–60.

47. Henry Gates Townsend, "The Political Philosophy of Hegel in a Frontier Society," in Shaub, ed., *William Torrey Harris*, pp. 70–72. Townsend also points out that "in 1860 one in every seven persons in the entire Missouri population was foreign born and one in fourteen was German born" (p. 71).

48. Ibid., p. 69.

49. In Goetzmann, ed., *The American Hegelians*, p. 20. The quotation is from Hegel's *Lectures on the Philosophy of History*.

50. Pochmann, *German Culture in America*, pp. 268, 282.

51. In Goetzmann, ed., *The American Hegelians*, pp. 160–61. See also pp. 184ff.

52. See Pochmann, *German Culture*, pp. 267, 643. As Townsend points out, Treitschke's interpretation of Hegel was not the one necessarily accepted at all times in America. Hegel was also seen as a liberal thinker ("Hegel in a Frontier Society," pp. 73–75).

53. "[George] Bancroft's ten-volume *History of the United States*, begun in 1834, was animated by this spirit, and the philosophical writings of [James] Marsh, [Frederic Henry] Hedge, [Carl] Follen, [Francis] Lieber, [James] Murdock, Emerson, [Freidrich Augustus] Rauch, [Francis] Bowen, H[enry] B[oynton] Smith, Phillip Schaff, G[eorge] S[ylvester] Morris, and especially the St. Louisians [Henry Conrad] Brokmeyer, Harris, [Denton Jacques] Snider, and [Adolf Ernst] Kroeger are imbued by the same principle." Pochmann, *German Culture in America*, p. 676.

54. See Goetzmann, *The American Hegelians*, pp. 29–30.

55. The quotations from and information on Whitman are drawn from Kathryne V. Lindberg, "Whitman's 'Convertible Terms': America, Self, Ideology," in Bainard Cowen and Joseph A. Kronick, eds., *Theorizing American Literature: Hegel, the Sign, and History* (Baton Rouge: Louisiana State University Press, 1991), pp. 247, 256, 252. My thanks to Prof. Lindberg for allowing me to consult the manuscript draft of her essay prior to its publication. She has located Whit-

man's unpublished lectures on Kant, Hegel, Schelling, and Fichte in the archives of the Humanities Research Center at the University of Texas, Austin.

56. As Walter Kaufmann has pointed out, "Fichte introduced into German philosophy the three steps of thesis, antithesis, and synthesis, using these three terms. Schelling took up this terminology; Hegel did not. He never once used these three terms together to designate three stages in an argument or account in any of his books. And they do not help us understand his *Phenomenology,* his *Logic,* or his philosophy of history; they impede any open-minded comprehenshion of what he does by forcing it into a schema which was available to him and which he deliberately spurned" (W. Kaufmann, *Hegel: A Reinterpretation* [N.Y.: Anchor, 1966], p. 154). And as R. J. Bernstein explains, not only do the concepts of thesis, antithesis, and synthesis "play an insignificant role in Hegel's philosophy, they are essentially static concepts and completely misrepresent what Hegel means by 'dialectic.' The dialectic . . . is essentially a dynamic and organic process. One 'moment' of a dialectic process, when it is fully developed or understood, gives rise to its own negation; it is not mechanically confronted by an antithesis" (Bernstein, *Praxis and Action* [Philadelphia: University of Pennsylvania Press, 1971], p. 20).

57. Pochmann, *German Culture in America,* p. 268. See also Townsend, "Hegel in a Frontier Society," p. 76; and Goetzmann, ed., *The American Hegelians,* pp. 28–29, 30–31, 160–61. Many of the members of the St. Louis Movement were German exiles, trained not only in the philosophy of Kant and Hegel but also in the arts of war. During the war they fought on the side of the Union.

58. Lindberg, "Whitman's 'Convertible Terms,' " p. 256.

59. Snider, *The St. Louis Movement* (1921), quoted in Pochmann, *German Culture in America,* p. 258, my emphasis. Pochmann also comments on the group's adaptation of Emersonian Transcendentalism along with Hegelian idealism.

60. Lindberg, "Whitman's 'Convertible Terms,' " p. 245. On Whitman, nationalism, and Hegel, see also Schneider, *History of American Philosophy,* pp. 146–49, 162–63.

61. John Gabriel Woerner, "An American War and Peace," an extract from *The Rebel's Daughter,* in William H. Goetzman, ed., *The American Hegelians: An Intellectual Episode in the History of Western America* (New York: Alfred A. Knopf, 1973), p. 332. Hereafter abbreviated *RD.*

62. Royce, *Spirit of Modern Philosophy,* pp. 213–14.

63. Frantz Fanon, *Black Skin, White Masks,* trans. Charles Lam Markmann (Fr. ed. 1952; New York: Grove Weidenfeld, 1967), p. 110.

64. Ibid., p. 220, n. 8.

65. Orlando Patterson, *Slavery and Social Death: A Comparative Study* (Cambridge: Harvard University Press, 1982), p. 99.

66. For further commentary on the usefulness or nonusefulness of Hegel's master-and-slave dialectic for thinking about actual slavery, see the *Cardozo Law Review* 10, nos. 5–6, part 2 (March–April 1989), a special issue devoted to "Hegel and Legal Theory." Four articles discuss whether Hegel can be helpfully used to think about American slavery. Guyora Binder, "Mastery, Slavery, and Emancipation" (pp. 1435–80), deals briefly with Woerner's *The Rebel's Daughter* and repeats

the equation of Hegel's account with the myth of the cowardly contract. There are three articles qualifying and criticizing some of Binder's premises: Kendall Thomas, "A House Divided against Itself: A Comment on 'Mastery, Slavery, and Emancipation'" (pp. 1481–1515); Jonathan Bush, "Hegelian Slaves and the Antebellum South" (pp. 1517–63); and Merold Westphal, "Hegel on Slavery, Independence, and Liberalism" (pp. 1565–73). Though Thomas's argument is rather crude in its literalism, his focus on the "inverted world" section of the *Phenomenology* (wherein Hegel writes of the "curtain" hanging before the world of appearances) and on the "unhappy consciousness" as more fruitful areas for exploration than the master-slave dialectic parallel as the focus of "Of Our Spiritual Strivings." Thomas mentions Du Bois's idea of "double-consciousness" at the very end of his article, though he does not pursue any possible comparisons or connections with Hegel. Nevertheless, this article, like the others mentioned here, has been helpful in clarifying some of the ideas in the present discussion. My thanks to Guillaume Balan-Gaubert for pointing me to this issue of the *Cardozo Law Review* and for all our conversations in Chicago about Hegel, Du Bois, and slavery. In the epilogue of his *The Problem of Slavery in the Age of Revolution: 1770–1823* (Ithaca: Cornell University Press, 1975), David Brion Davis argues for the utility of Hegel in thinking about the multifaceted nature of slavery.

67. Marx, *The Economic and Philosophic Manuscripts of 1844* (1959; Moscow: Progress Publishers, 1977), p. 132.

68. William T. Harris, *Hegel's Logic: A Book on the Genesis of the Categories of the Mind: A Critical Exposition* (Chicago: S. C. Griggs and Co., 1890), pp. 87–88.

69. Marx, *Economic and Philosophic Manuscripts*, pp. 133–34.

70. See the previous chapter of this study for a fuller outline of the other chapters of *Souls*.

71. For a succinct account of the new slavery, see Pete Daniel, "The Metamorphosis of Slavery, 1865–1900," *Journal of American History* 66 (1979): 88–99.

72. Marcuse, *Reason and Revolution*, pp. 4, 3.

73. For Du Bois's use of the biblical image of the veil, see also Werner Sollors, *Beyond Ethnicity: Consent and Descent in American Culture* (New York: Oxford University Press, 1986), p. 49.

74. Hegel, *Phenomenology of Mind*, p. 211.

75. Ibid., pp. 212–13.

76. On the *Atlantic Monthly*, see Ellery Sedgwick, "The Atlantic Monthly," in Edward E. Chielens, ed., *American Literary Magazines: The Eighteenth and Nineteenth Centuries* (New York: Greenwood Press, 1986), pp. 50–57.

77. See chapter 1 of David Levering Lewis, *W. E. B. Du Bois: Biography of a Race, 1868–1919* (New York: Henry Holt, 1993).

78. One of the pieces Du Bois wrote for an English composition course at Harvard in April 1891 was on the subject of "The American Girl," and it reveals the intensity of the personal experience that clearly lies behind the opening scene of *Souls*. The piece begins with the following paragraph and carries on in the same vein for about a page: "When I wish to meet the American Hog in its native simplicity; when I wish to realize the world-pervading presence of the fool; whenever I wish to be reminded that whatever rights some have I have none; when I wish, by a course

of systematic vulgarity, to be made to forget whatever little courtesy I have, when I wish to be doubly sure that the man lied who asserted that men's dead selves would furnish steps enough for a rise in the world: when I wish any of these things I seek the company of the American girl" (*AR* 19).

79. Sartre, *Being and Nothingness: An Essay on Phenomenological Ontology*, trans. Hazel E. Barnes (1953; New York: Philosophical Library, n.d.), p. 289. Hereafter abbreviated *BN*.

80. R. D. Laing, *The Divided Self: An Existential Study in Sanity and Madness* (1959; Harmondsworth: Penguin, 1965); see chap. 3, "Ontological Insecurity." Though not as complex a commentary as Sartre's, Laing's book is nevertheless useful for thinking about some of the issues raised in this chapter, not least because his existential psychology also works through a consideration of Hegel.

81. Fanon, *Black Skin, White Masks*, pp. 109, 111.

82. Joseph S. Catalano, *A Commentary on Jean-Paul Sartre's "Being and Nothingness"* (Chicago: University of Chicago Press, 1974), p. 166.

83. Jean Hyppolite, *Genesis and Structure of Hegel's Phenomenology of Spirit*, trans. Samuel Cherniak and John Heckman (Fr. ed. 1946; Evanston: Northwestern University Press, 1974), p. 189.

84. Ibid., p. 190.

85. Hegel, *Phenomenology of Mind*, p. 251. All emphases, except the first, are mine.

86. Georg Wilhelm Friedrich Hegel, *Phänomenologie des Geistes*, ed. Johannes Hoffmeister (Hamburg: Verlag von Felix Meiner, 1952), pp. 158–59. For the sake of reference let me also give A. V. Miller's translation of the passage, a more contemporary translation than Baillie's early-twentieth-century one:

> The duplication which formerly was divided between two individuals, the lord and the bondsman, is now lodged in one. The duplication of self-consciousness within itself, which is essential in the Notion of Spirit, is thus here before us, but not yet in its unity: the *Unhappy Consciousness* is the consciousness of self as a dual-natured, merely contradictory being.
>
> This *unhappy, inwardly disrupted* consciousness, since its essentially contradictory nature is for it a *single* consciousness, must for ever have present in the one consciousness the other also; and thus it is driven out of each in turn in the very moment when it imagines it has successfully attained to a peaceful unity with the other. Its true return into itself, or its reconciliation with itself will, however, display the Notion of Spirit that has become a living Spirit, and has achieved an actual existence, because it already possesses as a single undivided consciousness a dual nature.

G. W. F. Hegel, *Phenomenology of Spirit*, trans. A. V. Miller (Oxford: Oxford University Press, 1977), p. 126. My thanks to Professor Katie Trumpener of the German department at the University of Chicago for her help in comparing the translations with the original.

87. Hyppolite, *Genesis and Structure of Hegel's Phenomenology*, p. 156.

88. Gooding-Williams has argued that the trope of "second-sight" should be read as purely negative, a sign of the failure of black self-consciousness in gaining insight into the white world on the other side of the veil and also of seeing itself

through white eyes. This reading does not adequately address Du Bois's sense that "second-sight" is also a "gift," a meaning consistent with Hegel's sense of the self-consciousness of the slave. See Gooding-Williams, "Philosophy of History and Social Critique," p. 107.

89. These groups taken together make up 20.5 percent of the men over the age of twenty-one in gainful employment and 10 percent of the women in the equivalent category. All the other men are classed as "laborers" (divided into "better class" and "common class"), "servants," and "miscellaneous," and the women as "domestic servants," "housewives and day laborers," "housewives," and "day laborers, maids, etc." (see *PN*, pp. 101–3). The examples of this elite chosen for illustration in *Souls* are in fact from only two of the four categories given in *The Philadelphia Negro*. The choices are strategic. By concentrating on the "learned professions" and nonindustrial skilled labor Du Bois was able to maintain his Arnoldian or Carlylean moral stance against the gospel of wealth and also Washington's educational program.

90. W. E. B. Du Bois, *The Black North in 1901: A Social Study. A Series of Articles Originally Appearing in the New York Times, November–December, 1901* (New York: Arno Press and the New York Times, 1969), pp. 38–40.

91. Ibid., p. 41.

92. Ibid., p. 42.

93. Ibid., p. 46.

94. For these developments in the Progressive Era, see R. H. Wiebe, *The Search for Order, 1897–1920* (New York, 1967), and Richard Hofstadter, *Social Darwinism in American Thought* (1944; rev. ed., Boston: Beacon Press, 1955).

95. Alexandre Kojève, *Introduction to the Reading of Hegel: Lectures on the Phenomenology of Spirit,* trans. James H. Nichols, Jr. (1947; Ithaca: Cornell University Press, 1980), p. 68.

96. Ibid.

97. Ross Posnock, *The Trial of Curiosity: Henry James, William James and the Challenge of Modernity* (New York: Oxford University Press, 1991), pp. 96–97.

98. William James, letter to Henry James, 6 June 1903, *Letters of William James,* ed. Henry James, 2 vols. (Boston: Atlantic Monthly Press, 1920), vol. 2, p. 196.

99. Piotr Hoffmann, *The Anatomy of Idealism: Passivity and Activity in Kant, Hegel and Marx* (The Hague: Martinus Nijhoff Publishers, 1982), p. 5.

100. Bruce Wilshire, *William James and Phenomenology: A Study of "The Principles of Psychology"* (Bloomington: Indiana University Press, 1968).

101. These aspects of James's psychology are outlined in the chapter titled "The Consciousness of Self" in the first volume of *The Principles of Psychology.* They have been well noted by those who approach James as a phenomenologist or protophenomenologist, though the case for James as phenomenologist is uncritically overstated: see James M. Edie, *William James and Phenomenology* (Bloomington: Indiana University Press, 1987), and John Wild, *The Radical Empiricism of William James* (Garden City, N.Y.: Doubleday, 1969).

102. Santayana's course on modern French and German philosophy reflected the pervasive presence of European Romantic and idealist philosophy in the courses being offered at Harvard at that time. The survey course on modern

French and German philosophy included Leibnitz, Kant, and Hegel. Kant, Hartmann, and Schopenhauer formed the backbone of a survey of German philosophy since 1780. There was a course on the history of the philosophy of religion from Lessing to Schleiermacher. And Royce was offering his graduate course on Hegel's system, with special reference to the *Phenomenology*.

103. Du Bois recalled in his autobiography that he "sat in the upper room [of the Harvard Philosophical Club] and read Kant's Critique with Santayana" (*DD* 581). It may be worth noting here that, although Du Bois felt cut off from most of his fellow students by the color line, he felt he was well treated and supported by his teachers.

104. Rampersad, *Art and Imagination of W. E. B. Du Bois*, p. 74.

105. For a general survey of this area, see M. H. Abrams, *Natural Supernaturalism: Tradition and Revolution in Romantic Literature* (New York: W. W. Norton, 1971), esp. chaps. 3, 4, and 5.

106. William James, *The Principles of Psychology* (1890; New York: Dover Publications, 1950), 2 vols., vol. 1, p. 373. Hereafter abbreviated *PP*.

107. See Cynthia Eagle Russett, *The Concept of Equilibrium in American Social Thought* (New Haven: Yale University Press, 1966).

108. Clive Bush, *Halfway to Revolution: Investigation and Crisis in the Work of Henry Adams, William James and Gertrude Stein* (New Haven: Yale University Press, 1991), p. 147. Bush argues that James belongs, therefore, to a tradition of American social thought that includes Talcot Parsons among its later proponents (p. 430). Bush's critique of James is itself part of a larger cultural thesis that (building on Hannah Arendt's distinctions between *polis* and *societas*) characterizes late-nineteenth-century and early-twentieth-century America in terms of "a historical drift from a political view of the world to a social one" (p. 8).

109. Dorothy Ross, *The Origins of American Social Science* (Cambridge: Cambridge University Press, 1991), p. 155. See also Posnock, *Trial of Curiosity*, pp. 11–113, 119–21, for a discussion of possible alignments between James's thought and Edward Ross's theories of social control.

110. Daniel N. Robinson, *Towards a Science of Human Nature: Essays on the Psychologies of Mill, Hegel, Wundt and James* (New York: Columbia University Press, 1982), pp. 205–7.

111. Regarding the relationship of altruism and self-interest, James writes: "I should not be extant now had I not become sensitive to looks of approval or disapproval on the faces among which my life is cast. Looks of contempt cast on other persons need affect me in no such peculiar way. Were my mental life dependent exclusively on some other person's welfare, either directly or [in] an indirect way, natural selection would unquestionably have brought it about that I should be as sensitive to the social vicissitudes of that other person as I now am to my own. Instead of being egoistic I should be spontaneously altruistic, then" (*PP* 1:324). Bush has traced in great detail James's internalization of Darwinian natural selection. See "Psychologising a Social Pathology," chap. 8 of his *Halfway to Revolution*.

112. William James, *Varieties of Religious Experience* (1902; New York: Collier, 1961), p. 150.

113. On these two states of being, see lectures 4–7 of *The Varieties of Religious Experience*.

114. George Santayana, *Character and Opinion in the United States* (London: Constable, 1920), pp. 151, 153.

115. Ibid., pp. 151–52.

116. Ibid., p. 146.

117. Ibid., p. 148.

118. For a contemporary critique of the failure to theorize consciousness in the instrumentalism of James and Dewey that reaches conclusions similar to Santayana's (or Horkheimer's), see James Hoopes, *Consciousness in New England: From Puritanism and Ideas to Psychoanalysis and Semiotics* (Baltimore: Johns Hopkins University Press, 1989), pp. 205–26.

119. Santayana, "A General Confession," pp. 16–17.

120. Ibid., p. 16.

121. Ibid., p. 147.

122. George Santayana, "Apologia Pro Mente Sua" (1940), in Paul Arthur Schilpp, ed., *The Philosophy of George Santayana* (New York: Tudor, 1951), p. 556.

123. Daniel M. Cory, "Some Observations on the Philosophy of Santayana," in ibid., p. 96. Cory means this to be a criticism of the lack of philosophical rigor, but Santayana defends the utility of literary psychology against such critiques (see Santayana, "Apologia Pro Mente Sua," pp. 556–57).

124. Abrams, *Natural Supernaturalism*, p. 225. Royce is cited by Abrams (p. 229).

125. Ibid., pp. 230–31.

126. Arnold Rampersad's conclusion that in *Souls* Du Bois failed to fashion an autobiography to match Booker T. Washington's *Up from Slavery* misses the *Bildungsbiographie* structure of the book. See Rampersad, "Slavery and the Literary Imagination: Du Bois's *The Souls of Black Folk*," in Deborah McDowell and Rampersad, eds., *Slavery and the Literary Imagination* (Baltimore: Johns Hopkins University Press, 1989), p. 111.

127. Santayana, *Persons and Places*, p. 389.

128. Ibid., p. 393.

129. Santayana, "Apologia Pro Mente Sua," p. 557.

130. Flower and Murphey, *A History of Philosophy in America*, vol. 2, p. 780.

131. See George W. Howgate, *George Santayana* (1938; New York: Russell & Russell, 1971), pp. 21–22.

132. Santayana, *Persons and Places*, p. 389.

133. James, quoted in Posnock, *Trial of Curiosity*, p. 17.

134. William James, *Talks to Teachers on Psychology; and to Students on Some of Life's Ideals* (Boston: Henry Holt, 1899), p. 299.

135. On links between James and Emerson and on James's reading of Emerson, see Frederic Carpenter, "Points of Comparison between Emerson and William James," *New England Quarterly* 2 (July 1929): 458–74, and Carpenter's "William James and Emerson," *American Literature* 11 (March 1939): 39–57.

136. Emerson, "The Transcendentalist," in Stephen E. Whicher, ed., *Selections from Ralph Waldo Emerson* (1957; Boston: Houghton Mifflin, 1960), p. 204.

137. Emerson, *Nature*, in ibid., p. 24.

138. R. Jackson Wilson, *The Quest for Community: Social Philosophy in the United States, 1860–1920* (1968; Oxford: Oxford University Press, 1970), p. 6.

139. On the problematic of a "merely aesthetic dialectic," see David Punter, *Blake, Hegel and Dialectic* (Amsterdam: Rodopoi, 1982), pp. 24–25. On Emerson's reduction of dialectics to style, see Stephen Railton, "Seeing and Saying: The Dialectic of Emerson's Eloquence," in Stephen Donadio et al., eds., *Emerson and His Legacy: Essays in Honor of Quentin Anderson* (Carbondale: Southern Illinois University Press, 1986), pp. 48–49 and passim.

140. Stephen E. Whicher, *Freedom and Fate: An Inner Life of Ralph Waldo Emerson* (Philadelphia: University of Pennsylvania Press, 1953), p. 69.

141. Harold Bloom, *Figures of Capable Imagination* (New York: Seabury Press, 1976), p. 50.

142. Harold Bloom, *The Anxiety of Influence* (New York: Oxford University Press, 1973), p. 94.

143. For attempts to read Emerson within this version of dialectics, see William Torrey Harris, "The Dialectic Unity in Emerson's Prose," *Journal of Speculative Philosophy* 18 (April 1884): 195–202, reprinted in *Critical Essays on Ralph Waldo Emerson*, ed. Robert E. Burkholder and Joel Myerson (Boston: G. K. Hall, 1983), pp. 215–21; and Gustaaf van Cromphout, "Emerson and the Dialectics of History," *PMLA* 91 (1976): 54–65.

144. Harold Bloom, *A Map of Misreading* (New York: Oxford University Press, 1975), pp. 175–76.

145. Ibid., p. 176.

146. Quentin Anderson, *The Imperial Self: An Essay in American Literary History and Culture* (New York: A. Knopf, 1971), p. 5.

147. Sacvan Bercovitch, "Emerson the Prophet: Romanticism, Puritanism, and Auto-American-Biography," in David Levin, ed., *Emerson: Prophecy, Metamorphosis, and Influence* (New York: Columbia University Press, 1975), pp. 12–13. Comparing "The American Scholar" with *The Prelude*, Bercovitch writes: "Wordsworth hopes to reconstitute in himself all that had been divided, and so must deal with the specifics of his personal and historical condition. Emerson can bypass such considerations because he bears witness to the rising glory of America. Insofar as he projects himself in his hero, he recasts Romantic autobiography into auto-American-biography, reveals himself as harbinger of the nation intended 'by all prophecy, by all preparation . . . to fill the postponed expectation of the world'" (pp. 12–13). On Wordsworth and Emerson, see also Anderson, *The Imperial Self*, pp. 49–51. Anderson also contrasts Wordsworth and Whitman, pp. 95, 113.

148. Anderson, *Imperial Self*, p. 58.

149. For an elaboration of this point, see Wilson, *Quest for Community*, p. 9, and Hoopes, *Consciousness in New England*, pp. 173–74.

150. Hamilton Wright Mabie, quoted in John Higham, "The Reorientation of

American Culture in the 1890s," in Higham, *Writing American History: Essays on Modern Scholarship* (Bloomington: Indiana University Press, 1970), pp. 101–2.

151. See "The Plight of the Transcendental Individual," chap. 1 of Wilson, *Quest for Community*.

152. Wilson's thesis is borne out by the work of sociologists like William Graham Sumner. In *Folkways* (Boston: Ginn and Co., Atheneum Press, 1907), Sumner argues that traditional mores "very largely control individual and social undertakings" (p. iv). This becomes a basis for an aquiescence to the status quo.

Five

1. Quoted in Frank M. Kirkland, "Modernity and Intellectual Life in Black," *Philosophical Forum* 34, nos. 1–3 (1992–93): 140.

2. For further information on Crummell and an assessment of his influence on Du Bois, see Manning Marable, *W. E. B. Du Bois: Black Radical Democrat* (Boston: Twayne Publishers, 1986), pp. 32–40, and Eric J. Sundquist, *To Wake the Nations: Race in the Making of American Literature* (Cambridge: Harvard University Press, 1993), pp. 514–19.

3. Kirkland, "Modernity and Intellectual Life in Black," p. 158.

4. Max Horkheimer, *The Eclipse of Reason* (1947; New York: Seabury Press, 1974), p. 44. Horkheimer is quoting from John Dewey's "A Recovery of Philosophy" in his *Creative Intelligence: Essays in the Pragmatic Attitude* (1917). Dewey himself draws on James, and the alignments with James should be clear.

5. Jay Wright, "W. E. B. Du Bois at Harvard,'" in Wright, *The Homecoming Singer* (New York: Corinth, 1971), p. 32.

6. I am referring here to the discussion of consciousness in Johannes Fabian, *Time and the Other: How Anthropology Makes Its Object* (New York: Columbia University Press, 1983), p. 161. Fabian's argument is discussed in greater detail later in the final section of this chapter.

7. For the allegory, see Plato, *Republic,* VII.514A–521B.

8. Thomas Wentworth Higginson, *Army Life in a Black Regiment* (Boston: Fields, Osgood, 1870), p. 222. The essay was originally published in the *Atlantic Monthly* 19 (June 1867): 685–94.

9. New York: A. Simpson, 1867.

10. For a brief survey of these, see John David Smith, "The Unveiling of Slave Folk Culture, 1865–1920," *Journal of Folk Research* 21 (1984): 47–49, and 58, nn. 5 and 12. On early studies of African-American music, see also Bernard Katz, ed., *The Social Implications of Early Negro Music in the United States* (New York: Arno Press, 1969), and Dena J. Epstein, *Sinful Tunes and Spirituals: Black Folk Music to the Civil War* (Urbana: University of Illinois Press, 1977). On which contemporary sources Du Bois used, see Sundquist, *To Wake the Nations,* p. 1.

11. See Simon J. Bronner, *American Folklore Studies: An Intellectual History* (Lawrence: University Press of Kansas, 1986), pp. 10–11, 22–23.

12. Higginson's work, along with that of McKim Garrison, is given favorable mention in *Souls* (*SBF* 537).

13. Bernard Bell, *The Folk Roots of Contemporary Afro-American Poetry* (Detroit: Broadside Press, 1974), pp. 20–24, discusses the influence of the communalists on

Du Bois. My comments on Du Bois's relationship to the communalists and to the Herderian tradition here are indebted to Bell's work, particularly to his bibliographic apparatus. Although Du Bois did not study with any of the communalists, he did take subsidiary courses in English as an undergraduate at Harvard at a time when both Child and Kitteredge were offering many courses in that department. See Harvard course catalogs for 1888–89 and 1889–90. According to his Harvard course transcripts, Du Bois took four courses in the English department between 1888 and 1890, two in forensics, one in composition, and one in elocution (see also Du Bois's *Autobiography,* 144–45). For an account of the communalists, see D. K. Wilgus, *Anglo-American Folksong Scholarship since 1898* (New Brunswick: Rutgers University Press, 1959). For an outline of Herder's influence in America and on the Transcendentalists, see Constance Rourke, "The Roots of American Culture," in *Roots of American Culture and Other Essays,* ed. Van Wyck Brooks (New York: Harcourt, Brace & World, 1942), and Gene Bluestein, *The Voices of the Folk: Folklore and American Literary Theory* (Amherst: University of Massachusetts Press, 1972).

14. The comparison of Du Bois's primitivization of the black folk with the writings of realists such as William Dean Howells in Kenneth W. Warren's *Black and White Strangers: Race and American Literary Realism* (Chicago: University of Chicago Press, 1993), pp. 118–19, is useful here.

15. See Bernard Bell, "W. E. B. Du Bois's Struggle to Reconcile Folk and High Art," in William L. Andrews, ed., *Critical Essays on W. E. B. Du Bois* (Boston: G. K. Hall, 1985), 110. For a discussion of Du Bois's attempt to define culture in relation to other African-American thinkers at the turn of the century, see John Brown Childs, "Concepts of Culture in Afro-American Political Thought, 1890–1920," *Social Text* 4 (1981): 28–43.

16. For materials on Du Bois's conceptualization of race, see chap. 3, n. 99.

17. These are, in order of appearance, Arthur Symons, James Russell Lowell, Byron, Schiller, Whittier, Omar Khayyam (in Fitzgerald's translation), "The Song of Solomon," William Vaughn Moody, Elizabeth Barrett Browning (twice), Fiona McCleod (pseud. for William Sharp), Swinburne, and Tennyson.

18. In the Library of America edition of *Souls,* used throughout this study, the title of the final chapter is also printed as "*The* Sorrow Songs," not "*Of* the Sorrow Songs." This also differentiates the chapter from the preceding ones, which all begin with "Of." But the first edition of *Souls* prints the title of the chapter as "Of the Sorrow Songs," and I have retained that form.

19. Quoted in Bluestein, *The Voices of the Folk,* 8.

20. As the American poet Jerome Rothenberg puts it at the end of the Civil Rights decade and in the context of the Vietnam War, "Measure everything by the Titan rocket & the transistor radio, & the world is full of primitive peoples. But once change the unit of value to the poem . . . it becomes apparent what all those people have been doing all those years with all that time on their hands" (Rothenberg, "Pre-Face," in Rothenberg, ed., *Technicians of the Sacred: A Range of Poetries from Africa, Asia & Oceania* [1968; Garden City: Anchor Books, 1969], p. xix).

21. Fabian, *Time and the Other,* chap. 1 and passim.

22. Frederick Douglass, *Narrative of the Life of Frederick Douglass, an American Slave* (1845; New York: Penguin, 1982), p. 58.

23. Frederick Douglass, *My Bondage and My Freedom* (1855; New York: Dover, 1969), p. 362.

24. Douglass, *Narrative of the Life of Frederick Douglass*, p. 57.

25. Eric Sundquist has recently offered a lengthy reading of the final chapter of *Souls* and its treatment of the spirituals. He too notes the differences between Du Bois and the "folk" but offers a reading of the songs with which the present reading would take issue. For Sundquist *Souls* seems to be a prophecy of Du Bois's later Pan-Africanism, an effort "to recover ancestral roots" within the framework of a bardic black nationalism. While the present reading could find certain hesitant alignments with Sundquist's commentary, Sundquist's romantic critical rhetoric tends for the most part to ride a little too roughshod over the complexities and subtleties of Du Bois's writing in *Souls*. For examples, see Sundquist, *To Wake the Nations*, pp. 460–61, 464, 469, 488, 495, 507, 511, 526.

26. Wilson Jeremiah Moses, *Alexander Crummell: A Study of Civilization and Discontent* (New York: Oxford University Press, 1989), p. 281. For a brief history of the place of the Episcopal church in African-American culture and history, see the entry on Episcopalians in *The Encyclopedia of Black America*, ed. W. Augustus Low and Virgil A. Clift (New York: McGraw-Hill, 1981), pp. 372–77.

27. Du Bois's comments on African and African-American folk religion offer a less lighthearted qualification. Throughout the chapter on "the Faith of the Fathers" Du Bois's Victorian unease persists as he traces the development of African-American religion "through its gradual changes from the heathenism of the Gold Coast to the institutional Negro church of Chicago" (*SBF* 495). But at the same time the moralism that denigrates the African origins of African-American religion as "Voodooism" (*SBF* 498) is balanced by a political consciousness that sees the transition from "Obi worship" to Christianity as a transformation of the spirit of revolt into "passive submission" (*SBF* 499), though Du Bois also notes that, with the growth of the abolition movement and freedom, religion for the African American "became darker and more intense, and into his ethics crept a note of revenge, into his songs a day of reckoning close at hand" (*SBF* 501).

28. Du Bois provides musical notations along with the lyrics in *Souls*. These have been omitted here.

29. See Sundquist, *To Wake the Nations*, 528.

30. Du Bois taught sociology at Atlanta University from 1897 to 1910, and then returned to Atlanta in later life. The "Forethought" to *Souls* is signed "Atlanta, GA., Feb. 1, 1903."

31. *Souls* was published in 1903 and the chapter on the "sorrow songs" was written expressly for the book. This would make the setting of the final scene contemporary to the date of publication and would put Du Bois's age at thirty-five.

32. There are, again, similar contradictory tensions in Douglass's commentary on the slave songs in *Narrative of the Life of Frederick Douglass* (p. 57). Douglass notes that although the words to some of the songs "would to many seem un-

meaning jargon," they were, nevertheless, "full of meaning" to the slaves themselves. But then he goes on to state that he himself "did not, when a slave, understand the deep meaning of those rude and apparently incoherent songs." The reason for this was that the slave Douglass was himself "within the circle; so that I neither saw nor heard as those without might see and hear." The songs "told a tale of woe which was then altogether beyond my feeble comprehension." This lack of comprehension seems curious given Douglass's detailed and gruesome description of life as a slave. But Douglass is in fact, like Du Bois, suggesting a difference between alternative orders of understanding, between "meaning" and *"deep* meaning," between immediate response and retrospective reflection and analysis.

33. James Clifford, "On Ethnographic Allegory," in James Clifford and George E. Marcus, eds., *Writing Culture: The Poetics and Politics of Ethnography* (Berkeley: University of California Press, 1986), p. 113.

34. Ibid., p. 114.

35. Frederic Jameson, "Marxism and Historicism," *New Literary History* 11, no. 1 (1979): 51.

36. Higginson, *Army Life in a Black Regiment*, pp. 197, 198.

37. *The Republic of Plato,* trans. Francis MacDonald Cornford (1941; Oxford: Oxford University Press, 1945), p. 227.

38. Ibid., p. 234.

39. I am drawing here on J. A. Stewart, *The Myths of Plato* (1905; New York: Barnes and Noble, 1960), pp. 15, 81–82, 243–45.

40. See I. M. Crombie, *An Examination of Plato's Doctrines: II Plato on Knowledge and Reality* (London: Routledge and Kegan Paul, 1963), p. 85.

41. On the importance of biblical Jeremiad rhetoric in American culture, see Sacvan Bercovitch, *The American Jeremiad* (Madison: University of Wisconsin Press, 1978). For the impact of this typological tradition on American minority writing, see Werner Sollors, *Beyond Ethnicity: Consent and Descent in American Culture* (New York: Oxford University Press, 1986), pp. 40–65.

42. Arnold Rampersad, "Slavery and the Literary Imagination: Du Bois's *The Souls of Black Folk,"* in Deborah E. McDowell and Arnold Rampersad, eds., *Slavery and the Literary Imagination* (Baltimore: Johns Hopkins University Press, 1989), pp. 106, 121.

43. Ibid., p. 120.

44. Fabian, *Time and the Other,* p. 159.

45. Ibid., p. 160.

46. Ibid., pp. 161–62.

47. H. T. Wilson, *The American Ideology: Science, Technology and Organization as Modes of Rationality in Advanced Industrial Societies* (London: Routledge and Kegan Paul, 1977), p. 252.

48. Max Horkheimer, *The Eclipse of Reason* (1947; New York: Seabury Press, 1974), pp. 45–46.

49. Fabian, *Time and the Other,* p. 25.

50. *The Complete Poetry and Prose of William Blake,* ed. David V. Erdman, rev. ed. (New York: Doubleday, 1988), pp. 483–84.

51. S. Foster Damon, *A Blake Dictionary: The Ideas and Symbols of William Blake*, rev. ed. (Hanover, N.H.: Brown University/University Press of New England, 1988), p. 288.

52. Northrop Frye, *Fearful Symmetry: A Study of William Blake* (1947; Princeton: Princeton University Press, 1969), p. 59.

53. Ralph Waldo Emerson, *Nature*, in Stephen E. Whicher, ed., *Selections from Ralph Waldo Emerson* (Boston: Houghton Mifflin, 1957), p. 21.

54. Emily Dickinson, *The Complete Poems*, ed. Thomas H. Johnson (London: Faber and Faber, 1975), poem 258, p. 118.

55. Emerson, "The American Scholar" (1837), in Whicher, ed., *Selections*, p. 70.

56. See Kenneth Marc Harris, *Carlyle and Emerson: Their Long Debate* (Cambridge: Harvard University Press, 1978), p. 69.

57. Denis Donoghue, "Emerson at First: A Commentary on *Nature*," in Stephen Donadio et al., eds., *Emerson and His Legacy: Essays in Honor of Quentin Anderson* (Carbondale: Southern Illinois University Press, 1986), pp. 44–45.

58. Walt Whitman, *Leaves of Grass*, ed. Sculley Bradley and Harold W. Blodgett (New York: W. W. Norton, 1973), p. 50. Hereafter abbreviated *LG*.

59. Larzer Ziff, *Literary Democracy: The Declaration of Cultural Independence in America* (1981; New York: Penguin, 1982), pp. 235–36.

60. Joachim Hoeppner, "A propos du passage de Hegel a Marx," quoted in Louis Althusser, "On the Young Marx: Theoretical Questions," in Althusser, *For Marx* (1965), trans. Ben Brewster (London: Verso, 1990), pp. 54, n. 6; 55, n. 8.

61. Althusser, "On the Young Marx," p. 55, n. 8.

62. Ibid., p. 70.

Six

1. On Fanon's reading of Nietzsche, Hegel, the phenomenologists, and Sartre, see Peter Geismar, *Fanon* (New York: Dial Press, 1971), p. 43; Renate Zahar, *L'Oeuvre de Frantz Fanon*, trans. R. Dangeville (Paris: François Maspéro, 1970), p. 6; and Irene L. Gendzier, *Frantz Fanon: A Critical Study* (London: Wildwood House Ltd., 1973), pp. 13 and 22 and chap. 2.

2. Frantz Fanon, *Black Skin, White Masks*, trans. Charles Lam Markmann (Fr. ed. 1952; New York: Grove Weidenfeld, 1967), p. 222. Hereafter cited in the text as *BS,WM*.

3. There is an interesting discussion of Hegelian models of action in relation to *Native Son* that offers a different slant on the issues discussed here in chapter 12 of Gerd Hurm's *Fragmented Urban Images: The American City in Modern Fiction from Stephen Crane to Thomas Pynchon* (Frankfurt: Peter Lang, 1991).

4. Henry Louis Gates, Jr., *The Signifying Monkey: A Theory of African-American Literary Criticism* (New York: Oxford University Press, 1988). Hereafter cited in the text as *SM*.

5. The chapter on *Mumbo Jumbo* was first published as "The Blackness of Blackness: A Critique of the Sign and the Signifying Monkey" in *Critical Inquiry* 9, no. 4 (1983). See also *Signifying Monkey*, p. 218.

6. Quoted in Robert D. Pelton, *The Trickster in West Africa: A Study of*

Mythic Irony and Sacred Delight (Berkeley: University of California Press, 1980), pp. 144–45.

7. Ibid., p. 144.

8. For a historicized account of a trickster figure, see Norman O. Brown, *Hermes the Thief: The Evolution of a Myth* (Madison: University of Wisconsin Press, 1947).

9. Jacques Derrida, *Dissemination,* trans. Barbara Johnson (1972; London: Athlone Press, 1982), p. 93.

10. This alignment of deconstructionist theory and Emerson is not wholly fanciful. The Nietzschean inheritance of deconstruction has close and well-documented affinities with Emerson's thought. I am suggesting only affinities, and when I say Emerson I mean the author of the early prophetic essays, not the author of "Fate."

11. Much of the debate about the utility of Hegel has centered on the issue of whether the master-slave dialectic provides an accurate model for describing actual slavery in America. This debate has been discussed in chapter 4. Homi K. Bhabha has argued that in the context of colonial discourse Hegel offers a dualistic model of self and other, and that Fanon and Lacan provide more complex models of an internally split self and of the interpositioning of self and other (see Bhabha, "Signs Taken for Wonders: Questions of Ambivalence and Authority under a Tree outside Delhi, May 1817," in Henry Louis Gates, Jr., ed., *"Race," Writing and Difference* [Chicago: University of Chicago Press, 1986], pp. 163–84, and "Remembering Fanon: Self, Psyche and the Colonial Condition," foreword to Fanon's *Black Skin, White Masks* [London: Pluto Press, 1986], pp. vii–xxvi). Bhaba's argument is more complex than this, and Du Bois is not writing about the kind of colonialism that Bhabha is writing about, but the present discussion clearly tries to suggest that Hegel and the Hegelian tradition provide more complex models than either Bhabha or Fanon acknowledges. For a critique of the ahistoricism of the Lacanian model of alterity, see Anthony Wilden, *System and Structure: Essays in Communication and Exchange,* 2d ed. (London: Tavistock Publications, 1980), chap. 17. For a direct critique of Bhabha, albeit one that does not do full justice to him, see Abdul R. JanMohamed, "The Economy of Manichean Allegory: The Function of Racial Difference in Colonialist Literature," in Gates, ed., *"Race," Writing and Difference,* pp. 78–106.

12. Jacques Derrida's work, though one example among many, offers perhaps the best-known critiques. See his *Of Grammatology,* trans. Gayatri Chakravorty Spivak (Baltimore: Johns Hopkins University Press, 1976), pp. 24–26; *Margins of Philosophy,* trans. Alan Bass (Chicago: University of Chicago Press, 1982), pp. 69–108; and *Writing and Difference,* trans. Alan Bass (Chicago: University of Chicago Press, 1978), pp. 257–58.

13. Judith Butler, "The Nothing That Is: Wallace Stevens' Hegelian Affinities," in Bainard Cowan and Joseph G. Kronick, eds., *Theorizing American Literature: Hegel, the Sign, and History* (Baton Rouge: Louisiana State University Press, 1991), p. 269.

14. Marx, *The Economic and Philosophic Manuscripts of 1844* (1959; Moscow: Progress Publishers, 1977), pp. 133–34: "For Hegel," Marx writes, "the *human*

therefore *nothing* but *estrangement of self-consciousness*. The estrangement of self-consciousness is not regarded as an *expression*—reflected in the realm of knowledge and thought—of the *real* estrangement of the human being. Instead, the *actual* estrangement—that which appears real—is according to its *innermost*, hidden nature (which is only brought to light by philosophy) nothing but the *manifestation* of the estrangement of the real human essence, of *self-consciousness*."

15. Alexandre Kojève, *Introduction to the Reading of Hegel*, p. 5. My discussion here is indebted to Kojève's analysis of desire and activity throughout his first chapter.

16. Slavoj Žižek, *The Sublime Object of Ideology* (London: Verso, 1989), pp. 176–77. For the classic statements of the idea of the negation of the negation, see Engels's *Anti-Dühring*, pt. 1, chap. 13, and Marx's *Capital*, chap. 24, sec. 7. Unlike Engels, the present discussion is not invoking the negation of the negation as an absolute law of nature or history

Bibliography

A Note on Manuscript Materials

The following unpublished works by Du Bois are in the Du Bois papers at the University of Massachusetts at Amherst: "Bismarck," "Carlyle," the Philosophy 4 notebook, and "A Vacation Unique." Du Bois's thesis on ethics, "The Renaissance of Ethics," is in the James Weldon Johnson Collection at the Beinecke Library at Yale University. Francis L. Broderick's research notes on Du Bois, now at the Schomberg Library in New York, were also consulted. Du Bois's course transcripts and course descriptions were made available by the Harvard University archives.

Abbott, Edwin A. *Flatland: A Romance of Many Dimensions* (2d ed. 1884; New York: Dover, 1952).

Abrams, M. H. *Natural Supernaturalism: Tradition and Revolution in Romantic Literature* (New York: W. W. Norton, 1971).

Adams, Henry. *The Education of Henry Adams,* ed. Ernest Samuel (1907; Boston: Houghton Mifflin, 1973).

Allen, Ernest, Jr. " 'Ever Feeling One's Twoness': 'Double Ideals' and 'Double Consciousness' in *The Souls of Black Folk,*" *Critique of Anthropology* 12, no. 3 (1992): 261–75.

Allen, William F., Charles P. Ware, and Lucy McKim Garrison. *Slave Songs of the United States* (New York: A. Simpson, 1867).

Althusser, Louis. "On the Young Marx" (1960), in Althusser, *For Marx,* trans. Ben Brewster (1965; London: Verso, 1990), pp. 49–86.

Anderson, Quentin. *The Imperial Self: An Essay in American Literary History and Culture* (New York: A. Knopf, 1971).

Appiah, Anthony. "The Uncompleted Argument: Du Bois and the Illusion of Race," *Critical Inquiry* 12, no. 1 (Autumn 1985): 21–37.

Aptheker, Herbert. "*The Souls of Black Folk:* A Comparison of the 1903 and 1952 Editions," *Negro History Bulletin* 34, no. 1 (January 1971): 15–17.

Baker, Houston A., Jr. *Blues, Ideology, and Afro-American Literature: A Vernacular Theory* (Chicago: University of Chicago Press, 1984).

———. "Generational Shifts and Recent Criticism of Afro-American Literature," *Black American Literature Forum* 15, no. 1 (1981): 3–21.

Bannister, Robert C. *Social Darwinism: Science and Myth in Anglo-American Social Thought* (Philadelphia: Temple University Press, 1979).

Bell, Bernard. "W. E. B. Du Bois's Struggle to Reconcile Folk and High Art," in William L. Andrews, ed., *Critical Essays on W. E. B. Du Bois* (Boston: G. K. Hall, 1985), pp. 106–22.

———. *The Folk Roots of Contemporary Afro-American Poetry* (Detroit: Broadside Press, 1974).

Bellomy, Donald C. "Two Generations: Modernists and Progressives, 1870–1920," *Perspectives in American History,* New Series 3 (1987): 269–306.

Bentley, Eric. *The Cult of the Superman: A Study of the Idea of Heroism in Carlyle and Nietzsche, with Notes on Other Hero-Worshippers of Modern Times* (1944; Gloucester, Mass.: Peter Smith, 1969).

Bercovitch, Sacvan. *The American Jeremiad* (Madison: University of Wisconsin Press, 1978).

———. "Emerson the Prophet: Romanticism, Puritanism, and Auto-American-Biography," in David Levin, ed., *Emerson: Prophecy, Metamorphosis, and Influence* (New York: Columbia University Press, 1975), pp. 1–27.

Bernard, L. L., and Jessie Bernard. *Origins of American Sociology: The Social Science Movement in the United States* (1943; New York: Russell & Russell, 1963).

Bhabha, Homi K. "Remembering Fanon: Self, Psyche and the Colonial Condition," foreword to Fanon's *Black Skin, White Masks* (London: Pluto Press, 1986), pp. vii–xxvi.

———. "Signs Taken for Wonders: Questions of Ambivalence and Authority under a Tree outside Delhi, May 1817," in Henry Louis Gates, Jr., ed., *"Race," Writing and Difference* (Chicago: University of Chicago Press, 1986), pp. 163–84.

Binder, Gyora. "Mastery, Slavery, and Emancipation," *Cardozo Law Review* 10, nos. 5–6, part 2 (March–April 1989): 1435–80.

Blake, William. *The Complete Poetry and Prose of William Blake,* ed. David V. Erdman, rev. ed. (New York: Doubleday, 1988).

Bloom, Harold. *The Anxiety of Influence* (New York: Oxford University Press, 1973).

———. *Figures of Capable Imagination* (New York: Seabury Press, 1976).

———. *A Map of Misreading* (New York: Oxford University Press, 1975).

Bluestein, Gene. *The Voices of the Folk: Folklore and American Literary Theory* (Amherst: University of Massachusetts Press, 1972).

Boas, Franz. *The Ethnography of Franz Boas,* ed. Ronald P. Rohner (Chicago: University of Chicago Press, 1969).

———. *A Franz Boas Reader: The Shaping of American Anthropology,* 1883–1911, ed. George Stocking (Chicago: University of Chicago Press, 1974).

———. "The Limitations of the Comparative Method of Anthropology" (1896), in Boas, *Race, Language and Culture* (1940; Chicago: University of Chicago Press, 1982), pp. 270–80.

Bourne, Randolph. "Twilight of Idols," *Seven Arts* 2 (October 1917): 689–98.

Broce, Gerald. "Discontent and Cultural Relativism: Herder and Boasian Anthropology," *Annals of Scholarship* 2, no. 1 (1981): 1–13.

Broderick, Francis L. "German Influence on the Scholarship of W. E. B. Du Bois," *Phylon* 19, no. 4 (Winter 1958): 367–71.

———. *W. E. B. Du Bois: Negro Leader in a Time of Crisis* (Stanford: Stanford University Press, 1959).

———. "W. E. B. Du Bois: The Trail of His Ideas," Ph.D. diss., Harvard University, 1955.

Brodwin, Stanley. "The Veil Transcended: Form and Meaning in W. E. B. Du Bois' *The Souls of Black Folk,*" *Journal of Black Studies* 2 (March 1972): 303–21.

Bronner, Simon J. *American Folklore Studies: An Intellectual History* (Lawrence: University Press of Kansas, 1986).

Brown, Norman O. *Hermes the Thief: The Evolution of a Myth* (Madison: University of Wisconsin Press, 1947).

Browning, Don S. *Pluralism and Personality: William James and Some Contemporary Cultures of Psychology* (Lewisburg: Bucknell University Press, 1980).

Bruce, Dickinson D., Jr. "W. E. B. Du Bois and the Idea of Double Consciousness," *American Literature* 64, no. 2 (1992): 299–309.

Bush, Clive. *Halfway to Revolution: Investigation and Crisis in the Work of Henry Adams, William James and Gertrude Stein* (New Haven: Yale University Press, 1991).

Bush, Jonathan. "Hegelian Slaves and the Antebellum South," *Cardozo Law Review* 10, nos. 5–6, part 2 (March–April 1989): 1517–63.

Buss, A. R. "Development of Dialectics and Development of Humanistic Psychology," *Human Development* 19, no. 4 (1976): 248–60.

Butler, Judith. "The Nothing That Is: Wallace Stevens' Hegelian Affinities," in

Bainard Cowan and Joseph G. Kronick, eds., *Theorizing American Literature: Hegel, the Sign, and History* (Baton Rouge: Louisiana State University Press, 1991), pp. 269–88.

Cahan, Emily D., and Sheldon H. White. "Proposals for a Second Psychology," *American Psychologist* 47, no. 2 (1972): 224–35.

Carby, Hazel. "The Canon: Civil War and Reconstruction," *Michigan Quarterly Review* 28, no. 1 (1989): 29–40.

———. *Reconstructing Womanhood: The Emergence of the Afro-American Woman Novelist* (New York: Oxford University Press, 1987).

Carpenter, Frederic. "Points of Comparison between Emerson and William James," *New England Quarterly* 2 (July 1929): 458–74.

———. "William James and Emerson," *American Literature* 11 (March 1939): 39–57.

Catalano, Joseph S. *A Commentary on Jean-Paul Sartre's "Being and Nothingness"* (Chicago: University of Chicago Press, 1974).

Childs, John Brown. "Concepts of Culture in Afro-American Political Thought, 1890–1920," *Social Text* 4 (1981): 28–43.

Clifford, James. "On Ethnographic Allegory," in Clifford and George E. Marcus, eds., *Writing Culture: The Poetics and Politics of Ethnography* (Berkeley: University of California Press, 1986), pp. 98–121.

Commager, Henry Steele. *The American Mind: An Interpretation of American Thought and Character since the 1880s* (New Haven: Yale University Press, 1950).

Conn, Peter. *The Divided Mind: Ideology and Imagination in America, 1898–1917* (Cambridge: Cambridge University Press, 1983).

Cory, Daniel M. "Some Observations on the Philosophy of Santayana," in Paul Arthur Schilpp, ed., *The Philosophy of George Santayana* (New York: Tudor, 1951), pp. 93–112.

Coughlan, Neil. *Young John Dewey: An Essay in American Intellectual History* (Chicago: University of Chicago Press, 1975).

Cowen, Bainard, and Joseph G. Kronick, eds. *Theorizing American Literature: Hegel, the Sign, and History* (Baton Rouge: Louisiana State University Press, 1991).

Crombie, I. M. *An Examination of Plato's Doctrines: II Plato on Knowledge and Reality* (London: Routledge and Kegan Paul, 1963).

Cruse, Harold. *The Crisis of the Negro Intellectual: A Historical Analysis of the Failure of Black Leadership* (1967; New York: Quill, 1984).

Dale, Peter Allan. *The Victorian Critic and the Idea of History: Carlyle, Arnold, Pater* (Cambridge, Mass.: Harvard University Press, 1977).

Damon, S. Foster. *A Blake Dictionary: The Ideas and Symbols of William Blake*, rev. ed. (Hanover, N.H.: Brown University/University Press of New England, 1988).

Daniel, Pete. "The Metamorphosis of Slavery, 1865–1900," *Journal of American History* 66 (June 1979): 88–99.

Daston, Lorraine J. "The Theory of Will versus the Science of Mind," in William R. Woodward and Mitchell G. Ash, eds., *The Problematic Science: Psychology in Nineteenth Century Thought* (New York: Praeger, 1982), pp. 88–115.

Davis, David Brion. *The Problem of Slavery in the Age of Revolution: 1770–1823* (Ithaca: Cornell University Press, 1975).

De Marco, Joseph. *The Social Thought of W. E. B. Du Bois* (Lanham: University Press of America, 1983).

Derrida, Jacques. *Dissemination*, trans. Barbara Johnson (1972; London: Athlone Press, 1982).

———. *Margins of Philosophy*, trans. Alan Bass (Chicago: University of Chicago Press, 1982).

———. *Of Grammatology*, trans. Gayatri Chakravorty Spivak (Baltimore: Johns Hopkins University Press, 1976).

———. *Writing and Difference*, trans. Alan Bass (Chicago: University of Chicago Press, 1978).

Dewey, John. *The Early Works of John Dewey, 1882–1898*, vol. 1, 1882–1888 (Carbondale: Southern Illinois University Press, 1969).

———. "Kant and Philosophic Method," *Journal of Speculative Philosophy* 18 (1884): 170–73.

Dickinson, Emily. *The Complete Poems*, ed. Thomas H. Johnson (London: Faber and Faber, 1975).

Donoghue, Denis. "Emerson at First: A Commentary on *Nature*," in Stephen Donadio et al., eds., *Emerson and His Legacy: Essays in Honor of Quentin Anderson* (Carbondale: Southern Illinois University Press, 1986), pp. 23–47.

Douglass, Frederick. *My Bondage and My Freedom* (1855; New York: Dover, 1969).

———. *Narrative of the Life of Frederick Douglass, an American Slave* (1845; New York: Penguin, 1982).

Dove, Kenley R. "Hegel's Phenomenological Method," *Review of Metaphysics* 23, no. 4 (1970): 615–41.

Du Bois, W. E. B. *Against Racism: Unpublished Essays, Papers, Addresses, 1887–1961*, ed. Herbert Aptheker (Amherst: University of Massachusetts Press, 1985).

———. *The Autobiography: A Soliloquy on Viewing My Life from the Last Decade of Its First Century* (n.p.: International Publishers, 1968).

———. *The Black North in 1901: A Social Study. A Series of Articles Originally Appearing in the New York Times, November–December, 1901* (New York: Arno Press and the New York Times, 1969).

———. *Darkwater: Voices from within the Veil* (New York: Harcourt Brace, 1920).

———. *Dusk of Dawn: An Essay toward an Autobiography of a Race Concept* (1940), in Du Bois, *Writings*, pp. 549–801.

272 Bibliography

————. *The Philadelphia Negro: A Social Study*, with an intro. by E. Digby Baltzell (1899; New York: Schocken Books, 1967).

————. *The Souls of Black Folk* (1903), in Du Bois, *Writings*, pp. 357–548.

————. *The Souls of Black Folk: Essays and Sketches* (Chicago: A. C. McClurg, 1903).

————. "Strivings of the Negro People," *Atlantic Monthly* 80 (August 1897): 194–98.

————. *The Suppression of the African Slave-Trade to the United States of America, 1638–1870* (1896), in Du Bois, *Writings*, pp. 1–356.

————. "The Talented Tenth" (1903), in Du Bois, *Writings*, pp. 842–61.

————. *Writings*, ed. Nathan Huggins (New York: Library of America, 1986).

Easton, Loyd D. *Hegel's First American Followers. The Ohio Hegelians: John B. Stallo, Peter Kaufman, Moncure Conway, and August Willich, with Key Writings* (Athens: Ohio University Press, 1966).

Edie, James E. *William James and Phenomenology* (Bloomington: Indiana University Press, 1987).

Emerson, Ralph Waldo. *Selections from Ralph Waldo Emerson*, ed. Stephen E. Whicher (1957; Boston: Houghton Mifflin, 1960).

Epstein, Dena J. *Sinful Tunes and Spirituals: Black Folk Music to the Civil War* (Urbana: University of Illinois Press, 1977).

Evans, Henry Ridgely. "William Torrey Harris: An Appreciation," in Schaub, ed., *William Torrey Harris*, pp. 1–14.

Fabian, Johannes. *Time and the Other: How Anthropology Makes Its Object* (New York: Columbia University Press, 1983).

Fanon, Frantz. *Black Skin, White Masks*, trans. Charles Lam Markmann (Fr. ed. 1952; New York: Grove Weidenfeld, 1967).

Fine, William F. *Progressive Evolutionism and American Sociology, 1890–1920* (n.p.: UMI Research Press, 1979).

Fischer, Wolfram. "Gustav Schmoller," in *International Encyclopedia of the Social Sciences*, ed. David L. Sills (Macmillan and Free Press, 1968), vol. 14, pp. 60–63.

Flower, Elizabeth, and Murray G. Murphey. *A History of Philosophy in America* (New York: Capricorn Books and G. P. Putnam & Sons, 1977).

Fredrickson, George M. *The Black Image in the White Mind: The Debate on Afro-American Character and Destiny, 1817–1914* (New York: Harper and Row, 1971).

Frye, Northrop. *Fearful Symmetry: A Study of William Blake* (1947; Princeton: Princeton University Press, 1969).

Furner, Mary O. *Advocacy and Objectivity: A Crisis in the Professionalization of American Social Science, 1865–1905* (Lexington: University Press of Kentucky, 1975).

Gates, Henry Louis, Jr. *The Signifying Monkey: A Theory of African-American Literary Criticism* (New York: Oxford University Press, 1988).

Geismar, Peter. *Fanon* (New York: Dial Press, 1971).

Gendzier, Irene L. *Frantz Fanon: A Critical Study* (London: Wildwood House Ltd., 1973).

Giddings, Franklin Henry. *The Principles of Sociology: An Analysis of the Phenomena of Association and of Social Organization* (New York: Macmillan, 1896).

Glazer, Nathan. "The Rise of Social Research in Europe," in Daniel Lerner, ed., *The Human Meaning of the Social Sciences* (Cleveland: Meridian Books, 1959), pp. 43–72.

Goetzmann, William H., ed. *The American Hegelians: An Intellectual Episode in the History of Western America* (New York: Alfred Knopf, 1973).

Gooch, G. P. *History and Historians in the Nineteenth Century* (1913; 2d ed., London: Longmans, 1952).

Gooding-Williams, Robert. "Evading Narrative Myth, Evading Prophetic Pragmatism: Cornel West's *The American Evasion of Philosophy*," *Massachusetts Review* (Winter 1991–1992): 517–42.

———. "Philosophy of History and Social Critique in *The Souls of Black Folk*," *Social Science Information* 26, no. 1 (1987): 99–114.

Green, Dan S., and Edwin D. Driver. "W. E. B. Du Bois: A Case in the Sociology of Sociological Negation," *Phylon* 37, no. 4 (1976): 308–33.

Gunn, Giles. *Thinking Across the American Grain: Ideology, Intellect and the New Pragmatism* (Chicago: University of Chicago Press, 1992).

Harris, Kenneth Marc. *Carlyle and Emerson: Their Long Debate* (Cambridge: Harvard University Press, 1978).

Harris, William Torrey. "The Dialectic Unity in Emerson's Prose" (1884), in Robert E. Burkholder and Joel Myerson, eds., *Critical Essays on Ralph Waldo Emerson* (Boston: G. K. Hall, 1983), pp. 215–21.

———. *Hegel's Logic. A Book on the Genesis of the Categories of the Mind. A Critical Exposition* (Chicago: S. C. Griggs, 1890).

Harrison, Faye V. "The Du Boisian Legacy in Anthropology," *Critique of Anthropology* 12, no. 3 (1993): 239–60.

Hartz, Louis. *The Liberal Tradition in America: An Interpretation of American Political Thought since the Revolution* (New York: Harcourt, Brace & World, 1955).

Haskell, Thomas. *The Emergence of Professional Social Science: The American Social Science Association and the Nineteenth-Century Crisis of Authority* (Urbana: University of Illinois Press, 1977).

Hegel, Georg Wilhelm Friedrich. *Phänomenologie des Geistes,* 5th ed., ed. Johannes Hoffmeister (Hamburg: Verlag von Felix Meiner, 1952).

———. *The Phenomenology of Mind,* trans. J. B. Baillie (1807; trans. 1910; New York: Harper Torchbooks, 1967).

274   *Bibliography*

———. *Phenomenology of Spirit*, trans. A. V. Miller (Oxford: Oxford University Press, 1977).

Herbst, Jurgen. *The German Historical School in American Scholarship: A Study in the Transfer of Culture* (New York: Cornell University Press, 1965).

Herskovits, Melville J. *Franz Boas: The Science of Man in the Making* (New York: Charles Scribner's Sons, 1953).

Higginson, Thomas Wentworth. *Army Life in a Black Regiment* (Boston: Fields, Osgood, 1870).

Higham, John. "The Reorientation of American Culture in the 1890s," in Higham, *Writing American History: Essays on Modern Scholarship* (Bloomington: Indiana University Press, 1970), pp. 73–102.

Higham, John, Leonard Krieger, and Felix Gilbert. *History* (Englewood Cliffs, N.J.: Prentice-Hall, 1965).

Hinckle, Roscoe C. *Founding Theory of American Sociology, 1881–1915* (Boston: Routledge and Kegan Paul, 1980).

Hinton, C. H. *The Fourth Dimension* (London: Sonnenschein, 1904).

———. "What Is the Fourth Dimension?" (1884), in Hinton, *Scientific Romances* (London: Sonnenschein, 1884).

Hoffmann, Piotr. *The Anatomy of Idealism: Passivity and Activity in Kant, Hegel and Marx* (The Hague: Martinus Nijhoff Publishers, 1982).

Hofstadter, Richard. *Anti-Intellectualism in American Life* (Boston: Beacon Press, 1964).

———. *Social Darwinism in American Thought* (1944; rev. ed., Boston: Beacon Press, 1955).

Holt, Thomas C. "The Political Uses of Alienation: W. E. B. Du Bois on Politics, Race and Culture, 1903–1940," *American Quarterly* 42, no. 2 (1990): 301–23.

Hoopes, James. *Consciousness in New England: From Puritanism and Ideas to Psychoanalysis and Semiotics* (Baltimore: Johns Hopkins University Press, 1989).

Horkheimer, Max. *Eclipse of Reason* (1947; New York: Seabury Press, 1974).

Howgate, George. *George Santayana* (1938; New York: Russell and Russell, 1971).

Hughes, H. Stuart. *Consciousness and Society: The Reorientation of European Social Thought, 1890–1930* (New York: Alfred A. Knopf, 1958).

Hume, Robert A. *Runaway Star: An Appreciation of Henry Adams* (Ithaca: Cornell University Press, 1951).

Hyppolite, Jean. *Genesis and Structure of Hegel's Phenomenology of Spirit*, trans. Samuel Cherniak and John Heckman (Fr. ed. 1946; Evanston: Northwestern University Press, 1974).

Inwood, Michael. *A Hegel Dictionary* (Oxford: Blackwell, 1992).

James, William. *Letters of William James*, 2 vols., ed. Henry James (Boston: Atlantic Monthly Press, 1920).

———. *Manuscript Lectures* (Cambridge: Harvard University Press, 1988).

———. *A Pluralistic Universe* (London: Longmans, Green, 1909).

———. *The Principles of Psychology* (1890; New York: Dover, 1950).

———. *The Selected Letters of William James*, ed. Elizabeth Hardwick (New York: Farrar, Straus and Cudahy, 1961).

———. "The Social Value of the College-Bred" (1908), in *Memories and Studies* (London: Longmans, Green, 1911), pp. 307–25.

———. *Talks to Teachers on Psychology; and to Students on Some of Life's Ideals* (Boston: Henry Holt, 1899).

———. *Varieties of Religious Experience* (1902; New York: Collier Books, 1961).

———. "What Makes a Life Significant?" (1899), in *Essays on Faith and Morals* (Cleveland: Meridian Books, 1962).

———. *The Will to Believe and Other Essays in Popular Philosophy* (1897; New York: Dover, 1956).

Jameson, Frederic. "Marxism and Historicism," *New Literary History* 21, no. 1 (1979): 41–73.

JanMohamed, Abdul R. "The Economy of Manichean Allegory: The Function of Racial Difference in Colonialist Literature," in Henry Louis Gates, ed., *"Race," Writing and Difference* (Chicago: University of Chicago Press, 1986), 78–106.

Jordy, W. H. *Henry Adams: Scientific Historian* (New Haven: Yale University Press, 1952).

Kammen, Michael. "The Problem of American Exceptionalism: A Reconsideration," *American Quarterly* 45, no. 1 (1993): 1–43.

Kaplan, Harold. *Power and Order: Henry Adams and the Naturalist Tradition in American Fiction* (Chicago: University of Chicago Press, 1981).

Kaplan, Sydney. "Taussig, James and Peabody: A 'Harvard School' in 1900?" *American Quarterly* 7, no. 4 (1955): 315–31.

Katz, Bernard, ed. *The Social Implications of Early Negro Music in the United States* (New York: Arno Press, 1969).

Kaufmann, Walter. *Hegel: A Reconsideration* (New York: Anchor, 1966).

Key, R. Charles. "Society and Sociology: The Dynamics of Black Sociological Negation," *Phylon* 39, no. 1 (1978): 35–48.

Kierkegaard, Søren. *Concluding Unscientific Postscript,* trans. David F. Swenson and Walter Lowrie (Princeton: Princeton University Press, 1941).

Kirkland, Frank M. "Modernity and Intellectual Life in Black," *Philosophical Forum* 24, nos. 1–3 (1992–93): 136–65.

Kojève, Alexandre. *Introduction to the Reading of Hegel: Lectures on the Phenomenology of Spirit,* trans. James H. Nichols, Jr. (1947; Ithaca: Cornell University Press, 1980).

Kraus, Michael. *The Writing of American History* (Norman: University of Oklahoma Press, 1953).

Kucklick, Bruce. *The Rise of American Philosophy: Cambridge, Massachusetts, 1860–1930* (New Haven: Yale University Press, 1979).

Kuntz, Paul Grimley. "Rudolph Hermann Lotze, Philosopher and Critic," in George Santayana, *Lotze's System of Philosophy*, ed. Kuntz (Bloomington: Indiana University Press, 1971), pp. 48–68.

Laing, R. D. *The Divided Self: An Existential Study in Sanity and Madness* (1959; Harmondsworth: Penguin, 1965).

Lange, Werner. "W. E. B. Du Bois and the First Scientific Study of Afro-America," *Phylon* 44, no. 2 (1983): 135–46.

Lears, T. J. Jackson. *No Place of Grace: Antimodernism and the Transformation of American Culture, 1880–1920* (New York: Pantheon Press, 1981).

Lepenies, Wolf. *Between Literature and Science: The Rise of Sociology*, trans. R. J. Hollingdale (1985; Cambridge: Cambridge University Press, 1988).

Levenson, J. C. *The Mind and Art of Henry Adams* (Boston: Houghton Mifflin, 1957).

Lewis, David Levering. *W. E. B. Du Bois: Biography of a Race, 1868–1919* (New York: Henry Holt, 1993).

Lewis, J. David, and Richard L. Smith. *American Sociology and Pragmatism: Mead, Chicago Sociology, and Symbolic Interaction* (Chicago: University of Chicago Press, 1980).

Lindberg, Kathryne V. "Whitman's 'Convertible Terms': America, Self, Ideology," in Cowen and Kronick, eds., *Theorizing American Literature*, pp. 233–68.

Lipset, Seymour Martin, and David Reisman. *Education and Politics at Harvard* (New York: McGraw-Hill, 1975).

Logan, Rayford W. *The Negro in American Life and Thought: The Nadir, 1877–1901* (New York: Dial Press, 1954).

Lott, Tommy L. "Du Bois on the Invention of Race," *Philosophical Forum* 24, nos. 1–3 (1992–93): 116–87.

Low, Augustus, and Virgil A. Clift, eds. *Encyclopedia of Black America* (New York: McGraw-Hill, 1981).

McCosh, James. *Herbert Spencer's Philosophy as Culminated in His Ethics* (New York: Charles Scribner's Sons, 1885).

Marable, Manning. *W. E. B. Du Bois: Black Radical Democrat* (Boston: Twayne, 1986).

Marcuse, Herbert. *Reason and Revolution: Hegel and the Rise of Social Theory* (2d ed. 1954; Atlantic Highlands, N.J.: Humanities Press, 1983).

Marwick, Arthur. *The Nature of History* (London: Macmillan, 1970).

Marx, Karl. *The Economic and Philosophic Manuscripts of 1844* (1959; Moscow: Progress, 1977).

Meier, August. *Negro Thought in America, 1880–1915: Racial Ideologies in the Age of Booker T. Washington* (1963; Ann Arbor: University of Michigan Press, 1988).

Melville, Herman. *Moby Dick, or, The Whale* (1851; Harmondsworth: Penguin, 1972).

Meyer, Gerhard. "Adolf Wagner," in *International Encyclopedia of the Social Sciences,* ed. David L. Sills (Macmillan & Free Press, 1968), vol. 16, pp. 421–32.

Miller, Larry C. "William James and Twentieth-Century Ethnic Thought," *American Quarterly* 31, no. 4 (1979): 533–55.

Mills, C. Wright. *Sociology and Pragmatism: The Higher Learning in America,* ed. with intro. by Irving Louis Horowitz (New York: Paine-Whitman, 1964).

Mizruchi, Susan L. *The Power of Historical Knowledge: Narrating the Past in Hawthorne, James and Dreiser* (Princeton: Princeton University Press, 1988).

Moore, Jack B. *W. E. B. Du Bois* (Boston: Twayne, 1981).

Moses, Wilson Jeremiah. *Alexander Crummell: A Study of Civilisation and Discontent* (New York: Oxford University Press, 1989).

Moss, Alfred A., Jr. *The American Negro Academy: Voice of the Talented Tenth* (Baton Rouge: Louisiana State University Press, 1981).

Mottram, Eric. "Henry Adams: Index of the Twentieth Century," in *American Literary Naturalism: A Reassessment,* ed. Y. Hakutani and L. Fried (Heidelberg: Carl Winter Universitätsverlag, 1975), pp. 90–105.

Muller, Nancy Ladd. "Du Boisian Pragmatism and 'The Problem of the Twentieth Century,'" *Critique of Anthropology* 12, no. 3 (1992): 319–37.

Nicoloff, Philip L. *Emerson on Race and History: An Examination of English Traits* (New York: Columbia University Press, 1961).

Noble, David W. *The End of American History: Democracy, Capitalism, and the Metaphor of Two Worlds in Anglo-American Historical Writing, 1880–1980* (Minneapolis: University of Minnesota Press, 1985).

———. *Historians against History: The Frontier Thesis and the National Covenant in American Historical Writing since 1830* (Minneapolis: University of Minnesota Press, 1965).

Novick, Peter. *That Noble Dream: The "Objectivity Question" and the American Historical Profession* (Cambridge: Cambridge University Press, 1988).

Oppen, George. "Of Being Numerous" (1967), in Oppen, *Collected Poems* (London: Fulcrum, 1972).

Patterson, Orlando. *Slavery and Social Death: A Comparative Study* (Cambridge: Harvard University Press, 1982).

Paynter, Robert. "Afro-Americans in the Massachusetts Historical Landscape," in P. Gathercole and D. Lowenthal, eds., *The Politics of the Past* (London: Unwin Hynaman, 1990), pp. 49–62.

———. "W. E. B. Du Bois and the Material World of African-Americans in

Great Barrington, Massachusetts," *Critique of Anthropology* 12, no. 3 (1992): pp. 277–92.

Peel, J. D. Y. *Herbert Spencer: The Evolution of a Sociologist* (London: Heineman, 1971).

Pelton, Robert D. *The Trickster in West Africa: A Study of Mythic Irony and Sacred Delight* (Berkeley: University of California Press, 1980).

Perry, Palph Barton. *The Thought and Character of William James: Briefer Version* (1948; New York: Harper and Row, 1964).

Plato. *The Republic of Plato,* trans. Francis MacDonald Cornford (1941; Oxford: Oxford University Press, 1945).

Pochmann, Henry A. *German Culture in America, 1600–1900: Philosophical and Literary Influences* (Madison: University of Wisconsin Press, 1957).

———. *New England Transcendentalism and St. Louis Hegelianism: Phases in the History of American Idealism* (Philadelphia: Carl Schurz Memorial Foundation, 1948).

Posnock, Ross. *The Trial of Curiosity: Henry James, William James and the Challenge of Modernity* (New York: Oxford University Press, 1991).

Punter, David. *Blake, Hegel and Dialectic* (Amsterdam: Rodopoi, 1982).

Railton, Stephen. "Seeing and Saying: The Dialectic of Emerson's Eloquence," in Stephen Donadio et al., eds., *Emerson and His Legacy: Essays in Honor of Quentin Anderson* (Carbondale: Southern Illinois University Press, 1986), pp. 48–65, 231–33.

Rampersad, Arnold. *The Art and Imagination of W. E. B. Du Bois* (Cambridge: Harvard University Press, 1976).

———. "Slavery and the Literary Imagination: Du Bois's *The Souls of Black Folk,*" in Deborah McDowell and Arnold Rampersad, eds., *Slavery and the Literary Imagination* (Baltimore: Johns Hopkins University Press, 1989), pp. 104–24.

Ranke, Leopold von. *The Theory and Practice of History,* ed. Georg G. Iggers and Konrad von Moltke, with new translations by Wilma A. Iggers and Konrad von Moltke (New York: Bobbs-Merrill, 1973).

Reising, Russell. *The Unusable Past: Theory and the Study of American Literature* (New York: Methuen, 1986).

Richardson, Robert D., Jr. "Emerson on History," in Joel Porte, ed., *Emerson: Prospect and Retrospect,* Harvard English Studies 10 (Cambridge: Harvard University Press, 1982), pp. 49–64.

Robinson, Daniel N. *Toward a Science of Human Nature: Essays on the Psychologies of Mill, Hegel, Wundt and James* (New York: Columbia University Press, 1982).

Rose, Gillian. *Hegel contra Sociology* (London: Athlone Press, 1981).

Ross, Dorothy. *The Origins of American Social Science* (Cambridge: Cambridge University Press, 1991).

Rothenberg, Jerome. "Harold Bloom: The Critic as Exterminating Angel," *Sulfur* 2 (1981): 4–26.

———. "Pre-Face," in Rothenberg, ed., *Technicians of the Sacred: A Range of Poetries from Africa, Asia & Oceania* (1968; Garden City: Anchor Books, 1969).

Rourke, Constance. "The Roots of American Culture," in *Roots of American Culture and Other Essays,* ed. Van Wyck Brooks (New York: Harcourt, Brace & World, 1942).

Royce, Josiah. *The Spirit of Modern Philosophy* (Boston: Houghton Mifflin, 1892).

Rudwick, Elliot M. "Notes on a Forgotten Black Sociologist: W. E. B. Du Bois and the Sociological Profession," *American Sociologist* 4 (November 1969): 303–6.

———. *W. E. B. Du Bois: A Study in Minority Group Leadership* (Philadelphia: University of Pennsylvania Press, 1960).

———. "W. E. B. Du Bois as Sociologist," in James E. Blackwell and Morris Janowitz, eds., *Black Sociologists: Historical and Contemporary Perspectives* (Chicago: University of Chicago Press, 1974), 25–55.

Russett, Cynthia Eagle. *The Concept of Equilibrium in American Social Thought* (New Haven: Yale University Press, 1966).

Ryan, Judith. *The Vanishing Subject: Early Psychology and Literary Modernism* (Chicago: University of Chicago Press, 1991).

Santayana, George. "Apologia pro Mente Sua" (1940), in Paul Arthur Schilpp, ed., *The Philosophy of George Santayana* (New York: Tudor, 1951), pp. 495–607.

———. *Character and Opinion in the United States* (London: Constable, 1920).

———. "A General Confession," in Paul Arthur Schilpp, ed., *The Philosophy of George Santayana* (New York: Tudor, 1951), pp. 1–30.

———. *Persons and Places: Fragments of Autobiography,* ed. William G. Holzberger and Herman J. Saatkamp (Cambridge: MIT Press, 1986).

Sartre, Jean-Paul. *Being and Nothingness: An Essay on Phenomenological Ontology,* trans. Hazel E. Barnes (1953; New York: Philosophical Library, n.d.).

———. *What Is Literature?* trans. Bernard Frechtman (1948; London: Methuen, 1950).

Saveth, Edward N. *American Historians and European Immigrants, 1875–1925* (New York: Columbia University Press, 1948).

Schaub, Edward L. "Harris and the Journal of Speculative Philosophy," in Schaub, ed., *William Torrey Harris,* pp. 49–67.

Schaub, Edward L., ed. *William Torrey Harris, 1835–1935* (Chicago: Open Court, 1936).

Schneider, Herbert W. *A History of American Philosophy* (1946; 2d ed., New York: Columbia University Press, 1963).

Sedgwick, Ellery. "The Atlantic Monthly," in Edward E. Chielens, ed., *American Literary Magazines: The Eighteenth and Nineteenth Centuries* (New York: Greenwood Press, 1986), pp. 50–57.

Shapiro, Ian. *Political Criticism* (Berkeley: University of California Press, 1990).

Smith, Adam. *The Theory of Moral Sentiments* (1790, 6th. ed.), ed. D. D. Raphael and A. L. Macfie (1979; Indianapolis: Liberty Classics, 1982).

Smith, John David. *An Old Creed for the New South: Proslavery Ideology and Historiography, 1865–1918* (1985; Athens: University of Georgia Press, 1991).

———. "The Unveiling of Slave Folk Culture, 1865–1920," *Journal of Folk Research* 21 (April 1984): 47–62.

Snider, Denton J. *The St. Louis Movement in Philosophy, Literature, Education, Psychology, with Chapters of Autobiography* (St. Louis: Sigma, 1920).

Sollors, Werner. *Beyond Ethnicity: Consent and Descent in American Culture* (New York: Oxford University Press, 1986).

———. "A Critique of Pure Pluralism," in Sacvan Bercovitch, ed., *Reconstructing American Literary History* (Cambridge: Harvard University Press, 1986), pp. 250–79.

Spencer, Herbert. *The Data of Ethics* (London: Williams and Norgate, 1879).

———. *First Principles* (1862; 5th ed., London: Williams and Norgate, 1890).

Stanton, William. *The Leopard's Spots: Scientific Attitudes toward Race in America, 1815–59* (Chicago: University of Chicago Press, 1960).

Stepto, Robert. *From Behind the Veil: A Study of Afro-American Narrative* (Urbana: University of Illinois Press, 1979).

Stewart, J. A. *The Myths of Plato* (1905; New York: Barnes and Noble, 1960).

Sumner, William Graham. *Folkways: A Study of the Sociological Importance of Usages, Manners, Customs, Mores and Morals* (Boston: Ginn and Atheneum Press, 1907).

Sundquist, Eric. *To Wake the Nations: Race in the Making of American Literature* (Cambridge, Mass.: Harvard University Press, 1993).

Swingewood, Alan. *A Short History of Sociological Thought* (London: Macmillan, 1984).

Tallack, Douglas. *Twentieth-Century America: The Intellectual and Cultural Context* (London: Longman, 1991).

Taylor, Council. "Clues for the Future: Black Urban Anthropology Reconsidered," in Peter Orleans and William Russell Ellis, Jr., eds., *Race, Change and Urban Society* (Beverly Hills, Calif.: Sage, 1971), pp. 603–18.

Thomas, Brook. "The New Historicism and Other Old-fashioned Topics," in H. Aram Veeser, ed., *The New Historicism* (New York: Routledge, 1989), pp. 182–203.

Thomas, Kendall. "A House Divided against Itself: A Comment on 'Mastery,

Slavery, and Emancipation,'" *Cardozo Law Review* 10, nos. 5–6, part 2 (March–April 1989): 1481–1515.

Thompson, James Westfall. *A History of Historical Writing* (1942; Gloucester, Mass.: Peter Smith, 1967).

Townsend, Henry Gates. "The Political Philosophy of Hegel in a Frontier Society," in Schaub, ed., *William Torrey Harris*, pp. 68–80.

Trachtenberg, Alan. *The Incorporation of America: Culture and Society in the Gilded Age* (New York: Hill and Wang, 1982).

Van Cromphout, Gustaaf. "Emerson and the Dialectic of History," *PMLA* 91 (1976): 54–65.

Van Tassel, David D. *Recording America's Past: An Interpretation of the Development of Historical Studies in America, 1607–1884* (Chicago: University of Chicago Press, 1960).

Veblen, Thorstein. *The Place of Science in Modern Civilization and Other Essays* (1919; New York: Russell and Russell, 1961).

Warren, Kenneth W. *Black and White Strangers: Race and American Literary Realism* (Chicago: University of Chicago Press, 1993).

———. "Delimiting America: The Legacy of Du Bois," *American Literary History* (Spring 1989): 172–89.

West, Cornel. *The American Evasion of Philosophy: A Genealogy of Pragmatism* (Madison: University of Wisconsin Press, 1989).

Westphal, Merold. "Hegel on Slavery, Independence, and Liberalism," *Cardozo Law Review* 10, nos. 5–6, part 2 (March–April 1989): 1565–73.

Whicher, Stephen E. *Freedom and Fate: An Inner Life of Ralph Waldo Emerson* (Philadelphia: University of Pennsylvania Press, 1953).

White, Hayden. "On History and Historicism," introduction to Carlo Antoni's *From History to Sociology: The Transition in German Historical Thought*, trans. Hayden White (1940; London: Merlin, 1962), pp. xv–xxviii.

———. *Metahistory: The Historical Imagination in Nineteenth-Century Europe* (Baltimore: Johns Hopkins University Press, 1973).

White, Morton. *The Origins of Dewey's Instrumentalism* (1943; New York: Octagon Press, 1964).

Whitman, Walt. *Leaves of Grass,* ed. Sculley Bradley and Harold W. Blodgett (New York: W. W. Norton, 1973).

Wiebe, R. H. *The Search for Order, 1897–1920* (New York, 1967).

Wild, John. *The Radical Empiricism of William James* (Garden City, N.Y.: Doubleday, 1969).

Wilden, Anthony. *System and Structure: Essays in Communication and Exchange,* 2d ed. (London: Tavistock, 1980).

Wilgus, D. K. *Anglo-American Folksong Scholarship since 1898* (New Brunswick: Rutgers University Press, 1959).

Willey, Thomas E. *Back to Kant: The Revival of Kantianism in German Social and Historical Thought, 1860–1914* (Detroit: Wayne State University Press, 1978).

Williams, Raymond. *The Country and the City* (New York: Oxford University Press, 1973).

———. *Culture and Society: 1780–1950* (1958; New York: Columbia University Press, 1983).

Williamson, Joel. *The Crucible of Race: Black-White Relations in the American South since Emancipation* (New York: Oxford University Press, 1984).

Wilshire, Bruce. *William James and Phenomenology: A Study of "The Principles of Psychology"* (Bloomington: Indiana University Press, 1968).

Wilson, Daniel J. *Science, Community and the Transformation of American Philosophy, 1860–1930* (Chicago: University of Chicago Press, 1990).

Wilson, H. T. *The American Ideology: Science, Technology and Organization as Modes of Rationality in Advanced Industrial Societies* (London: Routledge and Kegan Paul, 1977).

Wilson, R. Jackson. *The Quest for Community: Social Philosophy in the United States, 1860–1920* (1968; Oxford: Oxford University Press, 1970).

Woerner, Gabriel. "An American War and Peace," an extract from *The Rebel's Daughter,* in William H. Goetzman, ed., *The American Hegelians: An Intellectual Episode in the History of Western America* (New York: Alfred A. Knopf, 1973), pp. 325–34.

Wolf, Eric. *Europe and the People without History* (Berkeley: University of California Press, 1982).

Woodward, C. Vann. *The Burden of Southern History,* 2d ed. (Baton Rouge: Louisiana State University Press, 1968).

———. *The Strange Career of Jim Crow,* 3d ed. (New York: Oxford University Press, 1974).

Wright, Jay. *The Homecoming Singer* (Washington: Corinth, 1967).

Zahar, Reante. *L'Oeuvre de Frantz Fanon,* trans. R. Dangeville (Paris: François Maspéro, 1970).

Ziff, Larzer. *Literary Democracy: The Declaration of Cultural Independence in America* (1981; New York: Penguin, 1982).

Žižek, Slavoj. *The Sublime Object of Ideology* (London: Verso, 1989).

Index